Instructor's Annotated Edition

Practical English Grammar

A Sentence-to-Paragraph Approach

Jean Anderson Embree

Evergreen Valley College

Mayfield Publishing Company
Mountain View, California
London ▾ Toronto

Instructor's Annotated Edition ISBN: 1-55934-349-4
Student Edition ISBN: 1-55934-348-6

Library of Congress Cataloging-in-Publication Data

Embree, Jean.
    Practical English grammar : a sentence-to-paragraph approach/
Jean Embree.
      p.   cm.
    Includes bibliographical references (p.   ) and index.
    ISBN 1–55934–348–6
    1. English language—Grammar—Problems, exercises, etc.
I. Title.
PE1112.E45   1995
428.2—dc20   95-10619
                                         CIP

Manufactured in the United States of America
10 9 8 7 6 5 4 3 2 1

Mayfield Publishing Company
1280 Villa Street
Mountain View, California 94041

Sponsoring editor, James Bull; managing editor, April Wells-Hayes; production editor, Lynn
Rabin Bauer; manuscript editor, Zipporah Collins; art director, Jeanne Schreiber; text and
cover designer, Claire Seng-Niemoeller; art manager, Robin Mouat; illustrator, Kevin
Opstedal; manufacturing manager, Randy Hurst. The text was set in 11/13 Sabon by
Thompson Type and printed on 50# Butte des Morts, PMS 2727, by Banta Company.

 This book is printed on recycled paper.

Page 306: "Silly Science" and "Muddled Medical Advice" from *More Anguished English* by
Richard Lederer. Copyright © 1993 by Richard Lederer. Used by permission of Dell Books, a
division of Bantam Doubleday Dell Publishing Group, Inc.

Welcome to the *Instructor's Annotated Edition* of Jean Anderson Embree's *Practical English Grammar: A Sentence-to-Paragraph Approach*. Developed by the author, the *Instructor's Annotated Edition* includes:

- a wealth of practical advice for organizing, scheduling, and teaching your course

- answers to all of the exercises, printed in a second color in your copy of the book

- additional commentary at the beginning of many chapters offering specific guidance for teaching the material in that chapter

- multiple versions of examinations covering each of the three parts of the book

- multiple versions of an evaluation and placement examination and of a final, comprehensive examination

- seven supplementary quizzes covering material in Parts Two and Three

- answers to *all* examinations and quizzes

- the complete student edition

We hope you find this material helpful. If you have any questions or suggestions for improving this annotated edition, feel free to write us or e-mail us at 74512.2233@compuserve.com. Thank you!

Preface to the Student Edition

This text is called "practical" because it works—as an innovative, entertaining, and comprehensive text that helps students learn and apply the rules of English grammar.

FEATURES

Creative solutions to grammar problems. *Practical English Grammar* reflects more than thirty years of teaching English grammar and writing to all kinds of students. The book is clearly grounded in the classroom and the culture of real students with real skills and real problems. Over the years, in the hundreds of grammar classes I've taught, I have been able to identify the most common problems students have learning grammar. More important, I've had the opportunity to experiment with various creative approaches to those problems. Some have worked better than others. *Practical English Grammar* embodies my best solutions to the many puzzles that come along with teaching—and learning—English grammar.

Grammar with a sense of humor! To help lighten the study of what students sometimes fear is boring, dense material, *Practical English Grammar* includes approximately seventy-five original cartoons and a light touch in its text examples.

Memory Pegs. Appearing throughout the book, these creative mnemonic devices help students remember the most frequently used rules and terms of grammar by highlighting the simplest version of each, often with an aural, visual, or logical memory hint attached. Examples: The *adverbs* usually *add* to action verbs, and the pre*positions* deal primarily with *position* and relationship.

Exercises. The text contains two types of exercises. The first, "Tryout" exercises (for which the answers are given in the text), appear after the introduction of each primary new idea and provide opportunities for students to test their knowledge before reading further. The second, "Practice" exercises, follow the Tryouts in each chapter. This organization allows students to read and listen to a quick preview, complete the Tryout exercise, check their answers in the back of the chapter, review problem areas, and then retest themselves with the Practice exercise and be ready to work with the instructor and the rest of the class on the material just covered.

Answers to "Practice" exercises only appear in this *Instructor's Annotated Edition,* not in the student edition.

Progressive Assignments. Both the grammar material and the "From Sentence to Paragraph" writing suggestions move from simple to complex, allowing students to gain confidence and competency as they move through the book. The middle chapters of the book, punctuation and usage, can be emphasized in varying degrees, depending upon student needs. The writing assignments are designed so that, by the last quarter of the text, students can use them as the basis for short but complete formal essays.

OUR CHANGING ENGLISH

For many centuries, books and oral histories have carried the knowledge of our civilization from one generation to the next. When parents teach their child, the child learns how to live by copying the parents' words and actions. Yet each generation has changed things a little, and in the twentieth century change comes rapidly. Gradually, even the most formal language must change to fit our new actions and ideas. We need to understand the traditions of our grandparents and yet fit ourselves into our current modes of living.

Does this mean that English is acceptable spoken in any way and in any style? The answer is no, because the purpose of the language is to communicate. To be able to make the meaning clear, to let other people know what we are thinking and feeling, we need to agree on the meanings and relationships of our words. For these reasons, the usage rules in this text will often be noted as fitting (approximately!) the following categories:

1. Standard English—the grammatically consistent, clear version of the language that is expected in most written nonfiction and in other relatively formal situations whether written or spoken.

2. Common Spoken English—a slightly less formal version of Standard English, used in relaxed everyday moments when absolute accuracy seems less important. As the culture changes, many of the less formal terms and phrases of Common Spoken English may become accepted in Standard English; the most recent dictionaries give updates that are reflected in several areas of this text, under the heading "Our Changing English."

3. Nonstandard English—grammatical errors that are technically incorrect but because of the sentence complexity are very commonly made, even by relatively educated people.

4. Major Mistakes—the illiteracies created by those who are not fluent in the language or who often speak a dialect. These are the errors that may grate on nerves of listeners and therefore put up barriers to communication. Again, these usages sometimes become accepted over many years of cultural change.

5. Dialects—the different versions of the language spoken by various cultural groups but not yet accepted as "Standard." A dialect may be an appropriate version in an informal situation, but speakers of dialects may need to learn, as they might learn any new language, how to speak and write Standard English when necessary.

TEACHING STRATEGIES

The order of presentation of the material has been thoroughly tested over thirty years. Once students truly understand basic sentences and parts of speech, they can easily learn to build effective sentences and to correct fragments and run-ons. They then move with relief into punctuation—a practical approach that enables them to write correctly quite early in the course.

The topic divisions are designed to provide "learning chunks" of digestible size, using ideas that are often related in students' minds. Each of the thirty chapters provides between half an hour and an hour of in-class material, depending upon the class level. Most students find that they like having the material previewed in one session, then discussed and checked—preferably by individual recitation—in a later session, after the homework or lab work has been completed.

Practical English Grammar is very flexible. For instance, students who have special problems in usage (Part Three), such as verb conjugation or agreement, can be assigned at any time to do earlier or extra work on that material. Part Three is discrete, and any part of it can be taught at any time after Part One.

The text can be covered more slowly for earlier developmental classes by deemphasizing or omitting all or most of Chapters 9 and 19 and the last parts of Chapters 29 and 30. Chapters 10, 20, and 30, the last chapters in each part, provide many review examples of the basic principles of each part. Assignments can be graduated either slowly or quickly by varying the length of the requested compositions and assigning extensive revisions or quick edits.

The text material has often been used as a review supplement for more advanced English composition classes. Business English students may write their assignments in letter form. All students can write occasional timed compositions in standard lab situations or on computers in electronic classrooms. The material has been taught in all these ways on all these levels over many years.

In any one class, students may use the material in a "modified individualized instruction" format. Those who need only a brief review of a certain section may find that doing and checking the Tryout is enough. Instructors may provide in-class guidance by going over both types of exercises with new learners but using just the Practices with the more advanced students, some of whom may be able to complete at least the last third of the text with help only from a lab assistant.

A full spelling and vocabulary unit can be easily developed from the Appendixes. All developmental students will benefit from Appendix B, Spelling and Pronunciation, particularly if the instructor can test one set of words per week. The other materials can be used as needed or assigned when time is available.

Five Useful Appendixes

Appendix A: Grammar Summary: Glossary of Terms (an alphabetical list of the most common grammatical terms, with definitions and simple usage examples)

Appendix B: Spelling and Pronunciation (the 250 most commonly misspelled words, divided into 10 manageable lists and annotated with Memory Pegs)

Appendix C: Homonyms and Pseudohomonyms (an alphabetical list of many of the most common homonyms, annotated with Memory Pegs)

Appendix D: Prefixes and Suffixes; Word Division (alphabetical lists of the most common prefixes and suffixes, with examples and definitions)

Appendix E: Recommended References; Proofreading Symbols

ACKNOWLEDGMENTS

The text materials have been developed over a teaching lifetime, with feedback from thousands of students and dozens of fellow teachers, writers, and publishing experts. You all know who you are—thank you!—including those who got me started early in my college major, by both encouraging and employing me:

Paul Engle and the other faculty and students of the Iowa Writers' Workshop at the University of Iowa;

Professors and Professors Emeritus James Cline, Josephine Miles, Charles Muscatine, and Mark Schorer from the University of California at Berkeley;

Harvey Birenbaum, James Clark, John Galm, James Harper, Virginia Larsen, Roland Lee, Nils Petersen, and David Van Becker from San Jose State University.

Detailed Contents

Resources for the Instructor

To the Instructor

Your new developmental English class looks at you expectantly. What now?

As a college instructor, you have a great advantage over the average high school teacher in the United States. All your current students are here because for one reason or another they want to be here. Some are eager to improve their English beyond the advanced level of ESL (English as a second language). Some may have been on the job for years and may be returning to school after long absences. Now they need to feel good about their plans and their choices. Your first step is to help them build a class spirit, to help them realize that they are not alone, that they can reach their own goals together, and that you are here to help.

SET THE TONE

Because so many developmental English students have histories of poor experiences in English classes, the tone of the beginning class is crucial. In general, you want to project an image of friendliness and humor but determination to get the job done. The students need to know that you'll expect them to work very hard, but that you think they can succeed and enjoy themselves at the same time.

Remind students that grammar is a means to an end. They may groan a little, but tell them that you'll use a minimum of terms and teach in a way that will quickly help them write and speak more accurately. Tell them that while no boss is likely to ask an employee to label a subordinate conjunction, many managers will be shocked if an employee writes fragments and run-ons because he or she can't identify the connecting words. Grade students accordingly; base the main grade on their writing, especially in-class writing.

GET ACQUAINTED

In the first class, then, you'll get acquainted. A sign-in sheet that indicates what English classes the students have completed (and when) can be a big help. Students can pick up and fill out these sheets with the detailed class outline or calendar while you write general class information on the board: your name, the class name and number, whether you have room for additional students, and a reminder about the textbook and other supplies students will need. You may immediately spot a few students who should be tactfully guided elsewhere. As soon as you've taken the roll, perhaps added a student or two from a waiting list, and picked up the sign-in sheets, you may find it useful to ask the students to move into a circle. You're ready to build the class into a unit.

Why a circle? You want the students to see one another if at all possible, to relate with one another as well as with you. Anybody tackling a new and difficult task feels encouraged by being in a helpful group that sets a pace and provides feedback. Working in a cooperative-competitive system prepares individual students for lifelong learning in a democracy. Here the students will be practicing both oral and written English, working together as they discover similarities and differences. At this first class, you may find it helpful to ask each student to "interview" the student next to him or her, discovering one thing they have in common and one thing that is different. Then you can ask each student to report on the person interviewed.

Students may be a heterogeneous group, but they should have been carefully tested for minimum English abilities before coming to you. During the last hour of the first or second class, you should test them again, with a simple grammar review and paragraph-writing test. These assignments can be much like the final examination for the class, perhaps just a little easier, but with much lowered expectations. You can tell students that they should be able to raise the grammar review test score (on a similar test) by 30 or 40 points in one term of work and to move from writing a half-page paragraph in an hour to writing a full-sized essay of two or three pages with few errors in the same time.

Another getting acquainted ploy that works very well and is also helpful to you is a "name chain." This name memorization activity works best in a circle, but it's possible even in a room with 40 people in rows of desks. Here's how: During the first or second class period (depending on class time and whether you are reasonably sure your class roster is now accurate), go around the room, asking each student to give his or her first name. Using groups of three or four names, have the whole class repeat the series, each time building on the series of three or four earlier names. Point out various memory devices; for example, if you get two names in a row that begin with the same letter or end with the same syllable, comment on that. Move on around the room in order, but go back frequently to the beginning of the "chain" as you knit the names together into longer and longer units.

After you've gone around the room completely, tell them you'll challenge anyone to repeat all the names after one more round. Do it once more as a class; then issue the challenge, telling them you'll help if necessary. Depending on the size of the class, you'll probably get a volunteer or two who can get most of the names right. The students need to hear the whole list three or four times during this first process, which may total 15 or 20 minutes. Remind them that this method is useful not only for learning names but also for learning any set of unrelated short materials.

At the next class, ask the students to sit in the same seats. Have the class repeat the names around the room, including names of students who may be absent and are represented by empty chairs. By the second or third week the process will take only five minutes, the students will begin to know each other's names even in the hall, and so will you. Of course, you'll need to learn the last names also, but it's a great beginning for everyone.

BUILD GROUP SPIRIT

You can encourage class spirit by at first allowing students to break into groups of their own choosing and later making the groups more heterogeneous as you do the choosing; asking students to exchange telephone numbers with at least two other students of their choice; and encouraging students to sign up for other classes and labs or study sessions together, to work on class projects together, and to plan a holiday or midterm or end-of-semester potluck or ?

As you encourage group spirit, keep a careful balance between cooperation and competition for a win-win quality-control attitude. Students can cooperate with each other and compete with their own records, challenging themselves and each other to grow. Encourage students to volunteer to answer questions when they're not quite sure of the answers. Applaud enthusiasm and the courage to participate in spite of mistakes. Expect and welcome teacher and textbook challenges. All learn new things by making mistakes. Demonstrate by admitting and correcting your own mistakes, laughing and going on.

Once you have your group formed, working together as a cooperative-competitive unit, you're ready for students to learn major batches of new material. The next three sections contain more specific teaching tips.

PREVIEW NEW IDEAS

Once everyone has a book, begin at the beginning of it. Skim over the material orally as they follow in the book, at the board, or on overheads. People learn in different ways; some do much better when they hear words as they see them.

Tell students that you are previewing the assignment for the next session and that they will be expected to read the assignment and do written work before the next session. (See "Instructors' Sample Schedules" on page xxi for suggested "chunks" of learning material.)

You may also want to quickly preview the first few chapters before students try the evaluation and placement (E&P) test; if you are teaching a three-hour class, preview the most important items in Part One during the second hour and give the E&P test in the third hour, or give the E&P test on the second day of a class that meets several times a week. Students often remember a great deal with a minimum amount of review. Tell them it may be buried deeply, but they can dig it up!

ENCOURAGE RECITATION

Even with relatively new material, involve students in the preview of the first few chapters by calling on the whole class to try a few oral answers in each Tryout exercise, saving much of the Tryout for later homework. As the class progresses and students get braver, you can ask for volunteers for an answer or two, then call on students who need a challenge (by the second or third class you'll know the students for whom the work is relatively easy but who want the fine details polished). In each preview, encourage the less-prepared students by giving them easier questions after they have had plenty of time for homework and hearing other recitations.

It is helpful to keep track of which students have contributed in class. One fairly reachable goal is to call on each student at least once each hour. After the first class session, you can call on each student to recite rather than simply taking attendance; just put a check mark by the name when the student gives an answer and a slash across that mark when you get a second answer. Such methods keep the students awake (if you don't go in alphabetical order!) and give you flexibility in asking difficult or easy questions geared to students' skills.

REVIEW

Review is a continuous process. All learning attaches to previous learning, enabling the learner to categorize and fit the new material to some item already in place. The ideal way to set up a three-hour developmental English class or week is to preview new material quickly, give the students time to read and do the written work, have them recite on the material in a separate session, review a little more before previewing the next new material, and review again before a midterm or final examination. Review tests for the students are placed at strategic spots throughout the text.

Some students will need less review than others. In fact, some students may not need to do all the homework. Just tell them you'll call on them frequently, and if they can do most of the answers "on the spot," the written homework in that section will not be necessary. Any students can get extra credit by doing long paragraphs or extra tests in areas not specifically assigned, if you like. There's plenty of material available.

GRADING

Although you may assign ungraded journals and other practice writing, you should mark all formal compositions turned in for grading, editing them to suggest correction of all the material covered in the class so far and concentrating on the most important points. Students need to learn by example and practice all the levels of proofreading, editing, rewriting, and revision—usually in that order. It's tempting to ask them to do everything at once, but that doesn't work.

My experience with these materials is that grammar and spelling or vocabulary test grades will have about a 50 percent carryover for non-ESL students and a 25 percent carryover for advanced ESL students; that is, an A average on grammar and spelling tests for non-ESL students will signal a probable A or B grade for composition; an A on grammar tests for advanced ESL students will probably signal a C or better for a final composition score. The reason for the difference is, of course, that ESL students must get past the idiom problem, the daily flow of the language that native speakers learn from constantly reading and hearing the language. ESL students must learn some grammar to attempt even basic English sentences; they can be encouraged and rewarded by A grades on grammar tests, but need weekly practice in writing focused compositions. At least half of this practice should be done in the classroom, and some of it should be timed.

ENJOY

Watch for moments of progress, the quick light in a student's eyes, a sudden "oooh!" sound or an "aha!" These all mean "I get it!" and they are the great rewards on your journey together.

INSTRUCTORS' SAMPLE SCHEDULES

Basic Weekly Semester Completion Goals

These schedules are based on three hours in class per week (a total of 48 hours) plus two hours of homework time for every hour in class. About half the numbered compositions should be written in class and timed, and students could write short paragraph answers to most in-text questions as practice journals. I recommend previewing and reviewing each topic during the weeks before and after these goals.

Week 1: Part One introduction; E&P test; practice composition 1

Week 2: Chapters 1–3; spelling list A (all spelling lists are in Appendix B)

Week 3: Chapters 4–5; practice composition 2; spelling list B

Week 4: Chapters 6–7; practice composition 3; spelling list C

Week 5: Chapters 8–10; Part One Examination; spelling list D; Part Two introduction

Week 6: Chapters 11–12; spelling list E

Week 7: Chapters 13–15; spelling list F

Week 8: Chapters 16–17; practice composition 4; spelling list G

Week 9: Chapters 18–20; practice composition 5; spelling list H

Week 10: Punctuation reviews; Part Two Examination; Part Three introduction; spelling list I

Week 11: Chapters 21–23; Sample Test 1 (plurals and possessives, in student edition); spelling list J

Week 12: Part Three Examination, Section 1 (plurals and possessives); Chapters 24–25; Sample Test 2 (pronoun usage, in student edition)

Week 13: Chapters 26–28 (verbs and agreement); Sample Test 3 (verb usage, in student edition); spelling test makeups on lists A–C

Week 14: Part Three Examination, Section 2 (verb/pronoun usage); preview Chapter 29; Sample Test 4 (agreement, in student edition); spelling test makeups on lists D–F

Week 15: Chapter 29; Sample Test 5 (modifiers, in student edition); Part Three Examination, Section 3 (agreement and modifiers); practice composition 6; spelling test makeups on lists G–J; preview Chapter 30; take-home E&P practice

Week 16: Chapter 30; review E&P take-home practice test; distribute an E&P alternate test as grammar final; last possible makeup grammar tests or in-class essays; timed final essay; party time!

Advanced Weekly Semester Completion Goals

Week 1: Part One introduction; E&P test; practice composition 1

Week 2: Chapters 1–4; test on spelling list A for extra credit at end of class (all spelling lists are in Appendix B)

Week 3: Chapters 5–7; practice composition 2; spelling list B

Week 4: Chapters 8–10; Part One Examination; Part Two introduction

Week 5: Chapters 11–13; practice composition 3; spelling list C

Week 6: Chapters 14–17; Part Two Sample Tests (in student edition); spelling list D

Week 7: Chapters 18–20; practice composition 4; spelling list E

Week 8: Complete Part Two Sample Tests (in student edition); Part Two Examination; Part Three introduction; Chapters 21–23 (plurals, possessives)

Week 9: Chapters 21–23; Sample Test 1 (plurals, possessives, in student edition); Part Three Examination, Section 1; Chapter 24 introduction; practice composition 5

Week 10: Chapters 24–25; library trip; Chapter 26 introduction; spelling list F; Sample Test 2 (pronouns, in student edition); assign research essay (practice composition 6)

Week 11: Chapters 26–28; Sample Test 3 (verb usage, in student edition); Part Three Examination, Section 2 (verb/pronoun usage); first version of research essay, spelling list G

Week 12: Chapter 29; research essay final copy due; Sample Tests 4 (agreement, in student edition) and 5 (modifiers, in student edition); Part Three Examination, Section 3; spelling list H

Week 13: Chapter 30, Part Three Sample Tests (in student edition) as wanted; spelling list I

Week 14: Appendixes A and C: Grammar Summary and Homonyms; practice composition 7 (in class); spelling list J and makeup tests

Week 15: Appendix D: Prefixes and Suffixes; vocabulary review; take-home practice comprehensive final; last makeup tests or essays

Week 16: Review of take-home practice; comprehensive grammar final; essay final; party time! (In-class essay makeups can be done during party time.)

Note: This completion speed requires a dedicated class of students who already know much of the material. You can give advanced ESL students a little extra time with Chapter 26, and you can vary the times spent on Chapter 30 and the appendixes.

Weekly Quarter Completion Goals

The quarter system is usually organized as 11 weeks of two-hour classes twice a week, for a minimum of 44 hours in class. Some Saturday courses are also designed in mini-semesters of about 44 hours. As "short" courses, these usually cannot be expected to cover advanced topics, although it would be possible to design a single quarter course covering approximately the first 25 chapters, except for Chapters 9 and 19 and much of the review material, and to put the rest of the material into an advanced course with much more writing practice, perhaps combining it with a short-essay reading text. You can also design schedules to fit specialized types of writing, with the grammar review being done concurrently with such classes as business writing or specialized reading.

In redesigning schedules to fit different levels and numbers of hours, think of total homework as well as class time; avoid giving students an at-home essay and a part examination during the same week, for example.

Completion goals for each four-hour week:

Week 1: Introduction; E&P; practice composition 1; Chapters 1–2; preview Chapters 3–5; spelling list A (all spelling lists are in Appendix B)

Week 2: Chapters 3–5; preview Chapters 6–8; spelling list B

Week 3: Chapters 6–8; practice composition 2 (in class); preview Chapters 9–10; spelling list C

Week 4: Chapters 9–10, Part One Examination; Part Two introduction; preview Chapters 11–14; spelling list D

Week 5: Chapters 11–14; practice composition 3 (at home); preview Chapters 15–17; spelling list E

Week 6: Chapters 15–17; practice composition 4 (in class); preview Chapters 18–20; spelling list F

Week 7: Chapters 18–20; Part Two Examination; Part Three introduction; preview Chapters 21–24; spelling list G

Week 8: Chapters 21–24; practice composition 5 (at home); preview Chapters 25–27; spelling list H

Week 9: Chapters 25–27; Part Three Sample Tests 1–3 (in student edition); Part Three Examination, Section 1; preview Chapters 28–30; spelling list I

Week 10: Review; Part Three Examination, Section 2; Chapters 28–30; Part Three Sample Tests 4–5 (in student edition); take-home final practice (version of E&P); practice composition 6 (in class); spelling list J

Week 11: Review; Part Three Examination, Section 3; timed final essay, grammar final (version of E&P); spelling makeups as desired; party time!

You'll cover each chapter in approximately one hour of class. They take about half an hour to discuss with another 10 minutes to review previous material and 10 minutes to preview the next chapter, including Tryout-based overheads if desired.

The Part Three Examination has been divided into three sections (approximately 15 minutes each), but you can give it all at once near the final exam if you prefer. Students seem to do better when it's divided.

For all but the most advanced students, you may decide to give retests with replaced or averaged scores. Length of writing can vary according to class progress, but students should have the experience of full-sized in-class essays before the class is over—preferably timed and with impromptu topics assigned.

Introduction

Why are you reading this book? Have you thought about goals you would like to reach? How many of them would be easier to achieve if you had a better education? How much of that education depends on your ability to communicate with others in the language of their culture? That's why you're studying English—to help make your dreams come true.

Nobody else can make your dreams come true, make you study and learn to reach your goals. No teacher can pour knowledge in: the word *education* comes from the Latin *educare,* which means "to lead forth" what's inside, not to pour anything in. Thomas Edison, who invented hundreds of modern devices, including the electric light bulb, said that "genius is 1 percent inspiration and 99 percent perspiration." So notice that bit of inspiration in your dreams, and then do the work to make them come true. Following are some steps to help you reach your goals.

KEYS TO REALIZING YOUR DREAMS

1. *Decide what your dream is,* and then set a first goal or a list of goals to reach, and write down the steps. Make your goal possible but not easy— challenge yourself.

2. *Set up a time line* to reach your goal. What's first, second, third? What are the priorities? What would be "nice if"? What is absolutely essential? Successful schedules must be flexible. Some days you can cross out many items from your "things to do" list; some days you just do what you can in the face of difficulty, but you keep moving on.

3. *Be ready to educate yourself almost anywhere, any time.* You can post a language vocabulary list on the popcorn stand at your part-time job; you can listen to audio tapes while you're driving or housecleaning or feeding a child; you can read a book or newspaper while you stand in line; you can read signs and repeat spelling words anywhere; you can watch people and listen to languages in the doctor's waiting room or on a bus; you can try problem solving before you go to sleep and discover that answers may appear in your dreams. A good student of life never goes out without material to study, just in case.

4. *Organize to suit yourself.* Many successful people organize materials into neat binders and file drawers and shelves, color-coordinated and labeled. Others find that although their work areas may look messy, the important materials are where they can find them, and they concentrate on organizing their minds. As long as you know what you want to do and where to find the

materials without wasted time, you can accomplish things. Want to work in bed? Mark Twain wrote all his books that way. Like computers? With a laptop, you might even manage *that* in bed. Use your ingenuity, and work out a system; after some trials and errors, it will be tailored for you.

5. *Find a study buddy,* or join (or set up) a companion group. Most people approach any new situation with some fear and self-doubt. If you go to school or start a business or reorganize your life or tackle any other new project alone, it's much easier to drop it, to stay home, to be discouraged. Get a friend to go with you, work with you, encourage you (including late at night when you can't find a specific answer), and give you a ride when your car won't start. If you can't find someone to work with you on exactly the same subject, try to find a *mentor,* someone who has already been through what you're doing and would be willing to help, provide feedback, give advice when you ask. Then be willing to do the same for someone else, because the best way to learn something well is to try to teach it.

LANGUAGE, THE KEY TO SUCCESS

1. *Reading is a key to language.* Learn to read rapidly when needed, to skim, to outline as you read. But also learn to read slowly when necessary, carefully and critically, to make marginal notes, to argue with the author, to ask questions of the author (and the teacher). Books (and magazines and newspapers) are meant to be savored, to be used, to be thought about and discussed. Exchange books with friends; write down titles recommended by teachers and in book reviews. The daily newspaper is one of the best sources of current events, current vocabulary, and new publications. Save interesting articles in a file; photocopy the best ones to exchange with friends.

2. *Speak the language you are studying*—whenever possible, wherever possible. Unlock your tongue (be willing to make mistakes), because we all learn by doing. If the language is your second or third, speaking it is most important—and try to listen to the language for many hours every day. A generally admired standard of United States English is spoken by the national news broadcasters, for example; they must have an accepted American accent, understandable to everyone.

3. *Take notes*—from reading, from lectures, from your own ideas, from discussions with friends, from television and movies, and from dreams.

Keep a note journal. It will provide a place for freewriting of thoughts and feelings as well as a resource for more formal writing in the future. Take careful notes in meetings and classes; teachers or other leaders may emphasize certain points in speeches, lectures, and examinations, which may clarify your reading and thinking. When you think you have the main ideas of assignments or discussions, try designing a test or a summary—you may discover things you want to study further.

4. *Know the basic structure of the language.* Knowing basic grammar is practical. When you find the subject and verb in an English sentence and

recognize a conjunction, for example, you can frequently tell where the sentence ends. You can avoid common problems, such as run-ons and fragments, that impair communication. You can organize paragraphs logically and polish essays and letters. You can get those good grades, those good jobs, those promotions and raises—because you make meaning clearer.

5. *Learn your way around your community,* business, schools, libraries, and the computerized world. Modern communication involves an explosion of information. Nobody is expected to know everything. Rather, you need to know where to *find* anything you want, and you need to eliminate all the unwanted information. Learn how to register to vote, how to get a teacher or class you want (a mentor may be a big help), how to submit a proposal, how to make up school work you didn't complete, how to communicate with a teacher about a missed class or with a business about a problem with a product or service, what to ask a counselor, how to use the library and other resources of your community, and (perhaps most of all now) how to use a computer. People who want to communicate in the twenty-first century will find the computer as valuable as the twentieth century found the automobile. The computer not only finds information for you but also helps you to present it in the neatest, clearest, and most efficient way; it saves you time and it saves the time of everyone else—and we all need time to follow our dreams.

On the first day of a new English class, when students are asked why they have come, they first say "because I need this course for a job," or "for graduation," or "to please my family." Then they begin to see that they need it for more long-term goals, to follow their dreams. So start your journey to the top.

Even a snail can reach the top.

All Tryouts, Practices, Examinations, and Quizzes in this instructor's edition contain suggested points per item, usually totaling about 100 points per test. Other scoring systems may be equally valid, of course, but I have found the suggested system useful.

A NOTE ABOUT FEATURES IN THE TEXT

Throughout the text you'll find Memory Pegs, which are designed to provide and mark relatively easy ways to remember key grammar points. All of the Memory Pegs are the simplest version of the most important parts of the rules.

The exercises within the text are of two types. Tryout exercises provide the first main practice for a topic division, and the answers are given at the end of the chapter. Practice exercises provide a second set for a topic. You can do the Tryout, check the answer key, review any areas in which you had problems, and then do the Practice as homework before the next class.

Chapters 10, 20, and 30, at the ends of the three parts of the book, also contain five Sample Tests each, covering the topics in the chapters of that part.

Part One
Structure

▼ ▼ ▼ ▼ ▼ ▼ ▼ ▼ ▼ ▼

Chapter 1

The Sentence
A Definition

Standard English sentences must include a subject and a verb.

Although some modern writing ignores standard sentence patterns, the sentence is the basic unit of English structure. Warn students that some instructors will give an F to any page of formal writing that contains a sentence fragment.

What is an English sentence? This may seem to be a simple question, but it isn't. Beginners learn that a sentence is a "group of words that makes sense by itself." Then they hear that a sentence "must have a subject and a verb." Both statements are true but a little vague—what does "sense by itself" mean? Beginners find themselves asking: What's a subject? What's a verb?

Are the following groups of words sentences? "He's coming today." "Jack climbing the beanstalk to see the giant." The first group of words is a sentence; the second one is not. Why? For answers, read on.

SUBJECT-VERB IDENTIFICATION

Find the Verb First

The verb is the key to the puzzle of the sentence, because it tells what's happening. If no verb exists, no sentence exists.

To find verbs, try the following . . . ask which word shows *action:*

    jump   sees   ran   thinks

or *state of being* (sometimes those words are called "linking verbs"):

    is   were   became

Decide whether the word shows the past, present, or future time of the sentence (tense).

Memory Peg

PAST	PRESENT	FUTURE
jumped	jump/jumps	will jump
saw	see/sees	will see
was/were	am/is/are	will be
ran	run/runs	will run
thought	think/thinks	will think
became	become/becomes	will become

The question of verb identification is troublesome because students tend to think only of action—even *visible* action—when they think about verbs. So the idea that a verb must show past, present, or future, that is, the tense of the sentence, is important.

7

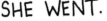

SHE WENT.

HE WILL GO.

THEY HAVE GONE.

The verb must show action or state of being and usually shows the time of the whole sentence.

She went.   He will go.   They have gone.

Memory Peg

Verbs show time (tense) in their form (usually by spelling changes).
Tense often refers to time, but there are exceptions—see Chapters 26 and 27 for a detailed discussion of verb usage in common and complex situations. A word that does not show time (a word such as *seeing* or the phrase *to see*) is not the full verb of the sentence. Phrases beginning with *to* and a verb are infinitives, not verbs, and "ing" words can't be verbs without helpers to show time.

The barking dog frightened the letter carrier.

Which word is the verb? Which word could change the time of the whole sentence if the word were changed? Try changing the sentence to future. The word that changes will be the verb.
Could these be sentences?

The barking dog.   The dog barking.   The dog to bark.

They aren't sentences because they don't have verbs. What about this one?

The dog bit.

What is the difference? The main difference is that true verbs show time. *Bit* shows past tense; *biting* does not show a tense.
Now try these:

The dog will bite.

Jack climbing the beanstalk.

He's coming today. [*He's* means what two words? Right: *he is.*]

The state-of-being verbs such as *was* and *are* show no action but do show time.

She *was* my first teacher.

She *will be* my next teacher.

If no verb exists, no sentence exists.

INCORRECT   The book on the sidewalk.

The book lying on the sidewalk.

These are not sentences! (Why not?)

Find the Subject Next

After you find the verb, the subject should become evident—it is usually the person or thing doing the action or being the rest of the sentence.

Fish swim in the ocean. [Do the fish swim? Or does the ocean swim?]

I ate my dinner last night. [Did my dinner eat? Did last night eat? I ate, so *I* must be the subject.]

Most people who have spoken or read English for some time can begin to tell whether the sentence sounds right. This textbook will give rules, but a good English student always tests the results against the sound. The more you read and hear standard English, the better your ear will become. Try saying just the simple subject with the verb you have found. Does it make sense?

INCORRECT   The boy run in the field.

The girls plays games.

When your ear is trained, you hear that something is wrong with these sentences. Either you have chosen the wrong subject, or there is a subject-verb agreement error.

The Rule of *S*: Most plural *nouns* have an *s* on them, but plural present tense *verbs* have no *s*. For singular present tense nouns it's the reverse. If the subject is *girl*, the verb is *runs*; if the subject is *dogs*, the verb is *see*: Sylvia types; Georgio writes; the teachers lecture; my brothers work; his sons eat. (See also Chapter 4, Verb Identification.)

Some "action" words (italicized in the examples that follow) can be used as subject-nouns.

Swimming is good exercise.

Studying is not always easy.

To swim is good exercise.

To study is not always easy.

SUBJECT AND PREDICATE

The main subject word in a sentence is sometimes called the *simple subject*. In Chapter 6, Identifying the Connectors, and Chapter 8, Clauses, Run-ons, and Fragments, we will discuss the *complete subject*, which includes

Don't tell a student "Don't trust your ear." Instead, say, "Train your ear by reading, listening, and speaking good English." Remind them that they'll often hear and see poor English in everyday life; they need to hunt for good language.

Memory Peg

Birds usually fly south in the winter.

the simple subject and the words surrounding it (modifying it). The *verb* also usually has extra words surrounding (modifying) it; this group of words including the verb is called the *predicate*. (The word *modify* means to "change," or "alter." Have you ever modified a car engine or a pattern or even an idea?)

One of the best ways to learn sentence structure is to label the parts of the sentence. Begin by labeling the verb and the subject. If you're used to underlining these, that's fine, but in more complex sentences, you'll need to label the function of each part with an abbreviation over it, like this:

> S   V
> Birds usually fly south in the winter.

This labeling system is simpler and easier than diagrams, seems to be just as clear for students, and takes much less space.

> S   S   V   V
> Jack and Jill jumped and ran.

SIMPLE, COMPLEX, AND COMPOUND SENTENCES

All the sentences noted so far are considered *simple* sentences because they contain only one subject-verb combination; however, sentences frequently come in the more complicated forms, *complex* and *compound*.

SIMPLE
> S V
> We wait impatiently for vacation each year.

COMPLEX
>   S V   S V
> Although we wait impatiently to travel each year, we are usually happy to get home again.

$$\overset{S}{}\quad\overset{V}{}\qquad\qquad\qquad\qquad\overset{S}{}\quad\overset{V}{}$$

COMPOUND   We wait impatiently to travel each year; however, we are usually happy to get home again.

A *complex sentence* contains two or more subject-verb combinations (clauses), with a subordinating conjunction on either clause. A *compound sentence* contains two or more subject-verb combinations joined by a coordinating conjunction or a semicolon. (See Chapters 6–8.)

Memory Peg

Tryout: Subjects and Verbs

Directions: Find the verb and then the subject in the following sentences. Watch for more than one of each. Label each subject with *S* and each verb with *V* placed above it. (Answers for Tryouts are always at the end of the chapter.)

1. Today we study English.

2. A little English is easy; fluent English is hard.

3. First lessons usually teach students to talk about daily things.

4. Many textbooks begin with pages about families.

5. They discuss mothers and fathers; they give names for family members.

6. Other important words concern transportation, communication, and money.

7. Language students read, write, and listen to new words often.

8. Students and teachers talk together for hours.

9. To learn, students listen carefully to their teachers, and then they try to repeat the words and phrases.

10. Soon they learn to write stories like the ones in this textbook.

11. A small child sees the world differently from you or me.

12. The boy sees the moon and cries to have it.

13. The moon is far away, but it looks like a ball to him.

14. The young girl's home is where her parents are.

15. Children grow very rapidly.

Five points per correct answer.

Try to go over the first third of each Tryout with students before you "turn them loose" on it. They need to go home or to a lab situation with a few examples of how to do the work. Caution them that when they recite answers for both Tryouts and Practices, you may ask them to tell the class *why* the answer is correct ("because it's a compound sentence," for example).

16. Time passes quickly for their parents.

17. To the child, each day is new.

18. The baby smiles at her parents and cries at strangers.

19. Each day brings laughter and tears.

20. Mothers and fathers work very hard to care for their children.

Practice: Subjects and Verbs

Directions: Label each subject with *S* and each verb with *V* above it.

Five points per correct answer.

                S   V
1. Don Lee is four years old.

         S   V
2. He lives in San Francisco.

         S   V
3. Don likes to ride on cable cars.

         S   V
4. He enjoys the colored lights of the city.

         S   S V
5. Don and his sister love watermelon candy.

         S   V
6. Mr. Lee is an accountant at a shop in Chinatown.

         S   V   S   V
7. Mrs. Lee studies English at night; Mr. Lee takes care of Don and his

    sister, Jan.

               S   V
8. The Lee children learn two languages, Cantonese and English.

               S   V
9. The children's grandparents speak to them in Cantonese Chinese.

       S   S V
10. Don and Jan go to Chinese school on Saturdays with their cousins.

         S   V
11. Mrs. Lee came from Hong Kong to the United States seven years ago to

    marry Mr. Lee.

Sentence 12: Ask why *majoring* is not the verb.

         S   V
12. Mr. Lee graduated from the University of California at Berkeley, major-

    ing in accounting.

         S V   S   V
13. They met when Mr. Lee went to Hong Kong to visit his grandparents.

             S   V
14. The Lee family's favorite holiday is Chinese New Year.

15. They have a favorite place to watch the parade, in front of Mr. Lee's workplace.
     s   *v*

16. Months ahead, they invite their friends to come to Chinatown for the festival.
                s   *v*

17. They bring folding chairs and raincoats, because sometimes it rains on the parade.
    s   *v*   *s* *v*

18. After they watch the bands, the marchers, and the dragon, they go to a Chinese family restaurant to celebrate with their friends.
          s *v*   *s* *v*

19. They eat a family-style feast of 12 dishes.
    s *v*

20. Then they all wish each other *Gung Hay Fat Choy*, Happy New Year.
         s   *v*

ANSWERS

Tryout: Subjects and Verbs

1. Today we study English.
           s *v*

2. A little English is easy; fluent English is hard.
       s   *v*   *s*   *v*

3. First lessons usually teach students to talk about daily things.
         s   *v*

4. Many textbooks begin with pages about families.
        s   *v*

5. They discuss mothers and fathers; they give names for family members.
   s   *v*   *s* *v*

6. Other important words concern transportation, communication, and money.
                  s   *v*

7. Language students read, write, and listen to new words often.
            s   *v*   *v*   *v*

8. Students and teachers talk together for hours.
   s   *s*   *v*

9. To learn, students listen carefully to their teachers, and then they try to repeat the words and phrases.
            s   *v*   *s* *v*

10. Soon they learn to write stories like the ones in this textbook.
         s *v*

11. A small child sees the world differently from you or me.

12. The boy sees the moon and cries to have it.

13. The moon is far away, but it looks like a ball to him.

14. The young girl's home is where her parents are.

15. Children grow very rapidly.

16. Time passes quickly for their parents.

17. To the child, each day is new.

18. The baby smiles at her parents and cries at strangers.

19. Each day brings laughter and tears.

20. Mothers and fathers work very hard to care for their children.

Chapter 2

Types of Sentences and Non-Sentences
Sentence or Fragment?

The four main sentence types are declarative, interrogative, exclamatory, and imperative. Fragments usually lack either a subject or a verb.

THE FOUR TYPES OF SENTENCES

By far the most common sentence type is the *declarative* sentence, or *statement,* which states a declared fact and ends with a period.

> California weather is relatively mild in most areas.
>
> The weather in the Midwest and Northeast has extremes of heat and cold.
>
> In winter, California has rain.
>
> Snow falls in New England but not in Florida.

The second most common type of sentence is the *interrogative* sentence. (The word *interrogative* is related to *interrogation*—if anyone has ever asked you many questions, you know what that is!) These sentences are more commonly called *questions* and end with a question mark.

> Does Saskatchewan have snow and ice?
>
> In summer, is New York City hot?
>
> Is Texas warm or cool?

The *exclamatory* sentence, or *exclamation,* shows strong feeling and ends with an exclamation point.

> Driving on ice is not easy!
>
> This is especially true on hills!
>
> How beautiful the snow and ice can be! [Note the word order in this exclamatory sentence.]

Remind students that these sentence types each have two names. Tell them which name you prefer or that you will accept either one.

Remind students that questions have a different word order from statements.

15

*Driving on ice
is not easy!*

Memory Peg

The most difficult sentence type to recognize seems to be the *imperative* sentence, or *command*. (**The word *imperative* is related to *imperial* and *emperor*. When you give commands, you're wearing your imperial crown!**) Imperative sentences have an *understood* subject, the word *you*. The subject is not said, but both the speaker and the listener know that it is *you*.

> Come to Florida for winter sunshine. [Who is supposed to come? *You.*]
>
> Try Minnesota lakes for summer boating and swimming.
>
> Read about the weather and then decide on your vacation.

Note: Many imperative sentences begin with the verb. Advertising copy uses these sentences often.

FRAGMENTS

The last group of words we'll discuss is sometimes called a *non-sentence* or *incomplete sentence,* but it is usually called a *fragment,* a broken piece of a sentence. We often speak in fragments and use them in informal writing or in answers to questions. Standard English, however, requires the usual subject-verb combination for declarative statements.

Fragments can occur for many reasons: no subject, no verb, a partial verb, an incomplete thought. In this chapter, we'll discuss the fragments that have missing parts.

INCORRECT   To come to Florida.

By the light of the silvery moon, shining on the pavement.

Singing and dancing in the street.

Do you see any true verbs, showing past, present, or future? The first two examples don't even have subjects. By adding words or combining fragments, can you make these word groups into sentences? (For more examples and discussion of other kinds of incomplete sentences, see Chapter 8, Clauses, Run-ons, and Fragments.)

Tryout: Type of Sentence

Directions: Label each group of words either declarative (dec), interrogatory (int), exclamatory (exc), imperative (imp), or fragment (fra). Use abbreviations if you wish.

Ten points per correct answer.

_____ 1. The world is changing very fast.

_____ 2. Did you see the Berlin Wall coming down?

_____ 3. What a party they had!

_____ 4. On my television screen, I've watched countries changing.

_____ 5. Dancing in the streets and seeing long-lost relatives.

_____ 6. Come watch the tapes with me.

_____ 7. Do you think television makes change come faster?

_____ 8. To see events as they happen.

_____ 9. It helps us to understand good or bad changes.

_____ 10. Don't forget!

Remind students that length has nothing to do with a sentence's type. Tell them it helps to label subjects and verbs.

Sentence 6: Ask why the sentence is imperative.

Sentence 9: Students may not notice *it* as the subject.

Look again at the word groups in the Tryout. On a sheet of paper (1) add words to any of the fragments and rewrite to make them complete sentences, and (2) answer the questions that were asked in the exercise. Are you writing a paragraph from these sentences? Could you rearrange and add things and have an organized paragraph?

Paragraph Assignment

The "From Sentence to Paragraph" sections appear after the main grammar discussion of each even-numbered chapter and lead toward related writing assignments.

FROM SENTENCE TO PARAGRAPH: ORGANIZATION

As you study sentences, you'll become more and more interested in combining them into paragraphs of connected ideas. You may have noted that some of the sentences in practice tests and examples in this text could be combined into paragraphs or short stories or essays.

Paragraphs were invented to simplify reading, to speed communication. Large blocks of print tend to make readers feel tired and resistant. So writers look for ways to divide groups of sentences into logical and more manageable chunks.

Some beginning writers feel that there must be a magic formula for creating perfect paragraphs. Certain suggestions and possible rules are available. However, paragraphs come in hundreds of varieties. As long as you can find any kind of logical or emotional break between two groups of sentences, feel free to divide them by using your writer's intuition as well as the following guidelines.

For the quickest communication, try the basic paragraph format: one general topic (main idea) sentence, usually at the beginning of the paragraph or after one introductory sentence, and followed by several more specific illustrations of the idea. Another common form reverses the pattern by putting the topic sentence at the end of the paragraph as a summary or conclusion. Here are some examples of typical paragraphs; watch for the topic sentences.

EXAMPLE 1

History books tend to be written by the winners, by those in control at the time of the writing. The English histories of the theater of Shakespearean times do not mention the 1,700 plays written by the great sixteenth-century Spanish playwrights, although they do discuss French authors. Most history books of the American West ignore the large numbers of African Americans, including cowboys, who helped settle the American frontier. And history books of all Western cultures contain very few references to the contributions of women.

EXAMPLE 2

Many otherwise health-conscious citizens have become discouraged about choosing healthy foods because the labels *light, low-fat,* and *healthy* seemed to mean little or nothing. However, a new labeling law recently enacted should help. The word *light* must now mean at least a 50-percent reduction in calories compared to the "regular" product, while *low-fat* must mean a 50-percent reduction in fat. In addition, exact amounts of fat and calories (per serving and by weight) must be listed in the nutrition panel on the package.

In more complex paragraphs such as Example 2, *transition devices* are often used within or between sentences to smooth the logical movement from one idea to the next. Note the use of *however* to show contrast, the use of *because* to show why, the use of *while* to show a related idea, and the use of *in addition* to show that another example is coming.

You may follow these basic paragraph guidelines not only for single paragraphs but also for longer pieces such as essay test answers, stories, and full-length essays.

Peg shows the effects of six countries in seven days.

Practice: Type of Sentence

Directions: Label each group of words either declarative (dec), interrogatory (int), exclamatory (exc), imperative (imp), or fragment (fra). Use abbreviations if you wish.

Five points per correct answer.

int	1.	Have you ever traveled in Europe?
dec	2.	On the first trip, people sometimes plan to do too much.
fra	3.	Six countries in seven days.
fra	4.	Jokes about Tuesday being Belgium.
imp	5.	Plan to stay at least two or three days in each place.
exc	6.	Then you won't forget where you are!
int	7.	Which country would you like to visit?
dec	8.	There are inexpensive ways to travel.
fra	9.	Youth hostels, elder hostels, student exchange programs.
imp	10.	Ask a travel agent about possibilities.
int	11.	Have you studied a foreign language?
fra	12.	Living in the country and speaking the language daily.
imp	13.	Don't be afraid to make mistakes.
int	14.	What's the best way to learn?
dec	15.	When we make a mistake and discuss it, everyone learns.

Some of our customs may seem strange to travelers!

_____fra_____ 16. In a new country, the differences in the architecture, art, music, language, customs, money, laws.

_____dec_____ 17. The country scenery of hills, forests, seashore, plants, and animals may seem like home.

_____int_____ 18. Have you looked at your own country through a visitor's eyes?

_____exc_____ 19. Some of *our* customs may seem strange to travelers!

_____imp_____ 20. When you travel, invite people to visit here.

Paragraph Assignment | Pick any question in the Practice exercise, and answer it in an organized paragraph.

ANSWERS

Tryout: Type of Sentence

Sentence 10: Give the same credit for either answer or both answers.

1. dec; 2. int; 3. exc; 4. dec; 5. fra; 6. imp; 7. int; 8. fra; 9. dec; 10. imp and exc.

Chapter 3

Noun and Pronoun Identification

Types and Functions

It pays to try to get the abstract, or idea, noun clear before discussing pronouns.

Subjects of sentences function as different types of nouns or pronouns.

IDENTIFYING NOUNS

A noun is often said to represent a "person, place, or thing." (Pronouns are treated on page 25 later in this chapter.) The most difficult nouns to recognize, however, are the "things" of the mind: ideas or abstract nouns. Perhaps the definition should be changed to persons, places, things, or *ideas*.

Abstract nouns often end in certain syllables that may be helpful in recognizing them:

-ty	-cy	-ance, -ence	-ness	-ment
liberty	adequacy	attendance	happiness	amusement
equality	efficiency	independence	business	announcement

-dom	-tion	-sion	-cion, -gion	-th
wisdom	notion	permission	suspicion	wealth
freedom	emotion	admission	religion	length

Other possible ending syllables include -tude, -ogy, -age, -al, -le. See also Appendix D, Prefixes and Suffixes; Word Division.

Can you think of more examples with these endings? Do you know any other "idea noun" endings?

Things that can be *counted* are usually nouns.

At the time, there were two *runs*, two *strikes*, and three *outs* in the baseball game.

Memory Peg

The italicized words are all nouns in this example. (They are not the only nouns in the sentence.)

If you see two or more words in a row that all seem to be nouns (no commas between), the last one is probably functioning as the noun.

We made a home run. [Did we make a home? No, we made a run.]

Many students need practice in home study skills. [*Skills* is the noun.]

Tony watched a Christmas television special. [Which word is the last possible noun, and which are the words describing it? Right—*special* is the noun this time. Why?]

Note: Some nouns are capitalized (proper nouns) because they are specific names. These are discussed further in Chapter 18, Capitalization. Capitalized nouns may often consist of several words, as in *José Marroquin,* but may be considered as one noun because they name one specific person or thing. Similarly dates, such as *Monday, February 26, 1996,* may be treated as one noun. *Collective* nouns are words that mean a group—*class, flock, jury, herd.* They are treated as singular when the members work together and as plural when the members work apart.

Words may be *count* nouns, such as *tables* or *girls,* or *mass* nouns such as *snow* or *homework.* Mass nouns are not made plural.

A sentence often has many nouns in addition to the one that is the subject (labeled S-N).

```
 S-N                V   N    N      N
People everywhere need food, clothing, and shelter.
```

```
 S-N     S-N  V                  N      N
Food and water are the most important requirements for life.
```

```
       S-N        N      N  V  N
However, half of the children in the world go to bed hungry.
```

```
 S-N   V        N    N        N
Famine begins because of drought or war in some countries.
```

```
       N    S-N  V        N         N
In other areas, people are hungry in streets near rich homes.
```

Keep in mind that a word is a certain part of speech, such as a noun, because of its position in the sentence in relationship to the other words, because of its function. The dictionary lists many different ways to use some words, because they can be many different parts of speech.

```
      V      N        N      V
I will paint the walk with new paint after I walk to the store.
```

The subject of a sentence *is* the subject because it works with the verb to make the basic sense of the sentence. If all descriptive words in the sentence are removed, including any material between commas, the subject and verb should still sound complete.

The man in the green suit called my brother. [Which is the subject-noun, *man,* or *suit?* Of course—the suit did not call my brother!]

Note: A subject can be either a noun or a pronoun. There are many other nouns and pronouns in most sentences, working not as subjects but as objects of verbs or objects of prepositions.

Remind students that the subject is not always the first noun or pronoun in the sentence.

Memory Peg

This will be clearer after you discuss prepositions, but students may be unable to handle all of it at once.

*The man in the green
suit called my brother.*

Watch for more than one subject or verb and for the switched word order of questions, with a split verb early in the sentence and the subject between the verb parts.

SPLIT VERB

V S V
Does Jim read the newspaper every day?

Tryout: Nouns

Directions: Label S, V, and/or N above all subjects, verbs, and nouns in these sentences.

EXAMPLE

S-N   V   N   N
People often talk about inflation in the United States.

1. National worries often cause problems for us.

2. The government budget changes because of the national debt.

3. The White House faces problems in this country, the Middle East,

    Africa, and Europe.

4. Leaders talk about Africa and Bosnia.

5. Which countries have freedom?

6. Do you follow current events on television or radio or in newspapers?

The next chapter discusses and lists helping verbs, but students can see now that the helper changes sentence time. Note that the examples include many idea nouns and proper nouns, including titles of more than one word, which may be labeled either as one large complex noun or as separate parts of speech.

Five points per correct answer. Partial credit for partially correct answers.

Variety is the spice of life!

7. Lela listens to music while she does homework.

8. When Hal stays up too late, his health suffers.

9. Can you get permission to travel to Egypt now?

10. Variety is the spice of life!

11. The Middle East is a fascinating area.

12. Western civilization probably began in an area near the Tigris River.

13. Baghdad, the capital of Iraq, is on the Tigris River.

14. The ancient nation in this area was called Babylon.

15. The magnificent Hanging Gardens of Babylon were known as one of the "Seven Wonders of the World."

16. Babylon, the capital of Babylonia, was on the Euphrates River.

17. The written records of Babylonia go back to a time before 3000 B.C.

18. The ancient Hebrews thought of Babylon as a very sinful place.

19. The Babylonians worshiped a goddess, not a god.

20. Visitors can see many of the old paintings, statues, and writings in museums.

Sentence 13: Baghdad is the subject. The material in the commas is an "extra" (appositive) that will be discussed later.

Practice: Subjects, Verbs, and Nouns

Two points per correct label.

Students find material more difficult in paragraph form, but that's more like real life.

Directions: Label S, V, and/or N above all subjects, verbs, and nouns in the paragraph.

             S-N   V   N   S-N   V

(1) Jenny Nguyen comes from Vietnam. (2) Her father died in the

N   S-N   V   N   N

war. (3) The Nguyen family helped the United States in South Vietnam.

      S-N   V   N   N   N   N

(4) <u>Phat Nguyen</u> came to this country with her daughter Jenny in 1974.

    S-N   V   N   S-N   V   N

(5) Pirates attacked their refugee boat. (6) The pirates stole jewelry and

 N   V   N   N   S-

food and took some refugee women to the pirate boats. (7) <u>Phat</u>

 N   V   N   N   V   N   S-N

<u>Nguyen</u> dressed Jenny like a boy and hid under a lifeboat. (8) Jenny

      V   N   N   N   N

remembers many things from Vietnam—the beautiful hills and rivers,

         N   N   N   N   N

the warm tropical forests and gardens, her cousins, her pets, the music,

   N   S-N   S-N   V   N

the food. (9) Jenny and her mother also remember great fear and

   N   V   S-N   V   N

hunger. (10) Why does Jenny miss Vietnam?

Remind students that dates like 1974 are *names* of periods of time and therefore are usually nouns.

In an organized paragraph, answer the question in sentence 10. Try to draw pictures with your words. Then label your own subjects, verbs, and nouns.

Paragraph Assignment

IDENTIFYING PRONOUNS

Pronouns are used in place of nouns. They are especially useful when you want to avoid repeating a noun, as in "Mary saw Mary's sister driving Mary's car." The common *personal pronouns* are listed below. (For more details and lists of other types of pronouns, see Appendix A, Grammar Summary, and Chapter 24, Pronouns—Common Usage and Agreement.)

SUBJECT

I   he   she   we   they   who

OBJECT

me   him   her   us   them   whom

SUBJECT OR OBJECT

it   you

POSSESSIVE

| my | his/her | our | their | your | its |
| mine | his/hers | ours | theirs | yours | its |

This is my book.   She is holding her book.
This book is mine.   That one is hers.

INTERROGATIVE (FOR QUESTIONS)

who, whom, whose, what, which, when, where, how, why

Note: The masculine pronouns are *he, him, his;* the feminine pronouns are *she, her, hers.*

The shorter possessive pronouns are often called *possessive adjectives* because they are used as modifiers before nouns. (See Chapter 5, The Modifiers.) The longer possessive pronouns are used at the ends of phrases and clauses.

Pronouns tend to be vague and indefinite because they refer to some noun already understood. If you see a specific picture in your mind when you say a word, it probably isn't a pronoun.

Pronouns, like nouns, are often used as subjects. (See Chapter 24, Pronouns—Common Usage and Agreement.)

S-Pro V   N   N
We argue often about the best methods of stopping poverty.

Keep in mind that many nouns are very general (abstract) words. Don't confuse those nouns with pronouns.

V S-Pro V   N   N
Can   we   help the homeless by giving food?

Notice the split verb in the question and the use of *homeless* as a noun.

S-N V   V   N   N   V Pro   N   V Pro
An old motto says, "Give a man a fish, and feed him for a day. Teach him to

V Pro   N
fish, and feed him for a lifetime."

Notice the verb position for the imperative sentence and the object position for *him.*

Pro   V   S-N   V
What does this saying mean?

Notice the interrogative pronoun, the split verb in the question, and the "ing" noun as a subject.

Tryout: Nouns and Pronouns

Directions: Label S, V, N, or Pro above all subjects, verbs, nouns, and pronouns.

EXAMPLE

S-Pro   V   N
He worries about earthquakes.

1. Earthquakes happen all over the world.

2. They often shake land near mountains and oceans.

3. The strongest earthquake on this continent was in Missouri.

Margin notes:

Remind students about infinitives.

One point per correct label.

Remind students about the list of interrogative pronouns on page 25.

Remind students about the list of possessive pronouns on page 25.

Tell students to use S-Pro to identify any pronoun that is the subject of a sentence.

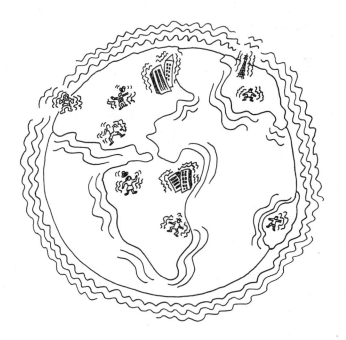

*Earthquakes happen
all over the world.*

4. Japan felt a very strong quake recently.

5. California laws require special earthquake standards for houses.

6. The most recent California quake shook my town.

7. Several people died when a bridge cracked.

8. It happened too fast for them to drive away.

9. My sister and I were lucky; we were watching television.

10. Many people stopped their cars at the side of the road.

11. They could not drive the cars because the road was shaking so much.

12. We worry when the earth shakes under our feet.

13. Have you or your relatives or friends ever been in a disaster such as a
    major earthquake, fire, flood, or hurricane?

14. We think that we should control our lives in every way.

15. We change the things that we can change.

Challenge students to find
a few two-part verbs
(discussed in detail in
Chapter 4).

In an organized paragraph, answer the question in sentence 13, using specific details.

**Paragraph
Assignment**

Five points per correct label.

Practice: Nouns and Pronouns

Directions: Label S, V, N, or Pro above all subjects, verbs, nouns, and pronouns.

                    N   S-N   V

1.   In a democratic government, people expect to vote.

      S-Pro V   N   Pro   N

2.   First we study the candidates and their ideas.

      S-Pro V   N   N   S-Pro V

3.   Then we decide which ideas and candidates we prefer.

      S-Pro V Pro   N   S-Pro V   N

4.   Sometimes we ask our friends what they think about the election.

Paragraph Assignment

    In an organized paragraph, answer one of the following questions, trying to include details in examples. The use of concrete (not abstract) nouns and action verbs will make your discussion of ideas much more vivid and memorable.

    Have you heard of some suggested solutions for poverty or homelessness?

    Have you ever voted in an election? If not, why not? Do you have some ideas about future possible votes?

ANSWERS

Tryout: Nouns

          S-N   V   N

1.   National worries often cause problems for us.

           S-N   V   N

2.   The government budget changes because of the national debt.

         S-N   V   N   N   N   N

3.   The White House faces problems in this country, the Middle East, Africa, and

        N

    Europe.

      S-N   V   N   N

4.   Leaders talk about Africa and Bosnia.

        S-N   V   N

5.   Which countries have freedom?

      V   S   V   N   N   N   N

6.   Do you follow current events on television or radio or in newspapers?

      S-N   V   N   S   V   N

7.   Lela listens to music while she does homework.

         S-N V   S-N   V

8.   When Hal stays up too late, his health suffers.

      V   S   V   N   N

9.   Can you get permission to travel to Egypt now?

Sentence 3: Students may later wish to call "White" an adjective.

10.   S-N V   N   N
      Variety is the spice of life!

11.   S-N   V   N
      The Middle East is a fascinating area.

12.   S-N   V   N   N
      Western civilization probably began in an area near the Tigris River.

13.   S-N   N   N V   N
      Baghdad, the capital of Iraq, is on the Tigris River.

14.   S-N   N   V   N
      The ancient nation in this area was called Babylon.

15.   S-N   V
      The magnificent Hanging Gardens of Babylon were known as one of the

                N
      "Seven Wonders of the World."

16.   S-N   N   N V   N
      Babylon, the capital of Babylonia, was on the Euphrates River.

17.   S-N   N V   N   N
      The written records of Babylonia go back to a time before 3000 B.C.

18.   S-N   V   N   N
      The ancient Hebrews thought of Babylon as a very sinful place.

19.   S-N   V   N   N
      The Babylonians worshiped a goddess, not a god.

20.   S   V   N   N   N   N
      Visitors can see many of the old paintings, statues, and writings in museums.

Tryout: Nouns and Pronouns

1.   S-N   V   N
    Earthquakes happen all over the world.

2.   S-Pro   V N   N   N
    They often shake land near mountains and oceans.

3.   S-N   N V   N
    The strongest earthquake on this continent was in Missouri.

4.   S-N V   N
    Japan felt a very strong quake recently.

5.   S-N   V   N   N
    California laws require special earthquake standards for houses.

6.   S-N   V Pro N
    The most recent California quake shook my town.

7.   S-N   V   S-N   V
    Several people died when a bridge cracked.

8.   S-Pro V   Pro
    It happened too fast for them to drive away.

9.   Pro S-N   S-Pro V   S-Pro   V   N
    My sister and I were lucky; we were watching television.

10.   S-N   V Pro N   N   N
    Many people stopped their cars at the side of the road.

11.   They could not drive the cars because the road was shaking so much.
S-Pro V   V   N   S-N ____V____

12.   We worry when the earth shakes under our feet.
S-Pro V   S-N   V   Pro N

13.   Have you or your relatives or friends ever been in a disaster such as a major
V S-Pro   Pro   S-N   S-N   V   N

earthquake, fire, flood, or hurricane?
N   N   N   N

14.   We think that we   should control our lives in every way.
S-Pro V   S-Pro ____V____ Pro N   N

15.   We change the things that we   can change.
S-Pro V   N   S-Pro ____V____

Verb Identification
Action and Being

Some of this chapter is a review of Chapter 1, but now we go into much more detail, and it's the hardest part of English on this developmental or remedial level.

Verbs of sentences may be of the action *or the* being *type.*

VERBS AND VERBALS

The verb is the key word in the English sentence. **The verb must tell either the action or state of being (linking verb) of its subject. It must also tell us by changes in spelling or form whether the time is the past, present, or future.** Therefore, such phrases as *to tell* (an infinitive—see page 72) or *telling* (an "ing" form, used as a noun or adjective—see page 70) will not work alone as verbs. Such parts of verbs are sometimes classed as *verbals* because they are derived from verbs.

Memory Peg

> I like pizza to go.

Which word is the sentence verb? Which word changes if you want the action to be in the past? You would say "I *liked* pizza to go," not "I like pizza to *went.*" Therefore, *like* must be the verb.

Never change a verb form after *to;* the infinitive is the idea behind a verb, not the sentence verb itself. Infinitives and "ing" forms (verbals) are used instead as other parts of speech. (See Chapter 9, How the Phrases Fit.)

Memory Peg

We conjugate and memorize sentence verbs by "person," according to which person is speaking:

PERSON	SINGULAR	PLURAL
First person	I speak	We speak
Second person	You speak	You speak
Third person	He/She/It speaks	They speak

Note: The only verb needing an *s* added is third person singular present tense.

HELPING VERBS, BEING VERBS, AND ACTION VERBS

Sometimes verbs have more than one part. The following *helping* or *auxiliary* verbs help change the time (tense) of the sentence:

am, is, are, was, were, be, been [being or helping]

will, shall, would, should, can, could, may, might, must, ought [usually helping]

do, did, has, have, had [action or helping]

I <u>am</u> a student. [being verb, with noun]

They <u>are</u> studious. [being verb, with adjective]

I <u>am</u> studying. [helping verb]

You <u>will</u> study the language. [helping verb, with noun]

He <u>did</u> study. [helping verb]

She <u>did</u> the test. [action verb, with noun]

To identify the verb of the sentence, try *using* a word as a verb and changing its time (tense).

Sara is tall.

Can you say "Sara talled"? No, you can't change the tense of *tall,* so it isn't a verb.

The *being* verbs, which are sometimes classified as *linking* verbs, show the subject of the sentence being a noun, pronoun, or adjective later in the sentence. Since the latter part of such a sentence "completes" the idea, it functions as a *complement,* with the second part of the sentence "equal to" the first part, much like the relationship in a mathematical equation.

Tom was captain of the team. [Tom = captain]

Sara is tall. [Sara = tall]

In questions, some of the helping verbs, such as *do, did,* and *will,* appear as the first words. (See pages 23, 26, and 234–235 for further use of verbs in questions.)

Will you come tomorrow?

Which words are verbs? Where's the subject? In identifying parts of speech, sometimes it helps to restate a question as a declarative sentence.

S AV
You will come tomorrow.

When these verbs are used as helping verbs, an action verb appears as the main action of the sentence.

A combination of a helper and an action verb is always considered an action rather than a being verb. Remind students that the last word of these verbs is the action.

Tom *was swimming* in the ocean.

Sara *is standing* at the door.

(See Chapter 5, The Modifiers, for more details.)

Take apart verb contractions such as *she'll* or *could've* and label them separately when you are analyzing sentences—sometimes they are two different parts of speech, especially in relatively informal spoken English. *I'll* is *I will*—subject pronoun and verb.

```
S-N      AV     N     Pro    S-Pro BV    N
```
Georgio creates a dessert for us when we're in town.

```
S-Pro    AV    AV    N         N
```
They would've eaten dinner at a restaurant.

Tryout: Verb Identification

Directions: Label S, N, Pro, BV, and AV above all the subjects, nouns, pronouns, being (linking) verbs, and action verbs in the following sentences.

One point per correct label.

Remind students that action verbs do not need obvious visual action—if you are *doing* something, including sleeping, you have an action. Otherwise, you are *being* something, such as a student.

1. We all enjoy good food.

2. Do you like to cook?

3. The best good food is cooked at home.

4. Fresh vegetables are nutritious and tasty.

5. They are plentiful in most United States grocery stores.

6. We cooked when we visited Grandmother for Thanksgiving.

7. She cooks the turkey; we bring sweet potatoes, potatoes to mash, squash, salad greens, rolls, cranberry sauce, and pies.

8. Grandma makes the best stuffing, but we all help with the cooking.

9. In my oven, two kinds of pie are baking, made from pumpkins and apples.

Sentence 9: Ask why *made* is not the verb.

10. My children like pumpkin pie the best.

11. They think that mince pie has "too many pieces in it."

12. My father asks for apple pie for his birthday.

Sentences 10 and 11: The verb *to like* is an action. A being verb won't work here; we can't say that the children *are* the pumpkin pie. And in sentence 11, *has* is an action. (Why?)

13. We light candles and sing "Happy Birthday" as my son takes photographs.

14. We will eat turkey for a week, or we'll freeze it for later.

My father likes apple pie for his birthday.

15. Most people think about good fortune in the autumn, when the food is stored for winter and the holidays are here.

16. Many countries have fall festivals much like the American Thanksgiving.

17. Have you read about holidays in other countries?

18. Do most cultures have a spring festival also?

Sentence 19: One *can be listed as either a noun or a pronoun here; in the dictionary it's both ways.*

19. Do you spend one of the holidays with your family?

20. Which holiday is your favorite?

FROM SENTENCE TO PARAGRAPH: DESCRIPTION

As you begin organizing your writing into paragraphs, you'll find that your first general statement, your *topic sentence,* frequently contains abstract ideas such as those listed as "idea" nouns at the beginning of Chapter 3. Good writing of nearly any kind will move quickly from this idea level into specific concrete examples. When Charles Schultz entitles a book *Happiness Is a Warm Puppy,* he is making the abstract-to-concrete shift immediately. The idea of "happiness" is hard to image: we can't touch or hold it in our hands, and yet we want it. So we need examples that we can touch, see, smell, hear, feel against our skin. We need specific examples involving the five senses.

Now look at the paragraph you just read. It begins with an introductory sentence. Then you see the topic sentence, then an expanded concrete example, then a concluding section that both restates the topic sentence and redefines it.

Any good writing that involves the five senses can be considered at least partially "descriptive," but we think particularly of descriptions of the scene of the writing, the setting, or the place. If you are asked to describe your favorite room, a holiday location, or an uncomfortable workplace, you'll need to engage the five senses of your readers.

Look at your recent writing assignments. Have you been using specific details in your descriptions?

Here's one special hint: try to write so that an artist or photographer could illustrate your piece. Use shape, color, sound, contrasts of light and dark, surface textures, relationships between objects and people. Be sure that your description, like a camera eye, moves in some kind of order, from one corner of the room to the next or from the most obvious parts to the smaller details. And remember that although the description consists of concrete examples, the result may create a mood or emotional reaction.

EXAMPLE 1

First come the feelings and the images. A newborn child's first experience has been of enclosed, safe warmth; then, of being thrust into a cold, bright, fearsome world, and, for the many lucky ones, the enclosed safety again of human arms. Voices that the child hears should seem familiar; they have been heard even before birth. The child opens eyes to images of light and dark that quickly become a human face. The fingers easily clutch long hair, clothing, the adult hand.

EXAMPLE 2

A description of the setting puts us into the emotional core of the story. If the night is dark and stormy, the action will probably be frightening. The wind will howl to match our feelings; the rain pouring down will foreshadow tears. Doors will creak and slam mysteriously, and running footsteps will echo down long hallways, as we feel the tingle in the spine that has meant fear since we were born. Everyone in the world is afraid of thunder, startled by lightning, drawn to a campfire to escape the dark.

EXAMPLE 3

Every part of this earth is sacred to my people. Every shining pine needle, every sandy shore, every mist in the dark woods, every clearing and humming insect is holy in the memory and experience of my people.
—Chief Seattle, *"Letter to the President of the United States"*

Notice that great communicators often follow the basic pattern. Chief Seattle did not learn this at the local college, but he first makes a general statement, then gives specific examples, then sums up with a slightly augmented and clearer version of his topic sentence. The sentence that concludes in this way is sometimes called a "clincher," because it ties the paragraph together. Look for these in the other paragraphs you read.

Write an organized descriptive paragraph answering one question in Try-out: Verb Identification. Remember to think of yourself as an artist illustrating or a camera photographing, as you include both description and narration (storytelling).

You'll find many "Paragraph Assignment" sections from here on. Use as few or as many as your schedule permits. You may expand some assignments to essay size or use them as extra-credit or writing journal additions for students who especially need the practice.

Paragraph Assignment

Two points per correct label.

Practice: Verb Identification

Directions: Label S, N, Pro, BV, and AV above all the subjects, nouns, pronouns, being (linking) verbs, and action verbs.

1.   N   S-N   AV   N
   Only a hundred years ago, more American citizens worked on farms
               N
   than in any other occupation.

2.   S-N   N   AV
   Families with eight or ten children worked together to harvest food for
        N
   local communities.

3.   S-N   AV   N   N
   Young people find little work now on small family farms.

4.   S-N   N   N   AV   N
   Many kinds of fruit and vegetables come from giant ranches using
        N
   expensive harvesting equipment.

5.   S-N   AV   N   S-Pro   AV
   Such large farms use machines very efficiently, but they may raise envi-
        N   N   N   N
   ronmental questions about soil erosion, water supply, and pesticides.

6.   S-N   N   BV   N
   Most people in this country are now city dwellers.

7.   S-N   AV   N
   Each person does a more specialized job than before.

8.   N   S-N   BV
   In large urban areas, most successful job applicants recently have been
        N
   high school or college graduates.

9.   S-N   N   AV   S-N
   Every new machine acquired by a business means that more applicants
    AV   N   N
   need specialized training for their jobs.

Sentence 3: Remind students that work *can be a noun. In this case it's the thing they* find.

Sentence 4: Ask students why using *is not the verb.*

Sentence 9: Ask students why acquired *and* training *are not the verbs.*

Paragraph Assignment

Have you ever seen a job (or even a whole occupation) change when a new machine was installed to do part of it? Write a paragraph explaining your reactions to a new job or occupation. Begin by describing the scene and changes in the scene.

ANSWERS

Tryout: Verb Identification

    S-Pro   AV   N
1. We all enjoy good food.

2. Do you like to cook?
     AV S-Pro AV

3. The best good food is cooked at home.
     S-N   AV   N

4. Fresh vegetables are nutritious and tasty.
     S-N   BV

5. They are plentiful in most United States grocery stores.
     S-Pro BV   N

6. We cooked when we visited Grandmother at Thanksgiving.
     S-Pro AV   S-Pro AV   N   N

7. She cooks the turkey; we bring sweet potatoes, potatoes to mash, squash,
     S-Pro AV   N S-Pro AV   N   N   N

     salad greens, rolls, cranberry sauce, and pies.
     N   N   N   N

8. Grandma makes the best stuffing, but we all help with the cooking.
     S-N   AV   N   S-Pro AV   N

9. In my oven, two kinds of pie are baking, made from pumpkins and apples.
     Pro N   S-N   N   AV   N   N

10. My children like pumpkin pie the best.
     Pro S-N   AV   N

11. They think that mince pie has "too many pieces in it."
     S-Pro AV   N AV   N Pro

12. My father asks for apple pie for his birthday.
     Pro S-N AV   N Pro N

13. We light candles and sing "Happy Birthday" as my son takes photographs.
     S-Pro AV N   AV   N   Pro S-N AV   N

14. We will eat turkey for a week, or we'll freeze it for later.
     S-Pro AV   N   N S-Pro AV Pro

15. Most people think about good fortune in the autumn, when the food is stored
     S-N   AV   N   N   S-N   AV

     for winter and the holidays are here.
     N   S-N   BV

16. Many countries have fall festivals much like the American Thanksgiving.
     S-N   AV   N   N

17. Have you read about holidays in other countries?
     AV S-Pro AV   N   N

18. Do most cultures have a spring festival also?
     AV   S-N   AV   N

19. Do you spend one of the holidays with your family?
     AV S-Pro AV N   N   Pro N

20. Which holiday is your favorite?
     S-N BV Pro   N

Sentence 20: Remind students about interrogative pronouns such as *which*.

Chapter 5

The Modifiers
Adjectives and Adverbs

Here's an area where even experienced English writers and speakers often falter. This chapter provides a few hints for proper usage. More detailed hints and practice appear in Chapter 29.

Modifiers are adjectives or adverbs used to enlarge and decorate nouns, pronouns, and verbs.

Memory Peg

To *modify* is to change or add to something in order to make it more interesting, more accurate, or more efficient. (Have you ever modified a recipe or a bookcase or your opinion of someone?)

The prefix *ad,* meaning "positioned nearby" or "aiding," is used in a similar way in the phrase *add to.* **For this reason, "adverb" means to "*add* to" a *verb,* especially an action verb. *Ad*jectives are the words *add*ed to the nouns or pronouns used as sub*ject*s and ob*ject*s.**

Adjectives and adverbs enlarge and decorate a sentence. Although important ideas, they are structural "extras." For this reason, the easiest way to find them is to label the nouns, pronouns, and verbs first.

ADJECTIVES MODIFYING NOUNS AND PRONOUNS

Most adjectives are positioned just before the nouns or pronouns they modify. These adjectives include descriptive words (such as colors and sizes), numbers, and the subgroup often called *articles—a, an,* and *the.* Adjectives are sometimes capitalized and called proper adjectives, as in "the English language." As noted in Chapter 3, Noun and Pronoun Identification, the possessive pronouns are also often used in adjective positions.

a big bear   two black bears   the Russian bear   my teddy bear

Note: Adjectives can also follow "being" verbs because the adjectives are complements, equal to the subject.

We were *tired.*

The cook is *creative.*

This soup will be *hot.*

You'll frequently find more than one adjective (or adverb) in a row. If you're hunting for adjectives, try each separately on the noun you think it

EVOLUTION OF THE ADJECTIVE

modifies. For example, a big brown bear is a big bear and also a brown bear, so both *big* and *brown* are adjectives modifying *bear*.

Some adjectives use hyphens to combine ideas, as in *no-fault* insurance.

Be careful not to use too many adjectives. They tend to lose effectiveness if overused.

ADVERBS MODIFYING VERBS

Adverbs are more movable than adjectives but usually sound natural next to the verb of the sentence. **Here's one helpful rule to memorize: Adverbs add to action verbs. They show how, when, where, or why actions are done.**

Memory Peg

> The bear is running *quickly* away with my lunch bag.
>
> He ran down the road very *quickly*.
>
> I crept *nervously* after him.

Some adverbs show place (here, there) or time (yesterday, tomorrow).

Adverbs are very versatile. We'll identify the ones that modify verbs first; then we'll see another variety. We'll label everything we've studied so far—subjects and verbs first. Adjectives and adverbs are often abbreviated in lowercase letters (adj, adv) to indicate that they are minor decorations.

Only after students understand the adverbs modifying action verbs, can they assimilate the other uses.

```
adj  adj   adj   S-N  adv      AV        adj adj adj  N      Pro
The big brown bear quickly climbed into the tall oak tree near me.
```

```
adj  S-N  BV  adj      adj
The bear was big and brown.
```

Tryout: Simple Adjectives and Adverbs

Directions: Label subjects (noun or pronoun), verbs (action or being), and all other nouns and pronouns. Then look for adjectives before the nouns and after the being verbs. Last, look for adverbs, which tell more about the verbs.

Two points per correct label.

1.   We drove eagerly to Yellowstone on a great vacation last year.

2.   The beautiful streams tumbled loudly over sharp rocks.

3.   Our big orange tent was carefully pitched under white birch trees.

4.   The fishing was great; the four of us caught 16 trout on the first day.

5.   Martha and Bob carried forty-pound backpacks!

ADVERBS AS INTENSIFIERS

Adverbs are versatile since they not only can add to action verbs (as adjectives cannot) but also can change the level of intensity of an adjective or other adverb. This is their other main use.

<pre>
        adj   S-N   BV   adj   N
The mountain weather was cold at night.
</pre>

<pre>
        adj   S-N   BV   adv   adj   N
The mountain weather was frequently cold at night.
</pre>

To illustrate levels of cold, it helps to move one's hand up and down as on a thermometer, from "cold" to "not cold" to "very cold."

Memory Peg

When you add words such as *frequently, very, not, somewhat,* or *slightly,* you change the level of cold. These words are all adverbs.

<pre>
adj adv adj adj   S-N BV   Pro
A very big brown bear is behind you.
</pre>

Level-changing adverbs are formally called *adverb intensifiers* because they make modifiers more or less intense. Adverb intensifiers can be used just as easily on other adverbs as on adjectives: very quickly, quite thoroughly.

Note: If you find two modifiers before a noun, try listening to them separately with the noun to see whether they are adjectives or adverbs. A big brown bear is both a big bear and a brown bear, but a very big bear is not a very bear. *Very* is an adverb modifying *big,* changing its level of intensity.

Tryout: Adjective and Adverb Intensifiers

One point per correct label.

Directions: Label S, AV or BV, N, Pro, adj, and adv. (Do you remember what they all stand for?)

1.   On the hike, Mel and Sue wore light hiking packs and helped the very

small children.

2. One hot afternoon, the men climbed the highest peak.

Sentence 2: Remind students about intensifiers.

3. When they eventually returned, they collapsed for two hours.

4. The big campfire dinner sizzled very temptingly.

5. After we had eaten like starving people, we told ghost stories.

6. The bedrolls in the tents were quite warm and very comfortable.

7. We slept soundly because we had taken a steep eight-mile hike.

8. The hike was extremely strenuous for us, but we are amateurs.

9. We are very eager to go back to Yellowstone in the winter.

10. We are eagerly waiting for deep snow.

Sentence 10: Note that the verb is split by the adverb, so the combination is AV.

Have you ever gone hiking or camping in the mountains or at the beach? Write an organized descriptive paragraph focusing on one of your experiences in outdoor activities such as these. Try to use several adjectives and adverbs in your description.

Paragraph Assignment

MOVING INTO LITERATURE

The next few practice pages are descriptive paragraphs excerpted from famous works of American and British literature. As you label parts of speech, you'll begin to notice the authors' different descriptive styles.

One point per correct label.

Tell students that they may be surprised at how easily they can label most of these pieces of literature.

Practice 1: Complex Adjectives and Adverbs

Directions: Label S, N, Pro, AV, BV, adj, and adv. Now you are labeling almost everything.

          S-N   Pro adj   N   N   adv
(1) New York, despite her first expression of disapproval, soon

 AV   Pro   adv   Pro adj   S-N   adv   adj
interested her exceedingly. (2) Its clear atmosphere, more populous

    S-N   adj   S-N   AV Pro adv   S-Pro
thoroughfares, and peculiar indifference struck her forcibly. (3) She

 AV   adv   AV adj adj adj   N   Pro   S-Pro adv   AV   Pro
had never seen such a little flat as hers, and yet it soon enlisted her

  N   adj   adj   S-N   AV adj   adj   N   adj
affection. (4) The new furniture made an excellent showing; the

   S-N   Pro   S-N   Pro   AV   AV   adv
sideboard which Hurstwood himself arranged gleamed brightly.

    adj   S-N   adj   N   BV   adj   adj   adj
(5) The furniture for each room was appropriate, and in the so-called

   N   adj   N   AV   adj   N   S-N   AV S-Pro
parlour, or front room, was installed a piano, because Carrie said she

     AV   S-Pro AV adj   N   AV
would like to learn to play. (6) She kept a servant and developed

   adv   adj   N   N   adj adj N
rapidly in household tactics and information. (7) For the first time in

 Pro N S-Pro BV   adj   adv   adj   adj N   N
her life she felt settled, and somewhat justified in the eyes of society as

S-Pro   AV   Pro
she conceived of it.

                             —Theodore Dreiser, *Sister Carrie*

Sentence 7: Felt is used like the being verb was, i.e., "she was settled."

One point per correct label.

Sentence 2: Turned is used like become here, so it's a BV.

Practice 2: Complex Adjectives and Adverbs

Directions: Label S, N, Pro, AV, BV, adj, and adv. (Review "Adverbs as Intensifiers" on page 40 if necessary.)

           AV   adj S-N   AV   S-Pro BV   adv   adj
(1) "Look, the sun's rising—this will be absolutely magnificent—

 AV   adv   AV   S-Pro AV adj N   adj N BV   adv
come quickly—look." (2) As she spoke, the sky to the left turned angry

 adj   S-N   AV   AV   adj N   N
orange. (3) Colour throbbed and mounted behind a pattern of trees,

     AV   N   BV   adv   adj   adv   adj   adj

grew in intensity, was yet brighter, incredibly brighter, strained from

                    adj   N   adj N   S-Pro   AV   adj   N

without against the globe of the air. (4) They awaited the miracle.

—E. M. Forster, *A Passage to India*

ANSWERS

Tryout: Simple Adjectives and Adverbs

    S-Pro AV   adv   N   adj adj   N   adj N

1.   We drove eagerly to Yellowstone on a great vacation last year.

    adj   adj   S-N   AV   adv   adj   N

2.   The beautiful streams tumbled loudly over sharp rocks.

   Pro adj   adj   S-N AV   adv   AV   adj   adj   N

3.   Our big orange tent was carefully pitched under white birch trees.

   adj S-N   BV   adj   adj S-N   Pro AV   adj N   adj adj N

4.   The fishing was great; the four of us caught 16 trout on the first day.

     S-N   S-N   AV   adj   N

5.   Martha and Bob carried forty-pound backpacks!

Tryout: Adjective and Adverb Intensifiers

    adj N S-N   S-N AV   adj   adj   N   AV adj adv adj

1.   On the hike, Mel and Sue wore light hiking packs and helped the very small

    N

children.

    adj adj   N   adj S-N   AV   adj   adj   N

2.   One hot afternoon, the men climbed the highest peak.

      S-Pro   adv   AV   S-Pro   AV   adj   N

3.   When they eventually returned, they collapsed for two hours.

    adj adj   adj   S-N AV   adv   adv

4.   The big campfire dinner sizzled very temptingly.

      S-Pro   <u>AV</u>   adj   N   S-Pro AV adj   N

5.   After we had eaten like starving people, we told ghost stories.

    adj S-N   adj N BV adv   adj   adv   adj

6.   The bedrolls in the tents were quite warm and very comfortable.

  S-Pro AV   adv   S-Pro   <u>AV</u> adj adj   adj   N

7.   We slept soundly because we had taken a steep eight-mile hike.

    adj S-N BV   adv   adj   Pro   S-Pro BV   N

8.   The hike was extremely strenuous for us, but we are amateurs.

  S-Pro BV adv adj   adv   N   adj N

9.   We are very eager to go back to Yellowstone in the winter.

   S-Pro AV adv   <u>AV</u>   adj N

10. We are eagerly waiting for deep snow.

Chapter 6

Identifying the Connectors

Prepositions and Conjunctions

Phrases are connected with prepositions and conjunctions; clauses are connected with conjunctions.

PREPOSITIONS: THE MINOR CONNECTORS

Point out that both *phrase* and *preposition* begin with *p*. Show students how the *pre* in *preposition* can remind them that the preposition comes first in a prepositional phrase.

Prepositions are connectors of smaller and/or less important parts of sentences. They connect nouns or pronouns to parts of the sentence and show word relationships, especially *position* relationships (note the word), such as "*in* the house," "*to* the store," "*from* the box," "*over* the hill."

Prepositions can also show *belonging* relationships. Some of the distinctions these make are quite significant: the man *of* the house is not necessarily the man *in* the house, who might be a plumber or a burglar.

Prepositions (abbreviated *prep* in labels) always are used in the word groups known as *phrases*. A prepositional phrase does not contain a verb. Phrases containing prepositions must begin with the preposition and end with the nearest logical noun or pronoun. Prepositional phrases are usually "decorations" on the sentence; like adjectives and adverbs, they modify the other sentence elements by adding details. The *simple* subject plus such modifiers creates the *complete* subject, just as the verb plus modifiers creates the predicate.

 Memory Peg

Prepositional phrases never contain the subjects or the verbs of sentences. Prepositional phrases can nearly always be removed without changing the basic sentence logic. A major exception is the prepositional phrase after a being verb, such as "He is in the house." The sentence meaning then isn't complete without the phrase.

Some Common Prepositions

about	below	except
above	beside	for
after	between	from
among	but (when it means "except")	in/into
at	by	like
before	down	off
behind	during	on

Some Common Prepositions *(continued)*

out	round	until	without
over	since	up	
past	through	with	

After, before, but, for, since, and *until* also appear on the conjunction lists (see pages 47 and 48).

When you analyze the sentences that follow, note the parentheses; it helps to put them around the prepositional phrases so that the structure stands out. Eventually the phrases may seem to appear magically.

S-Pro V   prep adj adj , N   prep adj adj   N
We hiked (into the dark forest) and (up the high trail.)

prep adj adj   N S-Pro AV adj ___adj___ N adj N prep adj
(On the long hike,) we   saw ten white-tailed deer, two otters (on the

adj   N   adj   adv   adj   N
river rocks,) and many beautifully singing birds. [Note the adverb used as an intensifier.]

Note: Prepositional phrases must end with the nearest logical noun or pronoun; however, they may contain two nouns plus *and*.

> Remind students that prepositional phrases may contain two or more nouns or pronouns, plus a conjunction such as *and*.

Tryout: Modifiers and Connectors

Directions: First label S, AV, BV, N, and Pro. Then label adj, adv, and prep and put parentheses around the prepositional phrases.

> One point per correct label.

1. In the winter, camping requires careful planning and extra gear.

2. You need special sleeping bags for below-zero temperatures.

3. Most people reserve tents with wooden floors for winter camping.

4. They greatly prefer campsites near hot showers and indoor plumbing.

5. On the breakfast table, the drinking water freezes.

6. Your milk and meat will be quite cold without an ice chest.

7. Cross-country skiing is now very popular in the mountains.

8. This sport will exercise every muscle in your body.

9. You ski down one small hill; then you struggle up the next hill.

10. After the skiing, you want a very warm fire and some hot cocoa.

> Sentence 6: Remind students that *will be* is a future tense being verb.

*Cross-country skiing
is now very popular
in the mountains.*

**Paragraph
Assignment**

How do you feel about various kinds of exercise? Write an organized paragraph describing at least one kind of exercise activity and your attitude toward it.

Practice: Modifiers and Connectors

Directions: Label S, AV, BV, N, Pro, adj, adv, and prep. Put prepositional phrases in parentheses. It helps to label subject and verb first, then all nouns and pronouns, then adjectives, adverbs, prepositions, and prepositional phrases.

One point per correct label.

1. Have you read any good books (about animals) lately?
    AV S-Pro AV adj adj N prep N adv

2. Many people like to go (on trips) to see animals (in their natural habitats.)
    adj S-N AV prep N N prep pro adj N

Give credit if students label possessive pronouns, such as *their* in sentence 2, as possessive adjectives.

3. Most countries are trying to save the natural environment and the ani-
    adj S-N AV adj adj N adj

    mals living (in it.)
    N adj prep pro

4. As people use more and more land, the animals have less and less space.
    S-N AV adj adj N adj S-N AV adj adj N

5. (In fifty years,) we may have no more wild animals (like the zebra or
    Prep adj N S-Pro AV adv adj adj N prep adj N

    giraffe, elephant or rhinoceros.)
    N N N

6. The grizzly bear is nearly extinct (in North America,) except (in Alaska.)
    adj adj S-N BV adv adj prep N prep N

7. When we cut down the rain forest (in Brazil,) we change our own climate
    S-Pro AV adv adj adj N prep N S-Pro AV pro adj N

    and the environment (of the animals.)
    adj N prep adj N

Sentence 8: Chapter 7 discusses *however* and other conjunctive adverbs. Students probably won't know how to label them yet.

8. However, people need space to live and work.
    adv S-N AV N

  adj   S-N   adj   S-N   AV   adj
9. Some governments and some companies are trying to solve these

      N
   problems.

       AV S-Pro AV   prep adj   N
10. Have you heard (about any solutions?)

In an organized paragraph, answer the question in sentence 1 or 10, including several descriptive sentences.

Paragraph Assignment

CONJUNCTIONS: THE MAJOR CONNECTORS

A conjunction is any word that is powerful enough to connect sentences. You might visualize conjunctions as strong connecting words—like the connectors that fasten train cars together.

Point out that *clause* and *conjunction* begin with *c*.

To decide whether a word can possibly function as a conjunction, try using it to join two short sentences. (Can you say, "I went to the store, *with* I wanted some bread"?) *With* can't be used as a conjunction because it can't join sentences.

Conjunctions come in three varieties: coordinating, subordinating, and correlative.

Coordinating Conjunctions

The coordinating (from *co-order*) conjunction, the most common kind, joins *equals*—equal sentences, equal phrases, equal single words—such as equal subjects, as in "Jack and Jill went up the hill."

The Main Coordinating Conjunctions

and	but	or
nor	so	for

She studies English constantly, *and* she knows it better each day.

Here the conjunction joins independent clauses—possible sentences—to create a *compound* sentence.

Subordinating Conjunctions

The second type of conjunction is the subordinating conjunction, which joins a subject-verb combination to another subject-verb combination but makes one part *subordinate* to or *dependent* upon the other. In other words,

Memory Peg

these conjunctions take possible sentences and turn them into "sub" sentences, something less than sentences, called *subordinate* or *dependent clauses*.

The Main Subordinating Conjunctions

after	before	provided that	when
although	even if	since	whenever
as	for	so that	where
as if	how	than	wherever
as soon as	if	that	whether
as though	in case that	unless	while
because	in order that	until	why

You probably noticed that some prepositions are also on these lists (pages 44–45 and above): *after, before, but, for, since, until.* When these words connect possible sentences, they are functioning as conjunctions and creating *complex* sentences. When they are not joining sentences, they are functioning as prepositions.

When dependent clauses are written as the *only* subject-verb combination, they are a type of fragment. Such fragments should be attached to simple sentences to create good complex sentences. Note the italicized conjunctions in the examples that follow.

It was almost time to go home. [sentence]

Because it was almost time to go home. [fragment]

If it was almost time to go home. [fragment]

Although it was almost time to go home. [fragment]

Although it was almost time to go home, we stopped to take one more picture of the valley. [complex sentence]

Note: Did an elementary school teacher tell you that you couldn't start a sentence with *because*? If so, that's because you were writing very short sentences at the time! You can begin a sentence with any conjunction, provided you connect it to another subject-verb combination (clause) in a way that makes sense.

Because my teacher says so, I can write this sentence.

Now write five more sentences beginning with subordinating conjunctions:

_____

_____

_____

_____

_____

Note: Any subject-verb combination that can stand independently as a simple sentence can also be used as part of a compound or complex sentence if it is properly connected, by a conjunction or semicolon, for example.

Correlative Conjunctions

Correlative (from *co-related*) conjunctions, the third type of conjunction, come in pairs. They are used to join equal words, phrases, or clauses (possible sentences) with one conjunction before one part and the other before the other part.

The Main Correlative Conjunctions

not only/but also   both/and
either/or   neither/nor

Sentence fragments are discussed *not only* in this chapter *but also* in Chapters 2 and 8.

Try writing five examples of sentences using correlative conjunctions:

_____

_____

_____

_____

_____

Tryout: Connectors

Directions: Label each word with an abbreviation for its part of speech (starting with S, AV, BV, N, and Pro), and then put prepositional phrases in parentheses. Label all types of conjunctions *con*.

One point per correct label.

1. Are you a good swimmer?

2. Swimming is good exercise for the whole body.

3. Many people learn swimming when they are very young.

4. Their parents have swimming pools, or they are taken to public pools or

   the homes of friends.

With the proper equipment, most people can enjoy both the beautiful underwater scenery and the tropical fish in warm vacation waters.

5. Small babies automatically hold their breath under water for short periods of time.

6. Some adults are afraid of the water, because they had frightening experiences when they were young.

7. They can still learn swimming, if they go to classes at the Y.

8. Swimming not only is fun but also increases safety.

9. All non-swimmers should learn "drown-proofing"—swimming and floating on the surface for fairly long periods of time.

10. With the proper equipment, most people can enjoy both the beautiful underwater scenery and the tropical fish in warm vacation waters.

FROM SENTENCE TO PARAGRAPH: NARRATION

When you tell a story about events in time, you are narrating. First this happened, then this, then this. (For one example, see the Jenny Nguyen story on pages 24–25 in Chapter 3.) Usually you describe events in chronological order. Since most of the events are in the past, you'll customarily use the past tense, although there are exceptions to this rule. Remember that most good narration also contains description, and, like many good paragraphs, it may move from the general statement to specific details. Here's an example using a famous old story opener:

> It was a dark and stormy night. As she drove along the freeway in her tiny battered car, Gina felt as if she were inside a roaring waterfall. The rain pounded the metal roof, streaked the lights glistening on the pavement, and poured down her windshield, making the freeway markers nearly invisible. The wipers slapped vainly left-right, left-right. Gina clutched the steering wheel and leaned forward, watching for the remembered exit.

Another type of narration describes happenings that frequently occur. (See the story about the Lee family's celebration of Chinese New Year on pages 12–13 of Chapter 1.) These narratives may often be told in the present tense, because they may still be continuing. Try not to shift from past to present tense within one sentence about one action. Your readers need a warning for such changes.

What have been your experiences with water—oceans, rivers, lakes, a swimming pool, or a small stream somewhere? Write a paragraph describing at least one of these.

Paragraph Assignment

Practice: Complex Labels

Directions: Label all parts of speech with the usual abbreviations.

```
          prep  N   adj  S-N    BV  adj  adj  S-N   BV  adj  con  adv S-Pro  AV
      (1)(At last,)the anchor was up, the sails were set, and off  we  glided.
```

One point per correct label.

```
       S-Pro BV adj  adj     adj        N        con con adj   adj    adj    N
      (2) It was a sharp, cold Christmas; and as the short northern day
```

Remind students that a prepositional phrase must end in a logical noun or pronoun and never contains the subject or a verb.

```
        AV    prep   N   S-Pro  AV    Pro    adv   adj  prep adj  adj
      merged(into night,)we found ourselves almost broad(upon the wintry
```

If students are not sure of a part of speech, they can try a word they do know in the same position in the sentence. For example, in line 3 they might try "we found ourselves *high* upon," or "we were *low* upon." In line 8 they might replace *all* with *completely.* (Remind students that a few adverbs are often used without the *ly,* such as *slow, fast,* and *deep.*)

```
        N    Pro     adj   S-N    AV  Pro prep N con prep  adj      N
      ocean,)whose freezing spray cased us(in ice,)as(in polished armor.)
```

```
          adj  adj  S-N  prep  N  prep adj    N      AV   prep adj    N
      (3) The long(rows of teeth)(on the bulwarks)glistened(in the moonlight;)
```

```
      con prep adj  adj   adj    N  prep adj  adj    N    adj   adj
      and(like the white ivory tusks)of some huge elephant,)vast curving
```

```
        N     AV    prep adj  N       adj  adj S-N  adv   AV  prep adj
      icicles depended(from the bows.)(4) The old craft deep dived(into the
```

```
       adj   N  con  AV  adj    adj      N    adv prep Pro con adj  S-N
      green seas)and sent the shivering frost all(over her,)and the winds
```

```
       AV   con adj  S-N    AV
      howled, and the cordage rang.
```

—Herman Melville, *Moby Dick*

Now see the musical extravaganza loosely based on Herman Melville's classic novel.

ANSWERS

Tryout: Modifiers and Connectors

1. (In the winter,) camping requires careful planning and extra gear.
   prep adj N   S-N   AV   adj   N   adj   N

2. You need special sleeping bags (for below-zero temperatures.)
   S-Pro AV adj   adj   N   prep   adj   N

3. Most people reserve tents (with wooden floors) (for winter camping.)
   adj S-N   AV   N prep adj   N   prep adj   N

4. They greatly prefer campsites (near hot showers and indoor plumbing.)
   S-Pro adv   AV   N   prep adj   N   adj   N

5. (On the breakfast table,) the drinking water freezes.
   prep adj   adj   N   adj   adj   S-N   AV

6. Your milk and meat will be quite cold (without an ice chest.)
   Pro S-N   S-N   AV   adv adj   prep adj adj N

7. Cross-country skiing is now very popular (in the mountains.)
      adj   S-N BV adv adv   adj   prep adj   N

8. This sport will exercise every muscle (in your body.)
   adj   N   AV   adj   N   prep Pro N

9. You ski (down one small hill;) then you struggle (up the next hill.)
   S-Pro AV prep adj adj N   adv S-Pro AV   prep adj adj N

10. (After the skiing,) you want a very warm fire and some hot cocoa.
    prep adj   N   S-Pro AV adj adv adj N   adj adj N

Tryout: Connectors

       BV S-Pro adj adj   N

1.   Are you a good swimmer?

       S-N   BV adj   N   prep adj adj   N

2.   Swimming is good exercise (for the whole body.)

      adj S-N AV   N   con S-Pro BV adv adj

3.   Many people learn swimming when they are very young.

      Pro   S-N   AV   adj   N con S-Pro   AV   prep adj   N   con

4.   Their parents have swimming pools, or they are taken (to public pools) or

      adj   N   prep   N

      the homes (of friends.)

      adj   S-N   adv   AV Pro   N   prep   N   prep adj   N

5.   Small babies automatically hold their breath (under water) (for short periods)

      prep N

      (of time.)

      adj   S-N BV adj prep adj   N   con   S-Pro AV   adj   N

6.   Some adults are afraid (of the water,) because they had frightening experiences

      con S-Pro BV   adj

      when they were young.

      S-Pro AV adv AV   N   con S-Pro AV prep   N   prep adj N

7.   They can still learn swimming, if they go (to classes) (at the Y.)

      S-N   con   BV adj   con   AV   N

8.   Swimming not only is fun but also increases safety.

      adj   S-N   AV   N   N   con   N

9.   All non-swimmers should learn "drown-proofing"—swimming and floating

      prep adj   N   prep adv adj   N   prep N

      (on the surface) (for fairly long periods) (of time.)

      prep adj adj   N   adj   N   AV   con adj   adj

10. (With the proper equipment,) most people can enjoy both the beautiful

      adj   N   con adj   adj   N prep adj   adj   N

      underwater scenery and the tropical fish (in warm vacation waters.)

Chapter 7

Interjections, Relative Pronouns, Conjunctive Adverbs, and Possessive Nouns

The four remaining parts of speech fulfill a variety of functions in sentences.

INTERJECTIONS

Words or small groups of words that are used before exclamation points to express strong feeling of any kind are interjections.

> Wow!   Hurrah!   Way to go!

Although these parts of speech are less common, we need them when we need them!

If an exclamatory group of words is too short to be called a sentence, call it an interjection, and write it separately from the main sentence.

> Congratulations! You've just won $10 million!
>
> Oh, sure! That comes in everybody's mailbox!
>
> Not mine! Do you really believe that?

Don't overuse interjections, or you may sound hysterical!

RELATIVE PRONOUNS

Certain pronouns seem to function as half pronoun and half conjunction—pronoun because they refer to a previous noun or pronoun, and conjunction because they can work as subordinating conjunctions do, to begin dependent clauses.

Memory Peg

The main relative pronouns are:

who	whose	whom
which	that	

You can easily memorize this short list.

54

The words *who* and *whom* are reserved in English for people, the word *which* is reserved for things, and the word *that* can be used for either. Don't say, "the teacher which I saw." You can, however, use *which* as an interrogative pronoun to ask a question meaning "which one?" about a person. In other words, you can say, "Which teacher is absent?"

> The teacher *whom* I had for the last class will be teaching it again this semester.
>
> The class *that* I took was very valuable.
>
> Ask *who* will be teaching the class *that* you are taking.

Note: Informal English sentences frequently contain an "understood" *that* to connect such clauses as the last one.

> She knew she was happy. ["She knew that" is understood.]

Be careful not to omit the *that* if the meaning is not clear.

> **INCORRECT**   She knew the boss would give her a raise.

What's the problem with meaning? Your reader may start by thinking, "She knew the boss." Is that what you meant?

CONJUNCTIVE ADVERBS

Adverbs that show some transition between sentence ideas are frequently confused with conjunctions. Like most adverbs, they can be moved to different parts of the sentence, however, because they are not connecting grammatical parts.

Memory Peg

> These words are called adverbs; *however,* they feel like conjunctions.

You can move the conjunctive adverb:

> These words are called adverbs; they feel, *however,* like conjunctions.

Common Conjunctive Adverbs

accordingly	likewise	then
consequently	moreover	therefore
furthermore	nevertheless	thus
however	otherwise	yet

Don't allow students to label these as conjunctions. They are adverbs, movable "extras"; they provide transitions but don't actually connect anything.

> Several of my relatives live in the Boston area; *therefore,* we often get together for holidays.
>
> One of my sisters lives in Cambridge; the other sister, *however,* lives in Wellesley.
>
> A few years ago, we drove to Springfield for Thanksgiving; *then* we got caught in a snowstorm on the way home.

The three italicized conjunctive adverbs are those that most often tempt writers into errors. People tend to use commas with them and think they have correct sentences. With no semicolons, the sentences above would be *run-ons,* with or without the commas. (See Chapter 8 for "run-on" details.)

POSSESSIVE NOUNS

As you've been labeling parts of speech, you may have noticed that there are seldom two nouns in a row—without commas, that is. The main exception involves the possessive noun. Possessives are nouns functioning like the type of adjective that shows ownership.

The possessive noun is shown with an apostrophe plus an *s* sound. When there is not already an *s* or an *s*-related sound, such as *x* or *ch,* an *s* is added. Plural possessives always carry an apostrophe after just the plural—whether the plural ends in *s* or not. (See Chapter 23, Possessive Nouns.)

Traditional possessive style always adds an extra *s* for short words that end in *s* sounds, as in "my boss's desk." A modern space-saving style uses "my boss' desk," because the *s* sound is already there. Know which version your group uses.

If you see two nouns in a row with the first one carrying the apostrophe and *s,* you have found a possessive noun.

my sister's baby	the boy's foot	a man's watch
the ladies' room	the boys' heads	the men's room

THE STORY OF THE DUCKBILLED PLATYPUS

In the grammar rules for labeling the functions of parts of speech, there are sometimes two correct answers; for example, some possessive pronouns are occasionally used as possessive adjectives. Such situations tend to make people nervous. They like to think that all of life falls neatly into the boxes they have organized for it. However, rules always have a few exceptions, and life sometimes brings surprises.

Consider the duckbilled platypus. You learned in science classes that mammals have hair and give milk and that water birds have bills like ducks and webbed feet and lay eggs. So we have scientific classifications of "mammals" and "water fowl." But after the classifications were designed, the duckbilled platypus and a few cousins were discovered in Australia. The platypus has hair, a duck bill, and webbed feet; it gives milk; and it lays eggs. Which box do we put this creature in? We need to design a small special box.

English grammar grew from English speech and later from English writing. As people's lives change, their language changes: new words are added to the dictionary every year, and new usages are accepted, although more slowly. Just be sure to check the most recent reference books when you're in doubt about a language question. Then you'll be communicating clearly with the largest number of people. You won't find yourself insisting that the platypus is only a mammal, or only a bird, or that a word can be used only a certain way.

Tryout: Full Labels

Directions: Label all parts of speech, starting with subjects and verbs. Use S, AV, BV, N, N(poss) (for possessive nouns), Pro, rel pro (for relative pronouns), adj, adv, prep, con, interj (for interjections), and inf (for infinitives—see pages 8, 31, 70, and 73). Put parentheses around prepositional phrases.

Two points per correct label.

1. Wow! That author's books make great practice materials.

2. Read the following chapters, and analyze them carefully.

3. At the library, Elena's children like to get books that have lots of

    pictures.

4. She says that the picture books nevertheless teach her children to read

    quickly.

5. The people who work conscientiously to improve their education have

    a good chance to succeed.

Practice: Full Labels

Directions: Label all parts of speech as S, AV, BV, N, N(poss), Pro, rel pro, adj, adv, prep, con, interj, or inf.

Two points per correct label.

By now, students may be ready to label infinitives. I've mentioned and defined them several times; Chapter 9 discusses them in detail.

          AV S-Pro adv AV adj   N   con   N   S-N   prep   Pro
(1) Have you ever kept a journal or diary? (2) Writing(about your

   N   N   con   N   AV   pro   inf   Pro   N
thoughts, plans, and dreams)may help you to improve your life.

    N (poss)   S-N   AV   adj   N   adj   N   N (poss)
(3) Mr. Rosa's students have kept a journal all semester. (4) Katrina's

  S-N   AV   adj   adj   N   con S-Pro AV   rel pro S-Pro
journal contains many interesting dreams. (5) When she knows that she

  AV   inf   prep Pro S-Pro   AV   Pro   N   adv   adv
wants to write(about them,)she remembers her dreams more vividly.

Katrina's journal contains many interesting dreams.

ANSWERS

Tryout: Full Labels

1. interj   adj   N(poss)   S-N   AV   adj   adj   N
    Wow! That author's books make good practice materials.

2. AV   adj   adj   N   con   AV   Pro   adv
    Read the following chapters, and analyze them carefully.

3. prep adj   N   N(poss)   S-N   AV   _inf_   N   rel pro   AV   N   prep   N
    (At the library,) Elena's children like to get books that have lots (of pictures.)

4. S-Pro   AV   con   adj   adj   S-N   adv   AV   Pro   N.   _inf_   adv
    She says that the picture books nevertheless teach her children to read quickly.

5. adj   S-N   rel pro   AV   adv   _inf_   Pro   N   AV   adj   adj
    The people who work conscientiously to improve their education have a good

    N   _inf_
    chance to succeed.

Sentence 4: Give students credit for labeling *that* as either a conjunction or a relative pronoun if it's attaching a clause.

Chapter 8

Clauses, Run-ons, and Fragments
Sentences or Not?

Independent and dependent clauses may become sentences, run-ons, or fragments.

INDEPENDENT CLAUSES

A *clause* must contain at least one subject and verb combination, but an *independent* clause must also make reasonable sense by itself.

The following are all simple sentences or independent clauses. Identify the subjects and verbs.

> Comedies are relaxing.
>
> Television and movies can keep people laughing.
>
> Mysteries and tragedies also absorb viewers.
>
> Why do people cry at movies?
>
> Some people like to be frightened by movies.

Sentences that include more than one independent clause are called *compound* (meaning "double or more") sentences. The clauses are usually joined by coordinating conjunctions, such as *and, but,* or *or.*

> Movies can make you laugh, but they can also make you cry.

The independent clauses in compound sentences can also be joined by semicolons or other major pieces of punctuation such as dashes, but never by commas alone (see "Run-on Sentences" on page 63).

Note: *Independent* means "able to stand alone." An independent child wants to do everything with no help. College students who are independent of their parents are paying their own way.

Write a short, organized paragraph, using and labeling a few independent clauses (in simple and compound sentences), answering the question, Why do people cry at movies?

Remind students that every sentence must have at least one independent clause, that is, at least one subject and verb combination.

Memory Peg

Paragraph Assignment

DEPENDENT CLAUSES

Dependent clauses also contain a subject-verb combination (or they wouldn't be clauses), but they cannot stand alone because they begin with connecting words such as subordinating conjunctions. A sentence that contains at least one independent and one dependent clause is called a *complex* (mixed) sentence.

There are three main varieties of dependent clauses: adjective, adverb, and noun clauses.

Adjective Clauses

The dependent clauses that describe nouns or pronouns start with the easily memorized relative pronouns: *who, whose, whom, which, that.*

> The house *that I saw* was for sale.
>
> People *who cry at happy movies* tend to be experienced in life.
>
> Shakespearian tragedies cause viewers to feel empathy for the characters *whom they admire.*
>
> The actor *whose work is good* will make us forget his occupation.

The italicized clauses are called *adjective* clauses, because they work in the sentence as a single adjective would; that is, the clauses identify which noun (house, people, characters, actor) is being discussed and give details about that noun. (Remember that a group of words can work as a single part of speech, the way capitalized nouns such as *United States* do.)

Try writing three sentences with dependent adjective clauses of this type. (They start with which words?) Then underline dependent clauses.

_____

_____

_____

Adverb Clauses

The second variety of dependent clause begins with the standard list of subordinating conjunctions, such as *because, since, although, if, when, before.* (See the complete list on page 48.)

> *When you see a movie or play,* you tend to relate it to yourself.
>
> *If you see an aspect of your childhood on television,* you may remember more details of your early years.
>
> Good plays, movies, and novels affect us *because they are true psychologically.*

Remind students that the "extra" adjective and adverb dependent clauses can be removed from their sentences, leaving only the necessary independent clauses.

Although people still read books, they may watch more stories on television.

Sometimes we read the book *after we have seen the movie.*

The italicized clauses are called *adverb* clauses because they seem to modify the whole independent clause, the most important word of which is the verb.

Adverb dependent clauses also tend to be movable, like most adverbs; they can usually be flipped from front of sentence to back and vice versa. Try moving the dependent clauses in the examples to the other ends of sentences.

Write three sentences with dependent adverb clauses in them. Remember, each dependent clause must contain a subject and verb and begin with a subordinating conjunction. It's possible to have a prepositional phrase in a clause. Then underline dependent clauses.

_____

_____

_____

Note that each sentence here contains at least one independent clause. Students need to practice using these terms; they tend to mix them up.

Noun Clauses

The third type of dependent clause is the one being used as a noun. These *noun* clauses stand (like any noun) for a person, place, thing, or idea. Noun dependent clauses are used as subjects, objects of verbs, objects of prepositions, or complements of being verbs. You can substitute a simple noun in such sentences for one of the noun clauses, although the meaning may change somewhat.

Noun clauses usually answer questions beginning with the words *what, who,* or *whom.*

> She said *that she understood.* [She said what? She said this idea—noun clause as direct object of verb *said.*]
>
> I know *that I can learn this.* [I know what? I know this idea—noun clause as direct object of *know.*]

All indirect quotes and clauses after *know* or *think* are likely to function as noun clauses.

> *What he said* is true. [What is true? This idea is true—noun clause as subject.]
>
> Give it to *whomever you see.* [Give it to whom? Give it to this person—noun clause as object of preposition.]
>
> Take pictures of *whatever you want.* [Take them of what? Take them of this thing—noun clause as object of preposition.]

(If you're curious about the correct use of *who* and *whom,* look at pages 217–220.)

Memory Peg

Note that noun clauses, because they function as key parts of the sentences such as subject or object, cannot be removed without destroying the basic *Memory Peg* sentence.

We often speak in noun clauses. Have you picked up the pattern? Try writing three sentences containing dependent noun clauses used as subjects or objects. Then underline dependent clauses.

_____

_____

_____

FRAGMENTS OF CONJUNCTIVE STARTS

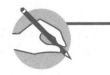

Memory Peg

Any dependent clause written without the rest of the sentence would be considered a sentence fragment. **Think of such clauses as *fragments of conjunctive starts*. In Chapter 2, Types of Sentences and Non-Sentences, we talked about the other type of fragment—the incomplete sentence—which we can call the *fragment of missing parts,* because it is missing the subject or the verb or both.**

Any dependent clause used alone is thus a fragment, and is considered a mistake in formal standard English. (Fragments are acceptable in dialogue, ads, letters to friends, poetry, or poetic literature.) All fragments are considered incomplete in idea, because they cause questions in the reader's mind; the reader is waiting for the rest of the sentence.

INCORRECT   How we did it.

Because I said so.

Whom you saw at the class.

Write several examples of fragments of either kind: clauses beginning with connecting words or partial clauses with key elements missing.

_____

_____

_____

Tryout: Fragments

Directions: Label the following clauses either S for sentence or F for fragment.

Seven points per correct answer.

____ 1. Because he was in the movie, he is recognized everywhere.

____ 2. Where did you go?

____ 3. Where you got the job.

_____ 4. Next week, we'll study plurals.

_____ 5. After we eat dinner, shall we talk?

_____ 6. If you know the answer.

_____ 7. Consequently, you will study.

_____ 8. Passing the test and therefore the course.

_____ 9. To study because you are interested.

_____ 10. Since summer, we have learned to write better.

_____ 11. The teacher who gave us clues to improved sentences.

_____ 12. Although we have practiced, we still can improve.

_____ 13. Which clause is dependent?

_____ 14. The one that starts with a subordinating conjunction.

_____ 15. The one whose meaning is not complete.

RUN-ON SENTENCES

Another major sentence mistake is the run-on sentence, which consists of two independent clauses connected incorrectly. **These clauses can be connected with a conjunction or semicolon or other major piece of punctuation such as a dash, but commas won't connect sentences—that's the type of run-on often called a** *comma splice.*

Memory Peg

	ind		ind

INCORRECT   We live in a complex society, it requires us to know many things. [run-on, comma splice]

Saul practiced every day, therefore he improved his free-throw success. [run-on, comma splice with conjunctive adverb]

I own several complicated appliances some of them are very hard to use properly. [run-on, no punctuation or conjunction; find the subjects and verbs; then decide where the sentence breaks]

CORRECT   We live in a complex society; it requires us to know many things. [compound, with semicolon]

	ind		dep

We live in a complex society, which requires us to know many things. [one clause made dependent; complex sentence]

Saul practiced every day; therefore he improved his free-throw success. [compound, with semicolon and conjunctive adverb]

ind | ind

I own several complicated appliances, but some of them are very hard to use properly. [compound, with coordinating conjunction]

Tryout: Run-on Sentences

Directions: Label each sentence either S (sentence) or R (run-on). It helps to label the subjects, verbs, and breaks between clauses first.

Five points per correct answer.

_____ 1. I've had some of these appliances for a long time, for example, my stove has a timer which I have never used.

_____ 2. I bought a VCR two years ago, I was hesitant to try to program it.

_____ 3. After about a year, I learned how to do it by asking someone to show me.

_____ 4. First you buy a great new thing then you spend the next week fussing with it.

_____ 5. When all else fails, read the manual.

_____ 6. Manuals are usually written by people who know the item very well.

_____ 7. They explain in technical language, they assume you know as much as they do.

_____ 8. Many companies are looking for good technical writers to improve their manuals.

*When all else fails,
read the manual.*

_____ 9. After you finish school, see whether you can get a writing job.

_____ 10. We study the language to improve our understanding and our communication.

_____ 11. We go to school, we study, then we get jobs.

_____ 12. We buy VCRs that we want to use.

_____ 13. We read the manual, finally we understand it.

_____ 14. Our cars are another problem, most of us can't repair them.

_____ 15. We don't even know what the funny noises are.

_____ 16. When we take the car to the shop, it behaves very nicely.

_____ 17. Like the computer, it knows when we are threatening it.

_____ 18. New cars, in fact, are becoming more like computers.

_____ 19. The computer chips figure the gas flow, they figure air mixture, they keep track of oil and water.

_____ 20. Now if they would just learn to avoid accidents, we might be really grateful.

FROM SENTENCE TO PARAGRAPH: THE JOURNAL

A journal is a very personal and informal piece of writing—a written record of parts of your life, written for yourself. There is no mysterious method for writing one. Just put pen to paper, or turn on the computer, and begin. Remember to use _I_—the first person—when writing about your own ideas and feelings and experiences. You are writing to understand yourself and others. The simple process of trying to put words onto paper often clarifies the mind, calms the emotions, and straightens out tangled thinking.

However, a journal can also be a form of _prewriting,_ if you are planning to communicate with others. For example, a letter to a friend can sound very much like a page from a journal. In such letters, you choose the parts from your personal journal (at least in your mind) and tell your friend (your audience) about the parts of your days you think would be of most interest to them. You choose which parts to include and which parts to edit out in the same way that professional writers edit books. Which parts are most interesting, sound best, communicate meaning best?

Let's say you've been jotting down notes somewhere—in a journal or as a response to a textbook or a teacher's assignment. Now you are asked to write and submit a paragraph that may eventually grow into a longer assignment such as an essay. (The word _essay_ means "a try" or "an attempt" to explain or communicate.) Can you see the advantages of having the notes as a beginning?

Write an organized paragraph explaining at least one of your own experiences with writing a journal or letters to friends.

I recommend that you encourage all kinds of journal writing. Without really "correcting" students' journals, you can make a quick check of them every month or two (perhaps during students' in-class writing or examinations) and give a little credit for extra effort.

Paragraph Assignment

Practice: Run-on Sentences

Directions: Label S or R in the blank following each sentence. First label the subjects, verbs, and breaks between clauses, if helpful.

(1) Because of computers, typing (now often called *keyboarding*) has become a necessary skill. __S__ (2) Anyone who wants to work in an office needs to use a keyboard efficiently. __S__ (3) You will use a computer at home, then you will need it in the office. __R__ (4) Salesclerks now use computers in most stores, even in the smallest businesses. __S__ (5) Young people learn to play games on computers, often they know more about computers than their parents do. __R__ (6) Changes come more quickly now, we all need to learn new things frequently. __R__ (7) When we learn to use the latest software programs, we can work more easily. __S__ (8) First, read the advertisements to see what employers need, next, study those subjects. __R__ (9) We study, we apply for jobs, however, we need luck too. __R__ (10) Ask your friends for help, see what they recommend. __R__

Practice: Run-ons and Fragments

Directions: Add the appropriate clause and sentence endings (semicolons or periods and capital letters) in these paragraphs to avoid run-ons and fragments.

Evidence is accumulating that the brain works a lot like a muscle. the harder you use it, the more it grows; its newly discovered ability to change and adapt is apparently with us well into old age. best of all, this research has opened up an exciting world of possibilities for treating strokes and head injuries and warding off Alzheimer's disease. recent research suggests that stimulating the mind with mental exercise causes millions of additional connections or synapses between brain cells. think of it as a computer with a bigger memory board.

Anything that's intellectually challenging can probably serve as a kind of stimulus for dendritic growth. here are some suggestions. do puzzles. try a musical instrument. fix something. try the arts. dance. date provocative people.

—Daniel Golden, "Building a Better Brain," *Life,* July 1994.

How do you relate to the machines of modern life? Write a paragraph explaining how you use one common modern machine.

Paragraph Assignment

ANSWERS

Tryout: Fragments

1. S; 2. S; 3. F; 4. S; 5. S; 6. F; 7. S; 8. F; 9. F; 10. S; 11. F; 12. S; 13. S; 14. F; 15. F.

Tryout: Run-on Sentences

1. R; 2. R; 3. S; 4. R; 5. S; 6. S; 7. R; 8. S; 9. S; 10. S; 11. R; 12. S; 13. R; 14. R; 15. S; 16. S; 17. S; 18. S; 19. R; 20. S.

Chapter 9

How the Phrases Fit

Prepositional, Participial, and Infinitive Phrases

The three main types of modifying phrases are prepositional, participial, and infinitive phrases.

This chapter can be postponed, assigned as reading only, or entirely omitted for early-level developmental classes. It is appreciated by early college students (those about ready for Freshman Composition) but is not included in the Part One Examination. (See "Instructors' Sample Schedules" earlier in this edition.)

PREPOSITIONAL PHRASES

Memory Peg

You have already practiced identifying prepositional phrases and noted that they never contain the subject or the verb. Prepositional phrases always begin with a preposition and end with the nearest logical noun or pronoun. **The preposition positions a thing, showing the relationship of the noun or pronoun that is its object to some other word in the sentence.**

Prepositional phrases always work in sentences as adjectives or as adverbs, because they give additional information. (A group of words can work as a single part of speech. For example, a person's full name works as a single noun.)

Long prepositional phrases may occasionally tempt you to punctuate them as sentences even though they lack a subject or a verb, but they are fragments and need to be attached to a main clause.

Adjective phrase means "adjective type of prepositional phrase," of course, but students don't need to keep repeating the long version.

> The house (on the corner) was a good buy. [adjective type of prepositional phrase, modifies *house*]
>
> My cat sleeps (by the window.) [adverb type of prepositional phrase, modifies *sleeps*]
>
> The doorway (with gold trim) is mine. [adjective phrase, modifies *doorway*]
>
> She climbed (up the ladder.) [adverb phrase, modifies *climbed*]
>
> He ran (across the road and field.) [adverb phrase, modifies *ran*—note that he ran across both areas]
>
> Bicycles (with lights or reflectors) are safer at night than those (without lighting.) [adjective phrases, modify *bicycles*]

In some sentences, a noun is used between the verb and the prepositional phrase modifying the verb, but the action verb is strong enough to connect with the prepositional phrase even across the noun.

He placed the ladder (against the house.) [Adverb: it's true that the ladder is against the *house*, but the phrase tells where he *placed* it.]

If the phrase makes sense with the verb, the verb takes it, and the phrase is functioning as an adverb. It tells how, when, where, or why the action was done.

This means "action verb," of course.

Some people paint walls (with a roller.) [Why is this phrase an adverb? It tells how they paint.]

Note: Words like *up* and *down* do not function as prepositions unless they are the beginnings of phrases.

Memory Peg

He climbed up.

Can you see that *up* is an adverb and not a preposition in that sentence?

Remind students that prepositions are always the first word of a phrase; they always attach something to the sentence.

Practice: Prepositional Phrases

Directions: Put each prepositional phrase in parentheses and circle the word it modifies. Then label it adj if it modifies a noun or adv if it modifies an action verb.

1. The (woman) at the desk) is the receptionist. *(adj)*

2. She usually (types) on a computer keyboard.) *(adv)*

3. The computer keyboard is (used) with a color monitor.) *(adv)*

4. Her (telephone) is (like a (computer) in miniature.) *(adj ... adj)*

5. It is a small (switchboard) with twenty flashing lights.) *(adj)*

6. Have you ever answered a (phone) with many lines?) *(adj)*

7. (At busy times,) you can easily (lose) people's calls. *(adv)*

8. The receptionist must watch every (light) on the board.) *(adj)*

9. Meanwhile, her computer (waits) for her.) *(adv)*

10. The (job) of a receptionist) is not a (piece) of cake!) *(adj ... adj)*

For each sentence give four points for labeling prepositional phrases correctly; three points for labeling types correctly; and three points for circling modified words correctly.

Note: The labeling of prepositional phrases as adjective or adverb helps in advanced writing projects and helps with punctuation but will not be covered further in Part One.

PARTICIPIAL PHRASES

Memory Peg

Do you remember the "ing" words that looked like verbs but were not? They are present participles. **Think of *participle* as meaning *part* of a verb.** Participles work as verbs only with helping (auxiliary) verbs such as *have* or *was* or *am.* The phrases containing only parts of verbs (that is, participles) are often mistakenly punctuated as sentences, but they are only fragments until they are attached to independent clauses.

Conjugating the Main Tenses of Verbs

All verbs (in most languages) are conjugated in ways that we memorize when we first learn new languages. In English the regular past tense verbs and past participles all end in *ed;* we memorize the tenses of irregular verbs. All present participles end in "ing."

INFINITIVE	PRESENT	PAST	PAST PARTICIPLE	PRESENT PARTICIPLE
REGULAR VERB CONJUGATIONS				
to look	look(s)	looked	looked	looking
to record	record(s)	recorded	recorded	recording
SAMPLE IRREGULAR VERB CONJUGATIONS				
to see	see(s)	saw	seen	seeing
to go	go(es)	went	gone	going
to write	write(s)	wrote	written	writing
to ring	ring(s)	rang	rung	ringing

For the full irregular verb list, see the extended discussion of verbs in Chapter 26, Verbs—Common Usage, and Chapter 27, Verbs—Complex Usage.

When the past or present participle is used with a helping verb (such as *has, have, was,* or *is*—see the complete list on page 31), the participle becomes part of the full verb. Full verbs are italicized in the examples that follow.

Labeling the full verb (AV or BV) of the sentence is enough, but students may begin here to use the label *part* for "participle" in verb phrases.

> We *have looked* at the evidence.
>
> It *was recorded* on tapes.
>
> *Have* you *seen* the judge's comments?
>
> We *have been going* over them very thoroughly.
>
> He *will be writing* carefully.

Participles Beginning Phrases

Present and past participles are also used to begin phrases. Such participial phrases are used as adjectives and are placed immediately before or after the nouns they modify. Sometimes the participial phrase consists of a participle plus a prepositional phrase.

Looking at the attorney's written notes, the word processor accurately typed the brief.

Recorded on tape, the testimony was damaging to the defendant's reputation.

The judge's comments, *heard by everyone,* startled the jury.

Going over the evidence, she made her decision.

The judge, *writing carefully,* has explained the legal principles.

Knowing the many correct ways of using modifying phrases will help students increase sentence variety.

Because adjectives need to be very near the nouns or pronouns they modify, there are only two "safe" places to put a participial phrase—just before the noun or just after the noun. The examples could be restated as follows.

The word processor, looking at the attorney's written notes, accurately typed the brief.

The testimony, recorded on tape, was damaging to the defendant's reputation.

Heard by everyone, the judge's comments startled the jury.

Now note what happens when participial phrases are put in the wrong position. (Ever hear of a dangling participle? For further discussion and practice with these, see Chapter 29, Adjective and Adverb Usage.)

INCORRECT   The word processor accurately typed the brief looking at the attorney's written notes. [Was the brief looking?]

The evidence was damaging to the defendant's reputation recorded on tape. [Was the reputation recorded?]

The judge's comments startled the jury heard by everyone. [Was the jury heard?]

These are very common errors, and students will enjoy watching for them in newspapers, for example. You might give extra credit for samples of errors they find.

These dangling or misplaced participles (also called *dangling modifiers*—and even prepositional phrases can dangle) can get ridiculous. Some sentences have to be completely rewritten; those with misplaced phrases can be fixed by simply moving the phrases.

Tryout: Dangling and Misplaced Phrases

Directions: Correct the dangling and misplaced participial phrases, rewriting if necessary.

Ten points per reasonable rewrite.

1. Running into the room, the typewriter fell over.

2. Boiling rapidly, the cook watched the eggs on the stove.

3. The lady got on the bus in the red dress.

4. After climbing to the top of the tower, the city lights gleamed below.

5. Blown across the room by the fan, we picked up the scattered papers.

6. The typewriters were returned by the repair technician, completely overhauled.

There are many Practice exercises and Sample Tests covering phrases in Chapters 10, 20, and 30.

The mountains were beautiful, rowing across the lake.

7. Traveling for days, our hotel was still many miles away.

8. Blooming in the desert, the travelers enjoyed the cactus.

9. The mountains were beautiful, rowing across the lake.

10. She was watching television, eating a snack.

Or you might add a *thing* needed for the action, as in sentence 2 in the Tryout on page 71 ("water is boiling"). Remind students that *rewrite* means to use any way to give the presumed idea of the sentence a logical interpretation.

Note: Some sentences with misplaced phrases can be repaired by simply moving the offending phrase. In others, a person doing the action <u>needs to be added</u> to the sentence. Be careful that you don't just create a new dangling modifier in your rewrite.

Even the best writers sometimes use phrases incorrectly. A while ago, a television reporter in a hurry gave us this example over the national news when he got a sudden bulletin about a major winter fire in a high-rise apartment:

> Filled with heavy water and covered with ice, the firemen had trouble lifting the hoses. [Yes, they would!]

How should the reporter have composed the sentence?

One more note about "ing" words: sometimes they are used as nouns, as we noted in Chapter 1, The Sentence. When they are used as nouns, their formal name is *gerund*.

INFINITIVE PHRASES

Memory Peg

The infinitive is the idea behind the verb, never the verb of the sentence. **The word is related to *infinite*, which means "without beginning or end, extending indefinitely," so the infinitive never shows past, present, or future time (tense), and its ending never changes. In English, infinitives always begin with the word *to*—to run, to study, to sleep, to think. Infinitives often function as adjectives or adverbs, much like prepositional phrases.**

The two important things to remember about infinitives are: They are not prepositional phrases (like "to the store"), and they are not verbs of sentences (we don't say "John to went" or even "John wanted to went").

> I like pizza *to go.* [adjective phrase; modifies the noun *pizza*]

> We have things *to do.* [adjective phrase; modifies what noun?]

Infinitives used as adverbs answer typical adverb questions: why, how, where, or when an action was done.

> Eric is studying *to pass the test.* [Why is he studying?]

> Mei told jokes *to make the students pay attention.*

Unlike prepositional phrases, infinitives are also often used as *nouns* because they represent ideas.

> S-N
> *To study* is not easy.

Note: This noun is much like a gerund. The sentence could be written "*Studying* is not easy."

> N
> We like *to laugh.* [object of verb *like;* answers the question what, which always elicits a noun answer]

Infinitives can also be modified by adverbs:

> adv
> To laugh happily was her usual response. [answers the question how to laugh]

Now you've learned all the structure of sentences. The lights should go on and stay on very soon—you just need practice. Think how far you've come in a short time!

Tryout: Phrase Identification

Directions: Put the prepositional phrases in parentheses; label the prepositions (prep), infinitives (inf), participles (part), and verbs (AV or BV). Be sure you can tell the difference!

Two points per correct label. Give credit for *part* label applied to last word in action verbs.

1. In the book is a fable from Aesop.

2. A boy was swimming in a river and sank into deep water.

3. He was in great danger of being drowned.

4. A man who was passing on a nearby road heard his cries for help.

5. Running to the riverside, the man began to scold the boy for his carelessness.

6. The man made no attempt to help the boy.

7. Nearly sinking into the depths, the boy yelled, "Help me first; scold me later!"

8. Aesop says, "In a crisis, give assistance, not advice."

9. Are you tempted to scold people in times of trouble?

10. Do you sometimes feel like the boy in the story?

Paragraph Assignment

In an organized paragraph, answer the question in sentence 9 or 10 or both.

ANSWERS

Tryout: Dangling and Misplaced Phrases

The idea is that a person was running, not the typewriter. Remind students that there are many acceptable answers; tell them to be creative.

1. [Possible answers] As I was running into the room, the typewriter fell over.
   John was running into the room when the typewriter fell over.

2. The cook watched the eggs boiling rapidly on the stove.
3. The lady in the red dress got on the bus.
4. [Possible answers] As we were climbing to the top of the tower, the city lights gleamed below.
    After climbing to the top of the tower, we saw the city lights gleaming below.
5. We picked up the scattered papers blown across the room by the fan.
6. [Possible answers] The completely overhauled typewriters were returned by the repair technician.
    The typewriters, completely overhauled, were returned by the repair technician.
7. [Possible answers] Traveling for days, we learned that our hotel was still many miles away.
    After we had been traveling for days, our hotel was still many miles away.
8. The travelers enjoyed the cactus blooming in the desert.
9. [Possible answer] The mountains were beautiful, as Susan was rowing across the lake.
10. [Possible answer] While eating a snack, she was watching the television.

Tryout: Phrase Identification

1. (In the book) is a fable (from Aesop.)
   prep BV *prep*

2. A boy was swimming (in a river) and sank (into deep water.)
   AV *prep* AV *prep*

3. He was (in great danger) (of being drowned.)
   BV *prep* *prep*
   part

4. A man who was passing (on a nearby road) heard his cries (for help.)
   AV *prep* AV *prep*
   part

5. Running (to the riverside,) the man began to scold the boy (for his carelessness.)
   part *prep* AV inf *prep*

6. The man made no attempt to help the boy.
   AV inf

7. Nearly sinking (into the depths,) the boy yelled, "Help me first; scold me later!"
   part *prep* AV AV AV

8. Aesop says, ("in a crisis,) give assistance, not advice."
   AV *prep* AV

9. Are you tempted to scold people (in times) (of trouble?)
   AV AV inf *prep* *prep*

10. Do you sometimes feel (like the boy) (in the story?)
    AV AV *prep* *prep*
    part

Chapter 10

Structure Review

Review and analysis of all kinds of sentence structure leads to English mastery.

WORD ORDER AND CONTEXT

You now know all the parts of speech and the ways that phrases and clauses fit together to make an English sentence. Have you noticed by now how important word order is in English? Let's try an experiment. Do you remember Lewis Carroll's *Alice in Wonderland*, the great English novel about a child's dream? Some of Alice's dream images and sayings seem to be nonsense (like many dreams), but the word order helps us to guess at the meaning. The famous poem "Jabberwocky," from Carroll's *Through the Looking Glass*, the second volume about Alice, begins:

> 'Twas brillig, and the slithy toves
> Did gyre and gimble in the wabe;
> All mimsy were the borogoves
> And the mome raths outgrabe.

Can you label the parts of speech in the poem? Use the word-order clues. What's the second subject of the first sentence? Right—it's *toves*.

Is the word singular or plural? How do you know? What's the verb? (What are these toves doing?)

The first clause begins with the old-fashioned contraction, *'Twas,* which stands for *it was.* The subject is what? Therefore, what part of speech is *brillig*? After a being verb, we have a noun or an adjective. It was a day; it was sunny; it was hot; it was brillig. What part of speech do you think this is?

Do you see the prepositional phrase at the end of the second line? What part of speech would *wabe* be?

Now try the other two lines. Do you see how important the word order is? A more complex term involving word order is *context*—the words around the other words. We get much of our meaning from the context of a word.

Incidentally, when the Disney artists illustrated *Alice,* they were asked to draw toves and mome raths. They decided that mome raths should look like giant, fluffy chrysanthemums.

And now, to continue the review, let's get on with our Practice and Tryout exercises. Do as many as you need to make the ideas clear, and then you should be ready for Sample Test 1. Good luck!

Sidebar notes:

Advanced students sometimes enjoy trying to label (or punctuate, for Part Two) the whole poem.

Brillig is an adjective.

Wabe is a noun.

Practice: Major Sentence Errors

Directions: In the blanks write S for complete sentence, F for fragment (incomplete sentence), or R for run-on—either with or without a comma to connect the two parts.

Four points per correct answer.

_F_ 1. The need to choose a career while in college.

_R_ 2. Marco has decided to become an actor he likes theater and the other arts.

_F_ 3. The students majoring in acting.

_S_ 4. Although he majors in theater, he loves to paint.

_F_ 5. To learn about acting and the study of Shakespeare.

_R_ 6. The students practice many hours, however, they still need to work on their lines.

_F_ 7. While Marco memorizes his lines.

_S_ 8. Marco memorizes his lines while he works as a janitor in a church near the college.

_F_ 9. Although he works hard at his job.

_S_ 10. Marco's work hours are long, but he can practice his lines while he cleans floors.

_R_ 11. A church janitor is called a *sexton,* it is a very old word.

_R_ 12. The first plays were held in churches, the plays were about religious ideas.

_R_ 13. Marco also works with a group of actors they put on plays in elementary schools.

_F_ 14. Because the children laugh at and learn from the plays.

Marco practices his lines while cleaning floors.

_F_ 15. These young actors from the college.

_S_ 16. Marco and his friends are getting valuable experience with the children in the audience.

_F_ 17. Much designing and creating of costumes and sets.

_R_ 18. First they sketch the ideas for the current play, then they create costumes and sets that can be easily moved.

_R_ 19. The actors do their own makeup and lighting, they need to be very versatile.

_F_ 20. Luis Valdez, who majored in theater at the local college and then started his own theater, Teatro Campesino.

_R_ 21. Sometimes the actors adapt children's stories for their plays, in fact, sometimes they write their own original scripts.

_S_ 22. Would you like to see a play?

_F_ 23. So that you can read about the plays at this theater.

_S_ 24. Every weekend the Sunday paper tells about them.

_S_ 25. All the world's a stage, and all the men and women merely players.

—William Shakespeare, *As You Like It*

FROM SENTENCE TO PARAGRAPH: CHARACTER

As you progress from writing about and trying to understand yourself, in journals and narratives about your life, you will feel the desire to understand and write about other people. Such writing is often labeled *character* writing, because it describes more than just the surface appearance of the people.

You may want to mention the many meanings of *character*, including in drama, in morals, and the like.

Good character writing shows the person's true being, the "inside" of the person. You may begin with a description of the person's looks, but then you should move quickly into showing the person in action, using details that show what the person's character is like. Choose details to illustrate a point about the person. If you want to "prove" that the person is generous, for example, show the person doing generous deeds.

Paragraph Assignment

One famous saying is, "You can't teach an old dog new tricks." You may agree or disagree. Using this idea as a main point, tell your readers in an organized paragraph about an older person you know who seems to be trying some surprisingly new things. Most of your paragraph will be in the *third person*—that is, using *he, she, they* with the proper verbs, rather than *I, you, we.*

Practice: Clause Review

Directions: Underline the *dependent* clauses.

Five points per sentence.

                           Dep (adv)   Ind

1. When management and labor cannot agree, a strike may occur.

2. We have some students **Ind** who work as telephone solicitors. **Dep (adj)**

3. I wanted rain **Ind** so that my garden would grow. **Dep (adv)**

4. That he had no money **Dep (N)** did not seem important.

5. Sue has a new watch, **Ind** which tells the date. **Dep (adj)**

6. The woman **Ind** whose recipe was tested **Dep (adj)** is not here today. **Ind**

7. He got the advice of his wife, **Ind** who knows a lot about cars. **Dep (adv)**

8. I always read his column, **Ind** although I often disagree with him. **Dep**

9. Give the money to whoever can use it. **Dep**

10. After I take this test, **Dep (adv)** I'm going to celebrate. **Ind**

Directions: In the blanks, write F for fragment or S for complete sentence.

__S__ 11. I should send her a thank-you gift.

__F__ 12. Such as a flowering plant.

__F__ 13. When I see her face.

__S__ 14. I feel like smiling.

__F__ 15. Expecting to get here on time.

__S__ 16. She drove slowly.

__F__ 17. If I can help it.

__S__ 18. Come see me.

__S__ 19. Cheese is nutritious.

__F__ 20. And costs very little compared to meat.

Tryout: Parts of Speech and Clauses

Directions: Label all the parts of speech in the sentences below, using S, AV or BV, N, N(poss), Pro, rel pro, adj, adv, prep, con, interj, inf, and part. Put parentheses around prepositional phrases. Watch especially for possessive nouns, adverb intensifiers, conjunctive adverbs, relative pronouns, and conjunctions—the hard ones. Then underline dependent clauses.

1. Aesop was a slave storyteller who probably lived six hundred years

    before the Christian era.

2. Croesus was an extremely rich king who lived at about the same time.

3. Aesop's fables always have a moral—usually the same moral.

4. The point of Aesop's stories is always to tell us that people should not

    believe very much in their own greatness.

This is a good review for the Part One Examination. Students don't need to label the types of dependent clauses, but they may ask for that information. Remind them that there should be an independent clause unless the noun clause is actually a subject.

Sentence 4: In this case a dependent clause is the subject of the sentence.

Sentence 6: The independent clause is split by the dependent clause.

Sentence 9: The dependent noun clause is a key part of the structure because it is the object of *to*.

If you decide to use both sections of this Practice exercise (pages 78–79), it might help to do the following Tryout first and go over it in class.

One-half point per correct label.

Remind students that when they label S and V and watch for connecting words, they will find the clauses and that the dependent clauses will begin with the conjunctions or relative pronouns. (This is the most difficult Part One Tryout exercise. Use it for upper-level developmental students.)

5. "Pride goeth before a fall" is one way Aesop says it.

6. Both Aesop and Uncle Remus told their best stories about beasts and birds.

7. The creatures stand for humans with certain characteristics.

8. The lion, therefore, is always stronger than the wolf.

9. The fox must necessarily be deceptive; however, the sheep must move blindly ahead, ignoring the signs of trickery.

10. Aesop also tells stories about people who make mistakes.

11. "The Goose That Laid the Golden Eggs" tells of a goose that was owned by a foolish man and woman.

12. We still talk about the story when we say that a person has "killed the golden goose."

13. The greedy couple killed the goose to get the eggs that had not been laid.

14. They found no eggs; therefore, they did not get rich immediately.

15. In addition, they got no more daily golden eggs.

Paragraph Assignment | In an organized paragraph, describe another greedy character who gets into trouble; use either a fictional character or someone from real life.

Sample Test 1: Parts of Speech

Directions: Label the part of speech of each word, using S, AV, BV, N, N(poss), Pro, rel pro, adj, adv, prep, con, interj, inf, and part, and put prepositional phrases in parentheses. Contractions should be split and labeled as two parts of speech.

Watch for adverbs of time and place. (Double-check the list on page 38 before you label these sentences.) Watch for verbs that have two parts. Don't forget that adverbs add to action verbs or intensify other adjectives and adverbs and that adjectives or nouns are used with being verbs.

These first four Sample Tests are much easier than the Tryout above (pages 79–80). These Sample Tests alone will provide a good review for early secondary-level students.

One point per correct label.

    adv pro S-N con S-Pro AV prep adj adj N
1. Yesterday my friend and I went (to three discount stores.)

            adj   S-N   prep   adj   N   AV adv   AV   adv

2. Many stores (with low-priced merchandise) are now located together.

      S-Pro AV   adv   AV   adj   N

3. These are often called "outlet stores."

             S-N   adv   AV   adj   N   prep adj   N

4. Manufacturers frequently send surplus products (to these stores.)

      interj S-Pro AV   adj   N   adv

5. Wow! We found great prices there!

      pro   adj   S-N   BV   adv   adj

6. Our charge cards were very tempting.

   S-Pro   AV   inf   pro   N   prep adj   N   adv   adv

7. I will have to plan my budget (for next month) quite carefully.

     interj S-ProAV adv AV   adj   adj   N

8. Hey! I don't like high interest rates.

     S-Pro AV   adj   N   prep pro   N

9. I keep careful records (of my purchases.)

           adv   S-Pro AV adj   N

10. Consequently, I get few surprises.

    S-Pro AV adj N   adv   con   AV   adj   adj   N   <u>rel pro</u> S-Pro   AV

11. I opened a bill yesterday and found one large item that I had forgotten.

       adv   S-Pro AV   adv prep pro   N

12. Tomorrow I'll look again (at my records.)

    prep   adj   N   adj   S-N   AV   pro

13. (At holiday times,) expensive items tempt me.

     adv S-Pro   AV   adv   inf   prep pro   N

14. Then, I must work harder to pay (for my purchases.)

Sample Test 2: Parts of Speech

Directions: Label the part of speech of each word using S, AV or BV, N, N(poss), Pro, rel pro, adj, adv, prep, con, interj, inf, and part, and put prepositional phrases in parentheses. Underline dependent clauses.

One point per correct label of word or dependent clause.

Memory Peg

             S-N   AV   adj   adj   N   prep pro   N   prep adj   N

Do you remember subordinating conjunctions? They connect dependent clauses to the main independent clause, thus making a sentence complex. Review the list of main subordinating conjunctions on page 48 and keep it in mind as you label the sentences.

(1) Children love the local park (beside my house.) (2) (In the spring)

adj   S-N   AV   prep adj   N   adj S-N   AV   adj   N

the ducklings hatch (near the pond.) (3) One duck hatched eleven babies

     adv   adj S-N con S-N AV   adj   N   prep adj   N

recently. (4) The boys and girls feed whole-grain crackers (to the ducks.)

     AV S-Pro AV   adj   adj   N   prep adj   N   adj-part prep adj N

(5) Have you seen the green heads (of the drakes,) shining (in the sun?)

     con   S-N   AV prep adj   N   adj adj S-N   AV   adv

(6) When visitors come (to the ponds,) all the ducks swim quickly

prep   N   S-Pro   AV   adv   adv   con S-Pro BV adv   adj

(to shore.) (7) They will move more slowly if they are not hungry.

          S-N   con   S-N   adv AV prep adj   N   S-Pro AV   N

(8) Tadpoles and frogs also live(in the pond.)(9) They eat mosquitoes

con   adj   N

and other insects.

— Sample Test 3: Parts of Speech —

Here are more good simple review examples.

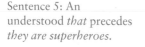

Memory Peg

One point per correct label.

See the discussion of the omitted *that*, for example, in the discussion of relative pronouns.

Directions: Label the part of speech of each word, using S, AV or BV, N, N(poss), Pro, rel pro, adj, adv, prep, con, interj, inf, and part, and put prepositional phrases in parentheses.

     Watch for infinitives, participles, and gerunds. They are formed from verbs but are not verbs of the sentences. Instead, they are used as adjectives, adverbs, or nouns. **Infinitives always begin with *to* and then contain a "verbal" (a word derived from a verb); gerunds (used as nouns) end in "ing"; present participles (used as adjectives) also often end in "ing."**

     Don't forget about imperative and complex sentences. Hint: Is it possible to have a complex sentence without saying the conjunction?

        adj   adj   S-N   AV   N   prep adj   N

1.   Most American parks contain playgrounds(for young children.)

        S-N AV adv   AV   inf   adj con prep adj N

2.   Swings are now designed to be safer(than in the past.)

        S-N   con   adj   S-N BV adj prep   N   prep adj N

3.   Slides and climbing bars are fun(for youngsters)of any age.)

        S-N   AV   N   rel pro   AV   prep N con   N

4.   Children like tunnels that are made(of logs and concrete.)

        con S-Pro AV   S-N   AV   S-Pro BV   N

5.   When they climb, children pretend they are superheroes.

Sentence 5: An understood *that* precedes *they are superheroes.*

6.
     S-Pro AV   N   adv con   N   adv
They like climbing up and jumping down.

7.
  con   S-N BV prep adj   N   S-N BV   adv   prep   N
When dogs are (in the park,) they are usually (on leashes.)

8.
     S-N   adv   AV   inf   N   con adj   N
Children also like to ride bikes and other vehicles.

9.
    AV prep adj adj   N prep   N   con S-Pro AV   adv   AV adj   N
Come (to a city park) (at sunset,) when you will probably see the children

   adj-part
playing.

> Remind students that participles and infinitives can be modified by adverbs, because they are created from verbs.

In an organized paragraph, name several ways in which having children changes a person's life.

> **Paragraph Assignment**

Sample Test 4: Parts of Speech

Directions: Label the part of speech of each word, using S, AV, BV, N, N(poss), Pro, rel pro, adj, adv, prep, con, interj, inf, and part, and put prepositional phrases in parentheses.

Do you remember what the helping verbs are? If you're not sure, check the list on page 32, and try to keep it in mind as you do the test. Also remember that words like *these* and *this* can be used either as adjectives before nouns or as pronouns.

> One point per correct label.

1.
   adj   S-N   AV prep N
Wise customers watch (for sales.)

2.
  S-Pro AV   N   prep N prep   N   con prep adj   N
You find advertisements (for sales) (in newspapers) and (in the mail.)

3.
    AV   N   adv   adv
Read ads very carefully.

> Remind students that a new preposition creates a new phrase.

4.
   adj   S-N   AV   N
Some ads claim bargains.

5.
    adj   S-N   BV   N   prep adv adj   N
"Loss leaders" are products (at very low prices.)

> Remind students to ignore quotation marks when labeling.

6.
   adj   S-N   AV   adj   N   prep adj   adj   N   prep adj   N
The store may have no samples (of the inexpensive products) (in the ads.)

7.
  S-Pro AV   adv   AV   adv   adj   N
You might regretfully buy more expensive things.

8.
   adj   S-N   AV   adj con   adj
Some products are labeled "lite" or "natural."

9.
    adv   adj   S-N   AV   Pro
Unfortunately, these words mean nothing.

> Remind students that so far they have studied only personal pronouns; they will study other types, such as indefinite pronouns, in Part Three.

10.
   adv   AV   adj   N
Always read nutritional labels.

11.
   adj   adj   S-N   AV   adv
The largest ingredient is listed first.

12. (In a fruit drink,)the first ingredient should be juice, not sugar.

    prep adj adj   N   adj adj   S-N   BV   N   adj   N

13. Most cities and states have laws(about advertising.)

    adj   S-N   con   S-N   AV   N   prep   N

14. Supermarkets usually have lower prices than small grocery stores.

    S-N   adv   AV   adj   N   con   adj   adj   N

15. A small store sometimes offers personal service.

    adj adj   S-N   adv   AV   adj   N

Tryout: Parts of Speech and Prepositional and Participial Phrases   *Quiz preparation*

One-half point per correct label or pair of parentheses.

Directions: Label all parts of speech, and put prepositional phrases in parentheses.

Capitalized nouns and titles may be labeled as if one word or labeled separately. A capitalized adjective is also possible. Participles, although often used in phrases, can be labeled either adj or part.

1. The United States is a country of immigrants.

2. The Native American Indians probably came first, walking over a land bridge into North America and then, through many centuries, moving gradually into the lower tip of South America.

3. During the days of the early Greek civilizations, the Phoenician traders sailed secretly into all the oceans.

4. In the Middle Ages, Vikings and other groups from northern Europe crossed the Atlantic frequently.

5. The first major evidence of European settlers in North America is from Vikings like Eric the Red in the tenth century.

6. However, traces of possible pre-Columbian trading posts or settlements from China have been found along the West Coast of North America.

7. Christopher Columbus sighted Western Hemisphere land on October 12, 1492.

8. Like many educated people of his time, Columbus believed in a round world.

This Tryout and Sample Test 5 are valuable for advanced students who really want to test themselves; they are not easy. You can use them as part of your course review or as a test to identify advanced students.

9. Columbus made several trips to his newly discovered land, bringing Native Americans and their belongings to Europe.

10. Why did Columbus call the Native Americans *Indians?*

In an organized paragraph, answer the question in sentence 10, or write a narrative about the immigration of someone in your own ethnic group.

Paragraph Assignment

Sample Test 5: Parts of Speech, Prepositional and Infinitive Phrases, and Independent and Dependent Clauses

Directions: Label all parts of speech; then put prepositional (prep phr), participial (part phr), and infinitive (inf phr) phrases in parentheses and label them; finally, underline dependent clauses (dep clause), and label them.

```
     adj    S-N      AV        adj      N   con   N  prep adj    adj
1.  The Puritans demanded religious freedom and reforms (in the sixteenth

     con    adj       N     prep    N
    and seventeenth centuries)(in England.)
```

This test is harder than the Part One Examination. For one thing, there are a few nouns used as appositives, which are discussed in Parts Two and Three. I sometimes use it as part of a final course review.

One-third point per correct label or parentheses.

2.
prep | N | adj | adj | adj | adj | S-N | prep | N
(In 1620,) the first permanent North American settlement (by Europeans)

AV | prep | prep adj | adj | N | inf | adj
was made (in Massachusetts) (by the Puritan Pilgrims) (to escape English

adj | N
religious persecution.)

3.
S-N | BV | N | prep | N | prep
William Bradford was Governor (of Plymouth, Massachusetts) (from

N | prep | N | con | adj | S-N | AV | prep pro | adv | adj | adj
1621) (to 1656,) when the colony was noted (for its extremely strict reli-

N
gious laws.)

4.
S-N | adj | N | S-rel pro | AV | prep | N | prep | N | prep
Roger Williams, a minister (who lived in New England) (from 1603) (to

N | AV | adj | N | prep | N | prep | N | inf | adj
1683,) founded the colony (of Rhode Island) (in 1636) (to escape Puritan

adj | N
religious persecution.)

Students can underline clause and phrase combinations separately if they desire.

5.
adj | S-N | adj | adj | S-N | S-rel pro | AV | prep adj | adj | N
The Inquisition, a religious tribunal which began (in the thirteenth cen-

AV | con | AV | N | prep | N | prep | N
tury,) convicted and executed thousands (of people) for heresy.)

6.
S-N | part prep | N | AV | adj | N | prep | N | prep
James Oglethorpe ((born (in 1696))) founded the colony (of Georgia) (to

rel pro | adj | adj | adj | S-N | AV
which) many French Protestant Huguenots fled.

7.
S-N | N | BV | adj | adj | N | rel pro | AV | N
William Penn (1644–1718) was the English Quaker who founded Penn-

prep | N
sylvania (in 1682.)

8.
N | part prep | N | BV | pro prep adj | adj | adj
Father Junipero Serra (born (in 1713)) was one (of the Spanish Catholic

N | prep adj | N | prep | N | S-rel pro | AV | adj | adj
priests) (on the West Coast) (of North America) who started the California

N | prep | N | adj | N
missions (along El Camino Real (the King's Highway).)

Sentences 8 and 9 contain noun phrases as appositives.

9.
S-N | prep adj | adj | adj | N | S-rel pro | AV | prep | N | prep | N
Hundreds (of the first black settlers) who came (to America,) (for example,

N | AV | prep adj | N | prep | adj | N
Crispus Attucks,) fought (for the colonies) (in Revolutionary times,) al-

con | adj | S-N | AV | prep | N | prep adj | N
though many others were brought (to New England) by slave traders.)

Sentence 10: Note the widely split verb and interrogative form.

10.
pro AV adj | S-N | AV | adj | N | prep adj | N
Why is the United States called "the land (of the free"?)

Paragraph Assignment | In an organized paragraph, give several possible reasons as an answer to the question in sentence 10.

ANSWERS

Tryout: Parts of Speech and Clauses

       S-N   BV adj adj   N   rel pro   adv   AV adj   adj   N   prep adj

1. Aesop was a slave storyteller who probably lived six hundred years (before the

       adj   N

    Christian era.)

       S-N   BV adj   adv   adj   N   rel pro AV prep adv   adj   adj   N

2. Croesus was an extremely rich king who lived (at about the same time.)

    N(poss)   S-N   adv   AV adj   N   adv   adj   adj   N

3. Aesop's fables always have a moral—usually the same moral.

    adj   S-N prep N(poss)   N   BV   adv   inf Pro rel pro   S-N   AV   adv

4. The point (of Aesop's stories) is always to tell us that people should not

    AV   adv   adv prep Pro adj   N

    believe very much (in their own greatness.)

      S-N   AV   prep adj N   BV adj   N   S-N   AV Pro

5. "Pride goeth (before a fall") is one way Aesop says it. [understood "that"]

    adj   S-N   con   S-N   AV Pro adj   N   prep   N con   N

6. Both Aesop and Uncle Remus told their best stories (about beasts and birds.)

    adj   S-N   AV   prep   N   prep   adj   N

7. The creatures stand (for humans) (with certain characteristics.)

    adj   S-N   adv   BV   adv   adj con adj   N

8. The lion, therefore, is always stronger than the wolf.

    adj   S-N   BV   adv   BV   adj   adv   adj   N-S   AV   AV   adv

9. The fox must necessarily be deceptive; however, the sheep must move blindly

    adv   part   adj N prep   N

    ahead, ignoring the signs (of trickery.)

     S-N   adv AV   N   prep   N   rel pro AV   N

10. Aesop also tells stories (about people) who make mistakes.

    adj   S-N   rel pro AV adj   adj   N   AV prep adj N   rel pro AV   AV

11. "The Goose That Laid the Golden Eggs" tells (of a goose) that was owned

                                                     part

    prep adj adj   N con   N

    (by a foolish man and woman.)

    S-Pro adv AV   prep adj   N   con S-Pro AV rel pro adj S-N   AV   adj

12. We still talk (about the story) when we say that a person has "killed the

                                                   part

    adj   N

    golden goose."

    adj   adj   S-N   AV adj   N   inf   adj   N   rel pro AV   adv AV AV

13. The greedy couple killed the goose to get the eggs that had not been laid.

                                                   part

    S-Pro AV   adj   N   adv   S-Pro AV adv BV adj   adv

14. They found no eggs; therefore, they did not get rich immediately.

    prep   N   S-Pro AV adv adj   adj   adj   N

15. (In addition,) they got no more daily golden eggs.

Students may choose to include the prepositional phrases in the underlined clause; give credit either way.

Sentence 2: *About* is like *approximately* here.

Sentence 5: The *that* preceding *Aesop* is understood.

Remind students that clauses must contain a subject and a verb, and that relative pronouns often serve as subjects as well as connecting words.

Point out that the relative pronouns in sentences 1, 2, 4, and 10–13 are subjects of dependent clauses.

Sentence 14: *Get* is a BV because it is used like *become.*

Tryout: Parts of Speech and Prepositional and Participial Phrases

1.
    adj   S-N   BV adj   N   prep   N
The United States is a country (of immigrants.)

2.
  adj   adj   S-N   adv   AV   adv   adj-part   prep adj adj   N
The Native American Indians probably came first, walking (over a land bridge)

  prep   N   con adv   prep   adj   N   adj-part   adv
(into North America) and then, (through many centuries,) moving gradually

  prep adj   adj   N   prep   N
(into the lower tip) (of South America.)

3.
     prep   adj   N   prep adj   adj   adj   N   adj   adj   S-N
(During the days) (of the early Greek civilizations,) the Phoenician traders

  AV   adv   prep adj adj   N
sailed secretly (into all the oceans.)

4.
  prep adj   N   S-N con   adj   N   prep   adj   N
(In the Middle Ages,) Vikings and other groups (from northern Europe)

  AV   adj   adj   adv
crossed the Atlantic frequently.

Sentence 5: Eric the Red can also be a single noun; credit either labeling.

5.
  adj   adj   adj   S-N   prep   adj   N   prep   N   BV prep
The first major evidence (of European settlers) (in North America) is (from

   N   prep N adj   adj   prep adj   adj   N
Vikings) (like Eric the Red) (in the tenth century.)

6.
      adv   S-N prep   adj   adj   adj   N   con   N
However, traces (of possible pre-Columbian trading posts or settlements)

  prep   N   AV   AV   AV   prep adj   N   prep   N
(from China) have been found (along the West Coast) (of North America.)

7.
            S-N   AV   adj   N   prep   N
Christopher Columbus sighted Western Hemisphere land (on October 12, 1492.)

8.
  prep   adj   adj   N   prep Pro   N   S-N   AV   prep adj
(Like many educated people) (of his time,) Columbus believed (in   a

  adj   N
round world.)

9.
    S-N   AV   adj   N   prep Pro   adv   adj   N   adj-part
Columbus made several trips (to his newly discovered land,) bringing

          N   con Pro   N   prep N
Native Americans and their belongings (to Europe.)

10.
  Pro AV   S-N   AV adj   N   N
Why did Columbus call the Native Americans *Indians*?

Part Two
Punctuation

▼ ▼ ▼ ▼ ▼ ▼ ▼ ▼ ▼ ▼ ▼

Chapter 11

End Punctuation
Period, Question Mark, and Exclamation Point

The ends of sentences and parts of sentences are shown with periods, question marks, and exclamation points.

Students who are trying to do a lot of writing seem very grateful to learn punctuation as soon as possible, although you can teach all or part of the Part Three usage material first if you like.

Did you know that punctuation is a relatively recent invention? When archaeologists find written versions of early languages, there are no periods, no commas to give clues to meaning. However, modern standard English has customary rules for punctuation, rules that keep words separated and indicate pauses, emphasis, and changes of expression. Although these rules are sometimes broken to change an effect, especially in informal writing, standard formal communication calls for rules that most people understand and accept. This book gives the most commonly used rules, with emphasis on those used in relatively formal situations such as business offices.

THE PERIOD (.)

Ends of Sentences

The period (called a full stop in some British areas) is the accepted ending for the declarative statement, the most common of English sentences. Most of the sentences on this page use periods. The period is also used in all imperative sentences except those that are also exclamatory.

By now, students should be familiar with the proofreading marks used in the answer keys and in their written compositions. Ask them to refer to the list at the end of Appendix E (page 332) if necessary.

Be sure to come on time.

See me for payment.

In typing, be aware of customary spacing rules—two spaces at the end of most sentences, one space after most abbreviations (such as *Mr.*), no space within an abbreviation, such as *a.m.* Spacing customs may vary if you are using computer or printer fonts.

Memory Peg

Abbreviations

Periods are used for many abbreviations.

91

Common Abbreviations with Periods

a.m.	ante meridiem (before noon)
amt.	amount
anon.	anonymous
ans.	answer
atty.	attorney
Ave.	Avenue
B.A./A.B.	Bachelor of Arts
Blvd.	Boulevard
Capt.	Captain
dept.	department
D.D.S.	Doctor of Dental Surgery
Dr.	Doctor
e.g.	for example (from the Latin *exempli gratia*)
et al.	and others (other people) (from the Latin *et alii*)
etc.	and other things (from the Latin *et cetera*)
i.e.	that is (from the Latin *id est*)
int.	interest
Jr.	Junior
lit.	literally
Lt.	Lieutenant (also Lieut.)
M.D.	Doctor of Medicine
Mr.	Mister
Mrs.	Mistress (original meaning was "adult woman"; now used only abbreviated to mean "married woman")
Ms.	Miss or Mrs. (may also be used without a period)
no./No.	number
p./pp.	page/pages
pd.	paid
p.m.	post meridiem (after noon)
recd.	received
Rev.	Reverend
sec.	secretary
Sr.	Senior
St.	saint
St.	street

viz.	namely (from the Latin *videlicet*)
vol.	volume

Abbreviations for measurements in technical writing and some other abbreviations are usually written without periods.

Common Abbreviations without Periods

ad	advertisement	**km**	kilometer
cm	centimeter	**l**	liter
COD	Collect (or Cash) on Delivery	**m**	meter
doz	dozen	**mg**	milligram
ft	foot	**ml**	milliliter
g	gram	**mm**	millimeter
in	inch	**oz**	ounce
IQ	Intelligence Quotient	**qt**	quart

For a full discussion of the appropriate places to abbreviate or spell in full, see pages 153–156. **In general, to communicate with the largest number of people, spell out instead of abbreviating, except for Mr., Mrs., Ms., and titles after people's names.** Technical writing uses many abbreviations, however, because in technical writing you are communicating with experts in the field or with people in your own group.

Memory Peg

Lists and Outlines

When each item in an outline is a separate sentence, the items should end with periods. Periods are also commonly used at the ends of outline items when each item completes a sentence started by the introductory phrase.

    A. This report contains:
        1. An abstract.
        2. The description of the project.
        3. The conclusions reached.
        4. A bibliography.

Do you see why there are periods in this outline? "This report contains an abstract" makes a complete sentence.

If no complete sentences are created, then the items should not end with periods.

    A. Contents of report:
        1. Abstract
        2. Description of project
        3. Conclusions reached
        4. Bibliography

Note: A period is used after each *number* in the outline. If the items were made into a sentence with parentheses around the numbers, periods after the numbers would not be needed.

The items in a run-in list might be (1) a series of nouns, (2) a series of phrases, (3) a series of sentence fragments of any kind.

Memory Peg

No periods are used:

1. **After sentence fragments, except in very informal writing.**
2. **After full titles of people (such as King George III) or written material.**
3. **After amounts of dollars (such as $50).**

Notice that each of the items in this list does complete a sentence and hence uses a period.

THE QUESTION MARK (?)

Memory Peg

Question marks are used after interrogative sentences—sentences that ask direct questions, expressed in exact words. Try saying the example sentences as if you were asking them.

Are you shopping for a new pet dog?

How much is that doggy in the window?

Did you see a price tag anywhere?

An indirect question is not word for word but rather a paraphrase or summary of the question. It ends with a period, not a question mark. Try saying the next example sentences.

He wondered how much the dog would cost. [Do you hear his exact words? This is an indirect question, so it does not end with a question mark.]

He asked where the price tag was.

Do not use the question mark if the wording is actually that of a polite command, from which you expect action, not an answer.

Would you please send your late payment as soon as possible.

Could you type up that report for me right away, please.

It is possible to use question marks on a series of sentence ends. This sometimes makes the possible answers much clearer.

Have you taken the advanced keyboarding class yet? the intermediate math class? the advanced English?

Three separate yes or no answers are requested, not one answer about three courses. If there is no *or* or *and* in the sentence, this punctuation may work beautifully. Notice that the alternative sentence endings are not capitalized.

One variation of the question sentence is called a "tag question":

> We use this kind in conversation frequently, don't we?

> This takes a comma before the end question, doesn't it?

The following example shows how a question and answer are punctuated:

> Do you understand these uses now? Of course.

THE EXCLAMATION POINT (!)

Exclamation points (or exclamation marks) are used in three ways:

Memory Peg

1. They are used on all interjections—words that show emotion and are punctuated separately from the rest of the sentence, such as "Wow!" or "Hurrah!"

2. They may be used on any full sentence that is said with considerable feeling, such as "I'm worried!" or "You're wonderful!"

3. They must be used on sentences with special exclamatory word order, such as "What a beautiful day!" or "How great you are to do that!" If exclamation points are omitted, these sentences seem sarcastic, as though the speaker (or writer) meant the opposite of what is being said. See how your voice usually increases in volume when you say these sentences; then read them with a decrease in volume—you'll hear the odd effect.

Tryout: End Punctuation

Directions: Add any necessary end punctuation. You may attach items together (with or without commas, as necessary), changing capitalization.

Ten points per correct numbered item.

1. Aesop was a famous storyteller in ancient Greece

2. One of his stories was about a hungry fox and some grapes

3. Hanging from a vine that was trained along a high trellis

4. Though the fox did his best to reach them by jumping in the air

5. It was all in vain

6. For they were just beyond his reach

7. Do you want the grapes, Mr. Fox

8. Of course not

9. I thought those grapes were ripe

The fox decides the grapes are no good.

10.   I see now that they are sour

Paragraph Assignment

What do you think Aesop meant by this fable? Write an organized paragraph answering this question.

Ten points per correct punctuation mark or capital.

Practice: Exclamation Points

Directions: Add exclamation points, other ending punctuation, and capital letters where necessary in the sentences.

1.   Wow! what a time that was!

2.   Don't run in the street!

3.   Stop!

4.   Can't you stop that irritating noise! (or ?)

5.   Far out! you really did it that time!

ANSWERS

Tryout: End Punctuation

1. Aesop was a famous storyteller in ancient Greece.
   ^

2. One of his stories was about a hungry fox and some grapes,

3. Hanging from a vine that was trained along a high trellis.
   ^

4. Though the fox did his best to reach them by jumping in the air,
   ^

5. It was all in vain,
   ^

6. For they were just beyond his reach.
   ^

7. Do you want the grapes, Mr. Fox?
   ^

8. Of course not!
   ^
                                    (or .)
9. I thought those grapes were ripe!
   ^

10. I see now that they are sour.
    ^

Chapter 12

Major Clause Connectors
Colon, Semicolon, and Dash

Many short Tryouts appear with the chapters in Part Two, but most Practices are in Chapter 20, labeled according to the punctuation material covered.

Three other ways to connect and punctuate sentence and clause endings use colons, semicolons, and dashes.

Memory Peg

When you want to write two or more independent clauses that seem to be related in idea, you have several choices. **You can write two sentences. You can join the two clauses with a conjunction (or a comma plus a conjunction), to make a compound sentence. You can also join independent clauses (possible sentences) with punctuation such as a colon, semicolon, or dash to make a compound sentence.** (You can join almost any non-sentence group of words with a comma.)

> We went to Hawaii at Christmas last year; the weather was warm and rainy. [two independent clauses]

> We went to Hawaii at Christmas last year; however, the weather was warm and rainy. [one independent clause, adverb, another independent clause]

> We went to Hawaii at Christmas last year, but the weather was warm and rainy. [one independent clause, conjunction, another independent clause]

> When we went to Hawaii at Christmas last year, the weather was warm and rainy. [one dependent clause—it starts with a subordinating conjunction—and one independent clause]

These are all correct versions of the sentence. Can you see that you make subtle differences in meaning, however, depending on which connectors you choose?

Here are other possibilities:

> We were a bit disappointed in our Christmas vacation in Hawaii: the weather was warm but quite rainy.

> We were disappointed in our Christmas vacation in Hawaii—the weather was warm but quite rainy.

We went to Hawaii at Christmas last year, but the weather was warm and rainy.

The choice of connectors becomes more a matter of exact meaning intended and less a question of correct or incorrect. Can you see that some versions are clearer? some stronger? some more tactful?

Here are the usage rules for the colon, the semicolon, and the dash.

THE COLON (:)

The colon was actually invented first. **It is used for a general statement followed immediately by one or more specific examples or details. Think of it as a pair of eyes looking at the rest of the sentence and saying: "Here are the examples, here's the explanation, here's what I mean."**

Memory Peg

> We traveled to four islands: Maui, Hawaii, Kauai, and Oahu.
>
> The helicopter flight was thrilling: we flew over waterfalls.
>
> My favorite Hawaiian foods are these: pineapple, fresh fish, and coconut.
>
> I can have them all together at one place: a luau.

When you use a colon, be sure that there are no words connecting the two parts.

> **INCORRECT**   We traveled to: Maui, Hawaii, and Oahu.

The colon is not needed because the preposition *to* is doing the joining.

> **CORRECT**   We traveled to Maui, Hawaii, and Oahu.

After a colon, any examples or explanation must follow immediately.

INCORRECT   We took some great photographs: Some were from the helicopter. Besides the waterfalls, there were a volcano and the shoreline.

CORRECT   We took some great photos from the helicopter: the waterfalls, a volcano, and the shoreline.

INCORRECT   We went to the following islands: They are all very beautiful. Maui, Kauai, Oahu, and Hawaii.

CORRECT   We went to the following islands: Maui, Kauai, Oahu, and Hawaii. They are all very beautiful.

Also remember this rule: Do capitalize after a colon if a full sentence is coming and you want to emphasize it.

There are two other common colon uses: on the salutation in most business letters (such as "Dear Ms. Johnson:") and in statements of hours and minutes (such as "7:15 a.m."). The colon and *00* are usually omitted at the even hours (such as "8 a.m.") unless there's a series of times, some with minutes.

THE SEMICOLON (;)

Memory Peg

The semicolon was invented after the colon. Can you see that the name means "half-colon"? **In actual use, however, it works more like a half-period and half-comma.**

Use a semicolon when you want to join two independent clauses, and you don't want to use a conjunction. The effect is that of a balanced or parallel arrangement.

> In winter, I like to travel to warm climates; in summer, I like the cooler areas.

Memory Peg

Note: *Conjunctive adverbs* are not conjunctions; therefore, we often see them after semicolons, because they give a feeling of transition between the two ideas. Here are a few common conjunctive adverbs: however, consequently, moreover, nevertheless, therefore, then, besides, thus. **You can identify them because adverbs are usually *movable*.** (See Chapter 7, page 55.)

> He *then* ran *quickly* down the road.
>
> *Then* he ran down the road *quickly*.
>
> *Quickly then*, he ran down the road.

(See page 48 for the true subordinating conjunctions, which are used without semicolons.)

Another practical way to use the semicolon is in separating pairs of items in a complex series. A series usually uses commas to separate the parts (see page 108), but when there are commas within a part, it gets confusing.

INCORRECT   In the past five years, she has traveled to Paris, France, London, England, Rome, Italy, and Geneva, Switzerland.

Are you lost yet? Since the first item in each pair is a city, and the second item a country, the sentence becomes much clearer with semicolons:

CORRECT   In the past five years, she has traveled to Paris, France; London, England; Rome, Italy; and Geneva, Switzerland.

Semicolons also work for people and their hobbies, banks and their amounts of money, candidates and their states, and similar double series:

We met Sally Jones, president; Tom Green, vice president; Mary Rojas, treasurer; and Lee Tran, secretary.

Either a colon or a semicolon can be used before phrases such as "for example," "that is to say," and "for instance," whether a full clause or a list is coming.

She has decided to get more exercise: for instance, aerobics and running.

She said she needs more complex carbohydrates; for example, whole-grain breads and potatoes.

Tryout: Colons and Semicolons

Directions: Add a colon or semicolon in the appropriate places.

1. Here is the main reason I did it I was happy for them.

2. She tends to stay up late to watch television then she has trouble getting up in the morning.

3. These are a few of my favorite things warm yellow mittens and soft yellow kittens.

4. I like bright blue skies and a turquoise ocean.

5. The weather has been quite changeable this fall however, winter will come eventually.

6. We really need the rain this year, although I'm not fond of driving in rainy weather.

7. The first rains make the streets slick, it pays to drive very carefully.

Ten points per correct sentence.

8. Car tires litter the streets with oil and bits of rubber, which cause cars to skid badly.

9. Driving carefully, however, will still prevent most accidents.

10. Will you ride with me in your car, mine, or Jim's?

THE DASH (—; TYPED --)

Memory Peg

Use the dash only when you get desperate! The dash is very tempting but relatively informal and tends to be overused. **Because the dash is a straight line, it works like an arrow, pointing straight to its goal, emphasizing whatever follows.** A dash is fast and easy, so we like it. We often fill friendly letters with dashes and not much else. We also tend to overdo underlining and exclamation points, for similar reasons: we want to emphasize, and our words don't seem quite enough.

Dashes tend to be very versatile, but it is impossible to emphasize everything. Save those dashes for places where you really need them. Then you can occasionally sprinkle one in (like an exclamation point) when you want it, to suggest a strong pause before moving to a climax, for example.

Dashes *are* needed in the following situations.

In a *verbatim* (word-for-word) transcription, you try to write down exactly what someone has said. People often don't talk in formal sentences. They interrupt themselves in the middle, break off and start a new idea, and then sometimes go back to the original. Use dashes to signal these changes.

> I'm trying to tell you what happened—Johnny, stop teasing the cat—but I'm having trouble concentrating.

> It was really a ghost—I was—I can't talk about it anymore!

Use dashes to point to an item at the end of a sentence, or even to a series of items (the way a colon would), if you want emphasis:

> Down the hall the footsteps came, one by one, and then—the door creaked open.

> There it was in the glove compartment—a gun.

> He hated only two things—waking up and going to sleep.

Memory Peg

A series at the *beginning* of a sentence can be attached only with a dash, not a colon or comma.

> Horses, rabbits, sheep—if you had a few acres, which would you raise?

In an unusual situation, you may put a question mark or exclamation point inside dashes, inside the sentence.

My new teacher—have you seen her yet?—tells a lot of funny stories.

My sister—she's the one with the six horses!—has put her house up for sale.

Notice that the "sentence" within the dashes is not capitalized.

In general, choices among the colon, semicolon, and dash as connectors will primarily change emphasis and subtleties of meaning.

Tryout: Major Clause Connectors

Directions: Add a colon, semicolon, or dash at the appropriate places. You may change a comma into something else if necessary.

1. Please order the following for my hotel breakfast,

    a. Orange juice

    b. Scrambled eggs

    c. Wheat toast

    d. Coffee

2. We brought her bacon, waffles, and cocoa.

3. The waves were high and rolling, perfect for surfing.

4. There is one good reason to study we might pass the test.

5. The new vice president have you met her yet? is younger than I.

6. The following ideas were put forth at the meeting be sure to study them carefully.

7. He suggested several possibilities, for example, cutting costs, increasing income, and working longer hours.

8. Put the flour, baking powder, and salt in a large bowl, add the eggs, sugar, chocolate, and vanilla, and beat well.

Ten points per correct sentence.

What is wrong with this statement?

9.   Colons, semicolons, dashes these are the major connectors in punctuation.

10.   There's one good rule in answering most requests don't just say no, say yes to something else.

FROM SENTENCE TO PARAGRAPH: CAUSE AND EFFECT— "HOW-TO" WRITING

One of the most common types of writing is the kind that gives directions or explains how a process can be or has been done. Many of your textbooks are written in this logical, cause-and-effect mode: When you do this, this happens; when they did that, the other thing happened. Modern science and ancient history texts are all based on logical thinking.

Let's say that you want to explain how to change the oil in your car or how to plant a rosebush. You name the basic equipment and supplies, describe the space needed, list the steps in chronological order—presenting a "linear" procedure, like an orderly outline. The result should be approximately the same every time.

However, if you are writing about relationships between people or about very complex situations like world hunger, the result will probably not be predictable. These topics lead to discussion of *possible* results.

Writing about people or world problems, since these are so complex, can easily be expanded beyond a paragraph into an essay. As you practice writing paragraphs and writing journals, letters, notes, and essay examinations (which are often paragraph length), you'll find that your ideas grow until you really want to write longer pieces. Or—sooner or later—you'll have an essay assignment. Don't panic! Essays are organized very much like paragraphs.

The standard formal essay begins with a *thesis sentence*. A thesis is simply a general statement of your main idea. Then you proceed, in some orderly fashion, to lay out your reasons for this idea. You give more specific details, remembering to use the five senses and to illustrate with words.

You may be able to divide your essay idea into three parts. It sometimes helps to write a simple outline before you get very far into the essay.

THESIS SENTENCE   I believe that school uniforms are a good idea.

PARAGRAPHS   1. Experience of school problems with clothing choices.

2. Experience of some schools that have had uniforms in the past.

3. Experience of a few schools that have recently chosen uniforms.

CONCLUSION   Summary of evidence that uniforms have a positive effect.

Many essays do not follow this simple basic pattern, but it's an excellent way to begin, especially with an assignment asking for an opinion. Notice how many of your textbooks have paragraphs like the ones described—and whole sections that look like typical essays.

Comment on the statement in sentence 10 in the Tryout: Major Clause Connectors. Can you think of several different situations, perhaps involving your home life, your school life, and your work, in which the motto would be helpful? Write either a long organized paragraph or a short essay, explaining how to follow the motto.

Paragraph Assignment

ANSWERS

Tryout: Colons and Semicolons

1. Here is the main reason I did it: I was happy for them.

2. She tends to stay up late to watch television; then she has trouble getting up in the morning.

3. These are a few of my favorite things: warm yellow mittens and soft yellow kittens.

4. OK.

5. The weather has been quite changeable this fall; however, winter will come eventually.

6. OK.

7. The first rains make the streets slick; it pays to drive very carefully.

8. OK.

9. OK.

10. OK.

Remind students to use proofreading marks such as "∧," "∪ ,"and "≡ ," and to use dark pencil or pen.

Tryout: Major Clause Connectors

1. Please order the following for my hotel breakfast:

    a. Orange juice
    b. Scrambled eggs
    c. Wheat toast
    d. Coffee

2. OK.

3. OK.

4. There is one good reason to study: we might pass the test.

5. The new vice president--have you met her yet?--is younger than I.

    (or ; but no capital)

6. The following ideas were put forth at the meeting. Be sure to study them carefully.

7. He suggested several possibilities; for example, cutting costs, increasing

   (or :) [over the semicolon] ^

   income, and working longer hours.

8. Put the flour, baking powder, and salt in a large bowl; add the eggs, sugar,

   ^

   chocolate, and vanilla; and beat well.

   ^

9. Colons, semicolons, dashes--these are the major connectors in punctuation.

   ^

10. There's one good rule in answering most requests: don't just say no; say yes to

    ^   ^

    something else.

Chapter 13

Commas with *And*

Commas are used with coordinating conjunctions in compound sentences and series of three or more items.

Teachers are often tempted to try to teach all the "comma" material at once, but students seem to understand it better if the practices are divided into similar types that they can work on separately for at least a few hours or days.

Do you use commas when they "feel" right? Many people think that commas are used in sentences whenever we pause to breathe. Although commas do sometimes indicate pauses, some very specific rules govern about nineteen out of twenty comma uses. It's that twentieth use that will require a decision, usually based on what emphasis or lack of emphasis you intend for a certain phrase.

COMMAS WITH COORDINATING CONJUNCTIONS

When should you use a comma with *and*? **First, use commas before all the coordinating conjunctions (primarily *and, but, or*) when you are joining two possible sentences.** A comma plus *and* will create an effect similar to that of a semicolon; it will show where the main break in the sentence comes, and it will cause a slight pause before the second half.

Memory Peg

> Pedro applied for the job; then he turned it down.
>
> Pedro applied for the job, and then he turned it down.
>
> Pedro applied for the job, but then he turned it down.
>
> Pedro applied for the job and then turned it down.

These are all correct sentences. What are the differences? In the first version, the semicolon joins the clauses; there is no conjunction (*then* is an adverb, remember?). In the second version, the comma is used with *and*. The third version substitutes a different conjunction, *but*. The fourth version uses no comma, because, although there is a second verb, there is no second subject. Therefore, the *sentence* is not compound; it simply has a compound *verb*.

COMMAS IN VERY SHORT OR LONG COMPOUND SENTENCES

A compound sentence that is extremely short (four or five words in each part) may be written without the comma, although the word *but* sometimes creates the need for a comma to show contrast.

She bought it and she used it.

She bought it, but she returned it.

An extremely long compound sentence sometimes needs a semicolon rather than a comma with the conjunction, in order to show where the main sentence break comes.

INCORRECT   She has worked in Des Moines, San Francisco, Hartford, and Minneapolis, and she is now working in Santa Clara.

Do you see the confusion of *and*s? The sentence would be better punctuated with a semicolon after Minneapolis, with *or without* the second *and*.

CORRECT   She has worked in Des Moines, San Francisco, Hartford, and Minneapolis; and she is now working in Santa Clara.

She has worked in Des Moines, San Francisco, Hartford, and Minneapolis; she is now working in Santa Clara.

COMMAS FOR A SERIES

A series is three or more items (not two). It may consist of clauses, phrases, or single words. Use commas to set off the separate items, including a comma before the conjunction (formal style).

Jack, Jill, and Mary went up the hill. [series of nouns as subjects]

Jack and Jill went up the hill. [two noun subjects only]

Jack fell down and broke his crown. [two verbs only]

Jill came tumbling after and then ran to the doctor, the store, and Jack's house. [series of nouns, objects of preposition]

Mary, the doctor, and Jack's mother all came to the hill and helped him; and then he felt better. [series of noun subjects, two verbs in first clause; compound sentence]

Mary brought food, Jill got vinegar and brown paper, and Jack's mother told him to get up. [series of full clauses—possible sentences]

The following comma rules may seem too easy to be useful, but they solve many problems in more complex sentences:

Memory Peg

Don't use a comma with a conjunction if just two items are joined. Don't use a single comma between a subject and verb or between a verb or a preposition and its object. (Most prepositional phrases don't need commas anyway.)

INCORRECT   Jack, and Jill went up the hill.

Jack and Jill, went up the hill.

Jack and Jill went, up the hill.

Jack and Jill went up, the hill.

Mary had a little lamb and a little roast beef.

Tryout: Commas with *And*

Directions: Add any necessary commas and delete any that are unnecessary. (It's helpful to find the subject first and be sure you aren't splitting it from the verb with just one comma.) This is a good time to practice using the proof-reading symbols shown in Appendix E.

Ten points per correct sentence.

1. Mary, had a little lamb.

2. Mary had, a little lamb.

3. Mary had a little lamb and a little roast beef.

4. Mary had a little lamb a little roast beef and some potatoes.

5. Mary Jill and Jack were having a dinner party.

6. Mary decided that they needed more vegetables and fruit.

7. They went to the garden to get peas carrots and lettuce.

8. Jack found some, good tomatoes grapes and pears at the store.

9. Jill, fixed a salad and a fruit tray.

10. Mary, Jill, and Jack worked played and ate.

ANSWERS

Tryout: Commas with And

1. Mary, had a little lamb.
2. Mary had, a little lamb.
3. OK.
4. Mary had a little lamb, a little roast beef, and some potatoes.
5. Mary, Jill, and Jack were having a dinner party.
6. OK.
7. They went to the garden to get peas, carrots, and lettuce.
8. Jack found some, good tomatoes, grapes, and pears at the store.
9. Jill, fixed a salad and a fruit tray.
10. Mary, Jill, and Jack worked, played, and ate.

Chapter 14

Introductory Commas

An introductory word, phrase, or clause is usually separated from the sentence by a comma.

INTRODUCTORY WORDS

Most adverbs and other introductory words (words that are not otherwise part of the sentence), especially the longer words at beginnings or ends of sentences, can be separated from the sentence by a comma if there is a feeling of a slight pause at those words.

Memory Peg

> Yes, I'll do that.
>
> No, we can't.
>
> Oh, I don't know about that.
>
> First, let's discuss it.
>
> Obviously, it's a problem.
>
> Well, here's the solution.
>
> Finally, we have the answer.

You may choose to omit some commas following adverbs. You can often decide "by ear."

INTRODUCTORY PHRASES

For introductory material longer than one word, the general rule that works best is this: **Use a comma after introductory words before the subject, if the material contains a verb, a verb part, or five or more total words. Otherwise, leave the comma out.** There are several kinds of these introductory phrases.

Memory Peg

Infinitive Phrases

The infinitive is part of a verb—the word *to* plus the idea behind the verb, remember? (See pages 8, 31, 72.) Introductory infinitive phrases take commas.

> To understand this rule, you must first find the subject of the sentence.

The subject is *you,* so the infinitive phrase is "extra" introductory material, this time working as an adverb. It can be removed without changing much meaning.

> To understand this rule is not simple.

Now what is the subject? Yes, the infinitive itself, acting as a noun! Do you need a comma? No, a comma would split the subject from the verb. Remember, it's possible for several words together to act as subject of a sentence. (If you're not following this discussion, you need to review pages 72–73.)

Participial Phrases

Participles are other parts of verbs—the third or fourth parts on the list when you're memorizing a conjugation, such as *ring, rang, rung, ringing.*

> Studying participles, we begin to understand commas. [The subject is *we.*]

> Studying participles helps us to understand commas.

Now what's the subject? Right: *studying!* It's an "ing" noun here, otherwise known as a gerund, remember?

> Learning these distinctions will improve our writing.

Now we have a participial phrase as the subject and a gerund (present participle acting as a noun) as the object.

Prepositional Phrases

Most prepositional phrases in English do not need commas. We use so many prepositions that, if we put commas on them all, we'd have exceedingly choppy sentences. However, a long prepositional group—five or more words, one or several phrases—placed before the subject should be set off by commas in most sentences.

> In the middle of the night at Sixth and San Carlos, he stopped traffic. [comma used to help reader find subject, late in sentence]
>
> In the classroom most students learn quickly. [clear without comma]

Occasionally a comma after a prepositional phrase is needed for clarity.

> At his home, computers were used extensively. [comma to clarify *home computers* isn't meant]

INTRODUCTORY CLAUSES

Dependent clauses before the main clause nearly always need commas to set them off. (Remember that all clauses must have subjects and verbs.) This rule occasionally avoids misunderstandings, including ridiculous ones.

> After the lions had finished eating the attendants left the zoo.

Do you see how desperately the attendants need a comma after *eating*? (The lists of subordinating conjunctions and relative pronouns that begin dependent clauses are on pages 48 and 54.)

> Because she was taking the exam over, this was her last chance.

This comma keeps the reader from saying *over this*.

Technically speaking, most quotations are also dependent clauses. They are usually set off from the rest of the sentence by commas.

> "I'd like to go to the zoo Saturday," he said.

> She asked, "Will you take me along?"

(See Chapter 17, Miscellaneous Punctuation, for more details about quotations.)

Dependent clauses at *ends* of sentences do not usually need commas. (See Chapter 15, Commas Around Interruptions.) Nor do phrases joined by several conjunctions (enough *and*s to go around) need commas. Conjunctions might be used instead of commas to emphasize total quantities.

> The boys ate hot dogs and pizza and hamburgers for lunch.

Tryout: Introductory Phrase and Clause Commas

Directions: Insert commas where necessary.

1. During our trip to the zoo we saw many healthy animals.
2. Surrounded by tropical plants monkeys were climbing ropes and chattering.
3. To see them you would think that they were quite at home.
4. When they swing the ropes seem like vines in a jungle.
5. To look at us must be strange for them.
6. As we go past do you suppose they talk about us?
7. Given food and water and care they are probably happy.
8. With the very best care they do live longer than in the jungle.

Ten points per correct sentence.

*To look at us must be
strange for them.*

9.   In the middle of the night perhaps some of them dream of the old days.

10.   Even for monkeys in the zoo life is not easy.

FROM SENTENCE TO PARAGRAPH: ARGUMENT

As you do assignments that require you to state an opinion and give your reasons for it, your paragraphs become more complex, more like an essay, as described on page 104. Your opinion will be more persuasive for your readers if you immediately state the common differences of opinion on the topic.

For example, if you feel that we need zoos to protect some animals because their habitats are endangered, you must also remind readers that many people feel that the average zoo treats animals poorly. In other words, you need to discuss at least two sides to present an argument, giving specific examples for each side. You may have to write a long paragraph or two paragraphs. Sooner or later such a paragraph assignment will grow into a formal essay, with the essay thesis sentence working much like a paragraph topic sentence, each paragraph providing more details, and your conclusion tying your ideas together.

**Paragraph
Assignment**

Do you approve of keeping animals in zoos? In an organized paragraph, explain why or why not.

Practice: Comma Review

Directions: Insert commas where necessary.

From 100 points subtract
5 points per incorrect
comma.

(1) When you or members of your family need a doctor, how do

you choose one? (2) In newspapers and magazines and on television, you can discover many new ideas about medicine. (3) As you listen or read, your choices of medical service may seem to be increasing. (4) For example, you may choose a specialist, a general practitioner, or a nurse practitioner. (5) You may decide to try alternative medical treatments: acupuncture, chiropractic, hypnosis, biofeedback, or herbal medicines. (6) The many new kinds of medical ideas create both confusion and optimism for us. (7) Fortunately, some of the alternative therapies are less expensive than more conventional drugs or surgery. (8) However, because some of the treatments are new and relatively unproven, consumers need to be careful in choosing health providers. (9) Although many supposedly new remedies have been used for centuries in other countries, our government uses lengthy procedures to protect us from unsafe medicines. (10) Therefore, we all need to educate ourselves thoroughly about health care.

ANSWERS

Tryout: Introductory Phrase and Clause Commas

1. During our trip to the zoo, we saw many healthy animals.

2. Surrounded by tropical plants, monkeys were climbing ropes and chattering.

3. To see them, you would think that they were quite at home.

4. When they swing, the ropes seem like vines in a jungle.

5. OK.

6. As we go past, do you suppose they talk about us?

7. Given food and water and care, they are probably happy.

8. With the very best care, they do live longer here than in the jungle.

9. In the middle of the night, perhaps some of them dream of the old days.

10. Even for monkeys in the zoo, life is not easy.

Chapter 15

Commas Around Interruptions
Drop Your Voice and Listen

Commas are used to set apart sentence interruptions, appositives, degrees, titles, dates, addresses, and nonessential phrases or clauses.

TYPICAL SENTENCE INTERRUPTIONS

The basic English sentence consists of a subject and a verb. Many times the sentence flows smoothly on, with prepositional phrases and other adjective or adverb modifiers. Sometimes, however, the sentence is interrupted for a change of pace, a change of emphasis, or additional information.

Memory Peg

If, when you are reading the sentence, you find yourself *dropping your voice* for a few words and then going back to your original tone, you are probably noting an interruption. Did you do that in reading the previous sentence? The kind of nonessential information read with a lowered voice is nearly always set off by commas.

Look at the sentence at the beginning of this chapter that begins with *sometimes*. Read it with an exaggerated voice drop. Then read it without dropping your tone. Do you see why the commas are needed here and below?

> Winter is a time, whether we like it or not, when we are very susceptible to colds and flu.
>
> We should, therefore, be particularly careful to eat nutritious foods and get enough sleep.
>
> These measures, in my opinion, help us to keep healthy.
>
> Most people, realizing the risk of illness, try to watch what they eat.
>
> At this time of year, however, people get enticed by high-calorie holiday food and celebrations lasting long into the night.

APPOSITIVES

Memory Peg

The appositive, a specialized type of interruption, is a renaming of a noun or noun phrase, frequently a person, that makes more "positive" or specific who or what is meant.

116

Her daughter-in-law, Amie Bernier, wants to go to medical school someday.

Jan Bernier, another daughter-in-law, works in a hospital as a nutrition expert.

These two women, Jan and Amie, keep her posted on medical information.

Note that commas surround the interrupting appositive. It's also possible to have an appositive or any other interruption at the end of a sentence, in which case there would be only one comma, of course.

You've met my other daughter-in-law, Angela.

Angela and her husband, my son Hal, both work as psychologists in the prison system, specializing in substance abuse.

In the latter sentence, note that the word *Hal* by itself is too short and too closely related to need commas. You don't drop your voice when you say, "My brother Tom is coming." (See also the comma rules about "essential" phrases on pages 118–119.)

DEGREES, TITLES, DATES, AND ADDRESSES

Degrees and titles offer important but "extra" information about people, information that could be removed without harming the sentence. As such, they are usually set off by commas.

Johara Mukerji, M.D.; Hal Marcos, M.S.; Shulamith Elias, M.A.

Memory Peg

We don't say "Dr. Johara Mukerji, M.D.," because this would give double credit for the same title. However, we could say "Professor Shulamith Elias, M.A." or "The Reverend John Winslow, S.J.," because the abbreviations stand for different titles from the earlier ones.

Abbreviated titles such as Jr., Sr., Inc., and Ltd. are commonly used after the names of people and corporations. The traditional usage is to surround these abbreviations with commas. Recently, however, a usage of omitting the commas has developed. Always write the name of anyone or any organization as requested—either by the person involved or by your superior. This is a matter of preferred style, not a matter of right or wrong, since there are two forms in use. Do remember, however, that on interruptions of any kind there should be two commas, not one, unless you reach the end of the sentence.

John F. Kennedy, Jr., is practicing law.

TIME Inc. has decided to use the simpler title.

Macy★s Department Stores, Inc., likes to use a star sometimes in its store trademark.

Dates and addresses have one thing in common—an easily remembered comma rule. **Put commas *around* the second and all following items in dates and addresses. (It's very easy to forget the second comma.)**

Memory Peg

Note: When only month and year are given, no commas are used because there is no possible number confusion. The other comma exception is requested by the Postal Service, which prefers the two-letter state abbreviations and no punctuation before the ZIP code numbers, to make addresses easier for machines to read. (See Chapter 19, Numbers and Abbreviations.)

He lived in Honolulu, Hawaii, for many years.

He lives in Nyack, New York, but he works in New York City.

They moved from Honolulu to 1621 West Hedding Street, Santa Clara, CA 95051, on May 12, 1996.

Since August 1, 1995, she has been a radiologist at Mercy Hospital, 1800 Oak Street, Springfield, MA 01010.

She was born in Des Moines, Iowa, in January 1932.

Tryout: Interruption Commas

Directions: Insert commas where necessary.

Ten points per correct comma.

Remind students to drop their voices to a lower tone as they read "interrupting" materials. See sentence 3 here, for example.

(1) We hear interesting stories in the morning when we come to school. (2) Sometimes however we have trouble believing these tales. (3) One student as I heard it said that a dog ate her book. (4) Another student, Jan Miller said her boyfriend Mickey poured ink on her books. (5) One receptionist Sally Johnston said it was all like a soap opera.

Paragraph Assignment

Have you heard or used any unusual excuses for absence from school or missing books? Write an organized paragraph explaining and giving examples.

THE ESSENTIAL/NONESSENTIAL INTERRUPTION RULE

Memory Peg

The common terms *essential/nonessential* or *restrictive/nonrestrictive* are often applied to clauses and phrases. These simply mean that the clause or phrase is either important or not important in identifying the items being modified.

Note: Clauses that start with *that* almost never take commas; clauses that start with *which* almost always need commas. In other words, we are more likely to use the word *that* on essential (important) clauses.

In the examples that follow, the dependent (subordinate) clauses are in italics.

The young woman *who is standing at the front desk* is applying for a job.

Ms. Alicia Rodriquez, *who is at the front desk,* is applying for a job.

In the first sentence, we don't know which woman is being discussed until we see the "who" clause, the dependent clause that identifies her. This clause does not take commas. In the second sentence, we already know *who* she is, so *where* she is becomes extra information, and therefore the clause takes commas.

Dependent (subordinate) clauses at the ends of sentences follow the same rules. If we separate an ending clause with a comma, it places less emphasis on it, making it seem like an afterthought, an "extra."

I'll call you in the morning *if I need a ride to work.*

I may call you about that, *if I remember soon enough.*

In the first sentence, there's a big *if*—I won't be calling unless that *if* occurs. The last clause is therefore important, and I may even raise my voice as I say it, rather than dropping my tone. The meaning of the sentence depends on the clause. Try reading the second sentence with a voice drop on the last clause. Doesn't it sound like an afterthought? (When in doubt, don't use commas before dependent clauses at the ends of sentences.)

Tryout: Essential/Nonessential Word Groups

Directions: Add commas around all *nonessential* (that is, extra) clauses or phrases. (This also applies to appositives—listen for the voice drop.)

Ten points per correct sentence.

1. Those green velvet gloves which are lying on the front table are on sale today.

2. The gloves that are lying on the front table are on sale today.

3. Her oldest sister Susan is head of the housewares department.

4. Have you seen my favorite television show "Sisters"?

5. I think that one of the actors looks like my son Don who teaches computers but my son Hal disagrees.

   Sentence 5: Since the writer has at least two sons, the names become more important to identify them and therefore don't take commas.

6. On the show that I saw last night two sisters were not getting along very well.

7. Some people don't like the show because it reminds them too much of real life.

8. My daughter who lives in Massachusetts likes "Murder, She Wrote" because the setting is in New England.

   Sentence 8: Assume the writer has one daughter. Does that make a difference?

9. Cynthia Lee a CPA works in a hospital in Boston Massachusetts.

10. My children a daughter and three sons all grew up and got married.

*One student said that
a dog ate her book.*

**Paragraph
Assignment**

Do the people in your family all do very different things at work or for recreation? Write an organized paragraph explaining your answers.

ANSWERS

Tryout: Interruption Commas

(1) OK (or comma after *morning*). (2) Sometimes, however, we have trouble believing these tales. (3) One student, as I heard it, said that a dog ate her book. (4) Another student, Jan Miller, said her boyfriend, Mickey, poured ink on her books.

(5) One receptionist, Sally Johnston, said it was all like a soap opera.

Tryout: Essential/Nonessential Word Groups

1.   Those green velvet gloves, which are lying on the front table, are on sale today.

2.   OK.

Interruptions and their commas run amok.

3. Her oldest sister, Susan, is head of the housewares department.

4. Have you seen my favorite television show, "Sisters"?

5. I think one of the actors looks like my son Don, who teaches computers, but

    my son Hal disagrees.
6. On the show that I saw last night, two sisters were not getting along very well.

7. OK (or comma after *show*).
8. My daughter, who lives in Massachusetts, likes "Murder, She Wrote," because

    the setting is in New England.
9. Cynthia Lee, a CPA, works at a hospital in Boston, Massachusetts.

10. My children, a daughter and three sons, all grew up and got married.

Chapter 16

Miscellaneous Commas
Commas that Clarify

Commas may be used to separate consecutive adjectives, phrases with omitted words, repeated words or phrases, terms of direct address, contrasting phrases, and numbers.

CONSECUTIVE ADJECTIVES

Sometimes two adjectives in a row move very smoothly, with one leading into the next: a big brown bear, a beautiful velvet bedspread. In such sentences the word order of the adjectives is important: we would never say "a brown big bear" or "a velvet beautiful bedspread."

Frequently, however, the adjectives separately modify the nearest noun. In these cases, try to insert the word *and* between the adjectives or even to reverse their order. If there's enough pause to insert the *and* mentally, use a comma: "an efficient and personable executive" or "an efficient, personable executive."

Of course, you wouldn't put *and* between an adjective and its noun—"a personable and executive," or "a beautiful and bedspread," so don't put a comma there either.

Note: Your ear will help here. You would not say "a big and brown bear." **If the *and* sounds good between adjectives, or if you could reverse them, use the comma.**

a rich, talented person   sharp, clean copy   the quick brown fox

OMISSIONS

Sometimes you can use a comma to keep from repeating words several times. The comma causes the reader to pause long enough to insert expected words mentally.

My daughter lives in Boston; my oldest son, in New York City; my second, in Des Moines; my youngest, in San Jose.

122

The commas are inserted where the word *lives* would be repeated, and the items are separated like clauses, with semicolons. As you write the sentence, you can mentally insert the omitted word or words, placing the comma in the right spot.

> Beginning January 2, Mr. Jones will be in charge of finances; Ms. Walker, speakers; Mr. Jackson, supplies; Ms. Brown, rooms.

Notice how much space is saved and how much smoother the sentence is when we avoid the bumpy repetition of "will be in charge of." Use just enough words so that the meaning is clear in the clauses that have omissions.

> When a job offer seems very good, we become optimists; when not, pessimists.

Notice that we don't use a comma between *when* and *not,* only where we need to pause for the omitted idea.

Tryout: Commas for Adjectives and Omissions

Directions: Insert commas where necessary. Assume that other punctuation is correct.

Ten points per correct sentence.

(1) We're buying some attractive nylon curtains today. (2) They're on sale at the new fabric shop on the corner. (3) This shop has many inexpensive durable materials. (4) Bright shiny glamorous fabrics are available for the holidays. (5) We'll buy colorful inexpensive items for decorating. (6) Tomorrow we'll put a tree into the living room; stockings onto the mantel; a wreath on the front door; and a manger scene on the table. (7) Candles will decorate my neighbors' table; corn their front door; wrapped gifts their mantelpiece. (8) The children are drawing exciting holiday pictures. (9) Blinking holiday lights illuminate dark winter nights. (10) Children look forward to Santa; parents holiday parties; the stores high sales volume.

Note: Meaning can change with the addition or omission of a comma. One year a federal law was incorrectly typed to read: "Tropical fruit, plants, and seeds are subject to tariff." It should have read: "Tropical fruit plants and seeds are subject to tariff." The tax people became extremely confused about the law, which cost some importers millions of dollars.

We know, Mr. Lumpkin, that you like to play golf.

REPETITIONS, DIRECT ADDRESS, AND CONTRAST

Sometimes you may deliberately repeat a word to emphasize it. In such cases, put one comma between the repeated words or short phrases.

Never, never split a subject from its verb with one comma.

Never, but never split a word from its object with one comma.

These rules will be very, very helpful.

When you speak or write directly to an individual, you may use the person's name to capture his or her attention. Since the name is not otherwise part of the sentence, set it off with commas.

We know, Mr. Lumpkin, that you like to play golf.

Mrs. Lumpkin, would you rather watch or play the game?

Most people would prefer to play, Mr. Lumpkin.

In the last example, if the comma is omitted, the meaning is changed completely. Here's another example of a meaning changed by placement of a comma.

Mary, Lou has the turkey ready for the oven.

Mary Lou has the turkey ready for the oven.

Commas are also used to show contrast by setting off the contrasting phrase.

She likes this pie, but not that one.

The paper is due today, not tomorrow, and no extensions will be given.

They came to party, not to work.

NUMBERS

In the United States, we use commas to separate each set of three digits in large numbers. You can think of the commas as a "thousands" comma, a "millions" comma, and so on. The commas in large numbers are typed with no spaces after them. (In Europe and Asia, periods and commas are used much differently in numbers; be very careful to note local custom. One version simply uses extra spaces where we insert commas.)

2,300,450 [two *million*, three hundred *thousand*, four hundred fifty.]

Try another few; notice what you say as you reach the comma in each case.

4,350,370,000 [What comes after million? Remember that numbers grow larger from right to left.]

$23,221,421

$1,450,360,990,967 [Now we're discussing the national debt—thousand, million, billion, trillion!]

Note: In numbers of four digits, such as 1400, you may omit the comma if you want the number to read "fourteen hundred." Be sure to use the comma, however, if you are typing related numbers with commas in them.

When you write unrelated numbers together, add the comma for clarity.

In 1996, 625 more students attended the business college.

Be sure to separate the numbers in a series with commas.

Her children are 1, 2, 3, and 11. [She could have a child of 12 or 23 if you're not careful.]

Note: In many common American number groups, commas are omitted. These groups are broken by hyphens if necessary; they include street addresses; years; ZIP codes; page numbers; Social Security, account, and policy numbers; RFD numbers; and decimals.

in 1996	1372 Fleming Avenue	Chicago, IL 60619
page 1234	Policy No. 2367-99842	RFD 24113
3.14159	413-20-4367 (Social Security number)	(213) 984-5838

In precise measurements of any kind, such as weight or capacity, be sure to note the difference between one weight (for example) and a series of them. The series will take commas, but note these examples of one weight or one period:

The baby weighed 7 pounds 20 ounces. [They had just one baby, not a series!]

The class period lasts exactly 1 hour 55 minutes. [We're not talking about two different periods.]

Tryout: Miscellaneous Commas

Directions: Add commas only where needed.

Ten points per correct
sentence.

(1) The full moon has an interesting confusing reputation. (2) Very old tales speak of werewolves coming out to prowl; hospitals of a surge in admissions. (3) Full harvest moons supposedly shine for ardent young lovers. (4) Many people laugh at such statements. (5) Scientists have researched the actual physical effects of the moon on both the tides and the human body. (6) The moon pulls on the earth at the times of changing tides. (7) It has also been recently proved to change mammal cell pressure. (8) This pressure change seems minor not major. (9) Even very minor increased cell pressure can cause major noticeable behavior changes. (10) When things go well under a full moon, they go very well; when badly very badly.

Very old tales speak of werewolves coming out to prowl; hospitals tell of a surge in admissions.

Tryout: Commas for Numbers

Directions: Add commas where necessary.

Ten points per correct sentence.

1. I'm looking at my budget for 1997.

2. The adjustable mortgage rate has changed to 8.1 percent.

3. Taxes on Ms. Ledoux's house will be $1123; its valuation $178000.

4. Invoice No. 11-254 for painting will be deductible.

5. I need to check All-Risk Insurance Policy No. 22788 for earthquake coverage.

6. That package will weigh 2 pounds 13 ounces.

7. In 1998 12 people are coming for a reunion.

8. The address is 1525 Lyttonville Road Silver Spring MD 20910.

9. The instructions on pages 1122 and 1123 are not clear.

10. We'd better send the letter to 22311 Center Street.

FROM SENTENCE TO PARAGRAPH: COMPLEX TOPICS AND PREWRITING

Always keep in mind that paragraphs are a matter of style. Longer paragraphs create a slow, contemplative effect, asking the reader to think carefully, engaging the reader in the feelings and ideas of the writer. Much shorter paragraphs—sometimes only a short sentence or two—are often used in dramatic situations or in periodical writing such as daily news stories, which are designed to be skimmed quickly. However, all these types of paragraphs follow the general-to-specific pattern. When short paragraphs are used, the specifics may each be a paragraph.

As you start writing about more complex topics, you may need to use long or short paragraphs or both. In complex discussions, you may need to break up the longer, more complex paragraphs, simply to make them easier to read.

For example, think about comparisons and contrasts. To compare is to find similarities; to contrast is to show differences. There are two main methods for writing comparison and contrast. You can take a topic—such as two different educational systems—and first discuss one system in great detail; then you compare and contrast it with the other system in the second half of your writing. Or, perhaps preferably, you can keep alternating between the two systems. The second method is more difficult to set up but usually easier for the reader to follow.

Note: To write about this topic you need to juggle four things: comparisons, contrasts, educational system 1, and educational system 2. Because your subject is complex, you need to begin with notes of some kind, in a process often called *prewriting*. One way is to write a brief outline.

Another way is to start jotting down notes in "clusters," patterns on the page, with the parts that seem to belong together in one area and other parts clustered in other corners of your page.

This pattern works much like an outline except that it can show more different kinds of relationships—not just linear, but across the page, slanted from one part to another, and the like.

Here's the way you might begin a cluster on the comparison/contrast of two educational systems:

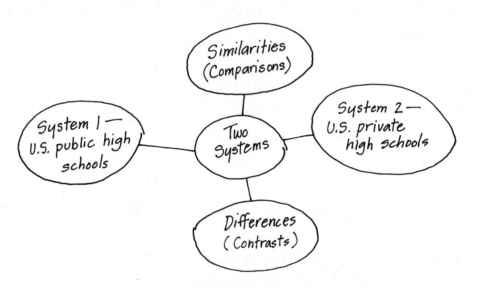

You can add details wherever they seem appropriate and draw lines from any one detail to any other detail as you decide how you want to organize the material.

The next time you are asked to write about a difficult topic or you have a problem getting started (sometimes the hardest part of writing), try one of these kinds of prewriting.

Paragraph Assignment

Have you ever noticed changes in behavior in your family or others during the few days before a full moon? Write an organized paragraph explaining your answer and your attitude toward the moon. Note that this assignment asks for your opinion about a rather complex subject. Try to give specific details from your own experience and your reading.

ANSWERS

Tryout: Commas for Adjectives and Omissions

(1) OK. (2) OK. (3) This shop has many inexpensive, durable materials. (4) Bright, shiny, glamorous fabrics are available for the holidays. (5) We'll buy colorful, inexpensive items for decorating. (6) Tomorrow we'll put a tree into the living room;

stockings, onto the mantel; a wreath, on the front door; and a manger scene, on the table. (7) Candles will decorate my neighbors' table; corn, their front door; wrapped gifts, their mantelpiece. (8) OK. (9) OK. (10) Children look forward to Santa; parents, holiday parties; the stores, high sales volume.

Tryout: Miscellaneous Commas

(1) The full moon has an interesting, confusing reputation. (2) Very old tales speak of werewolves coming out to prowl; hospitals, of a surge in admissions. (3) OK. (4) OK. (5) OK. (6) OK. (7) OK. (8) This pressure change seems minor, not major. (9) OK. (10) When things go well under a full moon, they go very well; when badly, very badly.

Tryout: Commas for Numbers

1. OK.
2. OK.
3. Taxes on that house will be $1,123; its valuation, $178,000.

4. OK.
5. OK.
6. OK.
7. In 1998, 12 people are coming for a reunion.

8. The address is 1525 Lyttonville Road, Silver Spring, MD 20910.

9. OK.
10. OK.

Chapter 17

Miscellaneous Punctuation

Quotation marks, ellipsis points, parentheses, and apostrophes are used for clarifying specific situations in sentences.

To clarify subtle differences in meaning, the punctuation marks we have already discussed will not be enough. Four other types of punctuation are used.

QUOTATION MARKS

Direct Quotations

Memory Peg

Quotation marks are used around *direct* quotations, the exact words someone has said or written. The quotation marks go immediately before and after the words said, as though wrapping up the quotations in ribbons. Printers use a different mark for opening and closing quotations. Typewriter keyboards have just one mark, the same for both opening and closing.

Note: To copy someone else's printed work (defined as five or more words in a row, or any original idea) as if it were your own is *plagiarism,* a serious ethical problem. To quote someone incorrectly and in a way that damages the person is *libel,* if written; *slander,* if spoken.

A Short Story

"I'm calling about the job opening you advertised," said she.

"That's still open," he replied. "Are you interested in it?"

"Tell me a little more," she said, "about the necessary qualifications."

"Well, you need to type 60 words a minute, handle a complex telephone setup, meet the public well, use Microsoft Word for Windows on the computer . . . "

"Oh, dear. I type pretty well, but I haven't learned the computer yet," she sighed. "I guess I'd better go back to school."

This example is a fairly standard quoted conversation, a dialogue. When the speaker changes, a new paragraph begins, regardless of whether the new speaker is named.

Notice that the quotation marks have little to do with whether a sentence is ending; you don't open and close quotation marks just because there's a

To help advanced students who need to do research papers soon, you might illustrate with examples of footnotes while teaching page 131, and take or send students on a library tour.

130

new sentence or a broken sentence. For sentence variety, quotations are frequently interrupted with a "he said" or "she replied," which switches from beginning to middle to end and back.

Capitalization of quotations is done according to the sentence structure of the quoted words, ignoring the interruptions. Commas usually attach the quoted pieces to the rest of the sentence. If the quotation is quite long or consists of more than one sentence, it may be attached with a colon. Small parts of sentences in quotation marks do not need to be attached with commas or capitalized.

Note: If you are not writing a direct quotation, don't use quotation marks!

He says that he is coming.

Is it a direct quotation? It must be word for word, remember. Watch for key clues that a quotation is indirect: *that* or *if,* for example.

She asked if dinner was ready yet. [What did she probably say?]

Occasionally, especially in research papers, you may have a "quote within a quote," that is, two different reasons for quotation marks in the same group of words.

"Did you say 'active verb' or 'action verb'?" she asked.

The main quotation marks are around her whole question. The "mini," or single, quotation marks are around her attempts to quote *you*. We also sometimes use quotes within quotes when we are quoting a critic's opinion of an author's words.

According to the critic, "Because Shakespeare's Polonius is a vain and foolish man, his 'to thine own self be true' speech is not to be taken quite literally as Shakespeare's opinion."

This quotation should be followed by a footnote giving the source. Footnotes are always numbered at the end of the material quoted, with the corresponding number at the beginning of the footnote itself. When formatting allows, type footnote numbers as "superscript" figures, one-half line up from the printed line.

Definitions, Translations, Unusual Terms, and Slang

The second major use of quotation marks is around phrases used as definitions, translations, unusual terms, slang, and deliberately poor grammar. These are used as though we were quoting a source such as the general public (slang) or a dictionary (definition or translation). **Words spoken of as though objects, and after phrases such as "called," "known as," "marked," or "signed," are often enclosed in quotation marks in typed documents and are printed in italics in printed documents.**

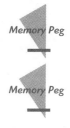

Memory Peg

Memory Peg

*Humpty Dumpty is
known as an
"egghead."*

The word *to* has several meanings and spellings.

The rattling package had been stamped *fragile*.

Capital means "of importance," as applied to money, cities, letters, and the like. *Capitol* means "a building housing the main elected officials."

The French term *comme il faut* means "as it must be done"; in other words, "done the proper way" or "fashionable."

When he calls this a "mod," he's abbreviating "module."

She "cain't say no."

Humpty Dumpty is known as an "egghead."

In a definition or translation, the defined or foreign words are usually set in italics; the English version is enclosed in quotation marks.

Titles of Short Works

Memory Peg

The third primary use of quotation marks is in titles of short published works. We customarily use two different formats for published titles, to help keep their identities straight. Larger works such as books or whole periodicals are underscored or set in italics; smaller ones, such as chapters or articles, are enclosed in quotation marks.

That chapter of *The Bonfire of the Vanities* is "Catching the Fish."

His article in *Life* magazine was "Air Pollution in China."

This chapter, entitled "Miscellaneous Punctuation," is the last punctuation chapter in the book *Practical English Grammar*.

An article entitled "Saving Our Planet" in the *Boston Globe* was illustrated with a globe labeled *This Side Up*.

The general rule is: If items are big enough to publish separately, put them in some form other than quotation marks—italics or underscoring, occasionally full capitals. Save the quotation marks for parts of books. Use quotation marks, therefore, for short stories and poems; italicize novels and plays. Quotation marks are not used around titles on a title page or other title position, just for references to those titles in a paragraph, a footnote, or a bibliography, for example.

Long Passages

Note: When you are quoting more than a few sentences from a written source, the standard format for manuscript material is single spacing, indented five spaces on each side. (Some style guides prefer double-spacing, indented.) For other material, manuscripts are usually double-spaced. In the indented, single-spaced format, quotation marks are not used at the beginning or end, because the format clearly indicates what is quoted.

> Dickens sets the scene in *Hard Times* vividly:
>
> It was a town of red brick, or of brick that would have been red if the smoke and ashes had allowed it; but, as matters stood, it was a town of unnatural red and black, like the painted face of a savage. It was a town of machinery and tall chimneys, out of which interminable serpents of smoke trailed themselves for ever and ever, and never got uncoiled.
>
> Clearly this will not be a tale of romance among the wealthy.

If you are quoting several paragraphs of speech by one speaker, you need opening quotation marks at the beginning of each paragraph, to indicate you're still quoting, but the closing mark is saved for the end of the whole quotation.

Placement with Other Punctuation

The main complication of quotation marks is the question of where to place the other punctuation. There are seven basic patterns:

1. She said, "That's true."
2. "No, it isn't," he responded.
3. "Why not?" she asked.
4. "Because I said so!" he shouted.
5. "But I asked, 'Why not?' and you didn't answer," she said.

6. Do you agree that he is being "unreasonable"?

7. I was reading Jackson's story, "The Lottery"; it still gives me chills.

Can you figure out the rules? The Memory Pegs that follow describe how to place punctuation at ends of quotes. Find the examples that illustrate each rule.

Americans always place periods and commas before the closing quotation mark. (Periods and commas are the small ones; they stay inside the fence.) British style treats periods and commas like question marks and exclamation points.

Semicolons and colons go outside closing quotation marks. (They're larger; they get to go outside!) (These memory devices may seem silly, but they work.)

Question marks and exclamation points are positioned according to sentence logic. **If the question *is* the quotation, the question mark goes inside the closing quotation mark. If the question is the sentence that contains the quotation, the question mark belongs outside the quotation mark. The same applies to exclamations.**

In the article, he was quoted as asking, "Why ask me?"

Have you read Faulkner's short story, "The Bear"?

At the end of the day, he fell onto the couch, muttering, "I'm exhausted!"

That's no excuse for "freaking out"!

ELLIPSIS POINTS

Ellipsis points are used to indicate that material has been omitted from a direct quotation. They are typed space, period, space, period, space, period, space (. . .). Leave out other punctuation at that place in the quotation unless essential. If the omission is preceded or followed by an end-of-sentence period, put one in, making a total of four.

Ellipsis points may also be used to show a thought break or a time break in narrative. A very large section omitted (more than one paragraph out) is sometimes shown with asterisks:

* * *

If an extra word is inserted within a quotation, to summarize the meaning of a section omitted, it is put in brackets, which look like squared-off parentheses [ ]. In newspapers, regular parentheses are used. Reporters frequently add clarifying or summarizing words to quotations.

The senator said, "I object to (the President's) . . . decision to use force in this situation."

Ellipsis points and bracketed insertions enable the writer to choose the key words from a quotation and yet indicate the main idea accurately.

PARENTHESES

Memory Peg

Parentheses are used much like dashes, with two major differences. **Parentheses are usually expected around phrases or sentences that the writer wants to *de*emphasize, to make less important—which is the opposite of dashes. The other difference is that parentheses are always used in pairs, even at the beginning or end of the sentence—unlike either dashes or commas.**

Writers use parentheses when they choose to use them. Once the choice of parentheses is made, however, there are definite rules about the other punctuation involved.

(Full sentences within parentheses are capitalized and have a period inside the final parenthesis.)

Parentheses around the latter part of a sentence may call for a period outside, to complete the sentence (as in this example).

Parentheses within a sentence may have punctuation following the interruption but not before (as in this sentence); the reader gets back on track with the semicolon or comma inserted after the closing parenthesis.

Punctuation within parentheses is done as usual except that the closing parenthesis seems to take the place of a closing interior comma, and a parenthetical expression inside another sentence never takes an end-of-sentence period, nor is it capitalized.

She couldn't decide on her vacation destination (she would probably see Lake Louise or Victoria, British Columbia), but she was enjoying thinking about it. [There would usually be a comma after *British Columbia,* but the parenthesis takes its place.]

In other words, in this example the second "dates and addresses" comma is omitted. The comma that appears after the closing parenthesis is, of course, a necessary compound sentence comma.

Note: Parentheses (like dashes) can contain full-sentence questions or exclamations. The result with the exclamation point is startling and effective emphasis.

He told me (still I don't believe it!) that he was a millionaire.

APOSTROPHES

You've practiced the two main uses of apostrophes, in contractions and possessives, on pages 33 and 56. Both of these are used very commonly for informal writing.

Another common use of the apostrophe is to show omission of the "19" in front of a year, as in "He was born in '22 and died in '96."

In contractions of words, such as *don't,* a common error is to put the apostrophe at the word break rather than at the letter omission. The apostrophe stands for the letter omitted: don't = do not.

For further discussion of contraction apostrophes and possessive apostrophes, see Chapter 21, Nouns, Singular and Plural, and Chapter 23, Nouns, Possessive.

Tryout: Miscellaneous Punctuation

Directions: Add any necessary punctuation and delete any that is unnecessary. Capitalize the beginnings of direct quotations. Ignore the sentence numbers when you are deciding how to punctuate the sentences.

From 100 points subtract 3 points per error.

Remind students of proofreading marks.

(1) A famous Aesop story is entitled "The Fox Without a Tail.

(2) The fable begins, "A fox got his tail caught in a trap. (3) Aesop then tells us that the fox managed to get free (but without his tail.)

(4) The fox called a meeting of all the foxes and advised them cut off your tails. (5) Theyre ugly things . . . heavy and tiresome to carry he said.

(6) "You wouldnt be so free to say that said one of the other foxes, if you hadnt lost your own."

(7) The fox seems to say, "If I cant have something, I think you shouldnt have it either.

(8) Id never behave like that says the student.

(9) Dont be so sure, says the teacher. (10) Have you ever heard a child say, 'If I have to go to bed early, so does my brother!?

Paragraph Assignment

Have you ever looked at a neighbor's house, car, or other belongings and wished you had something similar? Write an organized paragraph explaining your answer.

Practice: Miscellaneous Punctuation

Directions: Add any necessary punctuation and delete any that is unnecessary, but don't remove the quotation marks. Choose commas or parentheses for interruptions, but not both.

Ten points per correct sentence.

1. Do you know what the psychologists mean when they say "left brain behavior" or "right brain behavior"?

2. The left part of the human brain (in most people) seems to be connected to the right hand; the right part, to the left hand.

3. If you are predominantly a "left-brained" person, youre probably very logical, a bit like Data on "Star Trek: The Next Generation."

A left–brained person.

4. Predominantly left-brained people are usually right-handed and organized; according to the psychologists, they "like mathematics and puzzles."

5. If you are left-handed, you may be "right-brained," which to the psychologists means that you are intuitive and creative. OK

6. Because left-handed people are a minority, our culture, (not being very logical about these things) has tended to be prejudiced against them in the past.

7. Children were forced (in the "olden days") to use their right hands to write, or at least to put paper in the right-handed position.

8. The forced position of the paper caused many left-handed children to write "upside down," with the hand curled around the pen.

9. Arent you glad that prejudice is decreasing?

10. We still make scissors, can openers, and hundreds of other objects primarily for right-handed people; (the majority); but we realize that our "lefties" are some of our most creative citizens.

Do you belong to any group that (at least in the past) has experienced prejudice? Write an organized paragraph explaining one experience you have had involving prejudice.

Paragraph Assignment

ANSWERS

Tryout: Miscellaneous Punctuation

(1) A famous Aesop story is entitled "The Fox Without a Tail." (2) The fable begins, "A fox got his tail caught in a trap." (3) Aesop then tells us that the fox managed to get free (but without his tail).

(4) The fox called a meeting of all the foxes and advised them, "Cut off your tails. (5) They're ugly things, . . . heavy and tiresome to carry," he said.

(6) "You wouldn't be so free to say that," said one of the other foxes, "if you hadn't lost your own."

(7) The fox seems to say, "If I can't have something, I think you shouldn't have it either."

(8) "I'd never behave like that," says the student.

(9) "Don't be so sure," says the teacher. (10) "Have you ever heard a child say, 'If I have to go to bed early, so does my brother!'?"

Chapter 18

Capitalization
The Most Useful Rules

Capitalization is another useful way to emphasize.

Most young people start learning the alphabet with capital letters. Then they learn that "big letters" in formal standard English are saved for specific nouns, called *proper nouns,* and certain other situations. This chapter presents the most common rules.

BEGINNINGS

Capitalize the beginning of each sentence, each line of an outline, each line of most poetry, the first word of each individual direct quote, and at least the first word of each salutation and complimentary close in a letter.

> To be, or not to be: that is the question:
> Whether 'tis nobler in the mind . . .

> Shakespeare wrote, "To thine own self be true."

> Dear Ms. Cortines:

> Yours very truly,
> Jennifer Elias, M.A.
> Instructor

NAMES OF PEOPLE, PLACES, THINGS, AND IDEAS

Use the capital *I* for yourself.
Capitalize names (including nicknames).

PERSONS	PLACES	THINGS/IDEAS
Tom Cruise	Hollywood	Roman Catholicism
Aunt Bea	Des Moines, Iowa	the Senate
Sonny	Mount Madonna County Park	the Roaring Twenties
Sister Mary	the Great Lakes	the Muppets

Remember to capitalize to the end of the name of a place or organization.

Andrew Hill High School	the Empire State Building
the IBM Corporation	Apple Computer, Inc.

Don't capitalize *uncle* or the like unless it is used in place of a name or as part of a name.

My brother José bought a new house from Cousin Roberto.

Areas are also frequently called by nicknames, sometimes derived from specific descriptions, which are therefore capitalized.

the Midwest	the Far East	the Loop
the South	Silicon Valley	the East Coast
the South Pacific	the Back Bay	the Gold Coast

Note: Many of these names were given to the areas by visitors and are not geographically accurate. The South Pacific, for example, is not in the southern half of the Pacific Ocean, nor is the Midwest in the western half of the United States.

When used as directions, north, east, south, and west are not capitalized. They are capitalized only as parts of names.

He walked east on West Yonkers Street.

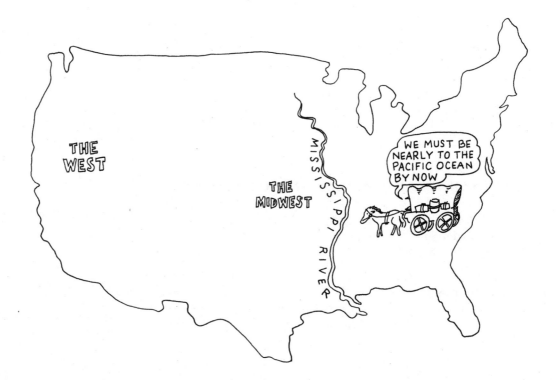

Capitalize names of the days of the week (Monday, Tuesday) and months of the year (January, June) but not the seasons (spring, summer) unless the seasons are personified ("Old Man Winter is blowing his icy breath").

Capitalize names of holidays (New Year's Eve, Labor Day, Passover).

Capitalize names of languages (French, Spanish, Vietnamese), because they usually are derived from the names of countries. Don't capitalize general subjects studied but do capitalize names of specific courses.

> I am taking a course in math.
>
> I am taking Mathematics 104.

Words such as *department* and *division* are capitalized when part of a specific title or when formal or polite emphasis is desired.

the Accounting Department	an accounting department
your Sales Division	that division of the company

Only specific commercial trade (product) names are capitalized—in other words, the product names that a specific company has a right to use.

General Electric vacuum cleaners	Ford Taurus sedan
Xerox photocopiers	Kleenex tissues
Apple Computer, Inc.	a Macintosh computer
a McDonald's restaurant	a Big Mac hamburger

City and *State* are usually capitalized after a name but not before, unless the name stands for a group of people. The words *federal* and *government* are not capitalized unless part of a specific organization's name.

Missouri State	FBI
Kansas City, Kansas	a federal government

I live in the city of Miami.
The City of Charleston has voted to build a new auditorium.
The state of Alaska is the largest in the United States.

TITLES

People's titles are capitalized before the name (Captain Janeway), but usually are not after the name unless emphasis is wanted for well-known elected or appointed officials (from big-city mayor up). People's degrees, however, are capitalized even though they come after the name.

> Sally Brown, editor of *New Woman,* was on the panel.
>
> Diane Cisneros, LL.D., Mayor of Houston, moderated the discussion.
>
> Yesterday Editor Brown went to see the Mayor.
>
> The President lives in the White House.
>
> Elizabeth Blackwell, M.D., was the first woman doctor in the United States.

Note: All titles are capitalized in envelope addresses.

In titles of printed matter, capitalize the first and last word (so readers will know where the title begins and ends), and capitalize all the other important words—that is, all words except small prepositions and coordinating conjunctions (four or fewer letters), and the article adjectives *a*, *an*, and *the*.

Of Mice and Men   The Declaration of Independence
Gone with the Wind   *Love Is Eternal*

The same rules are usually followed for people's names, even in foreign languages, as in *De la Cruz* or *Senator la Follette*. Write a person's name as that person prefers (but always capitalize at the beginning of a sentence).

OUR CHANGING ENGLISH

Remember the duckbilled platypus, who didn't fit the usual rules very well? (See Chapter 7.) Here are a few more examples of English usage that are correct two different ways.

Abbreviations of states in the United States have customarily been done according to a list that makes the meaning obvious: Calif. for California, for example. However, the two-letter, full-capital abbreviations requested by the United States Postal Service (CA for California, TX for Texas, and so on) are increasingly accepted even when the ZIP numbers are not used.

Titles of elected officials have in the past usually been capitalized even when printed separately from the name of the individual: the Senator, the Mayor. As our governmental practices become more informal, however, this capitalization has become less common. Now only the word *President* is usually capitalized, when it means the president of a country.

In titles of printed matter, there are two styles. In one, all words are capitalized except interior articles, prepositions, and conjunctions of four or fewer letters; in the other style, interior word length doesn't matter.

Don't be startled by such differences; the language evolves over time.

 —— Tryout: Capitalization ————————

Directions: Triple underline all letters that should be capitalized. Don't forget that the name of a specific group of people should be capitalized.

One point per correct capital.

1. when i went last thursday night to get my driver's license renewed, i had

   to park on third street because the department of motor vehicles lot was

   full.

2. inside the building, long lines of people stood at the counters.

3. i recognized mrs. silva, who lives around the corner from me on rose-

   wood avenue.

4. she and i hadn't seen each other since her daughter graduated from southeast business college in may.

5. my oldest uncle, bill baldwin, had warned me about the crowding at the dmv.

6. he works during the day at hewlett packard company nearby.

7. when i went to willow glen high school, i knew this area better.

8. now everything seems changed—there are many one-way streets, new buildings, the beltway, and a new parking garage.

9. i was born in the south, but my parents moved to the south bay when i was two years old.

10. since my birthday is near the fourth of july, and i usually go on vacation then, i need to get the license renewed now.

11. i should be studying for my algebra 2 test instead of talking to people in line.

12. maybe i should review the virginia driving laws again.

13. i forgot to bring the book i'm reading, *the catcher in the rye*.

14. there's someone else i know—mr. johnson, who teaches german.

15. here's a copy of the *albany mercury* newspaper, talking about george e. pataki, governor of new york.

16. the city of palo alto has just elected a new city council.

17. do you live in the city of santa clara or the county of santa clara?

18. if i don't get through here soon, i'll be late to meet mom at the corner of park and main.

19. i wonder what they'll call this decade—the nervous nineties?

20. oh. did you say "next"?

FROM SENTENCE TO PARAGRAPH: THE GIFT TO BE SIMPLE

A beginner in speaking or writing a language uses very simple sentences. A child writing sentences in the first or second grade will write them all in the same form.

I had a quarter.   I wanted candy.   I went to the store.

This form has one advantage: it is very clear. The main disadvantage is that it's so dull it's almost hypnotic—after three sentences, the reader begins to fall asleep. However, the opposite problem occurs among writers who are so concerned not to sound simpleminded that they smother meaning in bureaucratic jargon or gobbledygook. A classic example comes from the United States White House during World War II, when President Franklin D. Roosevelt discovered the following memo about air raid preparations:

> Such preparations shall be made as will completely obscure all Federal buildings occupied by the Federal Government during an air raid for any period of time from visibility by reason of internal or external illumination. Such obscuration may be obtained either by blackout construction or by termination of illumination. This will, of course, require that in building areas in which production must continue during the blackout, construction must be provided that internal illumination may continue. Other areas may be obscured by terminating the illumination.

Roosevelt wrote the following translation:

> Tell them that in buildings where they have to keep the work going, they should put something across the windows. In buildings where they can afford to let the work stop for a while, they should turn out lights.

Somewhere between the young child's sentences and the governmentese, there is a wide zone of good writing. It's possible to be formal on formal social or business occasions, to use standard English under most circumstances, and to be informal when you wish—all while maintaining clarity and interest.

Keep in mind clarity as a major goal. If a short word or phrase gives the intended meaning, use it unless it seems downright crude. (See Roosevelt's memo!) Using proper grammar and emphasis will also help clarity. Think through the exact meanings of individual words and phrases and their connotations; then organize them in clear patterns.

Beware of the "dummy subject," sometimes called an *expletive,* a word without meaning, masquerading as the subject of a sentence. You can recognize it by its "dead" and wordy way of beginning a sentence.

It is not easy to study English grammar.

There is no way to master English grammar without study.

What are the subjects of these sentences? In the first one, *it* sounds like the subject—but what does *it* mean? In the second, the subject is *way.* What purpose does *there* serve? The sentences should be revised to give a clear subject. Any of the following would be better:

The study of English grammar is not easy.

English grammar is not easy.

Studying English grammar is . . .

To study English grammar is . . .

No way exists to master English grammar without study.

Nobody can master . . .

The mastery of English cannot be done . . .

Mastering English cannot . . .

Can you think of any others? You can certainly improve on the original sentences.

Another clarity problem often arises at the ends of sentences. It is called *faulty predication,* which means saying that something "is" an extremely vague idea:

INCORRECT   Knowing English is when your teacher says you have the right answer.

The study of English is when you read lots of books.

Understanding English is where you don't make obvious mistakes.

Writers frequently have this problem when trying to define an idea. Let's just reword the examples slightly.

CORRECT   You know English when your teacher says you have the right answer.

The study of English is helped by the reading of books.

Your understanding of English is proved by your lack of obvious mistakes.

The confusing phrases are *is when* and *is where,* which are usually used incorrectly, so watch for them.

Keep in mind that you are usually writing to communicate ideas. The first step is to *have* a clear idea.

How do you spend your time while waiting in line? In an organized paragraph, describe a typical situation in which you might wait in line.

Paragraph Assignment

Practice: General Punctuation and Capitalization Review

Directions: Insert quotation marks where needed. Be sure to place the marks clearly before or after other punctuation marks.

Four points per correct item: partial credit possible in items 1–10.

1. Did the supervisor really say, "Type this as soon as possible"?

2. "Jane," asked Louis, "do you know where the application forms are kept?"

3. "What an interesting job you have!" exclaimed Brad to Ms. Samadi.

4. The article contained a quotation from her new book, *Modern Administration*, Chapter 2, entitled "The Art of Job Interviewing."

5. Terry shouted, "Watch out for the car!"

Directions: Insert colons and semicolons as needed in sentences below, and circle the ones already there that are correct.

6. The questions we ask ourselves are these: Have we served you promptly? Has our merchandise been satisfactory?

7. When you delay, you deny yourself the pleasure of owning a fine floor covering. OK

8. The union members have approved the new contract; therefore, they probably will be back to work by the end of this week.

9. We believe quality is more important than quantity; they believe the opposite.

10. Ms. Jackson made the following announcement to the committee: "The next convention will be held in Miami Beach."

Directions: Circle the letter of the correctly capitalized phrase in each group.

11. (a) at the Forest Avenue Baptist church
    (b) at the Forest Avenue Baptist Church
    (c) at the Forest Avenue baptist church

12. (a) for the Sunland oil company
    (b) for the Sunland Oil company
    (c) for the Sunland Oil Company

13. (a) to Ayer High School
    (b) to Ayer high school
    (c) to Ayer High school

14. (a) a Latin Holiday
    (b) a Latin holiday
    (c) a latin Holiday

15. (a) the McEnery building
    (b) the McEnery Building
    (c) the mcenery building
16. (a) the author of this Essay
    (b) the Author of this essay
    (c) the author of this essay
17. (a) a new elementary school
    (b) a new Elementary school
    (c) a new Elementary School
18. (a) on Thursday morning
    (b) on Thursday Morning
    (c) on thursday Morning
19. (a) to Lake Forest County Park
    (b) to Lake Forest county park
    (c) to Lake Forest County park
20. (a) with corn pops
    (b) with Corn Pops
    (c) with Corn pops
21. (a) in my Math Class
    (b) in my Math class
    (c) in my math class
22. (a) his new Ford Convertible
    (b) his new Ford convertible
    (c) his new ford convertible
23. (a) the new fall fashions
    (b) the new Fall fashions
    (c) the new Fall Fashions
24. (a) with Swedish Meatballs
    (b) with Swedish meatballs
    (c) with swedish meatballs
25. (a) the José Theater
    (b) the José theater
    (c) the josé theater

26. (a) in our Essay book
    (b) in our essay book
    (c) in our Essay Book

27. (a) read *Gone With the Wind*
    (b) read *Gone with the wind*
    (c) read *Gone with the Wind*

28. (a) in all Protestant churches
    (b) in all Protestant Churches
    (c) in all protestant churches

29. (a) to the James Lick High School
    (b) to the James Lick high school
    (c) to the James Lick High school

30. (a) on memorial day
    (b) on Memorial Day
    (c) on memorial Day

ANSWERS

Tryout: Capitalization

1. when i went last thursday night to get my driver's license renewed, i had to park on third street because the department of motor vehicles lot was full.

2. inside the building, long lines of people stood at the counters.

3. i recognized mrs. silva, who lives around the corner from me on rosewood avenue.

4. she and i hadn't seen each other since her daughter graduated from southeast business college in may.

5. my oldest uncle, bill baldwin, had warned me about the crowding at the dmv.

6. he works during the day at hewlett packard company nearby.

7. when i went to willow glen high school, i knew this area better.

8. now everything seems changed—there are many one-way streets, new buildings, the beltway, and a new parking garage.

9. i was born in the south, but my parents moved to the south bay when i was two years old.

10. since my birthday is near the fourth of july, and i usually go on vacation then, i need to get the license renewed now.

11. i should be studying for my algebra 2 test instead of talking to people in line.

12. maybe i should review the virginia driving laws again.

13. i forgot to bring the book i'm reading, *the catcher in the rye*.

14. there's someone else i know—mr. johnson, who teaches german.

15. here's a copy of the *albany mercury* newspaper, talking about george e. pataki, governor of new york.

16. the city of palo alto has just elected a new city council.

17. do you live in the city of santa clara or the county of santa clara?

18. if i don't get through here soon, i'll be late to meet mom at the corner of park and main.

19. i wonder what they'll call this decade—the nervous nineties?

20. oh. did you say "next"?

Chapter 19

Numbers and Abbreviations
Social Use and Business Use

Numbers and abbreviations are spelled out in many situations.

In standard English, both numbers and abbreviations are used in different ways for different circumstances. Numbers spelled out carry the feeling of formal social usage—on a wedding invitation, for example; in business reports, however, most numbers are written in figures (Arabic numerals). In daily informal use, these distinctions are less important than they are in formal or job-related situations.

When writing for the general public, always spell out any possibly unfamiliar or confusing abbreviations and define any necessary terms, especially the first time they are used. For similar reasons, use as few symbols as possible in writing for the general public. (The dollar sign is the only one that practically everyone knows!) If your writing includes many important unfamiliar terms, provide definitions in footnotes or a glossary (a list like a partial dictionary). **When in doubt, spell it out!**

Memory Peg

NUMBERS

Memory Peg

Words are usually used to express one-digit numbers. The number nine is only one digit; the numbers 10 and higher are two digits. Figures (Arabic numerals) are used for precise measurements, even small ones (under 10), and words are used for large imprecise numbers. In the humanities, numbers that can be written in one or two words are often spelled out.

Last week, we added four new courses. [small number]

The English Department now offers twenty-three courses. [humanities style]

About three-fourths of our students are parents. [fraction]

One student is about ninety years old now. [imprecise]

Words are used for any number at the beginning of a sentence.

We arrived at the hall at 8:30. Forty people had come to the meeting.

This shows where the new sentence begins and avoids a misreading of the end-of-sentence period and numeral as a decimal.

The use of figures (Arabic numerals) for numbers is considered business-oriented or relatively scientific or technical. Similarly, abbreviations are used more commonly in technical writing, which assumes that the reader has knowledge of the subject discussed.

Figures are usually used in situations that call for precision. They are used for precise numbers over nine, amounts of money, and percentages.

> We ordered 60 pies.
>
> The total was $662.38.
>
> That includes 17 percent annual interest.
>
> The pay increase will be 3.5 percent next year.
>
> We spent between $400 and $500 last year on cleaning supplies.

Large numbers (from millions up) are considered easier to read if they are partially in words. The word *thousand* is seldom spelled out, however.

$35 million	$3,200
3.5 billion people	$1,023.43
35 million pounds	57 cents
400 million bushels	$124.23

Note: A new international format now calls for using the term *thousand million* rather than *billion*, since the term is more exact. In international situations, the commas in long numbers are often replaced by spaces, as in the following: 300 251 225 would mean 300,251,225.

Related numbers should be treated alike.

> We spent $399,000 on advertising, $1,200,000 on salaries, and $800,000 on overhead.

Be sure you repeat *million* in phrases expressing a range: in the phrase *$3 to $4 million,* the first figure can be read as *three dollars.*

Use figures for mixed numbers because spelling them out takes much more space.

Memory Peg

> $3\frac{1}{2}$ [not *three and one-half*]

Use figures for the following types of numbers because they are precise or business-oriented.

DECIMALS	2.5	0.75 percent [Use the *0* to emphasize the decimal point.]
UNITS OF MEASURE	My desk is 3 feet by 5 feet.	

TIMES	7 a.m.	10:45 a.m. [For even hours, don't use 7:00 unless in a series with times giving minutes.]
AGES, WHEN SPECIFIC	He was 23 years old.	
YEARS	450 B.C.	A.D. 319 [formal style]

One recent trend is to write A.D. after the year. Another recent style changes B.C. to B.C.E. (Before the Common Era); A.D. then becomes C.E. (Common Era).

DATES, IN THREE DIFFERENT STYLES

May 19, 1997   the 19th of May, 1997   19 May 1997

A *th* is usually added to a date only if the month is not given before it. Note also one other modern style: 22d, 23d, rather than 22nd or 23rd.

Memory Peg

When one number is followed by another of a different meaning, spell out the first (or, alternatively, the shorter) of the two numbers.

They ordered five 50-page booklets.

They delivered 50 five-page booklets.

Note: Don't use a comma here or keep both numbers in the same format because these are not a series of similar items, such as "14 desks, 28 chairs, and 6 tables."

Memory Peg

Street names and building floors are spelled out from *first* through *ninth*; at 10th and above they are done in figures. House address numbers are done in figures except for the word *one*.

236 Fifth Street   One Madison Avenue   27 18th Street, Third Floor

A *th* is used on *18th*, because there is no other way to focus on the difference between the house number and the street address. If there is a word like *West* between, the *th* may be omitted, as in 16 West 27 Street; 293 South 11 Avenue.

Ten points per correct answer.

Tryout: Numbers

Directions: Circle any incorrect number forms, and rewrite them correctly in the blanks at the ends of the sentences.

1. There are only twenty-one shopping days left before Christmas.   _____

2. Why do we get so concerned about December 25th?   _____

3. I thought the religious holidays were for spiritual celebration, not to fill twenty-four hours with buying.   _____

4. Each year I resolve to donate ten % of my income
   to charities.   _____

5. Each year I run $100 dollars over my Christmas
   budget.   _____

6. My granddaughter says she is three and two-thirds
   years old.   _____

7. The best times to shop are before 7 a.m. and after
   eight p.m.   _____

8. There may be only two or 3 people at the supermarket then.   _____

9. School holiday vacation starts on the twenty-first. _____

10. These cards made from recycled paper are only
    $2.00.   _____

Do you know approximately how much (in percentages or dollars) you spend on the main items in your monthly or yearly budget? Try to explain in a paragraph approximately where your money goes. (This is one way to try to control it.)

This is a logical "how-to" assignment, not the more complex question of why you spend the money. Perhaps that would be a good topic for a longer essay later.

Paragraph Assignment

OUR CHANGING ENGLISH

The abbreviation B.C. seems to be going out of style, partially because it means "Before Christ" and therefore refers to one specific religion. The newer term is B.C.E., meaning "Before the Common Era."

The custom concerning dates for specific days also seems to be changing, and more than one way is acceptable, including the following:

May 17	May Sixth	the 23d of May
May 17th	May 6th	the 23rd of May
17 May 1996		

The most commonly used style is still "May 17, 1996."

ABBREVIATIONS

Use abbreviations only when you are extremely short of space or when you are writing technical copy for people who know your version of business or scientific jargon. All workplaces and many leisure places have their own language, spoken by the people "in the know." Many groups also have their own exclusive ways to communicate—think of teenagers! The specific customs in general standard English (neither technical nor extremely formal social situations, such as wedding invitations) are given here.

The preferred spellings for common titles before names are the following:

Mr. [plural is Messrs., from the French; it is uncommon and very formal]

Mrs. [plural is Mmes., from the French; uncommon and formal]

Miss [no period, not an abbreviation; plural is Misses]

Dr. [almost always abbreviated; plural is Drs.]

Ms. [used for either Miss or Mrs.; plural is Mss.]

Use the formal plural when addressing formal invitations:

Drs. John and Jan Jones   Mrs. Laura Boucher and Miss Veronica Boucher

Don't abbreviate other titles except in informal writing or when you are short of space, in which case the title may be abbreviated if it is very long or if the person's first name is given.

Senator Feinstein   Sen. Daniel Moynihan   Governor Brown
Brig. Gen. Redalia   The Reverend Rose Smith   Prof. Robert Beck

Titles showing special respect, such as *The Reverend* and *The Honorable,* are more often spelled out than such titles as *Superintendent.*

Titles after specific names, such as *Tom Iwashita, D.D.S.,* are capitalized, abbreviated, and surrounded by commas and periods. (See page 117.)

Don't use *Mr.* or the like before a name that has a title after it. Don't use the title both before and after (no double credit).

INCORRECT   Ms. Marlene McConnell, Attorney
                  Dr. Joel Fleischman, M.D.

CORRECT   Marlene McConnell, Attorney
                  Dr. Joel Fleischman   Joel Fleischman, M.D.

Call letters for radio and television are not abbreviations; therefore, they use no periods. This is also true of hypothetical names like *Mr. A* (in a math problem) and chemical symbols, such as *O* for oxygen.

Abbreviations that can be pronounced, such as NASA, are called *acronyms*. They are used in full caps with no periods.

Memory Peg

Memory Peg

Don't abbreviate days of the week or months except in tables and forms where you are short of space.

Don't use *a.m.* or *p.m.* with *o'clock;* use the abbreviations with figures only.

7 a.m.   10:30 p.m.   four o'clock

Abbreviation can lead to non-communication.

Don't abbreviate precise terms such as "inches" or "hours."

Don't abbreviate the names of any streets or cities except for the *St.* meaning "Saint."

Memory Peg

Fifth Avenue   West 10th Street   New York   St. Augustine

Words such as *Street* should be spelled out if there is space on the envelope. For state names, use the two-letter ZIP abbreviation—always with the ZIP code numbers—when addressing envelopes and in matching addresses elsewhere. The older traditional state abbreviations are used where ZIP codes don't matter, such as in bibliographies and newspaper articles. The newest postal recommendations use capital letters and special abbreviations for addresses—see the Postal Service manuals or a recent typing text for the approved style.

Spell out words such as *West* if they are early in an address; later compass points in addresses are usually abbreviated. A hyphen between home address and street name is an alternative style:

1621 West 69 Street   1621 69th Street   1621 - 69th NW

In general, any abbreviation you have heard as much as or more than the full title is properly abbreviated, usually without periods:

CBS   AT&T   UAW   FBI   USA   UN

The abbreviation *No.* for "Number" is used only before a figure and must be spelled out at the beginning of a sentence.

Note: Abbreviations are very different from contractions, which are words with letters omitted and apostrophes added at the point of omission. Here are common examples of contractions as a reminder:

we're = we are	don't = do not	he's = he is
they're = they are	isn't = is not	we'll = we will

Tryout: Numbers, Abbreviations, and Contractions

Ten points per correct answer.

Directions: Circle any incorrect forms, and rewrite them correctly in the blanks at the ends of the sentences. There may be more than one in a sentence.

1. Sen Smith gave the speech on Sat. _____

2. Dr. John Thomas, M.D., is my surgeon. _____

3. Mister Carrera knows him well. _____

4. Mr. Letterman worked for N.B.C. in Aug. _____

5. Vets should write to the gov't. about benefits. _____

6. Come at 8:30 o'clock a.m. _____

7. Bring 3 yds. of material. _____

8. The store is just 2 mi from my house. _____

9. No. 10 Downing St. is the British Prime Minister's address. _____

10. My address is Sixteen 4th St. Northeast. _____

Practice: Numbers, Abbreviations, and Contractions

Ten points per correct answer.

Directions: Circle any errors, and rewrite them correctly in the blanks at the ends of the sentences.

1. Water is made up of Ⓗ and Ⓞ. *hydrogen and oxygen*

2. He moved to Ⓜⓘⓝⓝ in Ⓢⓔⓟⓣ *Minnesota in September*

3. Have you been to Ⓟⓣ Reyes? *Point*

4. Ⓦⓔⓡⓔ moving to Ⓜⓣ Kisko Ⓣⓤⓔ *We're, Mount Kisko, Tuesday*

5. (Its) at the corner of (9th) (Ave.) (&) (Sixteenth).   *It's, Ninth Avenue and 16th*

6. (Hes) taking (Prin.) of (Mod.) (Acct.)   *He's, Principles, Modern Accounting*

7. (Rev.) Jones is talking with (Rep.) Stevens.   *Reverend, Representative*   Sentence 7: Preferred style
is "The Reverend."

8. Get off at the (5th) Floor.   *Fifth*

9. See me on (Dec.) (15th).   *December 15*

10. See me before the 16th of December.   *OK*

11. For a few (\$100,) you buy 92(%) of your food.   *hundred dollars, percent*

12. Go to 140 (W.) 12th (St.)   *West, Street*

ANSWERS

Tryout: Numbers

1. There are only (twenty-one) shopping days left before
   Christmas. _____21_____

2. Why do we get so concerned about December (25th)? _____25_____

3. I thought the religious holidays were for spiritual celebration, not to fill
   (twenty-four) hours with buying. _____24_____

4. Each year I resolve to donate (ten %) of my income to charities. _____10 percent_____

5. Each year I run ($100 dollars) over my Christmas budget. _____$100_____

6. My granddaughter says she is (three and two-thirds) years old. _____$3\frac{2}{3}$_____

7. The best times to shop are before 7 a.m. and after (eight) p.m. _____8_____

8. There may be only two or (3) people at the supermarket then. _____three_____

9. School holiday vacation starts on the (twenty-first). _____21st_____

10. These cards made from recycled paper are only ($2.00). _____$2_____

Tryout: Numbers, Abbreviations, and Contractions

1. (Sen) Smith gave the speech on (Sat). _____Senator, Saturday_____

2. (Dr. John Thomas, M.D.), is my surgeon. (or John Thomas, M.D.,)
   _____Dr. John Thomas_____

3. (Mister) Carrera knows him well. _____Mr._____

4. Mr. Letterman worked for (N.B.C.) in (Aug). _____NBC, August_____

5. (Vets) should write to the (gov't) about benefits. _____veterans, government_____

6. Come at (8:30 o'clock a.m.) _____8:30 a.m._____

7. Bring 3 (yds.) of material. _____yards_____

8. The store is just 2 (mi) from my house. _____miles_____

9. (No.) 10 Downing (St.) is the British Prime Minister's address. _____Number, Street_____

10. My address is (Sixteen 4th St. Northeast). _____16 Fourth Street NE_____

Chapter 20 _____

Punctuation Review
Rules and Tests

Now you're ready for a comprehensive punctuation review and testing. _____

SUMMARY OF IMPORTANT COMMA RULES

Commas with *And*

Use a comma to join two independent clauses with a conjunction, such as *and, but, or.*

Use commas to connect items in a series containing one *and.*

Do not use a comma to connect two items or to connect two possible sentences without a conjunction.

Introductory Words

Use a comma to set off any group of words containing a verb part, a verb, or five or more words before the main subject of the sentence.

Use a comma to set off an adverb if a possible pause exists.

Use a comma to attach a short quoted sentence.

Parentheticals (Interruptions)

Most items of "extra" information (such as appositives), most parenthetical clauses (such as "you know"), and any other information that can be read with a *dropped voice* (including use of the name of a person in direct address) should be surrounded with commas.

A specialized type of "interrupting" material includes dates and addresses. Use commas around the second and all following items in these.

Another subgroup of interruptions is nonessential clauses or phrases. **If the word group is likely to be read with a voice drop, it is not essential, and you should use commas around it.**

Memory Peg

159

Miscellaneous Commas

Use commas on repeats or to show omission of a repeated idea.

> The teacher made the point very, very clear.

> In these sentences, the teacher said to use commas; in those sentences, to omit them.

Use a comma between two adjectives that modify the noun separately enough so that you could insert the word *and* naturally between them.

Do not use commas on most prepositional phrases; however, occasionally a comma is needed for clarity.

Memory Peg

Never, never split subject from verb or verb from object with just one comma!

Tryout: Commas

Three points per correct answer.

Directions: Insert necessary commas and delete any unnecessary ones. Don't change other punctuation.

1. A guitar string broke as Rafael played but, he continued with the song.

2. We were attending a show at 1600 Pennsylvania Avenue Washington D.C.

3. Stan and Gloria parked their car near a store at 1450 Pennsylvania Avenue.

A guitar string broke as Rafael played . . .

4. Stan my brother-in-law, also plays guitar bass and drums.

5. Ben do you play a musical instrument, or sing in a choir?

6. In the show at the auditorium we saw Dave Bill and Linda.

7. When Rafael plays the guitar seems to sing.

8. He plays haunting beautiful melodies.

9. My son as you know, sings in a choir with the symphony.

10. After the show everybody went home and ate pizza and hot dogs and hamburgers.

11. You know, Stan that music makes people hungry.

12. The next show will be on January 22, 1997 at Davies Hall in San Francisco.

13. Because my son is singing I will probably go to hear him.

14. After the holidays, Lee, you'll have more time to practice, and to compose.

15. Lee replied, "My music teacher who knows me better than you do says I'll compose music but not practice enough."

Do you play a musical instrument or wish you did? Write an organized paragraph explaining one of your experiences with music. | **Paragraph Assignment**

Practice: Comma Review

Directions: Circle the correctly punctuated sentence.

Ten points per correct answer.

1. (a) Answer our letter now, Mr. Consumer, and save money.

   (b) Answer our letter now Mr. Consumer, and save money.

2. (a) The woman who bought the house was my sister, who can afford it.

   (b) The woman, who bought the house, was my sister who can afford it.

3. (a) This painting for example, is hung horizontally, not vertically.

   (b) This painting, for example, is hung horizontally, not vertically.

4. (a) In many houses in this city, children go to bed hungry.

   (b) In many houses in this city children go to bed, hungry.

5. (a) On October 12, 1492, Columbus is supposed to have sighted the Western Hemisphere, and a new world opened to European colonization.

   (b) On October 12, 1492 Columbus is supposed to have sighted the Western Hemisphere and a new world, opened to European colonization.

6. (a) If you don't study your schoolwork may suffer.

   (b) If you don't study, your schoolwork may suffer.

7. (a) "Yes!" "I signed the letter," said my boss.

   (b) "Yes! I signed the letter," said my boss.

8. (a) Walking down the sidewalk I saw a dime, and stopped to pick it up.

   (b) Walking down the sidewalk, I saw a dime and stopped to pick it up.

9. (a) The book stated, "He was born in Sioux City, Iowa, on December 24, 1925."

   (b) The book stated, "he was born in Sioux City, Iowa on December 24, 1925."

10. (a) Do you know Joan Smyth (Or is it Smythe?)?

   (b) Do you know Joan Smyth (or is it Smythe)?

Practice: Quotation Mark and Apostrophe Review

Directions: Insert or delete quotation marks, apostrophes, and related punctuation marks where needed. Be sure to place the marks clearly before or after other punctuation marks.

Three points per correctly marked sentence; partial credit possible.

1. "What an interesting course this is!" exclaimed Pat.
2. "Do you think you understand quotation marks yet?" asked the teacher.
3. "I think I do," said Pat, "but I'm not sure."
4. The teacher smiled. "Let's go over it one more time," she suggested.
5. They looked again at the review material in the chapter entitled "Miscellaneous Punctuation," from her book, *Practical English Grammar.*
6. "But Mary said this was 'very easy' for her," said James.
7. "Did she really say 'very easy?'" asked Jean.
8. "She said it." "Then she changed her mind," said Bob.
9. The teacher said she thought we should practice for one more hour. OK
10. "Then," she said, "you should be ready."
11. The bill for photocopying was four hundred two dollars ($402).
12. The students asked to review the discussion of parentheses (page 27). OK

13. The teacher criticized the text; (she mentioned the ambiguous test questions.

Practice: Punctuation Review

Directions: Supply the correct ending punctuation marks.

Two points per correctly marked sentence (total for items 1–25 is 50).

1. I will turn in the report next Friday.
2. At what time are you planning to go to dinner?
3. Please open your books to page 18.
4. *Help!Help!*
5. What time is it?
6. Will you please come on time tomorrow.
7. My mother asked me to buy a loaf of bread on my way home.
8. What was your grade in English?
9. Call a doctor!
10. He asked to borrow my eraser.

Directions: Add quotation marks where necessary.

11. Mai said, "I would like to go to the party."
12. My mother told me that I should be home by 10 p.m.   OK
13. "What," asked Bob, "do you intend to do about it?"
14. Did he ask if he could have permission to talk on that subject?   OK
15. The teacher asked, "How many will attend the conference?"

Directions: Add apostrophes where necessary.

16. Mary's sister came to the party, but she can't stay too late.
17. You're a fine person.
18. That's all I intend to say about the matter.
19. It's time that we left for John's house.
20. There's a sale on men's coats at Kelly's Department Store. , or Kelly's'

Directions: Add commas where necessary.

21. John, see me after class.
22. If you want to, help Mary.

23. Your teacher, Mr. Gomez, will answer questions.

24. Running out of the room won't solve the problem.   OK

25. Lee, Sally, and Jaime like to do games, puzzles, and crosswords.

Directions: Punctuate the following paragraph with periods, question marks, commas, and exclamation points, adding capitals where needed. Do not use semicolons. When correct, the paragraph will have 25 punctuation marks and capital letters (including the first capital).

Two points per correct mark (total for paragraph is 50).

What do you do when the motor of your car will not start some drivers make the mistake of pressing the starter until the battery goes dead as the trouble is usually caused by a minor difficulty isn't it more sensible to make a systematic check to see whether you can find the source of the difficulty stop investigate weak lights are a sign that the battery is low check your gas gauge and your spark plugs the smell of gasoline usually means that your carburetor is flooded turn off the ignition and wait a few minutes turn on the ignition and try again has your motor started excellent

---

FROM SENTENCE TO PARAGRAPH: GETTING STARTED CREATIVELY

You may begin using some of these ideas much earlier in the course, but the main problem seems to be in expanding from the short paragraph into longer forms such as the essay. Journals may help if you have the time for them.

In trying to put together almost any piece of writing, you may sometimes draw a blank. This is what some people call a writer's block, or "fear of the white page." Even professional writers and artists sometimes feel this anxiety, as though the first mark on the page would produce a mistake. All of us have felt this fear of making mistakes, so if you've had the problem, realize you're not alone.

The cure for writer's block is to decide that mistakes don't matter when you are starting to write. If you can just write anything, sooner or later you'll find something interesting to develop and polish. Here are some hints for getting started.

1. Any previous writing may provide a basis for future work. Look at your journals, notes, and letters.

2. Try what is called *automatic writing*. When you are very relaxed or sleepy—late at night or early in the morning or when you are just awakening from a nap—simply put pen or pencil to paper and let your hand move without thinking ahead of time about what you are going to write. You may repeat words and phrases such as "I can't think of anything," but sooner or later something will emerge from deeper in your mind.

3. Draw pictures—quick little sketches, doodles, and notes.

4. Try *word association*. Write one word and then all the other words that come into your mind in connection with it. Aim for visual, concrete nouns and verbs after the first word or two.

5. Try any of the common methods of meditation to get yourself thoroughly relaxed; then try one or more of the methods already listed for getting started.

The goal is to get past that blank sheet of paper. All of these suggestions are ways of contacting your right brain, the creative half (the one usually connected with the left hand). People who can't get started with artistic projects are often stopping themselves before they begin, by using the left brain (right hand) critical, logical half, the half that proofreads, edits, and sometimes says too quickly, "Oh, that's no good."

Keep the critical part of your brain locked away until you have let your creative ideas flow. Then, after you've covered several pages with notes, let The Critic out to polish up your good ideas. That's the time to make sure that you are being clear, that a reader can follow your thoughts through from beginning to end, and that you have cleaned up the details of spelling, punctuation, and grammar. Remember that the best writers do a lot of revision.

Sample Test 1: End Punctuation and Major Clause Connectors   *Refer to Chapters 11 and 12*

Directions: Insert or delete punctuation and capitals where needed. Do not assume emphasis is intended unless it is noted. Most marks will be end punctuation; a few, commas.

Two points per correct sentence; partial credit possible.

1. Ann is looking for pine she has found, however, that there is not much pine available.

2. Why he hasn't come is a mystery to me?.

3. The order arrived Friday, consequently, the book was sent on Monday.

4. Hurry We have only two minutes until takeoff time [Show emphasis.]

5. We need the following information: (1.) the order number, (2.) the amount, and (3.) the quantity.

6. Have you heard his offer it exceeds our wildest expectations, [Show emphasis.]

7. Can you estimate the cost of the roofing? The tile work? The painting?

8. Capitalize the first word of:

   a. Every sentence.

   b. Direct quotations of more than a few words.

   c. Items displayed in a list.

9. Will you be going to the play Of course

10. Sally misspelled the following words accommodate, convenience, and too.

11. Will you please let us have your decision as soon as possible?.

12. Please order the following items:

     1. Rubber bands,

     2. Paper clips,

     3. Staples,

13. We can count on your support, can't we.?

14. I plan to take that course for two reasons first, I am interested in math second, I have spare time.

Sentence 15: In both cases, the comma after *each year* is optional.

15. Each year, the number of applicants increased each year, the number of jobs decreased.

16. Ms. Tann asked whether we will attend?.

17. Why were you absent from class,?

18. We brought her, books, flowers, fruit, and magazines.

19. The snow was deep and crusty; perfect for skiing, [Show emphasis.]

20. Two courses are required: one for speed and one for accuracy. OK

21. The next design I can't wait to show it to you is in my folder.

22. Will you wait for me in, the car, the hall, or the garage?

23. We do a good job, and we do it fast [Show emphasis.]

24. Traffic may be heavy, be sure to leave on time.

25. There is one compelling reason for delay we lack sufficient funds to proceed.

26. Call Mike Adams he's with Smith Inc. and get his opinion.

27. We worked at headquarters all morning then we canvassed all afternoon.

28. He asked whether I had seen Ron.

29. The new director Have you met her yet will be here in an hour.

Sentence 30: Instead of a semicolon, students can use a period and a capital *B*.

30. The following reasons were given be sure to read them carefully.

Sentence 31: Students can use a colon instead of a semicolon.

31. She suggested several alternatives, for example, extending the deadline, rewarding prompt payment, or penalizing late payment.

32. Could you please be sure to include your $45 payment.

33. Will you be able to include this chapter in your book?

34. King Henry VIII, is famous for having many wives.

35. Several of the men, Joe and Al included are excellent speakers.

Sentence 36: Students can use a colon instead of a semicolon.

36. Our policy is clear, the customer is always right.

37. They had no plans for the summer therefore, we went to visit them.

38. Rice, pasta, potatoes, bread all of these are important foods for a runner.

Sample Test 2: Commas   *Refer to Chapters 13–16*

Directions: Add commas where necessary. Do not change other punctuation.

Two points per correct sentence; partial credit possible.

Sentence 2: This sentence would also be correct with no comma added.

1. Before Jan met with the real estate group, attorneys had given her advice.

2. Mr. Dolan realized the meeting was already over, because all the official cars had left.

3. The notices must be sent no later than 3:15 p.m. Friday, August 7, 1997.

4. Ms. Nancy Miller transcribed and typed that letter, but she did not write it.

5. In preparing such department reports, agents should use proper forms.

6. If you wish us to forward your mail, clerks have the forms you need to fill out.

7. Some firms provide cars for employees; others, a daily transportation allowance.

8. Having inspected the school, board members congratulated my boss.

9. Lincoln gave the address on November 19, 1863, at Gettysburg.

10. To be successful, managers must be courteous, accurate, and creative.

11. Incidentally, the return of students to campus in the fall will undoubtedly stimulate business, and we shall need additional help.

12. Miss Jones's idea is excellent; her statement, persuasive; her evidence, impressive.

13. The vice president, the manager, and the clerk submitted separate statements.

14. The Shipping Department hired seven new employees; the Finance Department, three.

15. After discussing investment policy, commission members took up taxes.

16. An announcer who mispronounces a word usually receives several telephone calls about the error.   OK

17. The policy committee, which is chaired by E. J. Rivera, turned in its report.

18. Mrs. Politsky's second suggestion, on the other hand, seems feasible.

19. Jack drew the suggestion to the attention of Mr. Branch,and the report convinced him.

20. Mr. Woo commented,"This room can be arranged more conveniently."

21. A meeting has been called for Friday,February 3,at 11 a.m. at Northeast Community College,200 Elm Street,Noank,Connecticut.

22. Inspecting the storerooms,closets,and hallways,the fire marshal found everything in order.

23. In addition,poise and self-confidence are extremely helpful.

24. Once apprised of the facts,the examiner studied the evidence.

25. Ms. De Angelo came from Mount Ayr,Iowa,but she moved to Harrisburg,Pennsylvania.

26. One reason that Mrs. Johnson,one of the leading educators in the Gulf Coast region,has such a keen interest in American schools is that she realizes that they are educating our future leaders.

27. After you proofread this contract,please see that it is mailed.

28. Mr. Meherin is a willing worker,and he is thoroughly capable of performing the duties assigned to him.

29. The secretary who ensures the accuracy,friendly tone,and completeness of every message she prepares is of great value.

30. In a rough draft,form is not important,for the layout can be changed later.

31. Students who apply themselves conscientiously will learn more than those who do the bare minimum of studying. OK

32. Returning by way of Dallas,Texas,Miss Pardo stopped at our office.

33. Sam Browne,who has taught at Eastside Community College,is now teaching in industry.

34. Ms. Hoover proposed adjournment; Ms. Mejia,continuation for as many sessions as needed.

35. Twenty-two firms are now using this plan; don't you think,Ms. Cate, that we should try it?

36. "In the next six months," said Ms. Hwang,"our business should double."

37. The assignment has been given to Celia Walsh,who is the Dean's assistant.

Sample Test 3: Quotation Marks and Parentheses

Refer to Chapter 17

Directions: Insert quotation marks and parentheses carefully where necessary, before or after other punctuation. You may want to practice using the proofreading marks in Appendix E at the end of this book.

Six points per correct sentence; partial credit possible.

1.   At the recreation center, the lifeguard asked, "Coming?"

2.   We wanted to swim, so we yelled, "Yes!"

3.   "You can't swim in the small pool," warned the lifeguard.

4.   We wondered why we couldn't do that.   OK

5.   Then the guard explained, "That's reserved for children."

6.   My younger sister laughed. "That means me!"

7.   "OK, OK," I agreed. "We'll meet you later."

8.   After we had swum for an hour, we called, "Time to go home."

9.   Cissie was still having fun. "Not ready yet!" she yelled.

10.   "But we're ready for hamburgers! Aren't you?" we asked.

11.   That changed Cissie's mind (she was getting cold anyway).

12.   Have you ever taken care of a little sister (a very stubborn little sister!) on a summer afternoon?

13.   (That's the problem with being the oldest one.)

14.   She always says, "Can I come too?"

15.   Sometimes we say "No." (That's the problem with being the youngest one.)

Sample Test 4: Capitalization   *Refer to Chapter 18*

Directions: Triple underline all letters that should be capitalized. Draw a slash through capital letters that should be lowercase.

From 100 points subtract 1 point per error.

(1) Have you ever gone back to visit a town or store or recreation center you last saw as a child? (2) The street in <u>d</u>es Moines, <u>i</u>owa, where I played when very young, seemed very small when <u>i</u> visited in <u>j</u>une. (3) The two-room /Elementary /School is gone; a new /High /School has been built nearby. (4) An old farmhouse still sits at the top of a hill where we took our sleds in /Winter. (5) At the bottom of the hill, where

Everything seems to have shrunk since I left!

the barbed wire fence once guarded the cattle, mcdonald's hamburgers are now served. (6) The United states post office was once part of a small general store. (7) Near that corner, where the union pacific railroad crosses the river, there is now a huge shopping center.

(8) We looked for the post office and finally saw the american flag in front of the building. (9) My Mother and aunt Sally wanted to buy stamps and local picture postcards. (10) Then Mother said she wanted to find a bookstore. (11) We discovered Green books just around the corner. (12) As we walked through the shopping center, we saw lots of the midwestern license plates we remembered—iowa, minnesota, missouri, illinois. (13) Next we needed a bank of America to get cash with our visa cards. (14) We ate lunch in denny's, one of the inexpensive chain cafés, near the church where Mom and dad were married. (15) Because my grandfather was a Protestant minister, he had officiated at the wedding. (16) The famous Little Brown Church in the Vale is in Nashua, iowa, not far from Des moines. (17) Later we mailed postcards showing the iowa State Capitol building and the Polk county courthouse, where dad worked. (18) On tuesday we visited my High School friend, Bonnie McAvoy, who is now teaching music at Drake university. (19) Across the street from drake is still the varsity

theater, where i sold popcorn—my first job as a student. (20) As we walked across the Campus, i remembered all the Buildings, the Classes, and the Professors from my first college year.

Have you ever gone back to an area where you lived when you were younger? What had changed? Write an organized paragraph answering the questions.

Paragraph Assignment

Sample Test 5: Numbers and Abbreviations

Refer to Chapter 19

Directions: Circle all errors in number and abbreviation usage, and write the correct forms in the blanks at the ends of the sentences. If you're not sure of spelling, guess—this isn't a spelling test.

From 100 points subtract 5 points for each error.

1. The cost of apples is $.28 per lb.   *28 cents, pound*
2. The price will go up on Tues. Jan. 15th.   *Tuesday, January 15*
3. Do you have 4 quarters for a $1?   *four, a dollar*
4. There's a less expensive store on 7th Street.   *seventh*
5. This store closes at ten p.m.   *10*
6. The manager's name is Karl Wilhelm Junior.   *Jr.*
7. Aisle Number Eight B is very crowded.   *No. 8*
8. The ad shows a quote from Sen. Mikulski.   *Senator*
9. Talk to the mgr. about a job application.   *manager*
10. I'll meet you at nine in the a.m.   *9 a.m.*

ANSWERS

Tryout: Commas

1. A guitar string broke as Rafael played, but he continued with the song.

2. We were attending a show at 1600 Pennsylvania Avenue, Washington, D.C.

3. OK.

4. Stan, my brother-in-law, also plays guitar, bass, and drums.

5. Ben, do you play a musical instrument, or sing in a choir?

6. In the show at the auditorium, we saw Dave, Bill, and Linda.

7. When Rafael plays, the guitar seems to sing.

8. He plays haunting, beautiful melodies.

9. My son, as you know, sings in a choir with the symphony.

10. OK (or comma after *show*).

11. You know, Stan, that music makes people hungry.

12. The next show will be on January 22, 1997, at Davies Hall in San Francisco.

13. Because my son is singing, I will probably go to hear him.

14. After the holidays, Lee, you'll have more time to practice, and to compose.

15. Lee replied, "My music teacher, who knows me better than you do, says

      optional comma for contrast
I'll compose music, but not practice enough."

Part Three

Usage

▼ ▼ ▼ ▼ ▼ ▼ ▼ ▼ ▼ ▼ ▼

Part Three of this text is very flexible to meet the many needs of developmental English students—whether they have been admitted to college but have serious reading and writing difficulties in English (especially beyond the sentence level) or are reading and writing at early high school level but need to brushup and review before probable success in college freshman composition class.

Students coming into the class direct from an advanced ESL (English as a second language) class will need more time and practice on Chapter 26, with its detailed discussion, diagrams, and reference materials on regular English verb usage. From the beginning of the course, you can assign ESL students to read and refer to this material.

Native English speakers, on the other hand, may need little time on the basics of Chapter 26 but more time to double-check the finer points of formal standard English, since they have grown accustomed to hearing so much informal, colloquial, and nonstandard English in advertisements, popular music, and conversation with their friends. So that such students can note individual problem areas in formal English usage and practice overcoming them, Part Three contains many short Tryout exercises complete with answers, and the instructors' test bank (at the end of this edition) includes many quizzes covering the main chapter areas. You can give the quizzes in any order to the whole class or to students who seem to need extra practice or would like extra credit. You can also use them as a review for the final examination.

More advanced developmental English students should move quickly through Chapters 21–28 and therefore have more time for the advanced writing topics—such as misplaced modifiers; parallel construction; and subtle differences in clarity, meaning, and style—covered in Chapters 29–30 and the vocabulary work in Appendixes C and D. Such advanced subjects are reflected in the comprehensive final examinations in the instructors' test bank. In addition, you should encourage advanced students to write longer compositions and get into standard essay structure as soon as possible, preferably relating their writing to work in their majors. For example, business students can write letters and reports, and psychology majors can begin writing short essays about their reading. You should, of course, encourage all students to read the whole text and save it for future reference.

For more information on course organization, see the section "Instructors' Sample Schedules" earlier in this edition.

Chapter 21

Singular and Plural Nouns
Person, Place, Thing, or Idea

English nouns are used as singulars, plurals, collectives, and possessives.

FORMATION OF PLURALS

Regular Forms

When children are two or three, they learn the first rule of English plurals, logically but incorrectly guessing "see two mans." Most noun plurals are formed just by adding *s*.

> boys   houses   thoughts   cats   books   absences

When the plural *s* cannot be easily pronounced, after *s* or *s*-related sounds (*x, z, ch, sh*), we add *es* at the end to form the plural.

Memory Peg

> boxes   waltzes   dishes   watches   glasses   Bushes

Note: The plural with *es* is the only spelling change ever made in people's names (such as the Bushes); we don't say "the Wolves are coming to dinner," unless we actually mean animals. If we are using people's names, it's "the Wolfs."

Nouns are used as subjects or objects in sentences, but sometimes they function as adjectives.

> adj   N   adj   adj   N
> a television program   a television program guide

In the adjective position they are formally called *attributive nouns,* but calling them adjectives is acceptable and easier. In English, unlike many languages, adjectives don't change from singular to plural—just nouns.

Attributive nouns function like adjectives.

Words ending in *y* change to *ies* for plural if a consonant comes before the *y*.

Memory Peg

> city/cities   community/communities   berry/berries
> ally/allies   penny/pennies   baby/babies

The Wolves are coming to dinner.

If a vowel comes before the *y*, just add *s*.

keys   valleys   attorneys   joys
journeys birthdays   monkeys   guys

Memory Peg

Never deliberately change a word to three vowels in a row to make a plural. (We don't spell it *monkeies*.)

The standard traditional plural rule for words ending in *o* is to add *es* to keep the *o* sound long.

heroes   cargoes   echoes   tomatoes

Memory Peg

In some more recent English plurals, the trend has been to drop the *e*. This occurs in words that have come from Italian, such as musical terms; words that have come from Spanish or Arabic; and informal shortened forms of familiar words.

solos   cellos   pianos   concertos
lassos   tacos   gauchos   zeros

autos (from automobile)   photos (from photograph)

Some plurals are currently listed in dictionaries with two spellings. It's best to use the first or the one labeled *preferred*. Whichever one you choose, be consistent in one piece of writing.

Memory Peg

If a vowel comes before the *o*, don't add the *e*. You want to avoid three vowels in a row.

    radios   folios   videos   shampoos

For plurals of nouns ending in *f* or *fe*, your ear will help. Most of these words change to *ves* at the end.

    calf/calves   hoof/hooves   thief/thieves
    knife/knives   wolf/wolves   leaf/leaves

The common exceptions will probably sound odd if you say them incorrectly:

    chiefs, *not* chieves   roofs, *not* rooves

Just because some words use *ve* as their verb ending doesn't mean they use it for their plural noun ending.

    He *saves* money in two *safes.*

Words that end in *ff* just add *s.*

    cliffs   plaintiffs   tariffs

Common Irregular Forms

Since the medieval beginnings of modern English, some very different but commonly used plurals have developed. Notice how many of these appear in nursery rhymes—perhaps so children can learn them.

    man/men   woman/women   child/children   tooth/teeth
    foot/feet   goose/geese   mouse/mice   louse/lice

Memory Peg

Another unusual pattern in English words dating from the Middle Ages involves hunting and fishing. When Dad brought home food for dinner, it didn't matter whether there were 16 little fish or 1 big fish—so the plural didn't change.

    one deer/two deer   one shrimp/two shrimp   one sheep/two sheep
    one moose/two moose   one fish/two fish   one tuna/two tuna

Note: The word *fishes* is a verb (as in "he fishes for salmon") but it can also be a double plural noun meaning "groups of multiple fish, species, or the like" (as in "all the fishes of the sea"). Another double plural is *people/peoples* (as in "the peoples of the world," meaning groups of people).

Compound nouns also sometimes create unusual plurals. The modern plurals *handfuls* and *cupfuls* still are listed in some dictionaries in their older

Sixteen little fish are about to become one big fish.

Memory Peg

Some common compounds have "lost" their hyphens. Check the dictionary to determine usage.

Memory Peg

forms, *handsful* and *cupsful*. Hyphenated and similar compound words such as *sister-in-law* add the plural *s* to the most important noun. A sister-in-law is a kind of sister, not a kind of law.

sisters-in-law	notaries public	men-of-war
mothers-in-law	attorneys-at-law	editors in chief
courts-martial	attorneys general	passersby

Some nouns are always written in plural form but treated as singulars; others are treated as plurals. Try a simple verb such as *is* or *are* after them.

SINGULAR (USE WITH *IS*)	PLURAL (USE WITH *ARE*)
athletics	earnings
economics	pants
measles	scissors
news	thanks
politics	proceeds

Similar English words with two separate meanings may have plurals that differ. For example, the word *bus* is a shortened form of *omnibus*. The usual plural is spelled *buses,* because we don't want to confuse it with an old English word *busses,* which means "kisses," either as noun or verb.

Plurals of Non-Words

Did you ever try to make a plural of a letter, a number, or an abbreviation? The traditional way has been to add an apostrophe plus *s* (as in "I got all

A's!"). The modern trend, however, is to add just *s* as long as the meaning is clear.

> 13s   Xs   CEOs   pros and cons

Only the plurals that could be confusing or pronounced as different words need to retain the apostrophe.

> A's   I's   *u*'s   O's

Common Foreign Plurals

Foreign plurals are used primarily in scientific and legal works. Some, but not all, have common English equivalents with the *s* ending (such as "television antennas" and "insect antennae"). The most common Greek and Latin plurals are divided into the following four groups:

Singular/Plural	Singular/Plural
ENDING *US/I*	**ENDING *A/AE***
alumnus/alumni [masculine or mixed]	alumna/alumnae [feminine]
locus/loci	vertebra/vertebrae
radius/radii	ulna/ulnae
ENDING *IS/ES*	**ENDING *UM/A* OR *ON/A***
parenthesis/parentheses	medium/media
crisis/crises	criterion/criteria
basis/bases	candelabrum/candelabra

If you concentrate on the most common word you know in each group and emphasize the endings, your ear will help you to learn the four patterns. Then you won't make the common mistake of writing "the media *is*" or "my criteria *is*"—because you'll know these two words are plural; always say "media are," "criteria are," and "criterion is."

The plural for *index* is spelled *indexes* when it means "back matter in books"; if spelled *indices*, it means "indicators," such as scientific symbols or economic indicators.

Other foreign languages also provide unusual plurals. Chinese, Japanese, Vietnamese, and Burmese don't change spellings for the plural. The word *corps*, from the French, doesn't change spelling but you do pronounce the *s* in the plural. (Never pronounce the *p*.) See Appendix B, Spelling and Pronunciation, for more hints on foreign words.

As you may already realize, one of the difficulties of spelling English is that the language has absorbed words from dozens of other common world languages, along with their spellings. This adaptability is, however, one of the reasons that English is used worldwide. It is relatively easy to speak and write "beginning" English. The challenge is to write and speak it well.

DOUBLED CONSONANTS

Memory Peg

Memory Peg

Memory Peg

Introduce this rule early in the course. If you don't assign the spelling lists and rules in Appendix B, at least assign this page and discuss a few other examples.

The most useful spelling rule in English is: when you add syllables, double the consonant after an accented short vowel. Because smaller dictionaries frequently don't list separately the plurals or endings such as "ing" or "ed," memorizing this rule really helps.

Vowels are *a, e, i, o, u;* and sometimes *y* or *w* functions as a vowel (as in *by* and *caw*). *Consonants* (the word means "sounded with") are all the other letters. **A *long vowel*** is any vowel that "says its own name." The sound is actually longer; the long *a* sounds almost like *aaaeee. Accented* means "emphasized." You can pronounce part of the word loudly, to check whether it is the accented part. You don't say "*ex*aggerate"; you say "ex*agg*erate."

Is the spelling rule beginning to make sense? Thousands of English words follow this rule. It helps not only in spelling but also in pronunciation of unfamiliar words. Just keep in mind the basic idea—**when there's *less* (a short vowel), use *more* (double the consonant).** Incidentally, if there are already two different consonants, nothing needs to be doubled: *bending* already has two consonants, so neither the *n* nor the *d* needs doubling. Let's try the rule.

fit/fitted [short *i*, double *t*]

benefit/benefited [one *t* because the accent is on the first syllable]

supper [short *u*, double *p*]; super [long *u*, one *p*]

written [short *i*, double *t*]; writing [long *i*, one *t*]

quizzes [short *i*, double *z*]

topazes [accent on first syllable, not before *z*]

curing [long *u*—sounds like *eeuuu*]

occurred [short *u*—definitely sounds different]

referred [short *e*, double *r*]

reference [accent on first syllable]

interfered [long *e*, one *r*]

Tryout: Common Plurals

Directions: Write the plural in the blank to the right of each word.

Four points per correct answer.

1. book _____

2. chair _____

3. city _____

4. fish _____

5. calf _____

6. key _____

7. radio _____

8. business   _____

9. thief   _____

10. reply   _____

11. mumps   _____

12. potato   _____

13. toy   _____

14. class   _____

15. mailman   _____

16. security   _____

17. tuna   _____

18. baby   _____

19. piano   _____

20. gentleman   _____

21. gravy   _____

22. hero   _____

23. handful   _____

24. sheep   _____

25. echo   _____

Practice: Plurals

Directions: Circle plural spelling errors, and write the correct forms above the incorrect ones.

Five points per correct answer.

(1) The English language has always used word endings to show

plurals   *languages*   *endings*

(plurales) (2) Some (languags) have no plural (endinges) (3) In Asian

languages

(languagees) plurals are shown by numbers before the noun, such as

persons

"two person," rather than the English form, "two (persones)" (4) In

times

medieval (tims) as the language was developing, some unusual plurals

women

were invented. (5) *Men,* (woman) and *children* are common irregular

plural   *days*   *people*

(plurals) forms. (6) In those (daies) most (peoples) lived on farms, which

animals   *farm*

had many (animales) (7) The (farms) animals seemed like members of the

families
~~familys.~~ (8) The farmers and their ~~wifes~~ *wives* and ~~childs~~ *children* named their animals and thought of them as individuals. (9) But when they went hunting or fishing, they thought of the animals they caught as simply ~~meats~~ *meat* on the *table* ~~tables.~~ (10) They relied on catching ~~trouts~~ *trout* and hunting ~~deers~~ *deer* to feed their ~~familys.~~ *families*

Paragraph Assignment

How do you feel about hunting and fishing? Write an organized paragraph in which you narrate one experience involving hunting, fishing, farming, or your attitude toward animals in general.

ANSWERS

Tryout: Common Plurals

1. books; 2. chairs; 3. cities; 4. fish; 5. calves; 6. keys; 7. radios; 8. businesses; 9. thieves; 10. replies; 11. mumps; 12. potatoes; 13. toys; 14. classes; 15. mailmen; 16. securities; 17. tuna; 18. babies; 19. pianos; 20. gentlemen; 21. gravies; 22. heroes; 23. handfuls; 24. sheep; 25. echoes.

Chapter 22 _____

Collective Nouns
Naming Groups

Collective nouns can be singular or plural without changing form.

SINGULAR OR PLURAL USAGE

Plural means "more than one." A *collective* noun stands for a group—usually of people, sometimes of animals—but it is not a true plural. **The fact is that groups can work either collectively as a single entity or separately as individuals. Therefore, collectives can work with either singular or plural verbs or pronouns without changing their form.** (For a list of collective nouns, see page 184.)

If a collective works as a single unit, it takes a singular verb or singular pronoun to refer to it. If the individuals are working separately, the noun takes plural verbs or pronouns.

> The jury was agreed on its verdict. [*jury* acting all together; singular verb and possessive pronoun]

> The jury were arguing about their views. [individuals on jury saying different things; treated as plural]

The singular verb and pronoun often sounds better with a collective noun. If that's so when the collective should be treated as plural, you can avoid the problem in many cases by using such phrases as "the jurors."

Note the differences in meaning in the following examples, all of which are correct.

> The faculty *are* moving into *their* new offices.

> The faculty *is* moving into *its* new office building.

> The audience *were* upset about *their* poor seats.

> The audience *was* extremely enthusiastic in *its* applause for the play.

> Most members of the audience *were* upset about *their* seats.

One member is not a group, so "members" is a regular plural, not collective.

For further discussion of and practice with collective usage, see Chapter 28, The Subject-Predicate Puzzle. For now, just try identifying collective nouns, so you'll know when the rules apply.

The audience were upset by their poor seats.

COMMON COLLECTIVE NOUNS

audience	class	herd	flock
mob	group	crew	family
faculty	jury	Board of Education	

Evergreen Valley College [when it means the group of people who govern it or go there—not when it means the place]

club [people, not place]

Senate [people, not place]

Try listing a few other examples below:

_____

_____

Tryout: Collective Nouns

Directions: Label *col* above each collective noun. Keep in mind that capitalized nouns can be considered one proper noun and that a group of people may have a capitalized title.

Four points per correct label (or from 100 points subtract 4 points per incorrect label)

Students are often tempted to label a plural as a collective. Remind them that one group may mean many people, but one car will never be many.

1. This company has decided to encourage car pooling.

2. The County or the State may vote to charge for parking at the workplace.

3. Each family must work out a schedule for using the family car.

4. Public transportation will have to be improved before the average staff can avoid using individual cars.

5. It's easy for a group to arrange to share a car for a sports event.

6. The car pool must just agree on a time and a team.

7. Southern College of Business has announced its vacation and graduation schedule.

8. Each class decorates a room of the college for the holidays.

9. Southern will graduate 200 students in January.

10. Have you considered moving to a different city or county to solve your transportation problems?

In an organized paragraph, answer the question in sentence 10, discussing any transportation problems you may have.   **Paragraph Assignment**

Tryout: Review of Difficult Plurals

Directions: Write the plural in the blank to the right of each word.

1. father-in-law   _____   Four points per correct answer.

2. series   _____

3. louse   _____

4. X   _____

5. chief   _____

6. moose   _____

7. cliff   _____

8. vertebra   _____

9. criterion   _____

10. medium   _____

11. parenthesis   _____

12. notary public   _____

13. silo   _____

14. half   _____

15. bus   _____

16. ox   _____

17. loaf   _____

18. roof   _____

19. quiz   _____

20. topaz   _____

21. trout   _____

22. alumnus   _____

23. basis   _____

24. gladiolus   _____

25. editor in chief   _____

Practice: Review of Difficult Plurals

Two points per incorrect plural circled plus two points per correct form.

Directions: Circle the incorrect plurals, and write the correct form above each.

(1) The *attorneys* ~~attorney~~-at-*law* ~~laws~~ who work in our building are trying two cases for *alumni* ~~alumnis~~ of our *colleges* ~~collegs~~. (2) In one case, two different *notaries* ~~notary~~ *public* ~~publics~~ were in *automobile* ~~automobiles~~ accidents. (3) The superior *court* ~~courts~~ judges are looking at the *diagrams* ~~diagrames~~ of the accidents covered with *Xs* ~~Xes~~ and *O's* ~~Os~~. (4) The media are treating these *cases* ~~casses~~ with masses of *publicity* ~~publicities~~. (5) The *editors* ~~editor~~ in *chief* ~~chiefs~~ use newspaper sales as a *criterion* ~~criteria~~ when deciding what *stories* ~~storys~~ to publish. (6) In one case, the plaintiff had broken two *vertebrae* ~~vertebres~~ in her back. (7) Both *plaintiffs* ~~plaintives~~ had *series* ~~serieses~~ of *injuries* ~~injurys~~. (8) If they get *half* ~~halfs~~ of the sums they have requested, they'll be lucky.

FROM SENTENCE TO PARAGRAPH: SENTENCE VARIETY

To keep your reader from falling asleep, try deliberate changes in sentence structure. Use introductory phrases and clauses, interrupting phrases and clauses, longer and shorter sentences and paragraphs.

Beyond the grammatical classifications of sentences as simple, compound, and complex, there is another set of types, categorized more according to stylistic effect and definitely providing variety.

Loose and Cumulative Sentences

The most popular modern types of sentences, those written to reflect the ways we talk, create a conversational tone on paper. These are put together informally and are called *loose* or *cumulative* (a little longer) sentences.

Most common is the sentence that starts with the independent clause and then adds phrase after phrase, clause after clause, until the reader and writer are both "done." Reread that last sentence for a good example. The danger, of course, is that you'll go on a bit too long. Variations of the pattern help, naturally.

> In the middle of the night, the officer stopped traffic at Sixth and San Carlos, because there had been an accident, causing injuries and drawing a crowd of onlookers from the neighborhood. [loose sentence with introductory prepositional phrase]

> For it is not meters, but a meter-making argument that makes a poem—a thought so passionate and alive that like the spirit of a plant or an animal, it has an architecture of its own, and adorns nature with a new thing. [loose sentence with long concluding appositive]
> —Ralph Waldo Emerson, "The Poet"

Here's an example of a cumulative (a longer loose) sentence, from a professional writer:

> The disaffected youth were refusing to participate in the system, having discovered that America, far from helping the underdog, was up to its ears in the mud trying to hold the dog down.   —Eldridge Cleaver, *Soul on Ice*

Can you see that this example begins with the subject-verb combination and adds from there? Because these sentences can get too long, many of them are combinations, with an introductory phrase, perhaps another one in the middle, and several at the end. Here's another great writer, accumulating:

> The cot the man lay on was in the wide shade of a mimosa tree, and as he looked out past the shade onto the glare of the plain, there were three of the big birds squatted obscenely, while in the sky a dozen more sailed, making quick-moving shadows as they passed.
> —Ernest Hemingway, "The Snows of Kilimanjaro"

Can you find all the phrases and clauses in Hemingway's sentence? Here's one more professional:

> [It is] as if our birth had at first sundered things, and we had been thrust up through into nature like a wedge, and not till the wound heals and the scar disappears, do we begin to discover where we are, and that nature is one and continuous everywhere.
> —Henry David Thoreau, *A Week on the Concord and Merrimack Rivers*

In the Thoreau example much of the loose material is at the beginning—another way to get variety. What about the sentence you just read in this paragraph? Is it a loose sentence? The last phrase of it can be considered an

Many students don't realize the difference between loose or cumulative sentences and run-on sentences. Remind them that full sentences cannot be joined by commas but almost anything else can be attached if it makes sense with a comma. The ability to use loose sentence forms well is one sign of a maturing writer.

"afterthought," since it seems to be tacked on as if the author had just thought of it. Another common structure.

What about the last three words you just read now? Usually such a word group unattached to a clause is a sentence fragment. But once in a while, especially in informal writing, an author may choose to use one. It gives the effect of afterthought or of emphasis, the way using a dash to connect a fragment does. Just be sure you know why you're using it.

One specific type of loose sentence is the comparison, especially the *simile,* in which the writer says that something is "like" something else. Similes frequently use combinations of conjunctions such as "as . . . as" or "than," or "as if."

> My love is like a red red rose.   —Robert Burns

> He looked as if he had lost his last friend.

In some comparisons, the author simply states that something "is" something else, using a poetic device called a *metaphor.* For example, Shakespeare says that Juliet "is the moon," and then extends the metaphor by having Romeo say "Arise, fair moon . . ." Marianne Moore defines poetry as "imaginary gardens with real toads in them" (in "Poetry"). And Edith Wharton writes, "There are two ways of spreading light: to be the candle or the mirror that reflects it" (from "Vesalius in Zante").

Memory Peg

A *simile* states that something is *similar* to another thing; a *metaphor* indicates that it *means* another thing.

Formal and Balanced Sentences

The other sentence styles are more obviously planned out, balanced, deliberately parallel. (Although loose and cumulative sentences may very well be planned ahead, they don't sound like it!)

One formal sentence style is the *emphatic* sentence, frequently a short, tight idea that contains a "saying" of some kind, such as these:

Many of the quotations in this chapter can be used as essay prompts or essay examination questions. Some are much more difficult than others; you might try discussing them first.

> Eat to live, and not live to eat.   —Benjamin Franklin, *Poor Richard's Almanac*

> A rolling stone gathers no moss.   —Publilius Syrus, Maxim 524

> The love of money is the root of all evil.   —I Timothy 6:10

> Every man desires to live long, but no man would be old.
>   —Jonathan Swift, "Thoughts on Various Subjects"

> A man can be destroyed, but not defeated.
>   —Ernest Hemingway, *The Old Man and the Sea*

Their very shortness emphasizes what is being said, sometimes shockingly.

> War is hell.   —William Tecumseh Sherman,
>   graduation address at Michigan Military Academy, 1879

> Parting is all we know of heaven, and all we need of hell.
>   —Emily Dickinson, No. 1732

Things are in the saddle and ride mankind.

—Ralph Waldo Emerson, "Ode to W. H. Channing"

Knowledge is power.   —Francis Bacon, *Sacred Meditations*

No one can make you feel inferior without your consent.

—Eleanor Roosevelt, *This Is My Story*

Whether you agree with them or not, you certainly notice emphatic sentences.

Other very carefully patterned sentences include these types and examples:

SENTENCE WITH SERIES   I came, I saw, I conquered.   —Julius Caesar

Man must evolve for all human conflict a method which rejects revenge, aggression, and retaliation. The foundation of such a method is love.

—Martin Luther King, Jr.,
speech accepting the Nobel Peace Prize

He [the writer] must teach himself that the basest of all things is to be afraid; and, teaching himself that, forget it forever, leaving no room in his workshop for anything but the old verities and truths of the heart, the old universal truths lacking which any story is ephemeral and doomed—love and honor and pity and pride and compassion and sacrifice.

—William Faulkner,
speech accepting the Nobel Prize for Literature

BALANCED SENTENCE   He who binds to himself a joy
Does the winged life destroy,
But he who kisses the joy as it flies
Lives in eternity's sunrise.   —William Blake, "Eternity"

INVERTED SENTENCE   Into the woods and out the other side ran the little dog. [Student sentence, ending with subject. Doesn't it make you search for the dog?]

PERIODIC SENTENCE   And so, my fellow Americans, ask not what your country can do for you; ask what you can do for your country.   —John F. Kennedy, inaugural address

You can think of such a periodic sentence as one that builds up to the period at the end of the sentence.

Practice: Sentence Style

Directions: Write at least two of each of the following types of sentences:

1. Loose sentences

2. Cumulative (longer loose) sentences

Six points for any good example.

3.   Sentences with similes

4.   Sentences with metaphors

5.   Emphatic sentences

6.   Sentences with series

7.   Balanced sentences

8.   Inverted sentences

9.   Periodic sentences

ANSWERS

Tryout: Collective Nouns

           col
1.   This company has decided to encourage car pooling.

          col   col
2.   The County or the State may vote to charge for parking at the workplace.

          col
3.   Each family must work out a schedule for using the family car.

                                              col
4.   Public transportation will have to be improved before the average staff can avoid using individual cars.

              col
5.   It's easy for a group to arrange to share a car for a sports event.

          col   col
6.   The car pool must just agree on a time and a team.

              col
7.   Southern College of Business has announced its vacation and graduation schedule.

          col
8.   Each class decorates a room of the college for the holidays.

          col
9.   Southern will graduate 200 students in January.

10.   None.

Tryout: Review of Difficult Plurals

1. fathers-in-law; 2. series; 3. lice; 4. Xs; 5. chiefs; 6. moose; 7. cliffs; 8. vertebrae; 9. criteria; 10. media; 11. parentheses; 12. notaries public; 13. silos; 14. halves; 15. buses; 16. oxen; 17. loaves; 18. roofs; 19. quizzes; 20. topazes; 21. trout; 22. alumni; 23. bases; 24. gladioli; 25. editors in chief.

Chapter 23

Possessive Nouns
Shortcuts for Ownership

There are some easy ways to remember how to form and use possessive nouns.

COMMON POSSESSIVES

Possessive nouns are noun forms that show ownership, possession, and similar relationships.

In the Middle Ages, noun possessives, called the *genitive* form, were made by adding *s* or *es*. The possessive of *man* would be *mannes,* so the current possessive is a contraction of that form: "that *mannes* wagon" became "that *man's* wagon."

> The squire's broadsword was too heavy.
>
> My father's coat needs replacing.

The coat belongs to my father; it is his, so **the apostrophe always goes after the word doing the "owning."**

The basic rule is this: **Watch for two nouns in a row, with an s on the first one.** If a noun follows another noun or noun phrase in a sentence, the first noun is usually a possessive and needs an apostrophe before or after the *s*.

To decide whether a noun should be possessive, say the second noun, say "belonging to . . . ," and say the first noun. The way you then pronounce the first noun will tell you where the apostrophe goes. Try it.

INCORRECT The boys foot was hurt. [Is it the foot belonging to the boy or the boys? You need to use a little logic. Can one foot belong to two boys?]

CORRECT The boy's foot was hurt.

INCORRECT The boys room needs cleaning

Can we tell from this sentence whether one boy or two have the room? Sometimes we need to ask questions, read the other sentences in the context, or guess. People who learn to guess well get promoted!

Memory Peg

Memory Peg

Now here's a real challenge. Suppose you have singular nouns but you want to change them to plurals, and then make them possessive. A few plural nouns need an apostrophe, but most plurals do not. (See page 179.) In a plural possessive, the apostrophe comes after the plural, whatever the plural is:

SINGULAR	the ear of the donkey	the donkey's ear
PLURAL	the ears of the donkeys	the donkeys' ears
SINGULAR	the eye of the man	the man's eye
PLURAL	the eyes of the men	the men's eyes
SINGULAR	a glove of one lady	one lady's glove
PLURAL	gloves of the ladies	the ladies' gloves

Just put the apostrophe on the last noun, move the other noun to follow it, and remove the *of*. Add *s* if you need the sound.

Tryout 1: Possessives

Directions: Place apostrophes where needed in the sentences.

Five points per correct placement.

1. The students minds are not fully on their work this week.

2. Sallys eyes have a dreamy look.

The students should try to keep their minds on their work.

3. Toms hands are idly sketching reindeer.

4. The teachers desk is covered with decorations.

5. Mrs. Ely is in Mrs. Greens office this month.

Directions: Change each phrase into a possessive in the blank that follows. You need to put the apostrophe on the last noun, switch the order of the two nouns, and remove the *of.*

6. the bike of the boy   _____

7. the bikes of the boys   _____

8. the car of my sister   _____

9. the car of my parents   _____

10. the mouse of the cat   _____

11. the mice of the cats   _____

12. the noses of the reindeer   _____

13. the head of the bear   _____

14. the pens of the girls   _____

15. the rooms of the men   _____

16. the cry of the wolf   _____

Directions: For each phrase on the left write a singular possessive form and a plural possessive form in the blank that follows.

wish of the princess   *the princess's wish, the princesses' wishes*

17. string of the piano   _____

18. sheep of the rancher   _____

19. schedule of the bus   _____

20. radio of the child   _____

Tryout 2: Possessives

Directions: Change the phrase on the left to the possessive form in the blank that follows.

1. the test of one student   _____

2. tests of two students   _____

3. a room of a woman   _____

Ten points per correct possessive.

4. the room of the children _____

5. the hat of one lady _____

6. the hats of two babies _____

7. the color of the fox _____

8. the dens of two foxes _____

9. an uncle of one monkey _____

10. the books of two boys _____

Tryout 3: Possessives

Directions: Add any necessary apostrophes.

Ten points per correct sentence.

1. "In my Fathers house are many mansions."   —John 14:2

2. This is one ministers favorite quotation.

3. The preachers idea is that there are many ways to live well.

4. "Whats food to one is to others bitter poison."
   —Lucretius, *De Rerum Natura*

5. My teachers thought is that this quotation is similar to the first one.

6. Could you give the meanings of the two quotations in your own words?

7. "Whats good for me may not be good for you."

8. The Buddha said, "There are many paths to right living."

9. "Whats sauce for the goose is sauce for the gander."

10. Is the meaning the same in this quotation as in the others?

Paragraph Assignment   In an organized paragraph, give the meaning of one or more of the quotations in the Tryout.

Practice: Possessives

Directions: Add apostrophes where necessary to form the correct possessive nouns. Watch for two nouns in a row. Every *s* doesn't require an apostrophe!

Ten points per correct sentence.

1. Some students in Mrs. Garcia's class are planning parties for the holidays.

2. Mark's job is to cut out paper hats.

3. Good manners include a person's thoughtfulness of others.

4. Gloria's kindness shows her good manners.

5. My family's thoughts on manners at home make sense.

6. Children should think of their parents. OK

7. Lee's sisters keep switching television channels.

8. Carrie says she is sorry if she hurts people's feelings.

9. The members of my family ask my father's permission to use the car.

10. The issue of manners is not uppermost in students' minds.

COMPLEX POSSESSIVES

Compound Nouns as Possessives

No matter how complicated the apostrophe situation, you can produce a possessive by asking, "belonging to . . . ?"—the word you say will take the apostrophe after it, plus an *s* if needed for the sound.

Let's say you want a possessive of a compound such as *mother-in-law*. **The house belongs to your mother-in-law. So you add the apostrophe after the whole word,** *mother-in-law:*

Memory Peg

mother-in-law's house	attorney general's address
district attorneys' cases	someone else's story

It's "the story belonging to someone else." Do you see why the apostrophe goes where it does? No matter how long and complicated the compound, the apostrophe (and often the *s*) will go at the end. Remember that compound *plurals* are different from compound possessives; plurals change the most important noun in the compound.

By the way, you sometimes may be tempted to write a compound plus plural plus possessive, such as "my sisters-in-law's babies." This is technically correct but so complicated to read that it's not really good style; therefore, don't use it—it's much better to say "the babies of my sisters-in-law."

Another example of poor style (because it's too confusing) is the appositive as a possessive. Try reading this example very quickly:

INCORRECT   This is John, my husband's, car.

Aren't you wondering whether the car is named John? This is technically correct but confusing. Avoid this use when at all possible.

Whenever your reader has to stop to analyze your sentence, muttering about whether your writing is right or wrong, you have lost communication. The reader should not be thinking about your writing but rather about the ideas you're presenting.

This is John, my husband's, car.

Memory Peg

Note: The modern tendency in writing is to simplify—to use simpler words, shorter sentences, the easier of two forms. For example, one trend in possessives is to use the added *s* as little as possible, even in short words, if there is already an *s* or *s*-related sound such as *x* or *ch*. The local newspaper may print a phrase such as "his boss' desk." However, traditionalists still write "his boss's desk." Know which way your boss or teacher prefers; look in your group's approved style manual or ask.

Joint or Separate Ownership

Possessives are, of course, ways of showing ownership. Sometimes you want to make clear whether items are jointly or separately owned.

Tom and Mary's wedding took place in the church on the corner.

Memory Peg

Since there's one wedding, one couple, a singular verb, use one apostrophe and one *s*.

Tom's and Jack's new jobs are nearby.

Memory Peg

There are two different jobs and a plural verb, so there are an apostrophe and *s* two times.

Now, let's say that Jack and Jill got married and had two children. How do we do the possessive?

Jack and Jill's two children were only a year apart in age.

But if the children are from previous marriages, the possessive would be different.

Jack's and Jill's two children . . .

Let's say Jack had been married to Mary before, and Jill, to Tom. Jack and Mary had a boy; Jill and Tom had a girl. Now let's talk about Tom and Mary's wedding again.

Jack and Mary's boy sat next to Jill and Tom's girl at the church.

Jack and Tom decided to go into business together. They opened a store selling pumpkins and pumpkin pies. Now, what do the following sentences mean?

Jack and Tom's store is doing great business.

Jack's doing a fine job at their store. [Jack's is not a possessive, it's a contraction!]

Tom's wife is making pumpkin pies by the dozen.

Tom's and Jack's wives are working in the store. [Each man has one wife.]

Implied Ownership

There is one more small complication. Sometimes the second noun, the one that is owned, is implied or hinted at, rather than stated. The meaning is still quite clear when you use the apostrophe.

I like your pies better than Jill's. [Jill's *pies* implied, not stated]

If you said, "I like your pies better than Jill," you'd either be comparing *your pies* to a person, *Jill,* which doesn't make sense, or you'd need to add *does* at the end to compare *I like* to what Jill likes.

Her ears were as large as elephants. [means each ear is the size of an elephant]

Her ears were as large as elephants'. [means each ear is the size of an elephant's ear—still not very kind but more likely]

Can you tell what the following sentences mean?

I'm going as far as Jack's. [probably *house* or *office* or the like implied]

That coat doesn't fit me; I'd rather borrow Tom's.

Yes, that's Dad's car; it's a little newer than Mom's.

Tryout: Complex Possessives and Contractions

Directions: Add apostrophes where necessary to make sense. Don't add or remove the letter *s*.

(1) Once upon a time there was a little girl named Red Riding Hood, who had some beautiful clothes. (2) Red Riding Hoods coat was made of silk; her mothers embroidery decorated it in gold patterns. (3) As Red skipped along to her grandmothers house one day, she

From 100 points subtract 2 points per incorrect answer.

In complex situations like this (where there are many possible incorrect choices), it's easier to subtract errors from 100 than to add correct points.

carried in her mothers picnic basket some tasty items for Grandma.
(4) Under the red and white checks of the napkin were Mamas very
best sweet rolls, red apples from Papas best apple trees, and two kinds
of Uncle Toms cheese.

(5) Suddenly from behind two big trees a wolf appeared.

(6) "Where are you going, my pretty one?" he asked.

(7) "To Grandmothers house, kind sir," said Red, who was very
polite.

(8) "And where might Grandmas be, Blue Eyes?" asked the wolf.

(9) Reds eyes grew wide as she thought, "I wonder why hes asking
so many questions." Then she said, "About two blocks down the path,
past Tom Thumbs."

(10) The wolfs teeth showed as he smiled. "See you later, Blue
Eyes," he said. Then he disappeared into the forest.

(11) Reds feet moved faster; she tightened her hands grip on the
basket. (12) At Grandmas front door, Reds fingers shook as she
knocked. (13) She heard Grandmas cough. "I hope shes getting over
her cold," Red thought.

(14) "Come in, Sweetie, the doors open," came the voice,
sounding deep and scratchy.

(15) Red opened the door; she saw Grandmas nightcap against
the pillows. (16) She thought to herself, "My, Grandmas voice sounds
awful, and her hair is all mussed up!"

Practice: Possessives and Plurals

Directions: Circle the correct plural or possessive form in the parentheses.

(1) Red Riding Hood was worried about more than (Grandma's/
Grandmas/Grandmas') voice and hair. (2) The (nightcaps/nightcap's/
nightcaps') ribbons could not conceal a very beastly face on
(Grandmas'/Grandma's) pillow.

(3) "What big (eyes/eyes') you have, Grandma!" said Red.

(4) "The better to see you with, my dear." The (wolfs/wolf's/
wolves') voice was soft and scratchy.

(5) "What a big mouth you have, Grandma!" Now (Reds/Red's/ Reds') voice began to tremble, and her (hands/hands') shook.

(6) "The better to eat you with!" growled the wolf, his (paws/ paws') throwing off the (sheets/sheet's) and (blankets/blankets').

(7) Red screamed, "(Wheres'/Where's) Grandma?" and ran for the door. (8) As she raced outside, (Red's/Reds) (cries'/cries) for help were heard by a man cutting (trees/trees'). (9) The (woodcutters/ woodcutter's) ax frightened the wolf. (10) The (wolfs/wolf's/wolves') yelps were heard throughout the forest as he disappeared.

(11) Then (Reds/Red's/Red) and the (woodcutters/woodcutter's) (mind/minds/minds') turned to Grandmother. (12) They heard muffled (sounds/sound's) from under the bed, where the wolf had tied and hidden Grandma for a late snack.

So . . . Red married the woodcutter, and they all lived happily at Grandma's house (Grandma cooked and cleaned). Or have you heard a different ending to the story?

In an organized paragraph, finish the Red Riding Hood story the way you feel it should end.

Paragraph Assignment

ANSWERS

Tryout 1: Possessives

1. The students' minds are not fully on their work this week.

2. Sally's eyes have a dreamy look.

3. Tom's hands are idly sketching reindeer.

4. The teachers' desk is covered with decorations.

5. Mrs. Ely is in Mrs. Green's office this month.

6. the boy's bike; 7. the boys' bikes; 8. my sister's car; 9. my parents' car; 10. the cat's mouse; 11. the cats' mice; 12. the reindeer's noses; 13. the bear's head; 14. the girls' pens; 15. the men's rooms; 16. the wolf's cry; 17. the piano's string, the pianos' strings; 18. the rancher's sheep, the ranchers' sheep; 19. the bus's schedule, the buses' schedules; 20. the child's radio, the children's radios.

Tryout 2: Possessives

1. one student's test; 2. two students' tests; 3. a woman's room; 4. the children's room; 5. one lady's hat; 6. two babies' hats; 7. the fox's color; 8. two foxes' dens; 9. one monkey's uncle; 10. two boys' books.

Tryout 3: Possessives

1. "In my Father's house are many mansions."

2. This is one minister's favorite quotation.

3. The preacher's idea is that there are many ways to live well.

4. "What's food to one is to others bitter poison."

5. My teacher's thought is that this quotation is similar to the first one.

6. OK.

7. "What's good for me may not be good for you."

8. OK.

9. "What's sauce for the goose is sauce for the gander."

10. OK.

Tryout: Complex Possessives and Contractions

(1) OK. (2) Red Riding Hood's coat was made of silk; her mother's embroidery decorated it in gold patterns. (3) As Red skipped along to her grandmother's house one day, she carried in her mother's picnic basket some tasty items for Grandma. (4) Under the red and white checks of the napkin were Mama's very best sweet rolls, red apples from Papa's best apple trees, and two kinds of Uncle Tom's cheese.

(5) OK.
(6) OK.

(7) "To Grandmother's house, kind sir," said Red, who was very polite.

(8) "And where might Grandma's be, Blue Eyes?" asked the wolf.

(9) Reds eyes grew wide as she thought, "I wonder why hes asking so many
questions." Then she said, "About two blocks down the path, past Tom Thumbs."

(10) The wolfs teeth showed as he smiled. "See you later, Blue Eyes," he said. Then
he disappeared into the forest.

(11) Reds feet moved faster; she tightened her hands [or hands] grip on the basket.

(12) At Grandmas front door, Reds fingers shook as she knocked. (13) She heard
Grandmas cough. "I hope shes getting over her cold," Red thought.

(14) "Come in, Sweetie, the doors open," came the voice, sounding deep and
scratchy.

(15) Red opened the door; she saw Grandmas nightcap against the pillows. (16) She
thought to herself, "My, Grandmas voice sounds awful, and her hair is all mussed
up!"

Chapter 24

Pronouns—Common Usage and Agreement

We use pronouns to avoid repeating nouns as we show subject, object, and demonstrative relationships.

AGREEMENT OF PRONOUNS AND ANTECEDENTS

Memory Peg

Pronouns are used in place of nouns to avoid repeating nouns. Instead of writing, "John put John's book on John's desk and then closed the door to John's room," you can write, "John put his book on his desk. . . ."

For clarity, pronouns must always refer to a specific noun or pronoun in the previous discussion. **The words to which the pronouns refer are called** *antecedents,* **which means "the words before."**

Pronouns must agree in number (she or they), in person (I, you, him), and in gender (he, she, it) with their antecedents. Here are the common personal pronouns:

Subject (Nominative)	Object (Objective)	Possessive
SUBJECT OR EQUAL TO SUBJECT WITH BEING VERB	**OBJECT OF ACTION VERB OR PREPOSITION**	**OWNERSHIP OF NOUN OR PRONOUN**
I	me	my, mine
you	you	your, yours
he	him	his
she	her	her, hers
it	it	its
we	us	our, ours
they	them	their, theirs

Memory Peg

The subject pronouns (except *it*) end in long vowels, making them easy to pronounce with verbs. Most of the pronouns with *m* in them are object pronouns, which are used at the ends of phrases, where the *m* is easy to pronounce.

to him   see them [object pronouns]

The possessives with consonant endings plus *s* are often used if there is no noun following, as in "the books are theirs." Possessives used before nouns are often called *possessive adjectives* because they are used to modify nouns, as in "their books."

There are three common types of pronoun agreement problems.

REFERENCE   Oscar and Jim went to Santa Cruz, and he bought a car.

Whom does *he* refer to? Either repeat one name, or—preferably—reword the sentence to use the pronoun after only one name: Oscar bought a car when he and Jim went to Santa Cruz.

NUMBER   One of the students ate their dinner early.

How many students ate? One. Change *their* to *his or her.*

GENDER   Mrs. Green wrote his book last year.

Whose book are we discussing? Mrs. Green's. Change *his* to *her.*

If students argue that one student could be greedily eating everyone's dinner, remind them to choose the more common situation, or to ask careful questions on tests.

PRONOUN CASE

The most common and difficult of the pronoun problems is that of *case.* The different case forms of pronouns in English show the pronouns' relations to verbs in the sentence—that is, as subject, object, or the like. (Be glad you're not writing Latin, where even nouns are spelled differently to match verbs and prepositions!)

All nouns and pronouns are used either as *subjects* (or complements, which are equal to the subject) or as *objects.* *Action* verbs (and prepositions) are followed by *object* nouns and pronouns. *Being* (linking) verbs are followed by *subject*-type (nominative) nouns and pronouns, sometimes called *predicate nominative* nouns and pronouns.

Memory Peg

   S BV   Pred Nom
She is the person speaking.

   S BV Pred Nom
This is   she   speaking.

S   AV   O
I will see him at dinner.

See me at the dinner.

   S   O
I gave the invitation to him.

    S   O
She is speaking for him.

    S   O
We will eat with them.

They will see us at dinner.

"They" is the subject; "us" is the object.

Can you label the rest of the pronouns?

Problems with Subject Pronouns

Memory Peg

Most problems of case occur with compound subjects or objects. The easiest way to solve these is to simplify the sentence. Your ear will tell you that the child who says, "Me go to the movies" is using the wrong pronoun. The pronoun *me* is never used as a subject. But how recently have you heard an adult say, "Me and John are going to the movies"?

To avoid this error, take one of the subjects out of the sentence (say each subject separately): "I'm going to the movies." "John is going to the movies." So: "John and I are going to the movies." The subject pronouns (listed on page 202) are used as subjects or equal to the subject of the sentence.

Note: It's customary in English to mention the speaker last: "John and I are going," rather than "I and John"; "give those to Sally and me" rather than "me and Sally."

    S   S
Don and she will drive to work together. [Don will drive; she will drive]

Memory Peg

Subjective case pronouns are also used with the being verbs, in which the subject and the noun or pronoun after the verb are interchangeable:

  S   S   equal to S   S   equal to S
Don and she are my children.   **She is my child.**

        S   equal to S   S   equal to S
My children are Don and she.   **My child is she.**

The being-verb pattern of pronoun use is also called the predicate nominative or *predicate pronoun* because a subject-type pronoun is used in the predicate of the sentence, after the verb. Although the pattern is followed in relatively formal English, it is frequently ignored in spoken English. In a formal oral or written situation, you would say, "This is she speaking," but informally, it's accepted to say, "This is her," or "It's me."

Problems with Object Pronouns

Object pronouns are used primarily after action verbs and after prepositions.

    O   O
See him or me about the payment. [Simplify to help your ear: "See him about . . ."; "See me about . . ."]

        O   O
I saw Mr. White and her at the restaurant. ["I saw Mr. White . . ."; "I saw her . . ."]

Don't change the action in the sentence when you simplify. She is not seeing anyone, and neither is Mr. White.

Try writing a few sentences with two pronouns in them:

_____

_____

_____

Tryout: Subject and Object Pronouns

Directions: Circle the correct pronouns in the parentheses.

Seven points per correct answer.

1. When Cecilia and (I/me) went to apply for jobs, we looked for (them/they) in the newspaper advertisements.

2. Cecilia said that she wanted to be a word processor, but (I/me) was more interested in jobs that might take (I/me) overseas.

3. (She/Her) applied for a computer job when (I/me) found (it/them) in an advertisement.

4. Everyone who applied except (she/her) didn't know WordPerfect.

5. The interviewers said (they/them) wanted an experienced worker for the job, but (he/they) couldn't find anyone.

6. Both Cecilia and (I/me) had excellent training in our business classes.

7. There was great competition between Cecilia and (I/me).

8. All of (us/we) had good references.

Cecilia got her wish and became a word processor.

9.   (She and I) (Her and me) have both been selected for new jobs.

10.   Now it's time for (us/we) to celebrate.

Paragraph Assignment | Have you found any newspaper ads describing jobs you would like to have? Write a paragraph giving the details of an ideal job for you.

Problems with Possessive Pronouns

Their and other possessive pronouns (not object pronouns, such as *them*) must be used before other nouns or pronouns, including "ing" nouns (gerunds).

> *Their studying* resulted in higher grades. [not "Them studying"]
>
> *His driving* was improving.
>
> I like *his driving*. [not "him driving"]
>
> I enjoy *their singing*.
>
> I enjoy *their voices*.
>
> They like reading *my writing*.
>
> They like reading *my books*.
>
> My children like *my cooking* pancakes for lunch.

They like my cooking, whether or not they like me at the moment, so the meaning is not "they like me cooking."

> I give them good nutrition without *their knowing* it.

Note: Beware of using "them" in an adjective spot—don't say "them books," "them people," "them clothes." Your ear should help you with this one.

Note: The possessive pronouns are complete possessive words and therefore don't need the possessive apostrophe. (See Chapter 23, Possessive Nouns.) The *it's* means "it is." It's a contraction. The possessive is *its*. **If the pronoun form doesn't mean two words, it doesn't need an apostrophe.**

Memory Peg

> The dog wagged its tail. [The dog wagged his (or her) tail. Would you put an apostrophe in *his* or *her*?]
>
> It's not easy to understand apostrophes. ["It is not . . ."]
>
> Who's going to answer the next question? ["Who is . . ."]
>
> Whose book is finished? [belonging to whom?]
>
> There's a large section left to do. ["There is . . ."]

This book is theirs. [belonging to them]

This room is ours. [belonging to us]

They're giving us good job leads. ["They are . . ."]

There're good job leads in their paper. ["There are . . ."; the paper belonging to them]

Note: *Their,* like *they're* and *there,* starts with *the* (not *thi*).

Memory Peg

DEMONSTRATIVE PRONOUNS AS POSSESSIVE ADJECTIVES

A relatively easy problem in English involves the use of *this, that, these,* and *those.* The first two are singular, the second two plural; *this* and *these* refer to items close to the speaker, while *that* and *those* refer to items farther away.

    this book   that rabbit   these books   those rabbits

Used in this way, these words are often classified as *adjectives* when they modify nouns. We often use the same words as simple pronouns, as in "this is my book," or "that is easy," but such usages are vague (the antecedents are not always clear), and therefore are not preferred.

Tryout: Possessive and Demonstrative Pronouns

Directions: Circle the correct pronouns in the parentheses.

Ten points per correct answer.

1. (That/Those) country is Mexico.
2. My friend Lisa recently interviewed (them/those) Indians who live in the mountains of central Mexico.
3. (They're/Their) stories are interesting.
4. Because Lisa speaks excellent Spanish, she was able to translate much of (this/these) material.
5. She doesn't speak an Indian language, so for (that/them) part she needed another translator.
6. (Who's/Whose) going to go to Mexico on vacation?
7. When you meet Mexicans, will you be able to understand (their/there) language?
8. Spanish spelling is easier than English spelling because (its/it's) nearly always the same as the pronunciation.

9. This map is (your's/yours); that one is mine.

10. (They're/Their) going to the museum in Mexico City first.

Paragraph Assignment   Which foreign country would you like to visit? Write an organized paragraph explaining why.

Practice: Pronoun and Contraction Review

Directions: Circle any incorrect pronoun usage and write the correct form of the pronoun or the word to which it refers above it.

From 100 points subtract 5 points per incorrect answer.

(1) When things in ~~you~~ *[your]* life seem dull or boring, what do you do about it? (2) Realize that when ~~your~~ *[you're]* bored, you are probably boring ~~others~~ *[other]* people. (3) Think about ~~you're~~ *[your]* life and decide to change ~~youself~~ *[yourself]*. (4) When my friend Louie decided to change ~~he's~~ *[his]* life, he began with ~~hisself~~ *[himself]*. (5) ~~Whose~~ *[Who's]* going to change ~~youre~~ *[your]* life but you? (6) His friend Maria and ~~him~~ *[he]* worked out an agreement to surprise each ~~others~~ *[other]* once a day. (7) Maria is one of ~~them~~ *[those]* people ~~who's~~ *[whose]* life will never be dull. (8) ~~Her~~ *[She]* and ~~him~~ *[he]* write notes and put them under their pillows and in their lunch bags. (9) Louie told me about ~~them~~ *[their]* laughing when they see the notes.

PRONOUN CHOICES

Pronouns Used After Conjunctions

A pronoun used after the conjunctions *than* and *as* can mean different things depending on the context. In your mind, complete the understood idea to be sure which pronoun to use.

Dad gave her more allowance than (I/me).

If you mean "gave her more than I did," you are probably her mother. If you mean "gave her more than he gave me," you are probably her sister or brother.

Some sentences can have only one logical meaning.

He is taller than I. ["than I am"]

The accident frightened the baby more than (us/we). [Are we frightening babies? No, so the meaning is "than it frightened us."]

You are as qualified as she. ["as she is"]

Pronouns with Appositives

When *us* or *we* is used immediately before a noun, the noun is an appositive (a renaming of the previous noun or pronoun); ignore the noun to decide how the pronoun fits.

(We/Us) women need to apply for good jobs. [Drop *women* and listen: "We need"; therefore, "We women need."]

Good jobs are available for (us/we) women. [Drop *women* and listen: "for us."]

Reflexive and Intensive Pronouns

Many people who are trying to speak well "by ear" make mistakes with the words *myself* and the other self/selves pronouns. These pronouns should be used in only two ways. **In both, the antecedent must be in the sentence. If you haven't said the *I*, you have nothing to "reflect" *myself* back on.**

Memory Peg

REFLEXIVE   I gave myself a shampoo. [action done to self]

INTENSIVE   I myself told you that. [used for emphasis]

A common mistake is to use the self pronoun when you aren't sure whether to use subject or object (*I* or *me,* for example), as in "They gave it to Tom and myself." That should that be "to Tom and me."

Another self pronoun problem appears when the pronoun is in the wrong spot in the sentence.

INCORRECT   She decided to ship herself when the mailroom was
                  overwhelmed with work.

How would you rewrite this to avoid a misreading? You could say "She herself decided to ship the package . . ." or "She decided to handle the shipping herself . . ."

She decided to ship herself when the mailroom was overwhelmed with work.

INDEFINITE PRONOUNS

Memory Peg

Indefinite pronouns do not refer to a specific noun. Some of them are often used as adjectives. **Some are singular, some plural, and some can be used either way depending on the noun or pronoun in the prepositional phrase that accompanies them. All the singular indefinite pronouns contain singular ideas such as "one," "body," or "thing" or can take the word *one* after them.** Keeping these points in mind, memorize the lists that follow.

SINGULAR			PLURAL	SINGULAR OR PLURAL
another	everybody	the number	both	all
anybody	everyone	one	few	any
anyone	everything	somebody	many	most
anything	many a	someone	others	none
each	neither	something	a number	some
either	nobody	this	several	fractions (such
every	nothing	that	these	as two-thirds)
			those	
			two, three, etc.	

A number are following.   *The number is* large.

Everybody was happy.   *Many a* student *is* happy.

Someone is coming soon.   *Both are* coming.

Most of the *pies were* eaten.   *All* of the *cake was* eaten.

The most common indefinite pronoun mistake is use of the plural possessive pronoun *their* to refer to one of the singular indefinite pronouns.

INCORRECT   Everybody studied their books.

However, this distinction is rapidly being relaxed in all but very formal English. Try to remember the standard correct usage when necessary, but don't be surprised at a use of *their* in an informal singular reference. It is often used because we don't have a good singular pronoun that can be either masculine or feminine, and writers hesitate to say "*his* book" when referring to a person who could be either male or female. They sometimes say "*his or her* book," but this gets awkward when it occurs frequently. To avoid repeating *his or her,* you can make the subject plural.

All the students studied their books.

Tryout: Pronoun Review

Directions: Circle the correct pronouns in the parentheses. (It helps to note the antecedent—the word to which the pronoun refers.)

1. Do you know that (you/your/yours) body language sends messages?

Five points per correct answer.

2. There is a universal body language, common to all cultures, that every human understands as (his or her/their) own.

3. When a child laughs, (she or he/they) is usually responding to laughter of others.

4. When a person travels, a frown is understood by (his or her/their) traveling companions in any country.

5. Everyone understands that tears are being shed when people wipe (his or her/their) eyes.

6. When Sarita and Roberto went to Spain, both (she and he/her and him) understood the verbal Spanish language, but not all the nonverbal gestures.

7. Roberto and (she/her) discovered that (they/them) had problems with some of the body language.

8. Although tears and laughter are universal, when Sarita waved (her/she) hand, (her/she) was misunderstood.

9. (She/Her) and Roberto had to explain very carefully, because a young man thought that Sarita had given (him/he) an invitation.

10. Sarita and (he/him) had an international misunderstanding, a very common problem.

11. (We/Us) travelers need to study our guidebooks very thoroughly to learn the customs of other countries.

12. It is important for (we/us) to help cross-cultural understanding, not hinder it.

13. (We/Us) students can practice with students from other countries so that (them/they) and (we/us) will learn each other's gestures and meanings.

14. Sarita told (me/I) that (she/herself) and Roberto were returning to Spain as soon as (he and she/her and him) complete their studies here.

Paragraph Assignment

Have any of your nonverbal gestures ever been misunderstood or have you misinterpreted someone else's? Write a paragraph describing gestures or other body language that may mean different things in different cultures.

Practice: Pronoun Review

Directions: Circle any incorrect pronoun usage and write the correct form above it. You may be able to correct an error by changing a subject or object—an antecedent—rather than by changing the pronoun.

From 100 points subtract 5 points per incorrect answer.

OK

(1) People all over the world look to this country as an answer to

their problems. (2) Everyone thinks that ~~their~~ *his or her* trouble is lack of material

OK

things. (3) Most American citizens have their houses filled with things.

Sentence 4: Another possible change is "Are all Americans happy with their lives, however?"

(4) Is everybody in the United States happy with ~~their~~ *his or her* life, however?

OK

(5) Does each person have his or her own problems? (6) Actually, one

American problem seems to be having too many things in our ~~life~~ *lives*.

(7) Two-thirds of Americans report that ~~he or she~~ *they* have too much to do.

Grammar and Grandpa

OK
(8) Many an American tries to escape his or her busy life by hiding in

front of the television screen. (9) Some of the people escape into alcohol

their   *OK*
or drugs to solve ~~his or her~~ problems. (10) Others try to escape through

OK
overeating or gambling or even overworking. (11) Many workers now

do two or three jobs during their work week. (12) Why does each of us

lives
feel that we need so much in our ~~life~~?

FROM SENTENCE TO PARAGRAPH: PERSUASION AND ARGUMENT

As you begin to write longer pieces on more complex topics, your writing will automatically approach the standard of the "essay" form. Keep the following hints in mind.

An essay, like a paragraph, needs to have a main idea. In the essay this idea is called the *thesis sentence*, and it usually appears at or near the beginning of the piece. You may be able to use an attention-getting sentence first, to startle and "hook" your reader, but very soon you need to give the reader at least a simple general version of your main idea.

Then you build your essay in the same way you build a standard paragraph, by adding specific details, such as individual examples of your theory, and including much material involving the five senses. If you have three main reasons for an argument, for example, you can use one paragraph for each reason, beginning with the general statement of the reason and illustrating with specifics as soon as possible.

Last, you'll conclude your essay by restating your thesis, not in the exact words of the original, but instead including some of the specifics you have developed within the essay.

In an argumentative essay, you have the extra problem of presenting both sides of the argument. (If you don't, your readers will automatically argue against you.) So an argumentative or persuasive essay contains some of the qualities mentioned in the discussion of comparison and contrast paragraphs (see pages 127–128).

In your conclusion, you may decide that you can't decide which argument is correct and you want to clarify both sides. If you truly have decided, you may want to persuade your readers, so yours will be a persuasive essay.

Let's take a topic of interest to many college students. Several colleges recently have proposed that every applicant admitted to the college must own or lease a personal computer. Certainly a computer would be very useful, and for scholarship students the computer, like books, would be paid for by the scholarship fund. However, many students are not eligible for scholarships, grants, or low-interest college loans. For at least some of them, the requirement would be a hardship. Do you think the requirement should be made?

Write a brief outline of the way you would argue the computer question. What would be your thesis sentence? What would you include in your paragraphs? How would you conclude?

Hint: This is the kind of argument that works much better if you use specific people, for example, typical students of various income levels and abilities, to speak for the various positions. You can describe these people, name them, note their financial situations and grade averages.

Once you have a brief outline or other notes about your points, you may be able to write a much better essay. Don't forget: when writing argument, carefully explain both (or all!) sides.

ANSWERS

Tryout: Subject and Object Pronouns

1. I, them; 2. I, me; 3. She, I, it; 4. her; 5. they, they; 6. I; 7. me; 8. us; 9. She and I; 10. us.

Tryout: Possessive and Demonstrative Pronouns

1. That; 2. those; 3. Their; 4. this; 5. that; 6. Who's; 7. their; 8. it's; 9. yours; 10. They're.

Tryout: Pronoun Review

1. your; 2. his or her; 3. she or he; 4. his or her; 5. their; 6. she and he; 7. she, they; 8. her, she; 9. She, him; 10. he; 11. We; 12. us; 13. We, they, we; 14. me, she, he and she.

Chapter 25

Pronouns—Complex Usage
Improving Your Ear

> *You can simplify sentences to help you use difficult pronouns correctly.*

REVIEW OF PRONOUNS WITH *BETWEEN* AND *THAN*

Although pronouns came into the language to make speech simpler, they are among the words most commonly misused. We need to retrain our ears to keep from making the common mistakes.

Of the pronoun usage situations already discussed in Chapter 24, there are two in which our ears tend to betray us most. Both involve the subject pronouns, especially *I*. We are tempted to think that *I* belongs at or near the beginning of the sentence. In Chapter 24, you saw the rules that govern the following examples; see whether you can pick up the mistakes.

> **INCORRECT**   Between you and I, this topic is not easy.
>
> He is taller than me.
>
> Yes, this is her speaking. [Review subjective case pronouns with being verbs on page 204.]

The first sentence contains an error that is very common in spoken English. Because *between* is a preposition, it must be followed by an object pronoun. You don't say "with I" or "to I" or "from I," so you shouldn't say "between you and I." It's "between you and me," "between you and her," "between you and them."

Next we have one of the sentences that begin clauses with *than* or *as*. The problem is that the clauses are not completed except in our minds. In the example, the clause would be "than I am." (A clause omitting written words, those that are to be understood by the reader or listener, is called *elliptical*.) The words *than* and *as* are not prepositions, but conjunctions. Often they express comparisons of two nouns or pronouns, as in the following sentences:

> She is as thoughtful as he. [meaning "as he is"]
>
> They were as excited as we. ["as we were"]
>
> You are busier than I. ["than I am"]

These omitted words, called *ellipses,* are left out because they are so easily understood. Sometimes the meaning of the sentence, and therefore the choice of pronoun, depends on them:

They gave him a bigger raise than (I/me).

Which should it be? It depends on whether I'm getting or giving the raise: either "than I gave" or "than they gave me."

Tryout: Review of Complex Pronoun Usage

Directions: Circle the correct pronouns in the parentheses.

Five points per correct answer.

1. Between you and (I/me), the winter holidays are sometimes disappointing.
2. My family and (I/me) always plan to get together sometime near the New Year.
3. Why do (we/us) always expect things to go perfectly for (we/us), just because it's holiday time?
4. First, there's the weather; for (I/me), a little cold goes a long way.
5. Small children love snow, but it quickly makes (they/them) feel cold.
6. Our photo album has lots of pictures of children frowning as the cold wet snow brings (them/they/their) chills.
7. Christmas and New Year's parties are fun; (they/them) also tend to bring flu and indigestion with (they/them).
8. Do you get as tired as (I/me) of eggnog and fruitcake?
9. When the family does get together, however, nobody is happier than (we/us) to be celebrating.
10. (We/Us) who live in the Philadelphia area have several birthdays near the winter holidays also.
11. This is for (us/we) an extra reason for anticipation.
12. Among (we/us) 12 members of the immediate family, there are seven birthdays in December and January.
13. Some of (us/we) have threatened to move our birthdays to June or July.
14. Daniel and (I/me/myself) are two of (those/they) involved.
15. The two most likely to do it, in fact, are Daniel and (I/me/myself).
16. Twin sisters have January birthdays, and we have a combined party for (they/them).

17. (They/Them) were the first twin babies of 1993, according to the newspaper.

18. That year, the first twins born in Philadelphia were (they/them).

WHO AND WHOM: THE BIG TWO

When speaking of problem pronouns, we must discuss the big ones—*who* and *whom*. If you can reproduce a very formal accent, your ear may be helpful here. Common spoken English tends to slur the phrases that use these words, so that people say *whoja,* as in "Whoja see at the party?" (Because the average speaker uses these pronouns so casually, *whom* may die out completely within the next 50 years, but you can't wait that long to take job placement tests.) You really can learn to use these two words correctly. There are only four main types of *who/whom* problems.

Rule Number One

Who is like *he* (or *she* or *they,* but *he* makes it easier to remember). Use it when you need a subject for a verb. *Whom* is like *him* (or *them*). Do you remember that most of the pronouns that contain *m* are objects? Use *whom* as the object of a verb or of a preposition, when you already have subjects for the only available verbs.

In questions, for example, answer each question, in your mind, with a *he* or *him* in the answer.

Memory *Peg*

> *Who* is coming? *He* is coming.
>
> With *whom* is he coming? He's coming with *him.*
>
> You gave it to *whom?* I gave it to *him.*
>
> *Whom* did you see? I saw *him.*
>
> *Who* saw you? *He* saw me.

Rule Number Two

Complex sentences often have dependent clauses in them that start with the *who/whom* choice. This type of clause is also called a *relative clause* because it begins with a relative pronoun. **Separate the dependent clause (in your mind) from the main clause, and follow rule number one.** (Remember that every sentence must contain an independent clause.)

Memory *Peg*

> The man (who/whom) was applying for the job has gone home.

Memory Peg

Can you find the dependent clause? It always *starts* with the *who/whom* choice. You just need to note where it *ends:* "who/whom was applying for the job." Now apply rule number one: "*He* was applying . . . ," so *who* is correct.

> The child (who/whom) was enjoying the snow was also getting cold. ["*he* was enjoying . . . ," so *who* is correct]

> Give the hot chocolate to the first child (who/whom) you see.

What's the dependent clause? Since it always starts with *who/whom,* it must be "who/whom you see." In that clause, is there already a subject for the verb? Yes, it's *you.* Now, apply rule number one: "you see *him.*" So *whom* is correct. (Forget the rest of the sentence—put your hand over it if necessary!)

Rule number two applies even if there is an extra subject and verb or other interruption inside the dependent clause. The important parts of the dependent clauses in the examples that follow are in italics.

> That young girl *whom* you think *you saw* is not the one.

> That young girl *who* I know *saw you* is my sister.

> That young girl *whom you* of course *know* is my student.

To focus on the actual subject and verb of the dependent clause, try the exaggerated voice drop we used for interruptions on page 116. Then you can decide about *who/whom.* Keep in mind that the dependent clause starts with the *who/whom* choice. Then look for the verb in that clause. Is there already a subject to match the only verb available in the clause? If so, you can't use *who.*

> She says hello to (whoever/whomever) she thinks will answer.

Is there an interruption in the *who/whom* clause? Drop your voice on it and focus on the rest of the clause: "whoever . . . will answer." The clause starts with the *who/whom* choice, not the *to*. When you apply rule number one, you answer the question, "*He* will answer," not "to *him* will answer."

Rule Number Three

Memory Peg

Being verbs always take **who**. Because being verbs make both sentence parts equal ("it is I," "it is she"), always say "Who is it?" or "It is who?"

> (Who/Whom) is here with you? ["*He* is here . . . ," so *who* is correct. This usually sounds right as a subject.]

> Your teacher is (who/whom)? [Predicate nominatives may not sound right, but *who* is correct: *teacher* equals *who*.]

Rule Number Four

Memory Peg

Verbs and prepositions always take *whom* as an object, including the form *whomever,* where necessary.

> The teacher (who/whom) I had last semester was very helpful.

Where does the dependent clause begin and end? It's "who/whom I had last semester." Do you already have a subject in that clause? Yes, *I.* Then what must you use? *Whom*—applying rule number one, "I had him . . . ."

> Give the chocolate to (whoever/whomever) you see. ["You see him . . . ," so *whomever* is correct. Remember to ignore the part of the sentence before the dependent clause.]

> Give the chocolate to (whoever/whomever) is there. [Is this example different from the preceding one? Why? "He is there," so *whoever* is the subject.]

> My nephews, (who/whom) are ski instructors, are happy to see snow. [You need to use *they/them* rather than *he/him,* to answer the question. It's the subject pronoun, *who.*]

Tryout: *Who/Whom* Choices

Directions: Circle the correct pronoun in the parentheses. (Review rules 1–4.)

1. (Who/Whom) is your ski instructor?

2. With (who/whom) do you ski?

3. The lift operator said to see (who/whom)?

4. That young girl (who/whom) is wearing beginners' skis is doing very well.

Nine points per correct answer.

One of the reasons
some parents with
small children don't
like the snow.

5. That young girl (who/whom) you saw on the slope is my granddaughter.

6. (Who/Whom) do you think is coming to the ski lodge?

7. Children (who/whom) may get a school holiday are usually glad to see snowdrifts.

8. The people (who/whom) like the snow less are those (who/whom) need to use shovels and snowblowers.

9. For (who/whom) in your opinion does snow represent fun?

10. (Who/Whom) is likely to think of snow as a problem?

11. (Whoever/Whomever) you are, you aren't alone.

Paragraph Assignment   Write a paragraph explaining how you feel about snow and cold weather.

Practice: Review of Complex Pronouns

Directions: Circle the correct pronouns in the parentheses.

Five points per correct
answer.

1. Cindy doesn't live as far from school as (we/us).

2. You can ride to school with the teachers or (we/us).

3. The twins and (they/them) are our closest friends.

4. My younger sister usually tags along with (we/us) girls.

5. Sally and (I/me) wear the same size dress.

6. The cards were sent by José and (**her**/she).

7. Was the audience cheering them or (**us**/we)?

8. The Rojas and (us/**we**) share the same driveway.

9. The thunder frightened the child more than (we/**us**).

10. (Him/**He**) and I belong to the same group.

11. We watched the dog wagging (**its**/it's) tail.

12. That style suits you much better than (I/**me**).

13. Tina is the student (**who**/whom) we think will win.

14. Counseling is available to (**whoever**/whomever) would like it.

15. She gives a big smile to (whoever/**whomever**) she sees.

16. (**Who**/Whom) do you think is ready to go back to school?

17. (**Who**/Whom) do you suppose will be chosen Student of the Month?

18. (**Whom**/Who) did you give the award to?

19. Between you and (I/**me**), English is not easy.

20. It's possible for you and (I/**me**) to learn this subject.

OUR CHANGING ENGLISH: THE RELATIVITY OF PRONOUNS

Several of the changes developing in English usage concern pronouns. Although pronouns usually simplify speech, we seem to want them to become even simpler. For example, the word *whom,* the object form of *who,* seems to be slowly dying out, especially in spoken English and other informal usage. We almost never hear *whom* in simple questions; instead, we have television programs such as "Who Do You Trust?" Yet we still expect careful usage in such phrases as "to whom it may concern." Don't be surprised at either usage. Just try to remember the formal style for use when you need it.

Another changing pronoun form is the predicate nominative "it is I" usage. People almost instinctively avoid using nominative pronouns near the ends of sentences. They don't stop to reason why this may be, so they toss *me* or even *myself* into technically incorrect spots. Sooner or later such usages may be accepted; so far, they're considered colloquial at best.

A third pronoun problem concerns the word *their.* We don't have a singular pronoun that means "his or her," and we are becoming more hesitant to use *his* to refer to a person who may be either female or male. Therefore, we are tempted to use *their* in sentences where the antecedent is a rather confusing singular such as *everybody.* The easiest way to solve the problem is to change the antecedent to an obvious plural such as *all,* but *their* increasingly seems to be used for either singular or plural.

ANSWERS

Tryout: Review of Complex Pronoun Usage

1. me; 2. I; 3. we, us; 4. me; 5. them; 6. them; 7. they, them; 8. I; 9. we; 10. We; 11. us; 12. us; 13. us; 14. I, those; 15. I; 16. them; 17. They; 18. they.

Tryout: *Who/Whom* Choices

1. Who; 2. whom; 3. whom; 4. who; 5. whom; 6. Who; 7. who; 8. who, who; 9. whom; 10. Who; 11. Whoever.

Chapter 26

Verbs—Common Usage
Agreement of Regular Verbs

Verbs change spelling to show person, singular or plural, and tense (past, present, future, or conditional).

Keep in mind that this chapter is especially useful for students of English as a second language. Refer them to it very early in the course if you like. The average native speaker of English will use it primarily as a reference.

In English, the verb of the sentence works with the subject to create the main idea of the sentence. It must show either action or state of being, and it must show time—past, present, or future. (See Chapter 1, The Sentence, and Chapter 4, Verb Identification.)

Note: The material in this chapter is of special importance to students of English as a second language, but it is also useful to all English students as a review or reference source.

Finding verbs is sometimes complicated because words that look like verbs are not verbs. The regular verb pattern is the following:

PRESENT	PAST	PAST PARTICIPLE	PRESENT PARTICIPLE
need/needs	needed	has/have needed	am/is/are needing

Verbs have different forms (tenses) to express different times of action or conditions of the subject. In forming these tenses, we start with the base form of the verb.

THE SIMPLE VERB TENSES

Simple Present

The simple present tense of all verbs (except *be*) is the base form, except for the third person singular. The third person singular—the form used when the subject is *he, she,* or *it,* or a word that one of these pronouns can replace—is formed by adding *s* to the base form of all verbs except *be, have,* and verbs that add *es.*

We add *es* to the following:

Base forms ending in *s* or *s*-related sounds—*ch, sh, z.*

Base forms ending in *o,* usually to keep the *o* long, as in *goes.*

Base forms ending in a consonant and *y;* we change the *y* to *i,* as in *carries.*

Memory Peg

223

She cat*ches* the ball.   He do*es* the laundry.   My sister hurri*es*.

Jan pass*es* the new store on that street frequently.

Every day he wat*ches* the clock.

The dog bur*ies* every bone he get*s*.

She ho*es* the weeds in her garden.

Present Tense Chart

	PERSON	SINGULAR		PLURAL	
Regular	First	I	play	we	play
Irregular			am		are
			have		have
Regular	Second	you	play	you	play
Irregular			are		are
			have		have
Regular	Third	he	plays	they	play
Irregular		she	is		are
		it	has		have

Occasionally other spelling changes also occur.

Present tense often indicates an action or condition that is occurring at the present moment.

I *jump* as high as I can without touching the goal.

Walking down the aisle, the bride *looks* like a picture from her mother's photo album.

The time (tense) usages of verbs can often be seen more easily in diagrams. In the one that follows and the others in this chapter, time is represented by a horizontal line; the moment of speaking is indicated by a vertical line; the time of the action, by an X or along an *a* and/or *b* line.

SIMPLE PRESENT TENSE

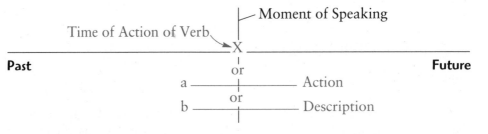

Try writing two sentences with present tense verbs of this type:

_____

_____

Present tense is used in another very common way, as an expression of a customary or habitual action or condition; it expresses continuous action or a condition or action occurring at intervals (that is, continual) up to the present and that will probably continue in the future.

> She *writes* with beautiful old-fashioned penmanship. [customary]
>
> Every summer he *fishes* for salmon in Oregon. [at intervals]

In the following diagram, the customary or habitual action of the present tense is represented by the area marked *a* or *b*, along a time line.

PRESENT TENSE, CUSTOMARY OR HABITUAL ACTION

```
                              ┌── Moment of Speaking
─────────────────────────────┼──────────────────────────────
Past                         │                        Future
                             │
             a ──────────────┼─── ◄── Continuous Action of Verb
                             │
             b |—|—|—┼—|—|   ◄── Action of Verb at Intervals
                             │
```

Try writing two sentences with present tense verbs of this type:

_____

_____

The present tense sometimes also indicates future time; the actual time is shown by words such as *tomorrow.*

> My friend *leaves* for Michigan tomorrow.
>
> The fall semester *begins* in four weeks.

In these cases, the X in the diagram shifts slightly into the future area of the time line.

PRESENT TENSE, REFERRING TO FUTURE

```
        Moment of Speaking ──┐│  Time of Action of Verb
                             ││            │
                             ││            ▼
──────────────────────────────┼────────X──────────────
Past                         │                    Future
```

Try writing two sentences of this type:

_____

_____

The present tense can also indicate timelessness—situations that are (more or less!) always true, such as those in directions, plot summaries, or narrations.

Mexico *borders* the United States on the south.

My children *are* good-natured.

Two and two *are* sometimes five.

Then Goldilocks *falls* asleep in the small bed.

PRESENT TENSE, TIMELESS ACTION

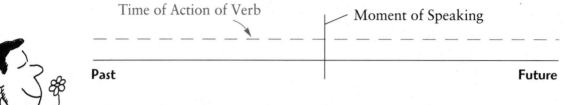

Time of Action of Verb · Moment of Speaking

Past · Future

Imperative

The base form of the verb is also used for imperative sentences (commands)—not to be confused with present tense declarative sentences.

Insert Tab A into Slot B.

Please *tell* me that you love me.

Stop to smell the flowers.

Try writing two command sentences:

_____

_____

Stop to smell the flowers.

Simple Past

Memory Peg

Simple past tense refers to a time before now, to an action *starting and ending* in the past.

SIMPLE PAST TENSE

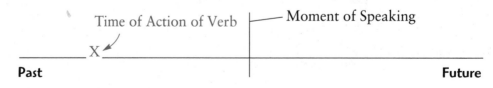

Time of Action of Verb · Moment of Speaking

X

Past · Future

The form is identical in singular and plural except for the verb *be* (which occurs as *was* with *I, he, she,* or *it,* and *were* with *we, you,* and *they*—this very irregular verb is a combination of two very old Anglo-Saxon words).

Regular verbs form the past tense by the following common spelling rules:

When the base form ends in *e*, add *d*.

When the base form ends in a consonant and *y*, change the *y* to *i* and add *ed*.

When the base form ends in an accented short vowel and a consonant, double the consonant (the way you do for plurals—see page 180) and add *ed*.

For all other regular verbs, add *ed*.

Yesterday we *experienced* an eclipse of the sun.

Birds *hurried* to their nests.

A flying saucer *appeared* over his manufacturing plant while Joe *was* there.

We *were* eager to hear his story, and he *compelled* our attention.

The time indicated may occur over a short or long period in the past and may be either continuous (not stopping) or continual (starting and stopping).

Freedom Anderson *attended* Columbia University during the late '90s.

When my parents *were* ill, I frequently *stayed* overnight at the hospital.

SIMPLE PAST TENSE, CONTINUOUS OR CONTINUAL ACTION

Time of Action of Verb
⟶ X
┌── Moment of Speaking

Past   **Future**

a ———————— Continuous Action

or b —|—|—|—| Continual Action

Try writing two sentences with simple past tense verbs:

_____

_____

We can also use the English idiom *used to* with the infinitive base form of a verb for expressing conditions over a period of time in the past. Notice the *d* ending; the idiom is *not* "use to."

Memory Peg

I *used to type* faster than I do today.

My children *used to walk* to school through an orchard.

Simple Future

The simple future tense is easy. We usually add *will* before the base form of the verb.

Note: A very formal usage requires *shall* with *I* or *we* (first person singular and plural) for ordinary intention, and *will* for determination; for *you, he,* *she, it,* and *they* (second and third person), the meanings switch. "You *shall* do it!" is emphatic, as is "I *will* do it, whether you like it or not." The distinction is not followed in most American writing anymore.

SIMPLE FUTURE TENSE

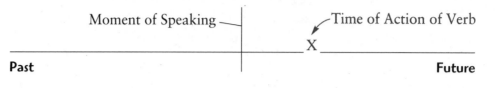

Moment of Speaking ⎯⏉ ⎯Time of Action of Verb

X

Past   **Future**

Try writing two sentences with future tense verbs:

_____

_____

Another common way of expressing the future is to use the phrase *am/is/ are going to* with a present tense verb.

I *am going to buy* a birthday gift for my boyfriend.

He *is going to take* a trip next week.

Memory Peg

Notice that this appears to create an infinitive after *going*—always the result in this future form.
Irregular verb usages are discussed in Chapter 27, Verbs—Complex Usage.

THE COMPLEX VERB TENSES

Memory Peg

Complex verbs are those that use more than one word to express the tense. (Even the simple future tense is complex in this sense, because it requires *will* or *shall,* but it is classified as a simple tense.)
The *helping verbs,* or *auxiliaries,* used to create the complex verbs, are the following:

am, is, are, was, were, be, been, being

have, has, had

do, does, did

will, shall

These can be used alone as complete verbs. When they are used with another verb form, they create *verb phrases;* the first verb in the phrase is always a helping verb; the last verb is the main verb.

helping V   main V
We have been studying hard.

Progressive Tenses

Memory Peg

Progressive tenses are those showing action over a period of time—that is, making progress.

Present progressive uses the present tense of *be* plus a present participle.

> We *are enjoying* the good summer weather.

> She *is* steadily *gaining* mastery of grammar.

On the verb time line, the action of a present progressive tense must be shown along a segment of the line—several instances, beginning before and continuing after the moment of speaking.

PRESENT PROGRESSIVE TENSE

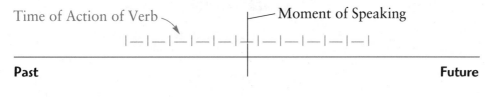

Time of Action of Verb   ┌— Moment of Speaking

|—|—|—|—|—|—|—|—|—|—|—|—|

Past   **Future**

Try writing two sentences with present progressive verbs:

_____

_____

Past progressive uses the past tense of *be* with the present participle. This tense shows one action occurring in the past over a period of time while another action occurs—either a single action or another progressive action.

> As she left the class, her friend *was* still *writing*.

> While she *was studying* last night, the radio *was playing* classical music.

PAST PROGRESSIVE TENSE

Time of Action of Verb   ┌— Moment of Speaking

|—|—|—|—|—|

Past   **Future**

Try writing two sentences with past progressive verbs:

_____

_____

Perfect Tenses

The other main group of complex tenses is called *perfect*. All use some form of the helping verb *have*. *Perfect* here means "completed." These tenses create a double tense in that they show one action in the past and another action in a different part of the past or in the present.

Present perfect describes something begun in the past but related to the moment of speaking—usually because the action continues into the present.

> Since she was a small child, Tina *has loved* summer weather.

> Because she *has* always *sunburned* easily, she goes out early or late in the day.

On the verb time line, the present perfect actions are all before the moment of speaking but are *expected to continue* into the future.

PRESENT PERFECT TENSE

Time of Action of Verb   ┌─ Moment of Speaking

Past   **Future**

Present perfect progressive verbs use a form of *have* plus *been* plus a present participle ("ing" form) of the main verb. The "perfect" or "have" part indicates some past action, but the present participle carries the continuous action into the present. One activity started before the moment of speaking and is still going on.

> Tina *has been swimming* all evening with her friends.

Memory Peg

Past perfect tenses, which use *had,* are quite useful to show the order of two happenings in the past—a sort of double past.

>   simple past   past perf
> By the time I *reached* the pool, Tina *had gone* indoors.

>   past perf   simple past
> The evening chill *had changed* her mind before I *arrived* to swim.

>   simple past   past perf
> When I *entered* the kitchen, Tina *had* already *started* the hamburgers.

The next two perfect tenses that we discuss are less commonly used. They are so wordy that we usually try to express the idea another way.

Past perfect progressive uses *had been* and the present participle, with a different past tense in a related clause.

>   past perf prog   simple past
> We *had been hoping* for a summer evening party; now we *were* ready.

>   past perf prog   past perf
> Tina *had been calling* us, but we *had* not *heard* her.

Future perfect progressive tense is formed with *will have been* plus the present participle. It emphasizes continuous action in the future.

By the time you reach this section, you *will have been studying* English for many weeks.

I hope that you *will* also *have been learning*.

Summary of Tenses

Remind students of the locations of all summaries.

Present Time	Present tense	I smile
	Present progressive	I am smiling
Past Time	Past tense	I smiled
		I used to smile
	Past progressive	I was smiling
	Present perfect	I have smiled
	Present perfect progressive	I have been smiling
	Past perfect	I had smiled
	Past perfect progressive	I had been smiling
Future Time	Future tense	I will smile
		I am going to smile
	Future progressive	I will be smiling
	Future perfect	I will have smiled
	Future perfect progressive	I will have been smiling

Note: In very formal usage and in questions, the word *shall* replaces *will* in the first person (I/we):

I shall go.   Shall we go?

Tryout: Verb Tenses

Directions: Underline the verbs in the following student memoir, and label their tenses as past, present, or future. Notice the careful combination of past and present tenses, depending upon whether the situation is still true. Remember that the present perfect tense (see page 230) is a present tense even though it may look a little like some past tenses.

Two points per correct verb word identification.

Note that the labels are limited to three choices: past, present, or future. Students don't need to differentiate beyond that.

Education Past and Present

I remember that my native village sits where two large rivers meet.

My house faced the home of my friend and neighbor, our English

teacher, who used to give us vegetables from his garden. As I walked

to school early each morning, the mist rose from the river and

surrounded me, and I heard the calls of thousands of birds.

Remind students that the storytelling present tense is allowed, but caution them not to shift back and forth frequently without a reason. You may also note that it confuses readers to "jump" tenses, that is, to go from past into future without using present in between.

Now see what happens when the author changes to the storytelling present tense.

Now in my mind I am that barefoot child in the schoolhouse. My teacher, Mr. Dinh, enters, and we all rise to greet him. He is wearing his classroom face, and his voice is serious. We are his obedient students, and his word is law. He will hit us with the ruler if we do not study, and many of our original age group have already decided to quit school and work in the fields. But I know that, after school, my friends and I will jump shouting into the river to practice swimming, while my father and my teacher fish to catch our dinner, and Mr. Dinh will smile at me again.

Today in my American classroom, there are jokes and laughter. Most of us are learning well, but some students do not want to work at all; they interrupt and talk while the teacher is explaining. I like the informality of learning this way, and I know that teachers do not hit students here, but I hope my teachers will tell the rude students to be quiet. When my teacher is only my friend, and not my leader, something is lost.

Paragraph Assignment   In an organized paragraph describe one incident from your own past as an example to compare or contrast two educational systems—from two different countries, cities, age levels, or teachers.

OTHER HELPING VERB USAGES

Usually helping verbs indicate various elements of time—that is, past, present, or future. You can use other helping verbs, however, to indicate your *attitude* about an action—your feeling about ability, possibility, probability, obligation, necessary conditions, or intended emphasis.

Modal helping verbs indicate possibilities and attitudes. They always come first in a verb phrase.

> You *can* write well if you practice. [capability]
>
> He *could* write if he wanted to. [capability]
>
> Mother says I *may* sell the car and buy a new one. [permission or possibility in the future]
>
> I just *might* do or *might* have done that. [possibility or permission in the future or the past]
>
> We *must* study to understand this well. [compulsion]
>
> At least we *ought* to study. [obligation]
>
> We *shall* overcome. [determination]
>
> Every citizen *should* pay taxes. [obligation]
>
> Every employee *shall* attend the meeting. [determination in formal style; ordinary intention would be "will attend"]
>
> He *would* come if he had a ride. [conditional]

Try writing one sentence with each of the above types of modal helping verbs:

_____

_____

_____

_____

_____

_____

Modals are sometimes combined with *be* and present participles or with the present perfect tenses.

> I *should be cleaning* my house, but I'll cool off with a swim first.
>
> I *would have cleaned* it sooner, but my grandchildren were visiting.
>
> I *could have been finished* with housecleaning by now, but I'm refreshed and ready to start.

The *emphatic helping verbs do, does,* and *did* plus a base verb form show emphasis, in either present or past.

> She *did study* for the test.
>
> The students *do want* to learn the material.

As a helping verb, *do, does,* and *did* are also used to form questions in the simple past or present.

> *Do* you *want* to take a break now?
>
> *Did* she *finish* the last quiz?

Always point out the Summary sections.

SUMMARY OF HELPING VERB USAGES

The auxiliary (helping) verbs come in three main types.

Tense Helpers

All forms of *be, have,* and *will/shall* are tense helpers. The forms of *be* are used as progressive tense helpers with participles.

> I am studying.

They are also used with passive (nonacting) subjects.

> Papers were passed.

Have/has/had are used as perfect tense helpers with participles.

> He has taken three courses; she had previously taken two.

Will/shall are used for future tenses with verb bases (the infinitive form, but without *to*).

> She will arrive tomorrow.   We shall overcome.

Emphasizers

Do/does/did adds emphasis to base forms, and are used especially for negatives or questions:

> Do you know?   I did not (know).
> I did pass, didn't I?   I do care.

Modal Helpers

Group A: *can, could, may, might, must, ought to, used to, should, would, will* are used with base forms. There are no tense changes and no subject-verb agreement changes.

> You can go.   She might come.   They should see.

Group B: *be able to, be going to, be supposed to, have to, have got to* (informal), are followed by the base form and do change with tense (for example, *was able to*).

I have got to run.   They used to go.
We were supposed to sing.   He will be able to see.

Group C: Certain modals have particular meaning in one tense—*had better* (advice, threat); *would prefer to* (preference); *would like to* (desire); *would rather* (preference). These are used with the base form and do not change further with tense.

I would prefer to have more time.

I had better study more.

He would like to review the material.

Note: In questions, the helping verb is usually placed before the subject of the sentence; the same verb may act as the only verb in the sentence.

Has she *given* you the answer?

Was she *swimming* last night?

Had she *gone* inside when you reached the pool?

Was he your first English teacher?

These verbs are also used to form questions in combination with the interrogative pronouns, *who, whom, whose, what, which, when, where, how,* and *why.*

Why did he *leave?*

Whose book *have* you *borrowed?*

Which teacher *was absent?*

CONDITIONAL TENSES

Conditional tenses show an action that depends on another action.

If she saves enough money, she will take the vacation.

If he *had* enough money, he *would buy* the boat.

If conditions are contrary to fact—that is, if they are impossible or nearly impossible—we use the *subjunctive tense,* a relatively rare tense in English. Watch for clues such as *if, as though,* or *wish.*

If I *were* you, I would make myself a study schedule. [subjunctive use—it's definitely impossible for me to be you!]

If I *were* in Paris today, I could visit the Louvre. [almost impossible]

He looked at me *as if* I *were* crazy.

I *wish* it *were* possible for us to visit the moon.

Try writing two subjunctive sentences:

_____

_____

The other common subjunctive use in English occurs in formal commands.

The judge ordered that the car *be returned* to the original owner.

PARTICLES AND IDIOMS

Remind ESL students about idiom collections in large or specialized reference books.

One confusing verb usage concerns the particle. Certain idioms in English use a combination of a verb and another word—usually a preposition or adverb—to create an entirely new meaning. The verb with the particle (the extra word) has a very different meaning from the meaning of the verb or that of the particle alone.

Sample Idiomatic Particle Usages

back up	There are many idiomatic meanings: in transportation, to reverse direction; in computer or legal language, to create a second copy of an electronic file or disk or create a second proof of a story.
call back	*To call* means "to contact, usually orally." *To call back* means "to return or repeat a call," usually a telephone call.
call off	*To call off* means "to cancel" something, such as a party, a debt, or a meeting.
drop by	*To drop* means "to let go." But *to drop by* means "to visit informally."
get off	*To get* means "to obtain." But *to get off* usually means "to exit" a means of transportation—an elevator, a bicycle, a bus, or the like. There are other slang meanings as well.
pass away	*To pass* usually means "to go by." But *to pass away* means "to die," and in some areas of the country the simple word *pass* also means "to die."
pass out	*To pass out* means "to faint"—frequently from exhaustion, drink, or illness.

For those not completely familiar with spoken or informal English, the study of idioms (such as these examples) is extremely important. Colloquial English uses thousands of such idioms—and only practice will make perfect.

FROM SENTENCE TO PARAGRAPH:
WRITING UNDER TIME PRESSURE

Many times in your writing assignments you will not have the luxury of several days to prepare. You will be asked to write under time pressure, after either a day or two of preparation or during one long class period or in an examination. Here are some suggestions for keeping yourself on track, using your time wisely.

First, relax. It's all right to make a mistake, even under time pressure. You'll have a chance to go back and polish later. Your first priority is to get something onto your paper. Begin with notes, clusters, an outline, sketches, as prewriting (see page 127). You may even be assigned a specific period of time for this.

Then, using your prewriting notes, try to decide on one main focused idea to fulfill the assignment or answer the test question. If you are being asked to *define* something, think of yourself as a dictionary editor. Use being verbs, synonyms, and descriptive words. If you are asked to *analyze* something, think of yourself as a scientist who is taking large ideas apart and discussing individual pieces. Your main idea should be workable as a *thesis sentence* and should be divisible into three or more subsidiary (lesser) ideas.

Now you should have the beginnings of an essay outline. Your main points may be topic sentences for paragraphs or for longer two-paragraph sections. Stay focused on those main points; if you are answering an essay question, remind yourself of the question.

Then give *specific examples*. Offer visual details or evidence from the other four senses, or readers will forget everything you say. Are there a few items in each paragraph that an artist or movie photographer could use to illustrate your writing? If not, you are being too general.

At the end of your writing, tie the parts into a *concluding sentence* or paragraph, which should reflect your main idea but make it more interesting, more understandable.

When you finish writing, put the other critical part of your brain to work. Reread your whole piece, slowly, checking for logic, clarity, unity of ideas, and for spelling, punctuation, grammar, and typographical errors. If you are doing timed writing in class, you need to use simple editing symbols on your paper. Don't take time to recopy completely if you are short of time. You are just as apt to make mechanical errors on the second copy, even if it seems neater. Instead, find errors on the original copy, and fix them in a readable style, using insertions and deletions. Be sure your directions and handwriting are legible.

Even the most skillful student writers sometimes write too much and save too little time for editing and proofreading. Some people seem to assume that "polishing" is not necessary, that an assistant editor or secretary will always be around to clean up their writing, like young princes or princesses who throw their clothing around, expecting the servants to pick it up. After all your hard work in this course, you know better, and you know how to polish your work yourself.

Writing done with less time pressure is held to even higher standards of neatness, of course. Neat work puts the reader in a good mood. If you have time, do a rough draft first, then a thorough revision, and then a final proof-reading. At that point you should have a completed product of which you can be proud.

Nobody's perfect. You do the best you can. Like the music student who asked how to get to Carnegie Hall, you've heard the answer: Practice, practice, practice.

ANSWERS

Tryout: Verb Tenses

                    present   present   present   past
I *remember* that my native village *sits* where two large rivers *meet*. My house *faced*

                                                                                     past
the home of my friend and neighbor, our English teacher, who *used to give* us vege-

                                            past   past
tables from his garden. As I *walked* to school early each morning, the mist *rose* from

                           past   past
the river and *surrounded* me, and I *heard* the calls of thousands of birds.

                                 present
Now in my mind I *am* that barefoot child in the schoolhouse. My teacher, Mr.

            present   present   present
Dinh, *enters,* and we all *rise* to greet him. He *is wearing* his classroom face, and his

            present   present   present   future
voice *is* serious. We *are* his obedient students, and his word *is* law. He *will hit* us with

                           present   present
the ruler if we *do* not *study,* and many of our original age group *have* already *decided*

                                                       present
to quit school and work in the fields. But I *know* that, after school, my friends and I

      future
will jump shouting into the river to practice swimming, while my father and my

            present   future
teacher *fish* to catch our dinner, and Mr. Dinh *will smile* at me again.

                                                 present   present
Today in my American classroom, there *are* jokes and laughter. Most of us *are*

present   present   present   present
learning well, but some students *do* not *want* to work at all; they *interrupt* and *talk*

                  present   present   present
while the teacher *is explaining*. I *like* the informality of learning this way, and I *know*

                  present   present   future
that teachers *do* not *hit* students here, but I *hope* my teachers *will tell* the rude

                                 present
students to be quiet. When my teacher *is* only my friend, and not my leader, some-

            present
thing *is* lost.

Chapter 27

Verbs—Complex Usage
Review and Agreement of Irregular Verbs

Complex verb problems concern irregular verbs, transitive and intransitive verbs, and pairs of verbs that are often confused.

IRREGULAR VERBS

The irregular verbs in English require the most memorization. You have probably seen the following very important list. You need it primarily to choose the various past tenses.

Common Irregular Verbs

PRESENT	PAST	PAST PARTICIPLE	PRESENT PARTICIPLE
am/is/are	was/were	been	being
bear (carry)	bore	borne	bearing
begin	began	begun	beginning
bid (command)	bade	bidden	bidding
bid (offer)	bid	bid	bidding
bite	bit	bitten	biting
blow	blew	blown	blowing
break	broke	broken	breaking
bring	brought	brought	bringing
burst	burst	burst	bursting (not busting!)
buy	bought	bought	buying
catch	caught	caught	catching
choose	chose	chosen	choosing
come	came	come (same as present tense)	coming
cost	cost	cost	costing
do	did	done	doing
draw	drew	drawn	drawing
drive	drove	driven	driving
eat	ate	eaten	eating
fall	fell	fallen	falling
fight	fought	fought	fighting
flee	fled	fled	fleeing

239

PRESENT	PAST	PAST PARTICIPLE	PRESENT PARTICIPLE
fly	flew	flown	flying
forget	forgot	forgotten	forgetting
freeze	froze	frozen	freezing
get	got	got (or gotten)	getting
give	gave	given	giving
go	went	gone	going
grow	grew	grown	growing
hang (put to death)	hanged	hanged	hanging
hang (suspend)	hung	hung	hanging
have/has	had	had	having
hide	hid	hidden	hiding
know	knew	known	knowing
lay (put)	laid	laid	laying
leave	left	left	leaving
lend	lent	lent	lending
lie (rest)	lay	lain	lying
pay	paid	paid	paying
ride	rode	ridden	riding
ring	rang	rung	ringing
rise	rose	risen	rising
run	ran	run (same as present tense)	running
see	saw	seen	seeing
set	set	set	setting
shake	shook	shaken	shaking
sing	sang	sung	singing
sit	sat	sat	sitting
speak	spoke	spoken	speaking
steal	stole	stolen	stealing
strike	struck	struck (or stricken)	striking
swim	swam	swum	swimming
take	took	taken	taking
tear	tore	torn	tearing
throw	threw	thrown	throwing
wear	wore	worn	wearing
write	wrote	written	writing

If you are not sure whether a verb is regular or irregular, check your reference manual or dictionary.

Did you notice that there are two different past tenses for *bid* and for *hang*, depending on the meaning? In the participles, did you see the spelling rule working—after an accented short vowel, double the consonant (compare *written* with *taken*).

Memory Peg

Irregular verbs use different forms for the past tense and the past participle. They don't follow the rules that the regular verbs do, so you must memorize these parts of the irregular verbs. **Keep in mind that the past participle is an incomplete verb *part*—it needs a helping verb because it doesn't tell us time (tense) without one.** Once you can recognize an irregular past participle, you'll know it needs a helping verb.

It's 2:47 a.m. on the day of the big test when Bob finally conjugates one too many verbs.

To avoid one common usage problem, remember to use the correct helping verbs with participles: a form of *be* with the present participle, a form of *be* or *have* with the past participle. It's I *am,* you *are,* he, she, or it *is,* for example, the most complex English verb we have; the verb *be* originally was derived from two similar early English words.

PRESENT	PAST	WITH PAST PARTICIPLE	WITH PRESENT PARTICIPLE
I begin	I began	I have begun	I was beginning
The girl sees	She saw	She had seen	She is seeing
We go	We went	We have gone	We are going

Note: The third person singular is *sees* because this singular subject takes an *s* added to the verb base; a plural subject, such as *we* or *boys,* takes *see.*

INCORRECT	Janet and I seen the movie last week.
	We had finally saw the ad in the paper after looking all week.
	Janet had flew in from Miami to spend the holidays here.
	She brought oranges that were grew in Florida.
	She has generously gave them to us.

Did you spot the mistakes immediately?

CORRECT   Janet and I saw the movie last week.

We had finally seen the ad in the paper after looking all week.

Janet had flown in from Miami to spend the holidays here.

She brought oranges that were grown in Florida.

She has generously given them to us.

Now check your verb memory by trying to reproduce the whole list of irregular verbs. Write down the present tense of each verb on a piece of paper; then see if you can fill in the parts. You probably know most of them, but a few may surprise you.

Tryout: Common Irregular Verbs

Directions: Circle the correct choice in the parentheses.

Ten points per correct answer.

1. What have you (did/done) to your car?
2. Mr. Fernandez has already (spoke/spoken) to me.
3. When we arrived, the car had already (striked/struck) the wall.
4. You should have (saw/seen) the street corner.
5. Be sure that the headlights are not (broke/broken).
6. The policeman has (began/begun) a thorough investigation.
7. Tom has (brung/brought) the insurance form.
8. One car had reached the corner and (begins/begun) to turn before the accident.
9. I wish that I could (have been/be) there to see what happened.
10. I understand that your car (ran/run) off the street to avoid hitting the other one.

TRANSITIVE AND INTRANSITIVE VERBS

To understand more complex verb usage, we need to know the difference between *transitive* and *intransitive* verbs. Action verbs are usually listed in the dictionary as *v.i.* or *v.t.* or something similar. These mean "verb, intransitive," or "verb, transitive." Now, why is that important to know?

In Chapter 4, Verb Identification, you read that verbs come in two main varieties—action and being. (Being verbs are sometimes called *linking*.) Action verbs are further divided into two groups.

Transitive Verbs

Some action verbs show an action *upon* a noun or pronoun in the sentence. These are transitive verbs. Others show action, but *not* on anything else. They are *intransitive* verbs:

> Birds fly.

This sentence has just a subject and a verb—no action upon anything. (It doesn't say that birds fly planes.) Transitive verbs are different:

> The boy hit the ball out of the park.

The subject is *boy,* the verb is *hit.* Now, *what* did the boy hit? *Ball* is the *direct object* (abbreviated DO) of the verb. If you can answer the "what" question with a noun or pronoun in the sentence, the verb is transitive. **Think of the transitive verb as rapid transit, directly from subject to verb to object.**

> S   AV   DO
> Many families in the United States enjoy sports activities together.

Is there an answer to the "what" question? Yes, this is another transitive sentence. Here's the rule: **Transitive sentences show something receiving action.**

Is that simple enough? There's only one small complication. It concerns the difference between active and passive sentences.

Active Sentences

The three sentences we've used as examples all show the subject of the sentence doing the action. These are called active sentences, and they are usually preferred, whether the verb is transitive or intransitive. The subject is acting, doing the verb action. In transitive verb sentences the object is receiving the action.

Passive Sentences

Sometimes the thing receiving the action is not the object of the verb but rather the subject.

> S   AV
> The ball was hit by the boy.

> S   AV
> Sports activities are enjoyed by many families in the United States.

In each case, is the subject *doing* the action, or is it *receiving* the action? The subjects receiving are called *passive* subjects, because they just sit there receiving, rather than doing anything.

Native-speaking students report that the transitive-intransitive distinction is not easy for them, but the explanation given here seems to work. For ESL students, of course, the distinction is absolutely essential, and they may already know it fairly well from ESL classes.

Note: The passive subject always takes a verb with at least two words, such as *was written* or *is being seen*.

The same ideas can often be rewritten using active subjects.

> The boy hit the ball. [still transitive, now *boy* is active subject, *ball* is object receiving action]
>
> Many families in the United States enjoy sports activities.

Passive sentences are usually considered rather dull and wordy compared to active ones. We prefer to show the subject simply doing the action, unless we are trying to soft-pedal a criticism or a tragedy and not remind everyone about who did it.

> S   AV
> A mistake was made. [kinder, more tactful than "Harry goofed"]

Another situation calling for the passive occurs when you want to focus attention more on the person or thing receiving the action than on the cause.

> The president was approached by reporters. [The reporters are not the main interest here.]
>
> Jack was struck by a car.

In some other passive sentences the cause is unnamed.

> The legislation was drafted early in the morning.
>
> Coffee was poured for everyone.

So, we have two versions of transitive verbs, one in which the action is done to the object of the verb, one in which the action is done to the subject. In both, something receives action—and that something must be a noun or pronoun.

Intransitive Verbs

Intransitive action verbs cannot take nouns or pronouns as direct objects—they can't move in "rapid transit" from the cause or doer to the nouns or pronouns receiving the action. Small children try to make all verbs transitive; they say, "Me go car." One can't *go* a car in English. One can push a car, pull a car, drive a car, go in a car, but one can't "go a car," because *go* is always intransitive—it can't take a noun or pronoun directly as its object.

To use an intransitive verb like *go,* we need a preposition to pull in the object—go in a car, to a car, or the like.

Let's try a few more examples:

> S AV
> Fish swim. [action, but not transitive, because nothing receiving]

     S   *AV*

Fish swim in the ocean. [intransitive, because prepositional phrases aren't objects; objects must be nouns or pronouns]

     S   *AV*

Fish swim easily in the ocean. [the same—action, but no object; remember that adverbs are "extras"]

     S   *AV*   *DO*

Mark swam the 100-meter race. [transitive; *race* is direct object of verb, answers "what" question]

The race was won by the Americans.

What is receiving action? It's *the race*. Is the subject doing the action? No. Is the verb transitive? Yes, it acts on a passive subject. If a noun or pronoun receives the action, the verb is transitive. It doesn't matter who or what is doing the action, once you see that something is receiving it.

      S   *AV*   *DO*

The boy hit the ball through the window.

Active? Yes. Transitive? Yes. Does the window matter? Not to anyone but the owner!

    Let's review transitive and intransitive verbs plus another type of verb here that you already know.

      S   *AV*   *DO*

Tom hit the captain.

Is this verb transitive? Yes.

      S   *AV*

The captain was hit by Tom.

The boy hit the ball through the window.

Is this one transitive? The captain is still receiving the action, so yes.

> Tom was the captain.

What kind of verb is this? It's a being verb, not an action verb, so it can't be either transitive or intransitive.

Keep the basic rule in mind: Transitive sentences show something receiving action.

TROUBLE PAIRS OF VERBS

Three pairs of action verbs cause us extra problems:

> sit/set   rise/raise   lie/lay

In each pair, one verb is transitive, the other intransitive. Trouble arises when we use the intransitive one in a transitive sentence or vice versa.

INCORRECT   Sit the chair next to the table.

It's time to rise the curtain.

He lay the child on the bed.

Memory Peg

In these sentences, we need the transitive verb in each pair—the verb that means "put"—because something is receiving the action.

CORRECT   *Set* the chair next to the table. Then I'll *sit* on the chair.

Raise the curtain when the show starts. The curtain *rises* slowly.

He *laid* the child on the bed. The child *lay* sleeping on the bed.

Of the three verb pairs, the most difficult is *lie/lay,* because the verb *lay* appears in both conjugations. People tend to overuse and misuse the words *laid* and *laying.* It doesn't help that we frequently hear the phrase *lay down* (which should be used only with an object) when *lie down* would be correct, or that it sounds like *laid down,* which is usually not correct. We also underuse *lain,* which has a meaning similar to *been lying.*

	PRESENT	MEANING	PAST	PAST PARTICIPLE	PRESENT PARTICIPLE
Intransitive	lie/lies	To recline	lay	lain	lying
Transitive	lay/lays	To *put* in resting position	laid	laid	laying
Intransitive	rise/rises	To go up	rose	risen	rising
Transitive	raise/raises	To *put* up	raised	raised	raising
Intransitive	sit/sits	To take a seat	sat	sat	sitting
Transitive	set/sets	To *put* into sitting position	set	set	setting

The *intransitive* verb in each pair has the "i" sound. Remember that intransitive means the verb can't take a noun or pronoun directly as object.

Memory Peg

To lay is to put something into position—a direct object, some thing (or person) is required. Therefore, we don't use the word *laid* or *laying* unless we mean "put" or "putting." Try these substitute words in the sentences of the Tryout that follows. The choice has nothing to do with whether we're discussing people or things.

Tryout: Trouble Pairs of Verbs

Directions: Circle the correct verbs in the parentheses.

1. Our dog is (sitting/setting) in the front seat of the car.

2. Brandy loves to (lie/lay) or (sit/set) in the car.

3. When we go to the veterinarian, Brandy (lies/lays) happily on the seat until we turn into the doctor's driveway.

4. Then we have to coax or drag him into the building and (sit/set) him on the examination table.

5. As he (lays/lies) on the table, he shakes, waiting for his shot.

6. Each time we have (laid/lain) him there, he has (laid/lain) there and acted this way.

7. When the doctor comes in, Brandy (raises/rises) his eyes with a pleading look, to no avail.

8. After the shot, he (raises/rises), looking dignified, and walks toward the door, his nose (raising/rising) proudly.

Ten points per correct answer.

Do pets and children have some qualities in common? Write an organized paragraph describing one experience you have had trying to get a pet or a child to do a necessary unpleasant thing.

Paragraph Assignment

Practice: *Lie/Lay*

Directions: Circle the correct verbs in the parentheses. Try substituting *put,* if that helps you decide.

1. Cathleen (lay/laid) her briefcase on the table.

2. The briefcase was (laying/lying) on the table.

3. If you (lie/lay) in the sun today, will you sunburn?

Ten points per correct answer.

4. When Cathleen (lies/lays) in the sun, she gets freckles.
5. Mike (lay/laid) his book on the bench.
6. The book has been (lain/laid) on the bench.
7. The book is (lying/laying) on the bench.
8. Now Mike will (lie/lay) in the sun too.
9. Mike and Cathleen are (laying/lying) towels out near the pool.
10. Now they have (lain/laid) on the towels in the sun for half an hour.

OUR CHANGING ENGLISH: PLATYPUS LAYS AN EGG

Because so few people understand the correct current usage of the words *lie* and *lay*, sooner or later *lay* may become formally accepted in phrases such as "they were just laying around on the beach." So far, that sentence means that they were "putting around." But don't be surprised if the usage changes—someday. Meanwhile, for correct usage of *lay* and *lie* in all their dozens of idiomatic and various other meanings, check your dictionary as well as your textbook.

Tryout: Labeling Verbs

Seven points per correct answer.

Directions: Identify the verbs as T for transitive, I for intransitive, or B for being verb in the blank that follows each sentence. You may first want to label subjects, other nouns and pronouns, action and being verbs, and direct objects of verbs.

1. The two boys sat on the bench.   ____

2. Their families were eating hot dogs at the park.   ____

3. The boys were cousins.   ____

4. Then Jamal was sent into the game.   ____

5. He hit a home run into the stands.   ____

6. The fans yelled and clapped.   ____

7. Jamal's team won the championship game.   ____

8. The last run hit by Jamal had won the playoff game.   ____

9. He and his family went to an Italian restaurant for a celebration. ____

10. They ordered linguine and a salad. ____

11. Jamal's cousin Tom bought root beer for the family. ____

12. Jamal wanted spumoni for dessert. ____

13. The spumoni was quickly eaten by Jamal's family. ____

14. Later, the whole family was tired. ____

15. They went to Jamal's house and watched a video of the game. ____

Does your family get together to celebrate with sports events or music or some similar hobby? In an organized paragraph, describe some activity that your family enjoys together.

Paragraph Assignment

LINKING VERBS

The being verbs (all the forms of *be* plus *am, is, are, was,* and *were*) are neither transitive nor intransitive because they don't involve action.

In addition, there are a few other verbs that sometimes work like being verbs. **These are often called *linking verbs.* They include most of the words involving the five senses, such as *look, smell, feel, touch, appear, sound, taste.***

Also working as linking verbs are a few words that mean "become," such as *grow.* When these words are used in sentences that mean some form of being, appearing, or becoming, they work like regular being verbs with adjectives—no action is involved.

Memory Peg

He seems happy.

He grew happier each day.

The popcorn tastes delicious.

It smells delicious.

Notice that the popcorn is just sitting there being delicious, not smelling anything or tasting anything. Is that true of the following sentences?

He looks happy.

He feels happy.

Yes, they have linking verbs. But most of these verbs can also be used to mean an action:

> The chef tastes the soup.
>
> He looks around the room.
>
> She grew vegetables that summer in her garden.

Look carefully at the meaning of these verbs in sentences; in each case, is the subject *being* something or *doing* something? Then you can tell whether the verb is being used as an action or being (linking) verb.

Practice: Irregular Verb Usage Review

Directions: Write in the blank to the right of each sentence the correct past form of the verb in the parentheses.

Five points per correct answer.

1. This biography was (write) for adults. _____written_____
2. The bone was (break) in two places. _____broken_____
3. The robins had (eat) most of the cherries. _____eaten_____
4. You should have (see) the two cars collide. _____seen_____
5. Uncle Louis (give) us his old computer. _____gave_____
6. The men just (come) to pick up the trash. _____came_____
7. Who (bring) all this mud into the house? _____brought_____
8. The jet had (fly) over the thunderstorm. _____flown_____
9. I discovered that my shirt was (tear). _____torn_____
10. Mr. Imiko had just (raise) the grades. _____raised_____
11. I had (swim) from the boat to the shore. _____swum_____
12. Anna must have (know) it was expensive. _____known_____
13. The car must have been (drive) without oil. _____driven_____
14. Some company (come) just as we were leaving. _____came_____
15. The dog (lie) down at my feet. _____lay_____
16. Yesterday I (lay) the records on the desk. _____laid_____
17. The dog was (lie) on the bed. _____laid or lying_____
18. I forgot where I (lay) my key. _____laid_____
19. Jim's coat was still (lie) on the chair. _____laid or lying_____
20. My sister had (sit) on the couch. _____sat_____

ANSWERS

Tryout: Common Irregular Verbs

1. done; 2. spoken; 3. struck; 4. seen; 5. broken; 6. begun; 7. brought; 8. begun;
9. have been; 10. ran.

Tryout: Trouble Pairs of Verbs

1. sitting; 2. lie, sit; 3. lies; 4. set; 5. lies; 6. laid, lain; 7. raises; 8. rises, rising.

Tryout: Labeling Verbs

1. I; 2. T; 3. B; 4. T; 5. T; 6. I, I; 7. T; 8. T; 9. I; 10. T; 11. T; 12. T; 13. T;
14. B; 15. I, T.

Chapter 28

The Subject-Predicate Puzzle
Agreement

Verbs and pronouns in the predicate must agree with the subject of the sentence.

You know how to find the subject and verb of the sentence, realizing that the subject and verb must make sense together. Now you can practice checking that the subject agrees with pronouns in the predicate. Begin by finding the subject and verb again. Keep in mind that third person singular verbs have an *s* at the end: goes, sees, runs, makes.

THE BASIC RULE OF AGREEMENT

Memory Peg

The subject of a sentence or clause is the noun or pronoun creating the main idea with the verb—usually it's the person or thing doing or being what the verb says. The predicate is the part of the sentence containing the verb and its modifiers—usually the latter part of the sentence.

The verb must agree with the subject.

1. A singular subject takes a singular verb.

    S   V

Nutrition has been recognized as important.

  S V

She wants to study.

2. A plural subject takes a plural verb.

     S   S   V

The boys in that room and the girls in this room are having a potluck lunch.

     S   S   V

Ms. Gordimer and Mr. Jensen have brought desserts.

3. A prepositional phrase may come between subject and verb, confusing matters. Still, the verb must agree with the subject, not a noun in the phrase.

      S   V

One of the students was asking questions.

          S   V

The teacher for the French classes is Ms. LaVoie.

4. When subjects are connected by *or* or *nor* the verb should agree with closest subject.

           S   S V

Neither the students nor the teacher is clear about this.

         S   S   V

Either the teacher or the students are bringing salads.

5. The word *and* is the only word linking two or more singular subjects that creates a need for a plural verb—and even *and* doesn't always do it, as seen in the following example:

My partner and friend is going on vacation with me.

Am I talking about one person or two? When only one modifier (*my*) is used, only one person is being discussed.

My partner and my friend are going.

Now two people are going. The verb is therefore plural. (For further discussion and examples, see page 274.)

6. A single item may sometimes sound plural but be treated as singular:

Athletics is my favorite subject.

Peas and carrots is her favorite vegetable combination.

If necessary, review Chapter 3, Noun and Pronoun Identification, Chapters 24 and 25 on pronoun usage, and the list of singular and plural indefinite pronouns in the next section.

REVIEW OF INDEFINITE PRONOUNS

Indefinite pronouns do not refer to a specific noun. Some of them are often used as adjectives. **To help you memorize them, notice that all the singular words contain singular ideas such as *one* or *body* or *thing* or can imply the word *one* after them, as in "each one."** The pronouns in the "Singular or

Memory Peg

Plural" column need to match the noun or pronoun in the prepositional phrase that follows them. Otherwise, ignore prepositional phrases.

	SINGULAR		PLURAL	SINGULAR OR PLURAL
another	everybody	the number	both	all
anybody	everyone	one	few	any
anyone	everything	somebody	many	most
anything	many a	someone	others	none
each	neither	something	a number	some
either	nobody	this	several	fractions (such
every	nothing	that	these	as two-thirds)
			those	
			two, three, etc.	

Try labeling the subjects and verbs in the sentences that follow:

All of the icicles have melted.

All of the snow has melted.

Some of the mud has been removed.

Some of the tracks have been cleaned.

Two-thirds of the cupcakes are gone.

Half of the angel food cake has been eaten.

Most of the students are studying tonight.

 ## Tryout: Subject–Predicate Agreement

Directions: Circle the correct words in the parentheses. It helps to label subjects first.

Five points per correct answer.

1. A fruit and a vegetable (is/are) needed to balance the meal.

2. The vegetables on this list (is/are) needed for the meal.

3. A fruit or vegetable (is/are) needed to balance the meal.

4. A low-calorie high-fiber dish (is/are) preferred here.

5. A high-carbohydrate dish with a vegetable (is/are) better.

6. Oranges and other citrus fruit (was/were) juiced and frozen rapidly.

7. Weather conditions (make/makes) food more or less expensive.

8. Baked beans and bacon (is/are) her favorite main dish.

9. We (like/likes) writing about food.

10. Writing (isn't/aren't) fattening, at least.

11. These grapes (were/was) (flew/flown) here from Chile.

12. Grapes, bananas, and apples (make/makes) good desserts.

13. People in this country (tend/tends) to eat junk food.

14. Junk food (is/are) the easy-to-cook dishes with high calories and low nutrient content.

15. One of the students (was/were) making popcorn.

Try a few of the tougher ones now.

16. Each of the students (is/are) looking at (his or her/their) (book/books).

17. Each woman and each man (is/are) looking at (his or her/their) (book/books).

18. Many a student (has/have) had trouble with this one.

19. The jury (is/are) arguing about (his or her/their) (idea/ideas).

How do you feel about food? In an organized paragraph, discuss food likes and dislikes. Include at least one collective noun (like the subject in sentence 19) and notice whether you use a singular or plural verb.

Paragraph Assignment

Tryout: Subject-Verb Agreement

Directions: Circle the correct verb in the parentheses. You may want to label subjects first.

Five points per correct answer.

(1) A major story on television today (is/are) about miracles.

(2) Miracles occasionally (happen/happens), even today. (3) One of the stories (is/are) about blindness. (4) There (is/are) many ways of seeing and not seeing. (5) Each of us (learn/learns) something new each day.

(6) During the holidays we (look/looks) for ways to live better.

(7) What (is/are) your two favorite holidays? (8) American children often (choose/chooses) Christmas. (9) Many American Christmas celebration customs (come/comes) from the nineteenth century, but winter solstice light festivals (is/are) much older.

(10) The first pictures of Santa Claus (was/were) drawn by Thomas Nast in 1832. (11) "A Visit from St. Nicholas" (" 'Twas the Night Before Christmas") (was/were) written by Clement Moore. (12) The first American Christmas trees (was/were) decorated in Massachusetts in the early 1800s as one version of a winter festival of lights. (13) The legend of St. Nicholas (go/goes) back to earlier times, to a time of another legendary visitor called "Father Christmas." (14) It seems that St. Nicholas (was/were) a monk who took surprise gifts to young people in need. (15) The name Santa Claus (is/are) just an unusual pronunciation of "St. Nicholas."

(16) Many European and other countries (mark/marks) the holiday by giving gifts at New Year's or on Twelfth Night, January 6. (17) On January 6, the day of Epiphany, the Three Wise Men (was/were) supposed to have (seen/saw) the Christ child.

(18) All of us (have/has) our own ways to celebrate holidays with our families. (19) Everyone (is/are) looking forward to some happy occasion. (20) Each of us (remember/remembers) holiday times and celebrations.

Point out that this is a summary even though it's not labeled.

Before you tackle the next Practice, review these basic rules:

The words *here* and *there* are never subjects.

Third person singular present tense verbs end with *s.*

Capitalized subject nouns can contain many words.

Collective nouns (such as *class* and *jury*) can be used as either singular or plural depending on whether members are acting together or separately—but the whole sentence must agree.

The words *all, any, most, none, some,* and fractions (from the Singular or Plural list of indefinite pronouns) must use verbs to match the nouns in the prepositional phrases that follow them.

Practice: Subject-Verb Agreement

Directions: Circle the correct choices in the parentheses.

1. Every one of these machines (need/**needs**) repair.
2. Where (is/**are**) the tools for this job?
3. The checks on this statement (is/**are**) not covered.
4. This desk (don't/**doesn't**) get enough light.
5. Either of these chairs (fit/**fits**) in the space.
6. There (was/**were**) two sandwiches left for us.
7. Each one of these students (**says**/say) hello each morning.
8. Here (is/**are**) the names of my family.
9. A scratch or cut sometimes (cause/**causes**) a visit to the nurse.
10. The weight of these boxes (**was**/were) listed on the bill.
11. June or July (**is**/are) a popular time for vacation.
12. The results of my test (was/**were**) fascinating.
13. The program (don't/**doesn't**) start until noon.
14. My practice on computers (go/**goes**) back to my childhood.
15. Every one of these keys (open/**opens**) a new lock.
16. The rules for this program (**don't**/doesn't) make sense at first.
17. One of the telephones (need/**needs**) fixing.
18. The marks on the paper (**show**/shows) how far you've proofread.
19. The color and sound on the video (is/**are**) quite good.
20. The tapes on this machine (is/**are**) worn out.

Five points per correct answer.

Remind students that in solving agreement problems it helps to find and label the subject first.

Tryout: Subject-Verb-Pronoun Agreement

Directions: Circle the correct choices in the parentheses.

1. Each of the students (is/are) working in (his or her/their) (notebook/ notebooks).

2. All of the students (is/are) writing in (his or her/their) (notebook/ notebooks).

Five points per correct answer.

3. The class (is/are) writing notes in (his or her/their) (notebook/notebooks).

4. Two of my classmates (is/are) reviewing notes together.

5. One of them (is/are) talking with (his/their) teacher.

6. Two-thirds of the year's work (has/have) been done.

7. Some of the icicles (has/have) melted.

8. Some of the snow (has/have) melted.

9. Everybody (is/are) waiting for Santa to put toys under (his or her/their) (tree/trees).

10. He won't come until everyone (is/are) asleep in (his or her/their) (bed/beds).

Paragraph Assignment | Some people maintain that a holiday brings out the child in each of us. Explain in an organized paragraph what you think this means.

Practice: Subject–Predicate Agreement _____

Directions: Circle the correct verb or pronoun in the parentheses.

Five points per correct answer.

1. In L. Frank Baum's most famous Oz book, the main characters (travel/travels) to the Emerald City on the Yellow Brick Road.

2. Along the road, this group (meet/meets) with unusual adventures.

3. First Dorothy and Toto, her dog, (encounter/encounters) the Munchkins, who tell her about the Land of Oz.

4. Then Dorothy (discover/discovers) the Tin Woodman, who (want/wants) a heart, the Scarecrow, who (need/needs) a brain, and the Cowardly Lion, who (is/are) afraid he (doesn't/don't) have enough courage.

5. Dorothy, of course, (want/wants) to get back to Kansas.

6. The Wicked Witch of the West (became/becomes) angry because Dorothy's house (had fallen/fell) on the Witch of the East.

7. As the travelers make their way to the Emerald City, the Witch (try/tries) to stop them.

8. The Winged Monkeys (carry/carries) them off, and soon they are (threw/thrown) into the trees.

9. The Cowardly Lion bravely (defend/defends) them all.

10. The Scarecrow without brains (is/are) smart enough to rescue (them/ him) from frequent mishaps.

11. The Tin Woodman with no heart (seem/seems) the kindest of them all.

12. In the field of magic poppies, as Dorothy and the Lion (lay/laid) sleeping, the Scarecrow went for help.

13. The friends had (laid/lain) down for a rest, but the flowers (was/were) dangerous.

14. They had (set/sat) their basket of food down for a picnic.

15. Dorothy had (laid/lain) a cloth out on the grass.

16. Now the field mice (is/are) going to help the travelers.

There will be only one more grammar topic covered on the final examination (the one like the evaluation and placement test). That topic, adjective or adverb choice, is covered early in Chapter 29 (see page 267). From this point on, you can easily vary the text for different levels of students, as noted in the Introduction to this edition. Students nearly ready for college composition classes can do discussion and writing assignments related to these last few chapters, and tests are available in the test bank at the end of this edition. Earlier levels of students can simply read the essay material and use it for later reference.

FROM SENTENCE TO PARAGRAPH: COMMUNICATING LOGIC AND EMOTION

How Do We Think?

How do you make your decisions? If you're like most people, most of your decisions are made quickly, without much logical thought. William Golding, author of the great novel *Lord of the Flies,* discusses his theory in his "Essay on Thinking."

His estimate is that over 90 percent of our decisions are made by sheer emotional or instinctive "gut" reactions to situations. This type of "thinking" he calls Grade 3. The next step up in the thinking process, for Golding, is Grade 2, which is the criticism of someone else's thought—the ability to say, "No, that's not right." Golding points out that college students are quite good at Grade 2 thinking. There seems to be a great scarcity, however, of Grade 1 thinking, which Golding describes as the process of creating a good new idea, of saying not only "that's wrong" but also "this would be better."

If you doubt Golding's percentages, try an experiment. The next time there is an election or a public debate about policy, watch newspaper and television reports for signs of a good new idea. When recent classes have tried this experiment, hundreds of people have looked for several weeks and found none.

Communicating Logic: Two Kinds of Reasoning

There are actually just two ways of coming to a logical conclusion about something. These are called *deductive* and *inductive* reasoning. Deductive reasoning, developed by the ancient Greek philosophers, begins with what they called a *major premise,* a main idea, such as "All men are mortal." The philosophers then stated a *minor premise,* such as "Socrates is a man." If the first two statements are true, then a third statement can be logically deduced: "Socrates is mortal." The series of statements is called a *syllogism,* and the result is a *conclusion.* The hard part is making sure both premises are true. If they are, the result is automatic. Notice that this structure—beginning with a large general idea and then developing with specific examples—is the most common pattern for writing essays.

Inductive reasoning is a method used by scientists, among others. They gather "in" many facts—counting the numbers of certain types of shells on a certain beach, for example. After gathering enough facts, they can come to the conclusion that the shellfish on this beach have changed in number and type over the past few years. Then they can look for reasons.

Logical Fallacies

It may be difficult to recognize good thinking because both types of reasoning can be short-circuited through what are called *logical fallacies.* You may have heard of some of these. The titles of many are in Latin, because the early Greek and Roman philosophers first classified them (yes, the problem is an old one!). Here's the list. As you go through the newspapers, try to identify and label some fallacies.

The Most Common Logical Errors (Fallacies)

Argumentum ad hominem or *ad personam.* This means that the idea must be right because a certain person (whom we trust) says so—an argument "to" or "because of" who said it.

Because I said so!

Argumentum ad populum. This is the argument "to" or "because of" the people—it must be right because "everybody says so."

But everybody does it that way!

Post hoc, ergo propter hoc. "After this, therefore because of this"—if something happened after something else happened, the first thing must have caused the second thing.

We never had this trouble before Jane came!

Non sequitur. "It doesn't follow"—one statement is followed by another as if they were related, but there's no real connection.

I like English, and my school is near the pizza parlor!

Begging the question. This means simply restating an argument in other words.

I don't like him because he's not my favorite person.

Self-contradiction. An argument states one thing and then its opposite.

This test is hard because the questions are the kind everyone should understand.

We never had this trouble before Jane came!

Hasty generalization. An argument gives one example and then assumes it as a general rule.

My brother throws his money around; all men do that.

Communicating Emotion: When Reasoning Isn't the Logical Response

Suppose a friend or coworker has recently suffered a tragedy. What's your reaction? Here's a hint of what *not* to say:

It could be worse.

Cheer up!

You'll get over it.

You think that's bad, wait till you hear about . . .

Forget about it. Let's just go . . .

Anyone who is feeling betrayed or destroyed—or even just sad—needs simply your expression that you are sorry a bad thing happened to him or her. You need to indicate you understand a little of the feeling the person has. This person has a right to the feeling, and expressions such as those we listed "discount" the feeling—imply that the feeling is not important.

But it also doesn't help to say, "I know just how you feel," because you probably don't. Listen to the person. Tell the person that you can imagine a little of the feeling. Try to encourage your friend to talk. Say or write things like this:

> I was really sorry to hear about . . . [your husband/your daughter/your job loss/your illness].

> Let me know when you feel like getting together—just call me and . . . [we can have dinner/I'll bring dinner over if you like].

It's helpful to suggest something specific.

Good communication always involves noticing and responding to the other person's feelings. If someone is sad about something that would not make you sad—that doesn't matter, does it? We're not talking logic here. A lost football game or an injured pet or a computer program ruined may wreck the month for someone—or may just be the "last straw"—on a load that has grown heavier over a long time. Encourage people to tell you how they feel, and then listen.

Denotation and Connotation

The total effect of both the logic and the emotion in a communication involves subtle differences in the meanings of words. Denotation and connotation are concepts that examine these subtleties.

In a study of vocabulary, you inevitably note many synonyms, most of which are not exact synonyms—that is, the meanings are not exactly alike. For example, *inexpensive* means *cheap.* However, you might call a person *cheap,* but you couldn't use *inexpensive* that way. Even referring to things, the meaning of the two words is not the same. If you say that a gift was *cheap,* you may mean "shabby," "thoughtless," or "insulting," under some circumstances, in addition to "inexpensive." *Denotations* of words are their dictionary definitions; *connotations* are the emotional connections carried by the word. Thus, denotations emphasize logic; connotations emphasize emotion.

If you write, "There was a knife lying by the plate at the dinner table," the reader will probably think "dinner knife." If you say "There was a dagger," no matter where you place the dagger, it carries many connotations and *dinner knife* is not among them. From that one word, the reader may deduce the time of day (it's after midnight, isn't it?), century, clothing the people in the scene are wearing, general atmosphere of danger, and so on. *Dagger* is an example of a "loaded" word, because it carries so many emotional connections.

Advertisers and politicians are especially careful about connotations. Do you know what *lanolin* is? It carries the connotation—that is, it "connotes" the idea—of something soft and smooth, good for the skin, an excellent ingredient for face cream or lotion. Would the advertisers sell much lotion if they called it *sheep fat?* Technically speaking, that's the definition!

Good writers choose words with the connotations that they want. Sometimes police or armies use innocent-sounding words such as *casualties* rather than *dead,* or neutral words such as *suspect* rather than *criminal,* or negative words such as *enemy* rather than *opponent*, who sounds more like a "human being." Yes, writing can be used for good purposes and bad purposes. Good writers recognize the good and see through the bad, because they become good critical thinkers and readers.

Because writing thus is a vehicle for communicating not only facts but also feelings and ethics, pieces of writing should be analyzed for their style and their persuasive powers. As you read advertising, political speeches, editorial columns—or even notes from family members or friends—decide what the communication goals are, and evaluate the writing with those goals in mind.

A Major Logical Fallacy: Prejudice and Stereotypes

We may think that we are without prejudice, but we all live with prejudice daily. A prejudice is simply a "prejudging"—a decision made about something or somebody because the thing or person reminds us of something else that we like or dislike. We have been trained from early childhood to make such judgments, which Golding would call Grade 3 thinking, an emotional reaction.

You see a boy playing at an anthill. The child has a long stick and is poking the stick into a hole in the anthill. What is he doing? If he is a child of Western culture, he's probably doing "scientific experiments"—he wants to see what the ants will do, to get them to run up the stick or cross over the stick. If he is a child of the African plains, he's probably trying to get a snack, because he knows that large termites taste like pineapple.

How did you react to the termite snack? Did you know that armed services personnel are taught to look carefully for insects to eat in emergencies—for example, if they are taken prisoner? But because Western culture is prejudiced against eating insects, some people would rather starve than eat grubs.

A group of prejudiced ideas about something is called a stereotype. Here's a common daily example of how stereotypes may affect our thinking.

You are in your classroom and have been told that your new teacher is arriving momentarily. Someone has seen him in the hall. He is said to be tall, strongly built, and middle-aged, and to have a short crewcut. The rumor immediately starts that he is a recently discharged serviceman, a sergeant or captain who will be very tough. What caused the rumor? What might this new teacher do to counteract the effects of prejudice? What can you as a student do to avoid being prejudiced against people?

The "tough teacher" example illustrates the idea of stereotyping, an example of prejudice against or for a certain group of people. Try a quick mental description of the following people:

accountants	ballplayers	teenagers
grandparents	young lovers	ballet dancers
doctors	artists	bosses

Now think about people you know; find several who fit one of the categories above. Do they all fit your first quick stereotype? Do all the accountants look and act alike? What about all the teenagers? Are all ballplayers the same

This topic is an excellent choice for discussion or writing or both. Students may hesitate to discuss race or religion, but they may be more comfortable with examples such as the ones in the list below. Let the students describe any of these or suggest or even illustrate others with role playing.

general type? Are all the bosses white males? Do all grandparents have a jolly laugh, gray hair, and ample lap?

These examples should be enough to illustrate the inaccuracies of stereotypes. We all need to relate to others as individuals rather than as members of any group.

Paragraph Assignment Write an organized essay explaining why we may at first try to limit certain people to certain activities.

ANSWERS

Tryout: Subject-Predicate Agreement

1. are; 2. are; 3. is; 4. is; 5. is; 6. were; 7. make; 8. is; 9. like; 10. isn't; 11. were, flown; 12. make; 13. tend; 14. is; 15. was; 16. is, his or her, book; 17. is, his or her, book; 18. has; 19. are, their, ideas.

Tryout: Subject-Verb Agreement

1. is; 2. happen; 3. is; 4. are; 5. learns; 6. look; 7. are; 8. choose; 9. come, are; 10. were; 11. was; 12. were; 13. goes; 14. was; 15. is; 16. mark; 17. were, seen; 18. have; 19. is; 20. remembers.

Tryout: Subject-Verb-Pronoun Agreement

1. is, his or her, notebook; 2. are, their, notebooks; 3. are, their, notebooks; 4. are; 5. is, his; 6. has; 7. have; 8. has; 9. is, his or her, tree; 10. is, his or her, bed.

Chapter 29.

Adjective and Adverb Usage
The Modifying Words and Phrases

Correct adjective and adverb usage provides clarity and subtlety of meaning.

THE ADJECTIVE/ADVERB CHOICE

Adjectives add to nouns or pronouns; that is, they modify, change, describe, make more interesting. **When we break the word *adjective* down into its parts and learn the original Latin meanings, the word is easier to remember. The "ject" part in Latin means "thrown"; it also occurs in *subject* and *object*. The "ad" part means "toward" or "near," or "adding." Therefore, adjectives are words "thrown near" or "adding to" the nouns or pronouns they modify. In this process, they answer questions such as which, what kind, and how many.**

Your imagination will help you to spot adjectives. Just find a noun or pronoun, see whether another word near it (usually before it) makes sense in describing the noun or pronoun, and you'll have discovered an adjective.

Memory Peg

the big brown bear	a spotted leopard	that hot dish
two short sentences	50 good ideas	The teacher is new.

In the last example, note that the adjective comes after the verb; this placement works only with being or linking verbs, not action verbs. We don't say, "The boy runs quick" (*runs* is an action verb; *quick* is an adjective). Nor do we say "The teacher is newly" (*is* is a being verb; *newly* is an adverb).

In fact, the main problem with adjective/adverb usage is to distinguish action verbs from being verbs and use adverbs to modify the action verbs and adjectives to modify nouns or pronouns only.

Adverbs add to action verbs. Many adverbs have been created from adjectives by adding "ly"; when you see the "ly," you have usually found an adverb. Listen to the phrases. That will also help train your ear.

Memory Peg

adj	adv
He is a quick typist.	He types quickly.

adj	adv
She is thorough.	She studies thoroughly.
adj	adv
The flowers are beautiful.	She skates beautifully.
adj	adv
He is a good worker.	He works well.

The last pair of sentences illustrates the most common adjective/adverb confusion. *Well* causes extra difficulty because it has several meanings. It's a mild interjection, as in "Well, maybe. . . ." It's a noun meaning a hole drilled for water. It's an adjective meaning "not sick." And it's the adverb related to the adjective *good*. The most common usage error is failure to use it.

People frequently say "I really type good," or "My car runs good," or "Brush your teeth good." These are officially nonstandard English. In careful standard English you say "I type well" (or quickly and accurately), "My car runs well," "Brush your teeth well." Think of *well* as an honorary "ly" word, usually.

Memory Peg

Adverbs add to *action* verbs; therefore, look at the sentence and decide: Is the verb *doing* something or *being* something? If it is doing, you need an adverb; it tells how, when, where, how much is happening.

My car starts *quickly*. [or *beautifully* or *badly*]

Brush your teeth *thoroughly*.

I type well. [or *slowly*—remember that *well* is like an "ly" word]

Memory Peg

Adjectives often follow *being* or *linking* verbs. When a verb is used in place of a being verb, it takes an adjective. Ask yourself, is the subject doing something, or being something?

Rita seems happy.

Does this mean "Rita *is* happy"? Yes—although the writer is not quite so sure about the statement.

Tom looks sad.

Does this mean that Tom is being something or doing something? He is being, so use an adjective.

Some verbs can be used either as linking verbs or as action verbs, so you need to think carefully about the meaning of the sentence. *Look* is an example.

Tom looks sadly up at the teacher.

Tom looks hesitantly at his paper. [He is not sure about the answers.]

Feel also can be used as either an action verb (meaning "to touch") or a being/linking verb (meaning "to have an attitude or belief").

I feel great about that.

I feel bad about that.

The last example sentence is very often worded incorrectly. Somehow we like to say "feel badly," although we never say "feel greatly." Both examples describe a state of being within the person. They don't have anything to do with the action verb meaning "to touch," as in "I felt the table hesitantly after the ink spilled." To say "feel badly" would be like saying "I touched something badly." Substitute the word *great* and your ear will probably give you the answers on sentences with *feel*, although "feel strongly" is being used.

Tryout 1: Adjective/Adverb Choice

Directions: Circle the correct word in the parentheses. In each case, ask yourself whether the verb is doing something or being something.

1. The roses smell (sweet/sweetly) on the evening air.
2. The chef smells the soup (hesitant/hesitantly).
3. The popcorn tastes (delicious/deliciously).
4. I tasted the soup (grateful/gratefully).
5. His band sounds (beautiful/beautifully).
6. The leader sounds the gong (loud/loudly).
7. I feel (good/well) about that.
8. I feel (sick/sickly) about that.
9. He feels (quick/quickly) for his shoes in the dark.
10. He feels (proud/proudly) that he can find them (quick/quickly).

Ten points per correct answer.

Tryout 2: Adjective/Adverb Choice

Directions: Circle the correct words in the parentheses.

(1) Adverbs and adjectives need to be studied (well/good). (2) Your ability to choose these words shows a (good/well) knowledge of usage. (3) When you study (thorough/thoroughly), you'll learn the correct usage. (4) A (thorough/thoroughly) knowledge of English helps your writing.

(5) After we study, we'll eat dinner (thankful/thankfully). (6) We'll taste the soup (hesitant/hesitantly) in case it's hot. (7) The hot and sour soup tastes (delicious/deliciously). (8) I feel (good/well) about the

Ten points per correct answer.

upcoming test. (9) I felt (good/well) after I recovered from the flu. (10) I have resolved to study (good/well) to pass the test.

ARTICLE ADJECTIVE USAGE

The words we used to call *articles* have now been grouped as a subclass of adjectives. There is a subtle difference in usage among the three—*a, an,* and *the.*

The words *a* and *an* are *indefinite* articles. They are used when naming a thing or person in general. Speak of "a book" when you mean no particular book—just any book. Use *an* rather than *a* with a noun that begins with a vowel sound—"an apple" is smoother than "a apple," which sounds a bit like stuttering.

Note: It's the *sound* that matters. We say "an hour" because the *h* is silent; we say "a union" because *union* sounds as if it begins with a *y.*

The *definite* article *the* is used to refer to a particular noun, usually one already mentioned or understood. If you say, "He put the book on the table," you're describing one specific item, not just any book on any table.

Some idiomatic differences in meaning occur with articles, however.

Memory Peg

> *a few* means "several"; *few* (without *a*) emphasizes a lack of items
>
> *a little* means "some"; *little* (without *a*) emphasizes a lack of size

ADVERB INTENSIFIER USAGE

Do you remember the adverb intensifiers? Adverbs are very versatile, and they can modify not only action verbs but also adjectives and other adverbs. They do this by intensifying the quality mentioned—making it more or less intense. (About one adverb use in twenty modifies something other than a verb.)

> a big brown bear   a very big bear   a slightly smaller bear

Both *big* and *brown* are describing *bear;* it's a big bear and a brown bear; we have two adjectives. It is not, however, a very bear. *Very* and *slightly* are intensifying adverbs, changing the level of "bigness." They modify the adjectives *big* and *smaller.* Adverbs commonly used in this way may include *more, most, quite, rather, somewhat, little, least,* and such regular adverbs as *really, surely, certainly,* and *definitely.* If you can substitute *very* for a word in a sentence, the word is usually this type of adverb.

COMPARATIVES AND SUPERLATIVES

The last complication of adjective and adverb usage is the choice between comparative and superlative modifiers.

To compare the degrees of a quality of two items, you add *er* to adjectives or adverbs of one syllable or one accented and one very short unaccented syllable; for longer words, you add *more* or *less*. This is called the *comparative* adjective or adverb.

When you want to discuss qualities of three or more items, you use the *superlative* form, which adds *est* to shorter words and *most* or *least* to longer ones.

In general, the preferred form is the shorter form.

Between French and Spanish, I think Spanish is *easier* to spell.

French, Spanish, and English are all popular languages, but Spanish is the *easiest* to spell. [But don't say *carefulest.*]

Some people say that the sound of Portuguese is the *most beautiful* of all. [You can say *prettiest.*]

Russian music sounds *sadder* than English music.

The Russian alphabet is *more difficult* for us than our own.

These examples are all regular comparatives and superlatives. A few adjectives and adverbs have irregular forms.

	COMPARATIVE	SUPERLATIVE
bad	worse	worst
good	better	best
many (counted items)	more	most
much (measured items)	more	most
little (measured items)	less	least
few (counted items)	fewer	fewest

Tryout: Complex Adjective and Adverb Usage

Directions: Circle the correct words in the parentheses.

1. My uncle gave me two computers; the (newer/newest) one is faster than the (older/oldest) one.

    Five points per correct answer.

2. This is the (fastest/faster) of all the computers I've used.

3. The gift was the (thoughtfulest/most thoughtful) gesture he'd ever made.

4. We want to earn (a/an) day's pay with (a/an) honest day's work.

5. This machine was (less/least) costly than that one.

6. That manual is (more/most) helpful of the ones I've seen.

7. I feel (good/well) about the purchase.

8. This program is the (easier/easiest) of the two.

9. That program is the (more productive/most productive) of the two.

10. This one is (least/less) helpful of all.

11. Because he types (bad/badly), he spends too much time keyboarding.

12. She bought (a/an) Apple PowerBook computer, even though it was the (more/most) expensive of the two brands.

13. She keyboards very (quick/quickly) on the job.

14. Mistakes can be corrected quite (easy/easily).

15. She seems (happy/happily) with her purchase.

16. He looks (happier/more happy) too.

17. I felt (bad/badly) about the lost time.

18. Now the program is running (beautiful/beautifully).

SUBTLETIES OF ADVERB USAGE

Understanding English requires much practice in reading, writing, and speaking. Many usages cannot be explained but must simply be learned. Here are helpful hints for some types of adverb usage.

An adverb can often be inserted in different places in a sentence, but its placement may change the meaning of the sentence. This is particularly true of a *limiting* adverb such as *only*, *just*, or *simply*. Note the differences in meaning in the following examples.

> Only my teacher has a computer in this room. [Nobody else has.]
>
> My teacher has a computer only in this room. [The teacher doesn't have one elsewhere.]
>
> My teacher has only a computer terminal in this room. [The rest of the computer isn't here.]
>
> My teacher has only a computer in this room. [The room contains nothing else.]

A limiting adverb such as *only* must go directly before the word or phrase to be limited, or the meaning will not be clear.

The adverbs *never* and *not* have different meanings. *Never* means "not ever" with long-term time implications. "He has never written to me" means that you have not received one single letter from him. "He never wrote to me last week" is almost nonsense, because the stated time period clashes with the idea of *never*. Don't use the word *never* with any idea of limited time. Use *not* to produce a simple negative effect.

The word *where* should be limited to ideas of placement and not used to substitute for *that*. Don't say "I read *where* you got a new job," unless you mean "I was reading in the place where. . . ." If you mean "the fact that you got a new job," say "I read *that* you got a new job."

Avoid using *badly* or *in the worst way* when you mean *very much*. You can mangle your meaning, making it seem negative. When you say "I wanted to pass the test badly," you're implying that you would be pleased to get a grade of 71 percent—a poor grade, but a pass. "I wanted very much to pass the test" or "I really wanted to pass" means that you were eager to pass.

Be sure to recognize *somewhat* (not *some*) and *almost* (not *most*) as the usual adverbs meaning "slightly" or "nearly." **In each case, the longer word is the adverb.**

Memory Peg

> He was somewhat tired. [not "some tired"]
>
> She was almost home. [not "most home"]

Also be careful of the often misused adjectives *real* (meaning "genuine") and *sure* (meaning "certain"). When you need adverbs, these must add "ly." Try substituting *very* or *certainly* in the sentence to help your ear.

> This is surely not easy. [not "sure not easy"; does "certain not easy" sound right?]
>
> He was really happy. [not "real happy"]

These two words are frequently misused casually in spoken English, but know what the correct usage should be.

Sometimes you have to choose between a two-word modifier and a similar one-word modifier, such as *already* and *all ready*. In nearly all these situations, your ear will tell you which way to spell if you remove the first word of the two-word version to see whether the second word makes sense alone or with a different word first. (Also see the list of word pairs in Appendix C, Homonyms and Pseudohomonyms.)

Memory Peg

> By the time I reached the store, he had (already/all ready) gone.

Does "he had ready gone" make sense? No. You need the full one-word modifier, *already*, meaning "sooner than expected."

> By the time he got home, we were (already/all ready) to go.

"We were ready to go" makes sense, so you need the two-word spelling.

> She was (altogether/all together) unhappy.

Was she "together unhappy"? No, so *altogether* is correct.

> We gathered the materials (altogether/all together).

"We gathered them together" or "completely together" makes sense, so it's the two-word spelling.

(Maybe/May be) we should study this.

Can you say "Be we should"? *Maybe* is correct.

We (maybe/may be) going.

Can you say "We be going"? Not really, but in this choice, you need a verb before *be*; try to substitute a different one—"might be," for example. You can hear that the one word *maybe* doesn't work. It doesn't provide a verb.

Tryout: Adverb Subtleties

Directions: Circle the correct words in the parentheses.

Ten points per correct answer.

1. You (never told/didn't tell) me that the mail had already come.
2. Because he had broken his leg, Don needed help (immediately/in the worst way).
3. Our income increased (some/somewhat) last year.
4. I do my best writing at a (real/really) quiet time of day.
5. (Only she/She only) knows about the winner; nobody else knows.
6. We are (most/almost) done studying modifiers.
7. I've heard (where/that) there is danger of pollution from automobiles.
8. I (badly/very much) want to graduate in May.
9. You will (sure/surely) need to study faithfully.
10. I read (where/that) you had won a prize.

DOUBLE-TROUBLE ADJECTIVES

Several situations involving adjectives have to do with using two words.

1. *Compound adjectives* are those created by putting two words together with a hyphen, creating a single adjective.

no-fault insurance   A two-year contract

a half-baked idea   a two-faced person

To decide whether to use the hyphen, ask whether the two words could both modify the noun separately. Is it "no insurance" and "fault insurance"? Definitely not. You need the two words together to create the adjective.

Sometimes the two words both modify the noun but create a meaning different from the one you intended. "Two year contracts" is different from "a two-year contract."

2. Avoid what is known as a *double comparison*. It is incorrect to say "more prettier." Either put an er/est ending on the adjective *or* use words such as *more* or *most*—not both. A double comparison is one of the telltale signs of poor or very colloquial grammar.

3. Avoid the *double negative*. In many languages, negatives used twice double the negative effect, but in English, two negatives cancel each other out. If you *haven't* got *no* money, you must *have some* money! This is another telltale sign of poor grammar.

Not only do we never use two negatives on the same idea, but also in standard English we never use a word that is almost a negative with a negative.

> The child *could hardly* reach the shelf. [not "couldn't hardly"]
>
> I *can scarcely* hear you. [not "can't scarcely"]
>
> We *will barely* make it to the concert on time. [not "won't barely"]

4. On the positive side, we have certain *absolute adjectives*, which, strictly speaking, mean 100 percent of the quality involved. Don't be tempted to increase them over 100 percent or decrease them below that, unless you use words such as *almost* or *nearly*. These words cannot formally be compared to greater or lesser amounts.

accurate	dead	immaculate	pregnant	supreme
complete	empty	perfect	round	unanimous
correct	full	perpendicular	square	unique

The standard way to compare these ideas is to use the phrase "more nearly" or "most nearly."

> I am perfect. You are almost perfect. He is more nearly perfect than she is. Well, actually, nobody's perfect. Can I be about 99 percent perfect?
>
> This jar is nearly full. That one is more nearly full. [If one was "fuller," it would overflow.]
>
> These flowers are nearly dead from the freeze. [Others can't be "deader"; they can be "more nearly dead."]

The word *unique* seems to offer the greatest temptation. People are apt to say something is "very unique." This would mean "very one of a kind," which is nonsense. Use "very unusual" or just "unique," instead.

ADJECTIVE AND PRONOUN PROBLEMS

When studying parts of speech, you learned that the possessive or indefinite pronouns (*his, any, their, all,* and the like) can also be used as possessive or indefinite adjectives. Several complications arise from these usages.

When you compare a person with a group, be careful not to eliminate that person from the group.

> **INCORRECT**   You are taller than *any person* in this room.

If you're speaking to an elephant, that's OK, but if you're talking to a person, it's insulting, because you are excluding the listener from the category of "persons in this room."

> **CORRECT**   You are taller than *anyone else* in this room.

When you say "my teacher and friend," you mean just one person. If you say "my teacher and my friend," repeating the modifier, you're probably talking about two people.

Be careful to use *this* and *that* as singulars, and *these* and *those* as plurals, even in adjective spots—"this book," "those books." A special problem arises when you add words such as *kind, type,* or *sort.* These should match the singular or plural as well.

these kinds of books	this kind of book
those types of people	that type of person

And don't ever use *them* as an adjective—"them books," "them people"—that's always a major grammatical error.

Tryout: Double-Trouble Adjectives

Directions: Circle the correct words in the parentheses.

Five points per correct answer.

1. This is the (greatest/most greatest) day of all.
2. Today is graduation day for all (that/them/those) lucky people who have worked so hard.
3. Those who studied (hardest/most hard) will get honors.
4. Their answers were the (most/most nearly) correct.
5. Their (grade point/grade-point) averages were (most high/highest).
6. Sue did better than (any/any other) woman in her class.
7. Carlos did better than (anyone/anyone else) in his class.
8. My best student and friend (has/have) written me a letter about her graduation experiences.

9. (This/These) (kinds/kind) of stories make graduation fun.

10. After the speeches, there will be a (30 minute/30-minute) refreshment period.

11. These (activity/activities) are fun for (these/them) students.

12. Those (kind/kinds) of events are planned by (this/these) group of students.

13. We (had/hadn't) scarcely any food left after the party.

14. Next time we should order a (larger/more larger) amount.

15. This occasion is (most/almost) unique.

16. The students are nervous before the ceremony; each graduate is (happier/more happier) once it's over.

17. Now the graduates begin knocking on all (them/those) employers' doors.

Practice: Review of Adjectives, Adverbs, and Pronouns

Directions: Circle any adjective, adverb, or pronoun usage problem, and write the correct form above it.

(1) I'm shopping for one of *them* (those) new backpacks for my niece.

(2) She's just old enough to want everything *almost* (most) perfect. (3) She's only six years old but more particular than *anyone else* (anyone) in her family. (4) Between the blue pack and the red pack, she likes the blue *better* (best). (5) Her brother likes the red one ~~more~~ *(delete word)* better. (6) My friend and roommate also likes these *kinds* (kind) of packs. (7) The two packs are both good, but the red one has *more* (the most) features. (8) The blue one is ~~more~~ *(delete word)* larger, however. (9) I've looked in several stores; this one has the *best* (better) bargains. (10) The store closest to my house is more convenient than *any other* (any) store in my town. (11) I'm asking that store to send me the pack by the ~~most~~ *(delete word)* fastest method. (12) Now that I've paid for the backpack, I haven't got *any* (no) money left.

From 100 points subtract five points per incorrect answer.

Tell students that words may need to be deleted to make the correct form.

DANGLING AND MISPLACED MODIFIERS AS ADJECTIVES

The dangling modifier, especially the dangling participle, was treated as a problem of grammar and logic in our discussion of adjective phrases. The basic rule is that any phrase that functions as an adjective must logically be identified with the noun or pronoun it modifies. It's identified mainly by its placement next to that noun or pronoun. When it is closer to another one, unintended meanings arise.

> **INCORRECT**   Running into the room, the chair fell against the table.

What's the problem here? *Running* is a present participle, a part of a verb but not the verb of the sentence. It's being used as an adjective, along with the prepositional phrase attached to it ("into the room"). The whole phrase, called a *participial phrase,* should be describing a noun, but the nearest noun is *chair.* The result in this sentence is that the chair has been running into the room. (Not!)

Memory Peg

A *dangling modifier* is any word or group of words that has no place to go—there is nobody in the sentence to whom it can be attached, so it dangles desperately in midair. To fix the sentence, you must add the missing noun or pronoun, either immediately before or after the modifier.

> **CORRECT**   As Sally ran into the room, the chair fell . . .
>
> Running into the room, we knocked the chair against the table.

Memory Peg

A *misplaced modifier* is one that can be fixed by moving it to a different spot in the sentence.

> **INCORRECT**   Sitting on the table, we saw a half-filled cup of coffee.

The modifying phrase is "Sitting on the table." What should it be modifying? Were "we" sitting on the table? How can we fix this sentence? Right—move the modifier to follow "cup of coffee."

A prepositional phrase or a clause can also be in the wrong spot.

> **INCORRECT**   My sister was cooking dinner in her new suit. [Was the dinner in the suit?]
>
> **CORRECT**   In her new suit, my sister was cooking dinner.
>
> **INCORRECT**   She ate dinner after she went to the party because she was so hungry. [Why did she go to the party? Do you know? Can you fix the sentence by moving the "because" clause or the "after" clause?]
>
> **CORRECT**   After the party she ate dinner because she was so hungry.

Even single adjectives or adverbs can cause confusion.

> **INCORRECT**   Silver women's chains are on sale today.

INCORRECT   Two-wheeled boys' bikes are also good buys. [Boys aren't two-wheeled!]

We just need to reverse the adjectives:

CORRECT   Women's silver chains are on sale today.

Boys' two-wheeled bikes are also good buys.

When they are caught with dangling or misplaced modifiers, some writers offer the excuse that readers can figure out what the meaning should be. That's not the point. Good writing is always clear and logical—if the intent is to communicate. There may be times when you don't want to communicate, when you deliberately want to soft-pedal a situation or avoid giving a precise statement, but dangling or misplaced modifiers don't accomplish that. When you want to be clear, you should know how.

Tryout: Dangling and Misplaced Modifiers

Directions: Correct the sentences using the proofreading symbols in Appendix E, if possible, or rewriting in the extra space, if necessary.

1. Shining brightly through the window, we saw the moon.

2. Flown here from Florida citrus groves, I appreciated the oranges.

3. Baked to a crisp, Grandma enjoyed the cookies.

4. In the newspaper she read the latest story.

5. Dripping down the window pane, Jack stared at the heavy rain.

6. We saw the bookcase, entering the room.

7. Eyes tightly closed, her thoughts drifted to her vacation.

8. After eating dinner, the clock struck seven.

9. Howling in the wind, the wolves' eyes gleamed.

10. When turning on the light, the room appeared brighter.

11. We ran up the stairs eating our snacks.

12. Touring the city, the skyscrapers loomed above the fog.

13. Nestled in the pillows, our thoughts turned to the baby.

14. Lying on the beach, the sun was burning.

Two points for each error found, two points for each logical correction.

Bouncing on the sidewalk, the boy caught the ball.

15. Bouncing on the sidewalk, the boy caught the ball.

16. Splashed across our television screens, we see violence.

17. He drove to Los Angeles with four new tires.

18. We finished the meal quickly swallowing and ran out the door.

19. Tightly curled, she liked her new permanent.

20. Cleaned and pressed, she hung the clothes in the closet.

21. Antique babies' cradles are a specialty of that store.

22. The child looked at the candy and then bought it longingly.

23. This test can be finished by students who have studied the book in 10 minutes.

Tightly curled, she liked her new permanent.

24. Laughing and waving, my mind filled with joy.

25. After running up the stairs, my heart was pounding.

COMPLEX PROBLEMS OF PRONOUN REFERENCE

Pronouns are very convenient shortcut words, but when the nouns to which they refer are not clear, the sentences can be very confusing. In the following examples, choose one meaning and then make it clear. (Assume that you know about the situation.) Correct examples are provided on page 280.

UNCLEAR   Tom and Jerry went to Santa Cruz last week, and he bought a new car. [Who is *he?*]

We have a new brochure about the school, which we'll send on request. [Will we send the school?]

We're ready to start the car now; when I raise my hand, floor it! [Should you floor my hand?]

Not satisfied with your new computer? Just fill out the guarantee form and send it back to us; we'll pay the postage. [Should you send the guarantee? or the computer?]

They say that we might be having a recession. [This sentence is grammatically correct but unclear—who are "they"?]

I keyboarded all day yesterday but printed only two of them. [You printed two of what?]

It is the clarity of the letters that determines their effectiveness. [What does *It* stand for? This is a wordy form that needs polish.]

UNCLEAR Karen told Barbara that if her work didn't improve she would be reprimanded. [Who has been warned? Are you sure?]

I was late because my alarm clock failed. This upset my boss. [What upset the boss?]

Memory Peg

Here's a basic pronoun rule: Don't use a pronoun unless you can say exactly which noun or pronoun is its antecedent. In other words, to which word or words does the pronoun refer?

The easiest way to fix most of the sentences above is to rename the mentioned noun, avoiding the pronoun. However, there are frequently better and shorter ways. Here are examples of rewrites of the sentences.

CORRECT Jerry bought a new car when he and Tom went to Santa Cruz last week. [Mention only one of the people before the *he*.]

The school has a new brochure, which we'll send on request. [Move the right noun nearer *which*.]

We're ready to start the car now; when I raise my hand, floor the gas pedal!

. . . Just fill out and return the guarantee form; we'll pay the postage.

The *Wall Street Journal* says that we might be having a recession.

I keyboarded all day yesterday but printed only two pages.

The clarity of the letters determines their effectiveness.

Karen told Barbara, "If my work doesn't improve, I'm in trouble."

My boss was upset because I was late when my alarm clock failed.

Note: The easiest way to rewrite indirect quotations is to make them direct.

Practice: Pronoun Reference Problems

Directions: Correct the reference mistakes, using the proofreading symbols in Appendix E, if possible, or rewriting in the extra space, if necessary.

Ten points per correct sentence.

1. To get the new catalogue, send in your order, this week, which will be filled immediately.

Sentence 2: An alternative is "After Mark returned from vacation, Mr. Brown sent him to the conference."

2. ~~Mr. Brown~~ *he* sent Mark to the conference after ~~he~~ *Mr. Brown* returned from vacation.

3. I'll plug in the computer; when I nod my head, turn ~~it~~ *the switch* on.

4. ~~Ben~~ *he* and Tomas revised the English outlines when ~~he~~ *Ben* taught English.

Sentence 5: An alternative is "The receptionist told Susana, 'I have a message,'" The rewrite must make clear which person gets the message.

5. When the receptionist ~~talked to~~ *told* Susana, ~~she said she had~~ *"You have* a message."

6. If you are a good student, please explain ~~it~~ *the fact* to your friends.

7. The teacher took the test from her desk, which everyone had been waiting to see.

   The newspapers
8. ~~They~~ say that classes will be less crowded next month.

   The
9. ~~In~~ fine print, it says in the contract that money will be refunded within 30 days.

   "My book will be ready soon."
10. Mrs. Black told the teacher, ~~that her book would be ready soon.~~

Sentence 8: "They say" could be replaced with "The administration says."

Sentence 10: An alternative is "Mrs. Black told the teacher, 'Your book will be ready soon.'"

ANSWERS

Tryout 1: Adjective/Adverb Choice

1. sweet; 2. hesitantly; 3. delicious; 4. gratefully; 5. beautiful; 6. loudly; 7. good; 8. sick; 9. quickly; 10. proud, quickly.

Tryout 2: Adjective/Adverb Choice

1. well; 2. good; 3. thoroughly; 4. thorough; 5. thankfully; 6. hesitantly; 7. delicious; 8. good; 9. well; 10. well.

Tryout: Complex Adjective and Adverb Usage

1. newer, older; 2. fastest; 3. most thoughtful; 4. a, an; 5. less; 6. most; 7. good; 8. easier; 9. more productive; 10. least; 11. badly; 12. an, more; 13. quickly; 14. easily; 15. happy; 16. happier; 17. bad; 18. beautifully.

Tryout: Adverb Subtleties

1. didn't tell; 2. immediately; 3. somewhat; 4. really; 5. Only she; 6. almost; 7. that; 8. very much; 9. surely; 10. that.

Tryout: Double-Trouble Adjectives

1. greatest; 2. those; 3. hardest; 4. most nearly; 5. grade-point, highest; 6. any other; 7. anyone else; 8. has; 9. These, kinds; 10. 30-minute; 11. activities, these; 12. kinds, this; 13. had; 14. larger; 15. almost; 16. happier; 17. those.

Tryout: Dangling and Misplaced Modifiers

Other correct answers are possible for most sentences.

1. Shining brightly through the window, we saw the moon.

2. Flown here from Florida citrus groves, I appreciated the oranges.

3. Baked to a crisp, Grandma enjoyed the cookies.

4. In the newspaper she read the latest story.

5. Dripping down the window pane, Jack stared at the heavy rain.

6. We saw the bookcase, entering the room.

7. *she felt*
   Eyes tightly closed, her thoughts drifted to her vacation.

8. *we ate*
   After ~~eating~~ dinner, the clock struck seven.

9. *As the wolves howled*   *their*
   ~~Howling~~ in the wind, ~~the wolves'~~ eyes gleamed.

10. *we turned*
    When ~~turning~~ on the light, the room appeared brighter.

11. We ran up the stairs, eating our snacks.

12. *As we toured*
    ~~Touring~~ the city, the skyscrapers loomed above the fog.

13. *we felt*
    Nestled in the pillows, our thoughts turned to the baby.

14. *As we lay*
    ~~Lying~~ on the beach, the sun was burning.

15. Bouncing on the sidewalk, the boy caught the ball.

16. Splashed across our television screens, we see violence.

17. *on his car,*
    He drove to Los Angeles with four new tires.

18. We finished the meal quickly swallowing and ran out the door.

19. Tightly curled, she liked her new permanent.

20. Cleaned and pressed, she hung the clothes in the closet.

21. Antique babies' cradles are a specialty of that store.

22. The child looked at the candy and then bought it longingly.

23. This test can be finished by students who have studied the book in 10 minutes.

24. *As I laughed and waved,*
    ~~Laughing and waving,~~ my mind filled with joy.

25. *I felt*
    After running up the stairs, my heart ~~was~~ pounding.

Chapter 30

Prepositions, Conjunctions, and Parallelism
Ways to Put Things Together

Prepositions and conjunctions can be used to balance and emphasize parts of sentences as well as joining them.

PREPOSITION PROBLEMS

Which Preposition to Use

Preposition usage is particularly a matter of the ear, of everyday usage, involving many *idioms,* little oddities of expression that arise from custom rather than logic. However, there are a few prepositional usages that can be explained logically and therefore remembered more easily.

The words *to* and *at* carry the meaning of direct one-way arrows.

Memory Peg

> I went to the store.
>
> I looked at the vegetables.

The store didn't go to me, and the vegetables didn't look back.

The word *with,* however, implies a two-way or more complex arrangement. See what happens to the meaning of certain phrases when the prepositions (italicized) change.

Memory Peg

> I was angry *at* the idea.
>
> I was angry *with* the person.
>
> She agreed *to* the suggestion.
>
> She agreed *with* the person.
>
> He talked *to* the teenager.
>
> He talked *with* the teenager.

Usually, the word *with* shows a more complex arrangement, frequently with a person. If we say we're *angry at* a person, we're treating that person as a thing, with no chance to talk back. Notice the difference in the meaning of the two sentences involving the teenager. When someone says "I'm going to speak to him" or "talk to him," you hear a tone of "I'm going to tell him what's what," rather than a tone of "He and I are going to have a discussion." The use of *with* tones down the anger and authority; it places the participants on an equal footing.

A related difference occurs between *compare to* and *compare with*. *Compare to* means to look at similarities only.

The teacher compared my writing to Kingsolver's.

Compare with means an examination of differences as well as similarities.

We compared our Tryouts with the Answers at the end of the chapter.

The word *with* is also often needed with the adjective *identical,* to hint at a complex comparison rather than a simple one.

This answer key is identical with that one.

While the prepositions *at* and *in* show position, *to, from,* and *into* show position in motion.

There are several different correct ways to say *regard to*.

In regard to your letter...

With regard to your idea...

As regards your proposal...[The *s* is used only here.]

Regarding your proposition...

Re your letter...[informal]

In re your letter...[informal]

Here are some other preposition distinctions.

Preposition Meanings and Usages

accompanied by is used for a person: She was accompanied by Joe.

accompanied with is used for a thing: The lasagna was accompanied with two vegetables.

account for is used for a thing or person: I can't account for the discrepancy.

agree on or *upon* means to "reach an understanding": We can't agree on a zoning plan.

agree with is used for a person or idea: Six of the members agreed with your proposal.

apply to is used for a person or thing: They applied themselves to the job.

argue about is used for a thing or idea: They argued about the legislation.

argue with is used for a person: He argued with his brother.

beside means "next to" a person or thing: The spider sat down beside her.

besides means "in addition to": Besides my mother, the rest of my family came to graduation.

choose between is used for two things: I had to choose between French and Spanish for my language requirement.

choose among is used for three or more things: We chose among 20 videotapes from our collection.

conform to is correct, not "conform with": The class content didn't conform to the outline.

consists in means "characterized or caused by": Job satisfaction consists in a sense of doing useful work competently.

consists of means "is made up of": This course consists of 48 class hours.

convenient for means "suitable": What schedule is most convenient for you?

convenient to means "near": Which bus stop is most convenient to your house?

correspond to means "match": This angle does not correspond to that one.

correspond with means "write to": I correspond with a friend in Japan.

differ about is used for a thing or idea: We differ about whether the economy is in a recession.

differ from is used for one thing and another: His position differs from mine.

differ with is used for a person: I differ with him on many economic issues.

different from is a prepositional phrase and the more common usage: This course is different from the grammar class I had in high school.

Tell students to remember the similar "fr" sounds in *different from*.

differently than consists of an adverb and a conjunction, used with an action verb: He studies differently than I do.

discrepancy in is used for a difference inside an item: The auditor found several discrepancies in the budget.

discrepancy between is used for a difference between two items (*between* is always used for two—never more or fewer): There was a discrepancy between income and expenditures.

independent of is correct, not "independent from": He wants to be independent of his parents.

interested in is correct, not "interested on" or "interested of": We are not interested in discussing that.

part from means to "say good-bye"—usually to a person: Sally was reluctant to part from her father.

part with means to "give up"—usually an object: Sally was reluctant to part with her spacious corner office.

retroactive to is correct, not "retroactive from": Your raise is retroactive to July 1.

When to Leave Prepositions Out

Memory Peg

When you're in doubt about whether an extra small word such as *of* (or *a*) is needed, the best guess is usually to omit the word.

inside the room [not "inside of the room"—*inside* is already a preposition]

outside the room

opposite the door

both the members

like to do it [not "like for to do it"]

plan to do [not "plan on doing"]

where she is [not "where she is at"]

where he went [not "where he went to"]

couldn't help asking [not "couldn't help but ask"]

behind [not "in back of"]

There are two major grammatical mistakes commonly made with *of* and *off*.

INCORRECT   I got the papers off the receptionist.

Was she wearing them on her shoulder? Always use *from* in these situations.

INCORRECT   I should of known better.

Oops! This person is trying to write *should've,* which would be written formally as *should have.*

Two Prepositions to Leave In

Although you can often trust your ears about when to leave out extra prepositions, watch out for phrases such as "a couple people" or "that type book"—the words *couple* and *type* can't be used as adjectives, so they must have the preposition *of.*

I saw a couple *of* cars in the driveway. [not "a couple cars"]

We need that type *of* windshield wiper. [not "that type windshield wiper"]

Try to avoid ending sentences with prepositions, but don't go to extremes. Avoid awkward constructions such as "up with which I shall not put."

To which city did you go?

That's the bench on which I sat.

His temper is hard to put up with.

Tryout: Preposition Usage

Directions: Circle the correct words in the parentheses.

1. I decided to speak (with/to) my boss about a raise.
2. When we added staff, he had to part (from/with) his corner office.
3. We found several discrepancies (in/between) the two reports.
4. This computer looks identical (to/with) the old one.
5. Is it really different (from/than) that one?
6. Can you load the new material (in/into) the computer today?
7. Where did the secretary (go/go to)?
8. My desk is (opposite/opposite to) hers.
9. Do you know where hers (is/is at)?
10. I guess I (should of/should've) studied a little more.

Ten points per correct answer.

Tryout: Choice of Preposition

Directions: Circle the correct words in the parentheses.

1. I hope my raise will be retroactive (to/from) the first.
2. If I apply myself (to/with) the job, I should succeed.
3. We didn't want to argue (about/with) the terms.
4. This salary doesn't conform (to/with) the contract.
5. My workday consists (of/in) 7½ hours.
6. This differs (from/with) my previous job.
7. The job stress is different (from/than) the previous stress.
8. Can you account (for/of) the difference?
9. I didn't want to agree (to/with) this arrangement.
10. I do agree (with/to) you about it.
11. Are you angry (about/with) it?
12. I was angry (at/with) my dog.
13. The job hours are convenient (to/for) me.
14. I would like to be independent (of/with) her supervision.
15. Their ideas are not well organized compared (to/with) mine.
16. I think I will ask to speak (to/with) my boss.

Five points per correct answer.

17. If I talk (to/with) him, we'll agree (upon/with) my job description.

18. When I correspond (to/with) him, his ideas correspond (with/to) mine quite closely.

CONJUNCTION USAGE AND PARALLELISM

Most conjunction choices have to do with logic. A primary problem is achieving parallelism—joining (with a conjunction) two or more words, phrases, or clauses that are equal in structure. The types of conjunctions that need to join equal word groups are the *coordinating* conjunctions (such as *and, but,* and *or*) and the *correlative* pairs (such as *not only/but also* and *either/or*). (For complete lists, see pages 47 and 49.)

Would you say, "I like fishing and to swim"? Your ear tells you that something is wrong. The conjunction *and* must join equals in form. We can fix the sentence by saying "to fish and swim" or "fishing and swimming." (It's not necessary to repeat the *to*.)

> **INCORRECT**   She was happier but suddenly sat down in the chair.
>
> He coughed, was smiling, and looked up at me.

Memory Peg

The first sentence joins a being verb and an action verb. The second sentence joins a simple past tense verb, a past progressive verb, and another simple past verb plus a prepositional phrase—a bit confusing. **When you're using coordinating or correlative conjunctions, join action verbs with same tense action verbs, being verbs with same tense being verbs, infinitives with infinitives, prepositional phrases with prepositional phrases, adjectives with adjectives, nouns with nouns, and clauses with clauses.**

> **CORRECT**
>
>   adj   adj
> She was *not only* happy *but also* tired.
>
> AV, past AV, past   AV, past
> He coughed, smiled, *and* looked up at me.
>
>   N   N
> They wanted *either* an exchange *or* a refund.

> **INCORRECT**
>
>   prep phr   prep phr
> The dog ran into the room, around the table, *and* then
>
>   clause
> he hid under the bed.

> **CORRECT**
>
>   prep phr   prep phr   prep phr
> The dog ran into the room, around the table, *and* under the bed.

Double-check sentences with correlative conjunctions to be sure you have the same kind of word group after each conjunction. Sometimes you may need to move the conjunction.

INCORRECT   I wanted to *either* eat at a restaurant *or* to order pizza.

The word *either* is followed by *eat,* but the word *or* is followed by *to.* Can you make the word groups alike by moving one of the conjunctions? Yes— either put the first *to* after *either* or take out the second *to.*

INCORRECT   He is *either* very smart *or* he studies many hours.

What comes after *either*? Does the same kind of word group come after *or*?

                    adj   adj
CORRECT   He is *either* very smart *or* very studious.

                   clause   clause
Either he is very smart *or* he studies many hours.

Tryout: Parallelism

Directions: Using the proofreading symbols in Appendix E, delete incorrect words and add correct ones in the proper places.

Five points per error located, five points per correction.

1. The photocopier requires simple weekly maintenance and a mechanic to check it thoroughly every month.

2. You may apply for the job by mail, by telephone, or coming into the office in person.

3. Both teachers seem to be helpful and have a lot of knowledge.

4. To study daily is important, but reviewing weekly also helps.

5. This quiz will help you understand the basics of parallelism and applying them to your writing.

6. Either this announcement was written by Mrs. Elias or by her aide.

7. The Dean hasn't decided yet whether Joanna will do that job or Wanda.

8. Ms. Powell likes both teaching accounting and computer science.

9. Mr. Martin neither agreed with Mrs. Lee nor Mrs. Carillo.

10. The staff all agreed either to have a picnic or a dinner dance.

CHOICE OF CONJUNCTION

The choice of conjunction to use depends sometimes on logic, sometimes on meaning. Here are some common problems.

The choice of *but* or *and* depends on the meaning. **Words such as *but*, *except*, and *although* set up a contrast. The word *and* means "in addition."** What do you think the following sentence means?

I put money in the machine, but no candy came out.

It implies that you were expecting candy and were disappointed not to get it. Suppose, however, that you were experienced with that machine and knew that it frequently gave trouble, so that you expected no candy. You might say:

I put money in the machine, and once again no candy came out.

There is no such conjunction as *being that*, although some people use the phrase incorrectly as one. Instead, use *since* or *because*.

| INCORRECT | Being that I know the answer, I'll speak out. |
| CORRECT | Since I know the answer, I'll speak out. |

However, don't use *since* or *because* if you've already used a word like *reason* or *why*—*because* means "for the reason that." You don't need to say the same thing twice.

INCORRECT	The reason I went to the gym was because I needed exercise.
CORRECT	The reason I went to the gym was that I needed exercise.
	I went to the gym because I needed exercise.

Be careful about the preposition *like*—it is not a conjunction! It can join prepositional phrases but not clauses. Therefore (although you hear such usages frequently, including in ads!), don't say, "I did the homework like I had planned." With words such as *pretend*, you may want to use *that*, but don't say "pretend like."

I did the homework as I had planned.

She looked as if she had had enough studying. [not "like she had"]

He decided to pretend that he was going to school. [not "pretend like he"]

The words *except* and *without* are also just prepositions, not conjunctions. In standard English we don't say, "I felt all right except I was hungry." We could say "except for my hunger" or substitute the conjunction *until* or *although*, changing the meaning slightly.

There is no such word as *anyways*, and no such phrase as "a long ways." *Anyway* is a common adverb that means "regardless of the consequences," and "a long way" means exactly what it says—the *s* makes no sense.

Tryout: Choice of Conjunction

Directions: Using the proofreading symbols in Appendix E, insert or delete words to correct the sentences. It helps to underline the conjunctions first.

1. Television can either be a time-waster or an educational tool.

2. She can't seem to study without she has music playing loudly.

3. She says the reason she does it is because she wants to shut out noise.

4. Mr. Whittiker gives homework like there is no tomorrow.

5. She can't seem to study without the loud music.

6. The teachers not only agreed on the hours but also on the schedule.

7. This book is both well written and has beautiful illustrations.

8. The test is tomorrow, and we are not worried about being ready.

9. Writing the paragraph is easy, but to correct it is harder.

10. She sets her clock ahead and pretends like the time is later.

Five points per error located, five points per correction.

HOW TO JOIN, BALANCE, AND EMPHASIZE

Balance with Conjunctions

When you want to show the relationship of ideas of equal importance, use parallel structure (see page 288)—join noun with noun, adjective with adjective, prepositional phrase with prepositional phrase, clause with clause, especially when you use coordinating or correlative conjunctions.

One of the major conjunction usage problems is the *incomplete comparison*.

INCORRECT   I like fish more than my husband.

I like fish more than my husband.

It's possible that I'm not at all fond of my husband and that I do like fish. The more likely meaning, however, is that I like fish more than my husband likes fish. If the meaning is not clear, complete the comparison that is in your mind. The phrases "as much as," "more than," and "less than" imply or state comparisons. Which one of the following examples needs to be made longer to be clear?

> He is taller than I.
>
> She types faster than Mary.
>
> She likes me better than Mary.

There's only one way to complete the first two sentences, so we don't need to add words. The third sentence, however, can have two meanings. Think about it, ask questions, and then make the meaning clear. It's either "than Mary does," or "than she likes Mary." (On a test, simply choose one meaning and make it clear.)

Here's another type of incomplete comparison.

INCORRECT   His salary is more than Mr. Smith.

Can you hear that this is comparing money and a person? To complete the idea, we need to say at least "Mr. Smith's" or "Mr. Smith's salary" (see the discussion of possessives on page 191), or we can say "that of Mr. Smith" or "the salary of Mr. Smith," although these phrases seem wordy and stiff.

Another lack of balance can occur when you join two nouns with *and* but use only one article or adjective. What's the difference in meaning between the following sentences?

Wanted: one receptionist and secretary for small office.

Wanted: one receptionist and one secretary for small office.

Be sure that you repeat the modifier if you truly mean one of each. Otherwise, your applicants will expect a one-person office job.

I saw a desk and clock on sale at the local hardware store.

Without an *a* before *clock*, this means a desk with a built-in clock.

Illogical Balances

Sometimes when writers try to save space, they make their sentences quite confused. One of the major problems occurs in a sentence that interrupts one thing with another, usually with commas around the interruption.

INCORRECT   I never have, and never will, see a purple cow.

What's the problem? When you remove the interruption—usually the part in commas—you'll hear the problem: "I never have see a purple cow." Each group of words must work with the surrounding words. You can't say "have see" or "will seen," so you need to add the other necessary word and move the commas a bit.

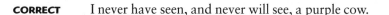

Memory Peg

CORRECT   I never have seen, and never will see, a purple cow.

Let's try another one.

INCORRECT   Your tests were corrected yesterday and the total grade recorded.

What's wrong here? The helping verb used in the first part of the sentence doesn't fit with the verb in the second part. You can't say "the total grade were recorded." So you must add the needed second verb.

CORRECT   Your tests were corrected yesterday, and the total grade was recorded.

Sometimes illogical balances involve prepositional idioms.

INCORRECT   Children should have confidence in and respect themselves.

"Confidence in" and "respect" don't fit with "themselves" the same way. Either repeat "themselves" in the first part or add "for" after "respect."

CORRECT   Children should have confidence in themselves and respect themselves.

Children should have confidence in and respect for themselves.

Questionable Balances

Memory Peg

Be careful about omitting words just to shorten the sentence. Sometimes the meaning slips away or confusion seeps in. Conjunctions or relative pronouns can often, but not always, be omitted in informal writing.

INCORRECT   We looked carefully and found the child had hidden the ring. [We found the child? No, we found *that* the child had hidden the ring.]

Parts of verbs or phrases can sometimes be omitted, but not always.

INCORRECT   Has he paid the bill or his wife?

Is he paying his wife? Or is his wife paying the bill? The sentence doesn't tell us. (On a test, just choose a meaning and make it clear.)

CORRECT   Has he or his wife paid the bill?

Shifts in Balance

Memory Peg

Related words or phrases joined by conjunctions need to be in the same form. Don't combine active and passive verbs. This is called a *voice shift*.

INCORRECT   He walked up to bat, and the first ball was hit by him.

I sent the letter Tuesday, and it was received the next day.

Do these sound awkward? Notice how much better the following sentences sound. They are shorter, more forceful, and definitely clearer.

CORRECT   He walked up to bat and hit the first ball.

I sent the letter Tuesday, and Don received it the next day.

The letter that was sent Tuesday was received the next day.

An even more common problem is the *tense shift*.

INCORRECT   I went to Fort Lauderdale yesterday. Now I'm on the beach.

The writer uses such simple language that the reader will easily understand the ideas.

These sentences would be clearer and simpler if parallel ideas were given parallel verb tenses.

CORRECT   I have been in Fort Lauderdale since yesterday. Now I'm on the beach.

The writer uses such simple language that the reader can easily understand the ideas.

A third frequent problem is the *person shift*.

INCORRECT   Tom wants to know where you can get a check cashed.

Is Tom really interested in where *you* can get a check cashed? Or does he want to ask where *he* can get it done, or where *one* can get it done?

Another common shift is from a general third person, such as *people,* to the second person *you*.

Emphasis Control

You can emphasize certain words in many different ways—for example, by using dashes or exclamation points. The way you arrange a sentence can also emphasize words.

When you try to memorize a list, do you find you remember the first part best, then the last part—and you tend to forget the middle? Keep this fact in mind when you think about emphasis. Where will you logically put the most important ideas, the ones that you want people to remember best?

The most important ideas are often at the beginning; the next most important, at the end. In the middle you can file away the unimportant things or the things you want to soft-pedal.

Memory Peg

You can also emphasize by putting the main idea in the main (independent) clause, and the less important idea in the dependent clause.

INCORRECT   There were many applicants, although Tom got the job.

Does this give the correct emphasis? I doubt that Tom would think so. What about this one?

INCORRECT   When the company president walked in, I had just started to open the mail.

Which is the more important idea? Where should it go, and in what kind of clause?

Here's an "interrupting" example.

INCORRECT   At Niagara Falls last week, when I got married, there was snow on the ground.

Could you improve the emphasis on this one by putting the most important idea in the main clause?

Certain conjunctions seem dull and uninspired, giving us little more information than a piece of punctuation might. They cannot be used for emphasis. Among the dullest are *and so* and just *and*. You can usually improve sentences and show connections better by using *since* or *because,* if this subordinate meaning is appropriate.

INCORRECT   We are almost finished with this chapter, and so we should be ready for a test.

CORRECT   Because we're almost finished with this chapter, we should be ready for a test.

Which sentence shows the connection of ideas more clearly and forcefully? Never use *and so* if you can think of a better conjunction.

Tryout: Balance and Emphasis

Directions: Using the proofreading symbols in Appendix E and rewriting, improve the sentences.

Five points per error located, five points per correction.

1. Mrs. Black never has, and never will, understand why some students are always late.

2. Our courses are better, not just equal, to theirs.

3. The students have great admiration and faith in that teacher.

4. The order was for a computer and desk.

5. Her report was more original than John.

6. I noticed the students in that class seemed very interested.

7. Should Ms. Hinkle sign the memo or Ms. Robertson?

8. Her first English class was six months ago, and so she needs to review before the comprehensive test.

9. I'd like to know where you can buy computer paper on sale.

10. I wrote the chapter, and then the tests were prepared by me.

Practice: Review of Plurals and Possessives

Directions: Circle the correct plural or possessive forms in the parentheses.

Four points per correct answer.

See Chapters 21–23.

(1) Fantasies, myths, folktales, either (children's/childrens') or (adults'/adult's) versions, occupy much of our leisure time. (2) Nursery school children dress up in (Supermans'/Superman's) cape, (Batmans'/ Batman's) hood, and the Ninja (Turtles'/Turtle's) masks. (3) (Super-

heroes/Superheroes') make children feel their own power. (4) Young (boy's/boys') aggressive instincts are channeled into a "fight for the good" against the "bad guys." (5) In the better (stories/stories') children are shown how to seek peaceful (solutions'/solutions) to conflicts.

(6) Because our culture is changing, recent (girls'/girl's) (story's/stories) show young (girls'/girls) bravery and strength. (7) (Girls'/Girls) and (woman/women) are no longer limited to keeping house and having (babies/babys). (8) Even some adult fantasies, for example (mens/mens'/men's) and (womens/women's/womens') scenes in ads, show the new message. (9) (Girls/Girls') dreams for themselves can now include jobs as police (officers'/officers) or (lawyers'/lawyers). (10) (Mens/Men's) strengths are now shown to include the difficult (arts/arts') of peacemaking, understanding (ones/one's) family, and caring for (one's/ones) children. (11) Look carefully at myths and tales to see the (culture's/cultures) messages.

In an organized paragraph or a longer piece, describe a modern story or ad that seems to be sending a new cultural message.

Paragraph Assignment

Tryout: Review of Adverb/Adjective Choices

Directions: Circle the correct words in the parentheses. (See Chapter 29.)

Five points per correct answer.

See Chapter 29.

1. Rosita dances very (graceful/gracefully).

2. Clean this table (good/well) before setting it.

3. This room looks (different/differently) since you painted.

4. Lee spent his money somewhat (foolish/foolishly).

5. This oven doesn't heat (good/well) anymore.

6. Dad's voice sounded (cheerful/cheerfully) on the phone.

7. Which ripen (faster/fastest)—oranges or lemons?

8. It was the (difficultest/most difficult) test we've had.

9. The woman wouldn't take (any/no) money for her work.

10. I've never had a (kinder/more kinder) advisor.

11. We couldn't find the answer key (anywhere/nowhere).

12. This model runs (good/well) on regular gas.

13. I tripped (awkward/awkwardly) on the doorstep.

14. This walkway looks (beautifully/beautiful) in the spring.

15. I can't type (good/well) on this old machine.

16. This pen writes (bad/badly), in my opinion.

17. Your travel plans sound (delightful/delightfully).

18. We didn't like (either/neither) of the shows.

19. Who lives (closer/closest)—Sally or Anita?

20. There weren't (any/no) easy answers.

Practice: Review of Advanced Grammar

Directions: Circle the correct words in the parentheses. (See Chapter 30.)

Five points per correct answer.

See Chapter 30.

1. Just (between/among) the three of us, she gave the (larger/largest) contribution.

2. Drop your money (in/into) the large container at the door.

3. (There/Their) are many animals that few people have seen.

4. The child's death was a (real/very) sad event.

5. This traveling circus is (good/well).

6. (Its/It's) clowns make children of all ages laugh.

7. There often is great rivalry (between/among) our two colleges.

8. The teacher is a (real/very) knowledgeable woman.

9. The custodian cleans the rooms (good/well).

10. We can't clean thoroughly, but we'll straighten our classroom (anyway/anyways).

11. (Almost/Most) everyone knows that the purpose of school is learning.

12. (Beside/Besides) the local community college, how many did you visit?

13. Did you hear the student talk (to/with) the teacher?

14. We walked (in/into) the classroom from the back hallway.

15. The teacher's desk is (beside/besides) the door.

16. We are (already/all ready) for the school celebration.

17. That cat looks (like/as) the cat we have at home.

18. It is a long (ways/way) to the new gym from here.

19. My coat is different (than/from) yours.

20. We (feel bad/feel badly) because we missed the baseball game.

In an organized paragraph, analyze which parts of your writing are your strengths and which are your weaknesses. (Then see whether your teacher agrees!)

Paragraph Assignment

Sample Test 1: Noun Usage

Directions: Form the correct possessives of the nouns in the following sentences by adding apostrophes and an *s* if necessary in the right places. Look for two nouns in a row. (See Chapters 21–23.)

Four points per correct numbered item.

See Chapters 21–23.

1. Some students in Mrs. Johnson's class are planning a party.

2. Jack's job is to send out invitations.

3. Good manners include a person's courteous voice on the phone.

4. My boss's desk is near the bookcases.

Sentence 4: Accept either "boss's" or "boss'."

5. The computers are easy for most employees to use.   OK

6. The work stations are designed for the secretaries' convenience.

7. These diskettes should not be removed from their cases.   OK

8. The problem of losing files is always in employees' minds.

9. I heard Ms. Lund's voice on the phone for several minutes.

10. My sister's new job will be very interesting.

Directions: Write the plural in the blank to the right of each word.

11. navy	*navies*
12. mailman	*mailmen*
13. tomato	*tomatoes*
14. attorney	*attorneys*
15. son-in-law	*sons-in-law*
16. solo	*solos*
17. spoonful	*spoonfuls*
18. utility	*utilities*
19. deer	*deer*
20. disk	*disks*

Directions: Write the possessive form in the blank to the right of each phrase.

21. clothing of the girls   *girls' clothing*
22. job of the editor-in-chief   *editor-in-chief's job*
23. fathers of Don and Ken   *Don's and Ken's fathers*
24. fashions of the women   *women's fashions*
25. house of the Joneses   *Joneses' house*

Sample Test 2: Pronoun Usage

Directions: Circle the correct pronouns in the parentheses. (See Chapters 24 and 25.)

Five points per correct answer.

See Chapters 24 and 25.

1. Hal doesn't work as long hours as (**we**/us).
2. You can share that job with Ken or (I/**me**).
3. The brothers and (**he**/him) are our closest friends.
4. My younger sister usually calls (**us**/we) girls on holidays.
5. John and (**I**/me) drive the same kind of car.
6. The cards were sent by Phyllis and (**her**/she).
7. Was the audience cheering them or (we/**us**)?
8. The noise frightened the child more than (I/**me**).
9. (Him/**He**) and I belong to the same employees' group.
10. We watched the dog wagging (**its**/it's) tail.
11. That chair suits you much better than (I/**me**).
12. (Them/**Their**) getting counseling is necessary before graduation.
13. Kris is the student (**who**/whom) will win.
14. She gives a big smile to (whoever/**whomever**) she sees.
15. (Who/**Whom**) did you want to give the speech?
16. You gave that book to (who/**whom**)?
17. (**Whom**/Who) would you choose to work with?
18. (**Who**/Whom) do you think will be chosen for the job?
19. (**Whom**/Who) did you give it to?
20. The Smiths and (**we**/us) share the same driveway.

Sample Test 3: Verb Usage

Directions: Write in the blank to the right of each sentence the correct *past* form of the verb in the parentheses. (See Chapters 26 and 27.)

1. You should have (see) the mud on the floor. _____seen_____

2. These oranges were (grow) in Florida. _____grown_____

3. The mailman (come) late this morning. _____came_____

4. The plate was (break) when we unpacked it. _____broken_____

5. *Gone with the Wind* was (write) by Margaret Mitchell. _____written_____

6. We should have (bring) more food to the party. _____brought_____

7. He must have (drive) there yesterday. _____driven_____

8. Mr. White (do) most of the cleaning. _____did_____

9. Fresh fruit is (fly) here from the valley. _____flown_____

10. The truck soon (run) out of gas. _____ran_____

11. Tony should have (eat) his salad. _____eaten_____

12. Some apricots had (fall) from the tree. _____fallen_____

13. I wish I had (know) that the paper was due. _____known_____

14. Jan has (take) many photos. _____taken_____

15. I had (spoke) to Ms. Rose about my grade. _____spoken_____

16. Julie has (sing) in the community chorus for years. _____sung_____

17. I (lie) back on the couch and relaxed. _____lay_____

18. Mary (lay) her books on the table. _____laid_____

19. David forgot where he had (lay) his pen. _____laid_____

20. The prices of groceries have (rise). _____risen_____

Five points per correct answer.

See Chapters 26 and 27.

Sample Test 4: Subject-Verb Agreement

Directions: Circle the correct forms of the verbs in the parentheses. Hint: Try the subject with the verb. (See Chapter 28.)

1. There (was/were) no dinner on the shelves.

2. Her parties (don't/doesn't) start until nine o'clock.

3. His interest in experiments (go/goes) back to his childhood.

4. January or February (is/are) a good time to visit Hawaii.

5. The results of her study efforts (was/were) amazing.

6. A sandwich or a small salad (make/makes) a good lunch.

7. One of her keyboards (need/needs) fixing.

8. His excuses for lateness (doesn't/don't) make sense.

9. Here (are/is) the names of the people to invite.

10. Every one of these employees (have/has) an interesting story.

Five points per correct answer.

See Chapter 28.

11. There ((wasn't)/weren't) any work left for you.

12. The grade in the book (show/(shows)) what tests you took.

13. The number of diskettes (were/(was)) printed on the box.

14. Either of these sweaters (are/(is)) a bargain at that price.

15. The size and price of these books (has/(have)) increased.

16. Every one of these items (need/(needs)) to be ordered.

17. Where (is/(are)) the vegetables for our dinner?

18. The emeralds in that necklace (is/(are)) not genuine.

19. This set of tires ((doesn't)/don't) cost much.

20. Each one of these pens (produce/(produces)) a different shade of red.

Sample Test 5: Adjective and Adverb Usage

Directions: Circle the correct modifiers in the parentheses. (See Chapter 29.)

Five points per correct
answer.

See Chapter 29.

1. If you brush your teeth (good/(well)), you'll probably have less decay.

2. Did you ever see anyone dance more (graceful/(gracefully))?

3. Her spaghetti tastes ((delicious)/deliciously) on a cold night.

4. My car runs (good/(well)) now that it's had a tune-up.

5. Laura knows her program almost (perfect/(perfectly)).

6. As the couple walked home, they noticed that the gardenias smelled ((sweet)/sweetly).

7. The driver stopped the car too (sudden/(suddenly)).

8. We thought the guitar sounded ((terrible)/terribly).

9. Dad felt ((terrible)/terribly) about losing the job.

10. Her friend Gus calls her quite (regular/(regularly)).

11. Why did Eric spend his allowance so (foolish/(foolishly))?

12. The living room looks ((different)/differently) with the new rug.

13. Which is (farthest/(farther)) north, Portland or St. Paul?

14. She is thinking quite (serious/(seriously)) about her job.

15. Would you like to join ((a)/an) union?

16. The size doesn't make ((any)/no) difference to me.

17. Ginny's story sounded ((suspicious)/suspiciously) to her friends.

18. The new tax laws on deductions are ((stricter)/more stricter) than the old ones.

19. This hamburger tastes (delicious/deliciously) with onions.

20. She felt very (bad/badly) about the wrecked car.

OUR CHANGING ENGLISH: A FINAL NOTE

"When I use a word," Humpty Dumpty said, in a rather scornful tone, "it means just what I choose it to mean—neither more nor less."

"The question is," said Alice, "whether you can make words mean so many different things."

"The question is," said Humpty Dumpty, "which is to be master—that's all."

—Lewis Carroll, *Through the Looking-Glass*

FROM SENTENCE TO PARAGRAPH: LEARNING LAUGHTER

Why is humor—the other side of feelings—so hard to communicate? How often have you heard (or said), "That's *not* funny"?

Each of us has an individual slant on what's funny, but in general, humor has several qualities:

1. The situation should be at least slightly unexpected—a play on words, for example.

2. It may involve conflict, including mild pain or confusion or discomfort, but the pain must be somewhat removed in time or relationship from the reader. Only if the reader doesn't immediately feel the pain will he or she see it as humorous.

3. It often involves "a little guy winning against a big guy"—a leveling effect, like that produced when a snowball knocks off a top hat or a dignified person slips on a banana peel. This is the effect that the king's jester (the Fool) tries to create.

4. Humor always offers the relief of feeling by making the conflicted situation more objective and therefore more bearable. "I had to laugh so I wouldn't cry." This shift of feeling makes it possible to adjust to difficult situations—even very fearsome, emotional situations like war, or sex, or final exams, or a visit from our in-laws. Humor makes us forget fear. It is therefore very important in our lives. Humans are perhaps the only creatures who can laugh. We laugh when we stand back just far enough. When we are too close, when we are very involved, it's often "not funny." But stand back, wait just a little, and the laughter bubbles up.

5. You may have noticed that teachers (and textbook writers) sometimes use (or try to use) humor in teaching or explaining. There's a very good reason. Humor helps communication.

People remember a funny rule or commercial long after a logical one. (Right now, think of an effective commercial—isn't it a humorous one?) Humor helps people to listen and remember.

Intentional humor isn't easy. But unintentional humor comes easily to us all. To see the funny side, we need to realize that we are all (deep inside) children, we are all (deep inside) fools, and certainly none of us is perfect. Then it's possible to laugh at most of our mistakes and therefore relax enough to learn from them.

High school English teacher Richard Lederer has collected funny mistakes in his books *Anguished English* and *More Anguished English*. On the next few pages are examples—most of them unintentionally hilarious. As you read these, try to decide whether the writer was trying to be humorous or simply slipped into miscommunication—and try to see how. Some of these examples from real life are dangling modifiers. Others are simply illogical. As you read them, have a good laugh, and then proofread your own writing to prevent unintentional humor. But remember that we all make mistakes, and that's how we learn. Keep an upbeat attitude, and learn even more.

Let's hope we can all laugh when things go slightly wrong—even when the joke is on us.

Letters to the Welfare Department from Applicants for Support

I am forwarding my marriage certificate and six children I have on half a sheet of paper.

I am writing the Welfare Department to say that my baby was born two years old. When do I get my money?

I am very much annoyed to find you have branded my son illiterate. This is a dirty lie as I was married a week before he was born.

I am forwarding my marriage certificate and three children, one of which is a mistake as you can see.

Unless I get my money soon, I will be forced to live an immortal life.

You have changed my little boy to a girl. Will this make a difference?

In accordance with your instructions I have given birth to twins in the enclosed envelope.

Humorous Headlines

Pocatello Mattress Factory Plays Important Role in City's Growth *(Pocatello State Journal)*

Most Lies About Blondes Are False *(Cincinnati Times Star)*

Drowning Can Ruin Fun in Water *(Marshallton Times-Republican)*

Traffic Dead Rise Slowly *(Hobbs, New Mexico, New-Sun)*

Car Leaves Road, Suffers Broken Nose *(Los Angeles Times)*

Weather Is Chief Cause of Drought *(Philadelphia Bulletin)*

Police Baffled by Suicide, Say Dead Man Had No Motive as He Was Unmarried *(Portland, Oregon, Reporter)*

Plane Hits Three Autos, Killing One *(Carlsbad Current-Argus)*

Man Shot in Head Accidentally Dies *(New Orleans Times-Picayune)*

Bridegroom of Three Months Dies in Action *(San Antonio Express)*

Escaped Leopard Believed Spotted *(Springfield, Massachusetts, Union)*

Miami Man Admits Taking His Own Life *(Orlando Sentinel)*

Divorces Are Fewer Among Single People, Chicago Figures Show *(Chicago Tribune)*

She Likes Babies but Doesn't Care About the Details *(Saginaw News)*

Father of Six Children Places Blame on Wife *(Lansing State Journal)*

Insuring Humor

Coming home, I drove into the wrong house and collided with a tree I didn't have.

I pulled away from the side of the road, glanced at my mother-in-law, and headed over the embankment.

I had been shopping for plants all day and was on my way home. As I reached an intersection, a hedge sprang up, obscuring my vision, and I did not see the other car.

My car was legally parked as I backed into the other vehicle.

An invisible car came out of nowhere, struck my car, and vanished.

The pedestrian had no idea which direction to run, so I ran over him.

The indirect cause of the accident was a little guy in a small car with a big mouth.

I was thrown from my car as it left the road. I was later found in a ditch by some stray cows.

The telephone pole was approaching fast. I attempted to swerve out of its way when I struck my front end.

Silly Science

When you smell an odorless gas, it is probably carbon monoxide.

The tides are in a fight between the Earth and the moon. All water tends toward the moon, because there is no water in the moon, and nature abhors a vacuum. I forget where the sun joins in this fight.

Three kinds of blood vessels are arteries, vanes, and caterpillars.

The moon is a planet just like the earth, only it is even deader.

Muddled Medical Advice

For nosebleed: Put the nose much lower than the body until the heart stops beating.

For dog bite: Put the dog away for several days. If he has not recovered, then kill it.

For asphyxiation: Apply artificial respiration until the patient is dead.

For drowning: Climb on top of the person and move up and down to make artificial perspiration.

To keep milk from turning sour: Keep it in the cow.

Paragraph Assignment   Have you noticed along your journey through this book that occasionally a voice seems to be speaking directly to you? Now's your chance to answer. Choose a quotation, and in an organized composition, explain how it relates to your life.

ANSWERS

Tryout: Preposition Usage

1. with; 2. with; 3. between; 4. with; 5. from; 6. into; 7. go; 8. opposite; 9. is; 10. should've.

Tryout: Choice of Preposition

1. to; 2. to; 3. about; 4. to; 5. of; 6. from; 7. from; 8. for; 9. to; 10. with; 11. about; 12. at; 13. for; 14. of; 15. with; 16. with; 17. with, upon; 18. with, to.

Tryout: Parallelism

1. The photocopier requires simple weekly maintenance and a mechanic. *thorough monthly checkup by* ~~to check it thoroughly every month.~~

2. You may apply for the job by mail, by telephone, or ~~coming into the office~~ in person.

3. Both teachers seem to be helpful and ~~have a lot of knowledge.~~ *knowledgeable*

4. To study daily is important, but reviewing ^to^ weekly also helps. [Or, Studying . . . , but reviewing. . . .]

5. This quiz will help you understand the basics of parallelism and applying them to your writing.

6. Either this announcement was written by Mrs. Elias or by her aide.

7. The Dean hasn't decided yet whether Joanna will do that job or Wanda.

8. Ms. Powell likes both teaching accounting and computer science.

9. Mr. Martin neither agreed with Mrs. Lee nor Mrs. Carillo.

10. The staff all agreed either to have a picnic or a dinner dance.

Tryout: Choice of Conjunction

1. Television can either be a time-waster or an educational tool.

2. She can't seem to study ~~without~~ ^unless^ she has music playing loudly.

3. She says the reason she does it is ~~because~~ ^that^ she wants to shut out noise.

4. Mr. Whittiker gives homework ~~like~~ ^as if^ there ~~is~~ ^were^ no tomorrow.

5. OK.

6. The teachers not only agreed on the hours but also on the schedule.

7. This book is both well written and ~~has~~ beautiful ^ly^ illustrations ^ed^.

8. The test is tomorrow, ~~and~~ ^but^ we are not worried about being ready.

9. Writing the paragraph is easy, but ~~to~~ correct ^ing^ it is harder. [Or, To write . . . ,
   but to correct. . . .]

10. She sets her clock ahead and pretends ~~like~~ ^that^ the time is later.

Tryout: Review of Adjective/Adverb Choices

1. gracefully; 2. well; 3. different; 4. foolishly; 5. well; 6. cheerful; 7. faster; 8.
most difficult; 9. any; 10. kinder; 11. anywhere; 12. well; 13. awkwardly; 14.
beautiful; 15. well; 16. badly; 17. delightful; 18. either; 19. closer; 20. any.

Tryout: Balance and Emphasis

1. Mrs. Black never has, and never will ^understood^ understand, why some students are
   always late.

2. Our courses are better, not just equal, to, theirs. *than*

3. The students have great admiration and faith in that teacher. *for*

4. The order was for a computer and desk. *a*

5. Her report was more original than John. *'s*

6. I noticed the students in that class seemed very interested. *that*

7. Should Ms. Hinkle sign the memo or Ms. Robertson?

8. Her first English class was six months ago, and so she needs to review *since (or Because)*

    before the comprehensive test.

9. I'd like to know where you can buy computer paper on sale. *I (or one)*

10. I wrote the chapter, and then the tests were prepared by me.

Appendix A

Grammar Summary: Glossary of Terms

Active and passive voice:	Terms that describe the relation of an action verb to the subject of a sentence. When the subject does the action ("People ate the fruit"), the sentence is active; if the subject is acted upon ("The fruit was eaten"), the sentence is passive.
Adjective:	A word used to describe or modify (*add* to) a noun or pronoun (the words used as sub*ject*s or ob*ject*s).
	A *young* dog a *big brown* bear a *worn* coat The dog is *small*.
Adjective clause:	A dependent clause that works like an adjective to describe or identify something or someone. Adjective clauses nearly always begin with a relative pronoun: *who, whom, whose, which, or that. See also* Clause.
	He consulted people *who are important*. [modifies *people*]
Adjective phrase:	A phrase, often prepositional, used as an adjective. *See also* Phrase.
	People *in good health* are lucky. [modifies *people*]
Adverb:	A word used to modify (*add* to) an action verb, adverb, or adjective—in other words, to modify the words that an adjective does not modify. Adverbs often end in "ly."
	A *very* small dog ran *quickly*.
Adverb intensifier:	A special class of adverbs—those that change the degree or intensity of an adjective or adverb: *very, quite, too, rather, somewhat,* and often *more* and *most. See* the example at Adverb.
Adverb clause:	A dependent clause that does the work of an adverb. Adverb clauses usually answer questions about action verbs, such as when, where, how, and under what conditions. The *adverb clause signal words* (subordinating conjunctions or markers) include:
	while, when, whenever, as, before, after, since (tell when)
	where, wherever (tell where)
	as if, as though (tell how)
	because, since, as, so that (tell why)
	if, unless, although, though (tell under what conditions)
	Pete awoke *when I called him*.

Note: An adverb or adjective clause standing alone produces one kind of incomplete sentence, a serious error in formal English sentences. *See also* Clause.

Adverb phrase:	A prepositional or similar phrase used as an adverb.
	The dog ran *into the house*.

Such phrases usually modify the verb of the sentence and may seem to modify the whole sentence. They can often be moved to a different part of the sentence (such as the beginning) without loss of meaning or style: *Into the house* ran the dog.

Ambiguous:	Having two or more possible meanings.
	five Spanish teachers two green boys' bikes

Appositive: A noun or pronoun phrase set after another noun or pronoun to rename it, to make more *positive* what is meant.

> Archibald, *our cat*, bit me.
> Jerry, *my locker partner with the red hair,* lost his key.

Clause: A group of related words containing a subject and a predicate (verb). There are two main kinds: An *independent clause* expresses a complete thought and can stand alone as a sentence. A *dependent clause* does not express a complete thought and cannot stand alone; its meaning is dependent upon or subordinate to the main, or independent, clause. It seems to lean on the main clause.

> Independent | Dependent
> We sent the telegram after we got his letter.

See also Adjective clause, Adverb clause, and Noun clause; these are the three kinds of dependent clauses.

Clause signal words (markers): *See* Conjunction.

Comma splice: The sentence error made when two independent clauses are joined as one sentence, with only a comma between them. This is insufficient punctuation; a semicolon, colon, or dash is required. This error may be marked CS, CF (for comma fault), or RO or RS (for run-on sentence) on corrected papers or copy.

> **INCORRECT**   The boy ran all the way home, he had forgotten his books.

See also Run-on sentence.

A comma splice can also be corrected by the addition of a conjunction such as *and* or *but* or a clause signal word such as *because* at the beginning of either clause.

Note: Merely adding words surrounded by commas does not correct the comma splice:

> **INCORRECT**   He was unhappy, therefore, he went home early.

Therefore is not a conjunction and doesn't help the situation at all.

It, although vague, can be a sentence subject and hence may incorrectly begin the second half of a comma splice sentence:

> **INCORRECT**   The weather was gloomy, it was raining.

The comma should be replaced by a semicolon:

> **CORRECT**   The weather was gloomy; it was raining.

See also Run-on sentence.

Complement: *See* Subject complement.

Complex sentence: A sentence containing an independent clause (possible sentence) and a dependent clause, such as an adjective or adverb clause. Think of *complex* as like "mixed."

> Tony can play the piano, although he has never had lessons.

See also Compound sentence and Simple sentence.

Compound sentence: A sentence containing two or more simple sentences joined with coordinating conjunctions (such as *and, but,* or *or*) or with a semicolon. Only related ideas of equal importance should be combined into a compound sentence.

> Our craft class made birdhouses, and the church sold them.

See also Complex sentence and Simple sentence.

Compound subject: Two (or more) subjects in a clause. *See also* Subject.

> *John* and *Marsha* sing together.

Compound verb: Two (or more) verbs in a clause. *See also* Verb and Predicate.

> Jack *ran* toward and *jumped* onto the steps.

Conjunction:	A word used to connect almost any words or groups of words into larger groups. The *coordinating* conjunctions are *and, but, or,* and *nor;* these join parts of equal importance. The clause signal words used for adverb clauses are sometimes called *subordinating* conjunctions; these join ideas of unequal importance. *See also* Adverb clause.

Fragment: A part of a sentence mistakenly punctuated as a whole sentence—usually a dependent clause or a phrase. Fragments are occasionally used in informal writing, such as advertising. The error may be abbreviated Frag; it is also called a "period fault."

> **INCORRECT**   My sister lives in Dania. *Although she works in Miami.*

This error can usually be corrected by joining the fragment to the related main clause, often with a comma between them.

See also Adverb clause, Adjective clause, and Noun clause.

Gerund: An "ing" form of a verb, used as a noun. A gerund can never be the complete verb of the sentence, because it does not show time.

> Singing is fun.
>
> His favorite exercise is swimming.

Grammar: The rules of structure and usage of a language.

Infinitive: The idea behind a verb, always with *to—to go* or *to see,* for example—often used as a noun. An infinitive can never be the verb of a sentence because it does not indicate past, present, or future—it is *infinite.*

Inflection: Any change in spelling that changes word meaning: singular to plural, present to past tense, or the like.

Intransitive verb: *See* Verb.

Noun: A person, place, thing, or idea. Common nouns, such as *boy, town, food,* and *woman,* are lowercased. Proper nouns, such as *Jim, Salinas, Pepsi,* and *Miss America,* are capitalized. Ideas are abstract nouns, such as *independence, beauty, kindness, confusion,* and *ignition* (note the typical endings). Collective nouns are words that mean a group, such as *class, flock, jury,* and *herd.* Some are "count" nouns, such as *tables* and *girls;* some are "mass" nouns such as *applesauce* and *homework,* which are not pluralized. Any word or phrase used as a noun is called *nominal.*

Noun clause: A clause used as a noun, as a subject or object in the sentence.

> He said *that he would go.* [object of *said*]
>
> *When he would go* was the question. [subject]

Object, direct: A noun or pronoun receiving the action of the verb or showing the result. It is abbreviated DO.

> S   AV   DO
> Dad repaired the motor. [answers the question, repaired what?]

Direct and indirect objects can be used only with action verbs. *See also* Verb. Objects are also forms of complements. *See also* Subject complement.

Object, indirect: A noun or pronoun placed before the direct object of the verb, to show to whom, from whom, for whom, or for what the action is done, without saying the *to, for,* or the like. An indirect object (abbreviated IO) can be used only in *front* of a direct object.

> S   AV   IO   DO
> Pam told Helen a secret.

Object of preposition: The noun or pronoun following the preposition in a phrase.

> in the *house*   to the *store*   between the two *trees*

See also Preposition.

Participle:

A *part* of a verb, used with a helping verb to form past or present tenses and sometimes used alone or in a phrase as an adjective.

CORRECT The coat is *torn* at the elbows. [part of verb]

the *torn* coat [adjective]

The girl was *singing*. [part of verb]

the *singing* girl [adjective]

The typewriter *sitting* on the desk is mine. [adjective (participial) phrase]

When used as an adjective, the participle must be next to the noun or pronoun it modifies.

INCORRECT *Running into the room*, the typewriter fell over. [dangling participle—no logical noun or pronoun to modify]

I heard the dog bark, *eating my lunch*. [misplaced participle—not next to pronoun modified]

Phrase:

A related group of two or more words that does not contain a predicate, that is, it has no verb. The most common is the prepositional phrase.

Predicate:

The part of the sentence containing the verb and its modifiers. It usually (but not always) begins with the verb and is the second half of the sentence. *See* Verb.

Predicate adjective or noun:

See Subject complement.

Preposition:

A word that usually relates the noun or pronoun that follows it to a previous noun or pronoun or to the verb in the sentence. Prepositions show primarily *position* (note the word relationship)—in time, direction, and possession. All prepositions in formal English begin phrases. *See* Prepositional phrase.

Prepositional phrase:

A group of words that begins with a preposition and ends with its object. It is usually said to modify (change or expand the meaning of) the closest noun or pronoun in the sentence or the verb.

```
          AV   prep  obj of prep
```
Fred works *for   his uncle*. [modifies verb]

He came *into the house*. [modifies verb]

The man *of the house* is my uncle. [modifies noun]

Prewriting:

Preliminary planning and outlining before making a rough draft of formal writing.

Pronoun:

A word used in place of a specific noun previously mentioned. It should be used only when the noun (antecedent) is quite clear.

My sister started *her* car.   Then *she* drove away.

The *personal pronouns* are:

I   he   she   we   they [subject pronouns]
me   him   her   us   them [object pronouns]
you   it [both subject and object]

The main *relative pronouns* are:

which   that   who   whose   whom

The following words are either pronouns or adjectives, depending on use:

this   some   many   both   these   all   each

The *possessive pronouns* are:

mine   yours   his   hers   ours   theirs   its

For a discussion of the *indefinite pronouns*, such as *each, every,* and *somebody,* see page 210.

Relative pronoun:	A "clause signal" word that begins an adjective or noun dependent clause: *who, whose, whom, which, that, whoever,* and the like. These words both connect (like conjunctions) and refer (like usual pronouns).
Run-on sentence:	The sentence error made when two independent clauses are joined together as one sentence with no punctuation or insufficient punctuation (such as a comma) between them. It is abbreviated RO or RS. *See also* Comma splice and Clause.
Rule of *s:*	A present-tense verb that has *s* added to its base is always singular. When you add an *s* to a subject to make it plural, do not add an *s* to the verb. When you add an *s* to the verb, do not add *s* to the subject. The subject and verb in English do not match, as they would in Spanish, Italian, and some other languages.

Boys run.   The boy run*s*.   Girl*s* climb.   The girl climb*s*.

Sentence patterns:	One modern way of labeling and classifying sentence structure.

SUBJECT–ACTION VERB

S   AV
Birds fly.

SUBJECT–ACTION VERB–DIRECT OBJECT

S   AV   DO
Tom hit the ball.

SUBJECT–BEING VERB–SUBJECT COMPLEMENT

S   BV SC
The road through town is short.

Simple sentence:	A sentence consisting of one independent clause and no other clauses.

S   V
John plays the piano.

A simple sentence *may* have a compound subject and/or a compound verb but cannot be divided into separate clauses with a subject and verb in each.

S   S   AV   AV   AV
Tom and his sister Angela can play the piano but have never taken lessons.

See also Complex sentence and Compound sentence.

Subject:	A word or group of words naming the thing or person spoken about or doing the action. *See also* Verb.

Max is my dog. [simple subject]

The clock on the wall tells time. [complete subject]

To find the subject, ask who or what did the action of the verb or equals the word after a being verb. Who is my dog? Max. What tells time? The clock on the wall.

Subject complement:	A word that follows a linking or being verb and describes or further identifies the subject of the sentence. It is abbreviated SC. It may be an adjective (also called a *predicate adjective*) or a noun (also called a *predicate noun* or *predicate nominative*).

S BV SC
John is *tall*. [adjective type]

S   V   SC
Bob will be *captain*. [noun type]

Subordinating conjunctions:	Also called clause signal words or markers. *See* Adverb clause.
Transitive verb:	*See* Verb.

Verb:	A word or group of words showing *action* or state of *being* and time. Being verbs are also called *linking* verbs. Verbs show by a change in spelling whether the action or being is past, present, future, or conditional (that is, they change tense). They are called *finite* because they show time. To find the verb, change the time of the sentence; the word or words that change will be the verb.

Birds *fly*.   Birds *flew*.   Birds *will fly*.   Birds *have flown*.
Arthur *is* happy.   Arthur *was* happy.   Arthur *will be* happy.
Arthur *has been* happy.

After finding the verb, you can find the subject easily by asking who or what did the action or who or what equals the word after the verb. You can also find the direct object easily by asking what noun or pronoun received the action of an action verb.

Verb, action:	A verb that shows action in the sense of doing. Action verbs that can take a direct object are called *transitive*; those that need a preposition between verb and object are called *intransitive*. Transitive verbs can also show action received by the subject.

$$\text{S} \quad \underline{\text{AV}}$$
The book was laid on the table.

For conjugations of regular and irregular verbs, see Chapters 26 and 27.

Verb, being or linking:	Any form of *be* plus verbs such as *seem, look, become, grow, taste,* and *feel,* when these carry a meaning like "is."
Verb, helping or auxiliary:	An "extra" verb used before a participle to create a complete verb by showing the tense. The helping verbs are *shall, will, may, can, could, would, should, did, does, do, done, must, might, ought, have, has, had* (when used with participles), and all forms of *be—is, am, are, was, were, been.*
Voice:	*See* Active and passive voice.
Who, whom:	The most difficult of the pronouns to use correctly. *Who* is used when the pronoun is the subject (much like *he*); *whom* is used when it is an object (much like *him*). Try substituting *he* or *him* either in the sentence or clause or in answer to the question the sentence is asking.

I have a cousin *who* visits my sister. [*He* visits.]
I have a cousin *whom* my sister visits. [She visits *him*.]
To *whom* did you send the box? [I sent it to *him*.]

Whom is dying out in *spoken* English except after prepositions such as *to*.

Appendix B: Spelling It Out

English spelling is difficult for some developmental English students; for others, relatively simple. (Some people seem to have been born with a "spelling gene.") But there are ways of solving the problem. Research shows that the average person's memory works in the following ways. We tend to remember: 10 percent of what we read, 20 percent of what we hear, 30 percent of what we see (film, pictures), 40 percent of what we experience (kinesthetic), 70 percent of what we see *and* hear. The best ways to memorize seem to use as many combinations of the above methods as possible. In addition, students who have difficulties in the average classroom seem to be less visually oriented than average. For these students, memory aids using pictures, aural previews, and kinesthetic practice are especially important.

In a developmental English class, previewing and testing about 25 words weekly (the number in each of the lists in this appendix) seems to be a good average pace. Remind students that passing spelling tests is much less important than using and spelling these words correctly in their writing. After students have had a chance to review and practice missed words, schedule certain days for makeup tests to give students one more chance to pass.   Because students will need to use their dictionaries less, the lists in this appendix will save much writing and editing time and will in the long run raise students' grades and confidence.

Appendix B

Spelling and Pronunciation: Rules and Lists

Review of Basic Spelling and Pronunciation Rules

1. Separate syllables ending in vowels usually carry the long vowel sound (they "say their own name").

gra-vy   *be*-cause   *hi*-jack   *go*-ing   *mu*-sic

However, sometimes the *a* is short, especially when unaccented.

ga-rage

2. Two vowels together usually carry the sound of the first one.

bead   coat   braid   lie

3. When syllables are added to a word that ends with a silent *e*, the *e* is usually dropped.

tune, tuning   face, facing   save, savable   love, lovable.

4. The letters *g* and *c* in English are usually hard before "deep throat" vowels such as *a*, *o*, and *u* and soft before the "higher" vowels, *e*, *i*, and *y*.

go   cat   gut   cut
city   gem   gym   cell

5. For *ie/ei* syllables that are pronounced like a long *e*, put *i* before *e* except after *c*.

grieve   relief   receive

6. **This is the most useful spelling rule: After an accented short vowel, double the consonant that follows the vowel when you are adding a syllable to the word. Don't double the consonant if the short vowel isn't accented.**

shop, shopping   defer, deferring   refer, reference

Memory Peg

Lists of 250 Commonly Misspelled Words with Memory Pegs

The words are presented in lists of 25 to allow for memorization and practice. They are alphabetized so you can find a word easily. Use the space at the bottom of each page to include your own individual spelling demons.

List A	Memory Pegs	List A	Memory Pegs
acceptable	has one hard and one soft *c*	accompanying	to "keep company" with; the *y* must be pronounced
accident	has one hard and one soft *c*	accounting	related to *count*
accommodate	to make comfortable, as in *commode;* has a double *c* too	accumulate	like *cumulus* clouds—gathered in

ache	needs a silent *e* for the long *a*
achieve	*i* before *e*
acknowledgment	like *knowledge*; may also be spelled with an extra *e* by some style guides
acquaintance	like *quaint*
acquire	has a common *ac* prefix
across	like *cross*
advantageous	needs an *e* to keep the *g* soft (*g* is soft before *e*, *i*, and *y*)
affidavit	"fi" means "faith" or "sworn to"—a sworn statement
all right	still the only accepted spelling
almost	means "nearly," not *all most*

List B	Memory Pegs
appropriate	means "proper"
argument	already has a long *u*, so doesn't need an *e*
arrangement	like *arrange*
assistant	like *assist*
athlete	two syllables only
automation	like *auto* or *automatic*
auxiliary	means "helping" (also one *l*) or "extra"
baggage	has an accented short *a*, so double the *g*
banquet	related to *bank*
beginning	has an accented short *i*, so double the *n*
believable	*i* before *e* with a long *e* sound; drop the silent *e* in *believe*
beneficial	like *benefit* and Latin for "good"

List C	Memory Pegs
comparative	like *compare* without the *e*
comprehensive	sound out the syllables: com-pre-hen-sive
compromise	to *promise* "with"
confident	like *confide*—if you have faith in someone, you confide and are confident
confidential	like *confide*
congratulate	not like *graduate*
conscience	like *science*
conscientious	like *science* and *scientific*; related to knowledge within
contagious	the *g* is soft before an *i*
container	like *contain*

already	it's an adverb, meaning "sooner than expected," not *all ready*
always	means "forever"—not *all ways*
amendment	means "mended"
analysis	like *analyze*
analyze	like *analysis*
annuity	like *annual*
answered	in Old English all the letters were pronounced; now the *w* and *e* are silent
apparent	related to *appear* but with an *a* spelling and sound
appearance	like *appear*

List B	Memory Pegs
bookkeeping	has three double letters in a row
brilliant	means "shining"
bulletin	like *bullet*
business	from *busy* with "ness"
calendar	"dar" ending for the word with "dates"
can't	the apostrophe shows where one or more letters are omitted
ceiling	"except after *c*"
certain	from the French word; the *a* is silent in English
changeable	needs an *e* to keep the *g* soft
collateral	*collected* to one side (*lateral*)
color	pretend it's pronounced Spanish style with long *o*'s
coming	has an odd old pronunciation
committee	has an accented short *i*, so double the *t*; this word has three doubles

List C	Memory Pegs
contingent	the *g* is soft; *contingent on* means "based on" or "depending on"
continuous	sound out the four syllables: con-tin-u-ous
convenience	separate into syllables: con-ve-ni-ence
convenient	con-ve-ni-ent
coordinate	going together—co-order
could	an Anglo-Saxon word; the *l* used to be pronounced
country	like *count*—we measure borders
courteous	related to *court*, where etiquette began
criticism	like *critic*
criticize	like *critic*

definitely	like *finite*
deliberate	sound out the syllables: de-lib-er-ate
delinquent	note the *n* before the *q*

List D	Memory Pegs
description	"de" plus "scription" (*not* "dis")
desirable	drop the silent *e* of *desire* before adding a vowel
development	like *develop*, which has no *e* at the end
dictionary	like *diction*, related to words
didn't	use the apostrophe where the letter is left out
difference	like *differ*
different	it "differs"
dining	has a long *i*, so no double *n*
disappear	"dis," meaning "not," appear
disappointed	"dis" plus *appointed*—because not appointed?
dissatisfied	"dis" plus *satisfied*
divide	*di* means "two"
document	sound out the syllables: doc-u-ment
does	not like a dose of something

List E	Memory Pegs
excellent	in a "cell" by itself
exorbitant	"ex-orb" means "out of orbit"—beyond the usual
experience	sound out the syllables: ex-pe-ri-ence
explanation	from *explain*, but there is no accent on the first *a* so no extra vowel
extension	like *extend*, but note the *s*
familiar	like *family*
fascinating	related to *fascist* (group)—means "tightly drawn toward"
feasible	means "practical," not just "possible"
February	listen for the first *r*
finally	*final* plus "ly"
foreign	not a long *e*, so it doesn't follow the *i* before *e* rule
forty	drop the *u* in *four* and spell this in short style

List F	Memory Pegs
hoping	has a long *o*, so don't double the *p*
immediately	*immediate* and "ly"
inconvenience	sound out the syllables: in-con-ve-ni-ence

depreciate	is the opposite of *appreciate*
describe	not "dis" anything—"de"

List D	Memory Pegs
doesn't	like *does*
don't	use the apostrophe where the letter is left out
elementary	like *element*
eligible	accented on the first letter, unlike *illegible*; *i* after soft *g*; means "qualified"
eliminate	related to *mini*
embarrass	double both the *r* and the *s* or you'll be embarrassed
endorsement	*endorse* means "to guarantee value"—of a check, a person, or a product
enough	has an Anglo-Saxon guttural ending that is often pronounced *f*
equipped	has an accented short *i*, so double the *p*
especially	like *special*
every	like *ever*

List E	Memory Pegs
friends	*i* before *e*
fulfill	one single *l* and one double; don't double both
furniture	like *furnish*
generally	*general* and "ly"
government	pronounce it carefully—like *govern*
grammar	like *grammatical*, it has an *a* after the double *m*
guarantee	"gu" is always a hard *g*
guess	"gu" is always a hard *g*
half	has a silent *l*
having	drop the silent *e* of *have* before adding a vowel
hazard	not like Hazzard County, Kentucky
height	*i* before *e* doesn't work here because there isn't a long *e*
hoarse	when you're ill and ho*a*rse, you open your mouth and say "*a*h"(!)

List F	Memory Pegs
independent	no *a* in any related words (such as *dependent*, *independence*, *dependence*) except *pendant*
instead	"in stead" means "in place"

interesting	sound out the syllables: in-ter-est-ing
interfere	accented on "fere"—long *e*
isn't	use the apostrophe where the letter is left out
itinerary	sound out the syllables: i-tin-er-ar-y; means "a trip schedule"
knowledge	things you *know*
laboratory	where you *labor*
lady's	belonging to one lady
laid	the long *a* needs a "helping vowel"
language	sound out the syllables: lan-guage; "gu" is always a hard *g*
ledger	like *ledge*
legitimate	accent the second syllable as you sound it out: le-git-i-mate

List G	Memory Pegs
maneuver	the *eu* comes from the French *oeuvre*, which means "work"
many	has an odd pronunciation
meant	has an odd old pronunciation as a short *e* although it looks like a long *e*
minimum	like *mini*
minute	there are two pronunciations and two meanings: with a short *i* and *u*, "60 seconds"; with a long *i* and *u*, "tiny"
miscellaneous	has *cell* in the middle
mortgage	like Latin and French *mort*, which means "death"
ninety	like *nineteen*, has an extra *e*; not like *ninth*
ninth	you don't hear an *e* anyplace in the word, so don't use one
nonessential	like *essential*
noticeable	needs the *e* to keep the *c* soft, not like *cable*

List H	Memory Pegs
pleasant	almost like *please*
possession	the "ssion" is pronounced like "shun"
practical	like *practice* without the *e*
preceding	like *precede,* but drop the last *e* before adding a vowel
predictable	*predict* means "say ahead of time"
preferred	has an accented short *e*, so double the *r*
principal	has three meanings: "main," "main person," and "main amount of money"

liaison	li-ai-son; a French word, meaning "a confidential meeting" or "persons who meet"
library	sound out the syllables: li-brar-y
license	always starts with "lic"; British spelling is "licence"
lien	this spelling means "legal claim"
losing	drop the silent *e* of *lose* before adding a vowel
loving	drop the silent *e* of *love* before adding a vowel
maintenance	no accent on the middle syllable, so shorten it
making	drop the silent *e* of *make* before adding a vowel
management	needs an *e* to keep the *g* soft

List G	Memory Pegs
occasion	"sion" with one *s* is pronounced "zhion"; with *ss*, as in *mission*, it's pronounced "shun"
occurrence	accented short *u*, so double the *r*—not pronounced like *cure*
off	not *of*
often	either silent or sounded *t*
omitted	has an accented short *i*, so double the *t*
opportunity	like *port*—an opening
original	like *origin*
pamphlet	"ph" sounds like *f*
parallel	has two parallel lines in the center
partial	in part
performance	like *perform*
permanent	sound out the syllables: per-ma-nent
personnel	each *person* in the office staff
persuade	sound out the syllables: per-suade

List H	Memory Pegs
privilege	means "private *leg*al right"—see the "leg"?
probably	not *probable*
procedure	like *proceed* but move one *e* to the end
prohibit	means forbid
pronunciation	sound out the syllables: pro-nun-ci-a-tion
pursue	you pursue a stolen *purse*
quantity	listen to the sound of *t* twice

questionnaire	the only word like this that doubles the *n*; *millionaire* has fewer letters
really	*real* plus "ly"
receive	"except after *c*"
recommend	"re" plus *commend*—to commend again
reference	like *refer*
referred	has an accented short *e* so double the *r*

List I	Memory Pegs
separate	divide into *parts*
shining	has a long *i*, so no double *n*
similar	sound out the syllables: sim-i-lar
since	pronounce the *i* carefully
sincerely	like *sincere*
specifically	sound out the syllables exactly: spe-cif-i-cal-ly
speech	not like *speak*
stopped	has an accented short *o*, so double the *p*
straight	has an old guttural sound that is now silent
strength	has seven consonants and one vowel
stretch	has six consonants and one vowel
studying	you must pronounce the *y*
succeed	has one hard and one soft *c*

List J	Memory Pegs
threw	past tense of *throw*
through	a preposition, with an old Anglo-Saxon guttural ending that is now silent
tired	has a long *i*, so only one *r*
together	not *gather*
tonight	like *night*
toward	like *forward*—"ward" means "general direction"
trouble	from the French; has a silent *o*
truly	long *u* does not need an *e* because of the *y*
Tuesday	abbreviated "Tue"
undoubtedly	like *doubt*
unnecessary	"cess" is the common spelling for this sound
until	unlike *till*
used	pronounced often with a *t* sound, as in "used to"

repetition	the short *e* after *p* is unaccented
sandwich	like a British county—sound out the syllables: sand-wich
schedule	has a hard *c* and a silent *h*
secretary	keeper of *secrets*
securities	has the standard plural ending for a consonant and *y*

List I	Memory Pegs
success	has one hard and one soft *c*; this is the most common spelling for the "cess" sound
sufficient	like *suffices*, it's enough
sugar	has a common but odd pronunciation
summarize	like *summary*
surprise	not like *prize*—some surprises are not good!
taking	drop the silent *e* of *take* before adding a vowel
territory	a little like *terra*, which means "earth"
than	like *as*, it's a conjunction
then	means "later"; it's an adverb
therefore	this spelling means "for this reason"
thorough	has two syllables and a silent ending
though	has an Anglo-Saxon guttural sound that is now often silent

List J	Memory Pegs
usually	*usual* and "ly"
voluntary	like *volunteer*
Wednesday	pretend it has three syllables: Wed-nes-day; named after the old Norse god Woden
where	sounds like "hw" (in Old English it was spelled that way!)
which	beginning pronounced like "hw"
woman	like *man*
women	pronounced oddly, spelled to match *men*
won't	has a long *o*; the apostrophe stands for the omitted *o* of *not*
wouldn't	an old silent *l*; use the apostrophe where the letter is left out
writing	has a long *i*, so use only one *t*
written	has an accented short *i*, so double the *t*
wrote	has a long *o*, which needs a silent *e*

Appendix C

Homonyms and Pseudohomonyms

Homonyms are words that sound alike; pseudohomonyms sound almost alike (*pseudo* means "fake"). Here's an annotated list of some of the most common word pairs that confuse people. For further lists, consult a large reference manual. Memory pegs for parts of words are in italics.

Word	Meaning	Word	Meaning
addition	noun: the process of taking a sum; a thing that has been *add*ed	bare	adjective: empty, plain, nude, open
edition	noun: a publication that has been *edit*ed by an *edit*or	bear	noun, a large furry animal; verb: to carry or withstand ("He bears a heavy burden"); also to give birth to ("She will bear a child in April")
affect	verb: to change ("Cold weather affects me")		
effect	noun: a change ("The weather had *an* effect on me")	berth	a place of rest, for example, on a ship or sleeper train
aisle	a walkway, as in a church or school	birth	the process of bringing forth, for example, a child or an idea
isle	an island		
allusion	a reference to a related thing or idea ("The poem made an allusion to a line in *King Lear*")	born	past participle of the verb *bear* meaning "give birth" ("The child was born at 2:27 a.m.")
illusion	a vision, frequently mistaken ("He was under the illusion that he was irresistible")	borne	past participle of verb *bear*, meaning "carry or withstand" (She has borne many hardships in her lifetime")
altar	the place at the front of a church that is the focal point of worship		
alter	to change	brake	noun: a mechanism for stopping a car or process; verb: to stop
are	present tense plural of verb *be*	break	noun: a respite; a separation; verb: to come apart forcefully
our	possessive pronoun: belonging to us		
ascent	noun: a climb, a movement upward	canvas	noun: a coarsely woven tough material, used for tents and the like
assent	verb: to agree; to say yes		
bail	noun: a deposit or bond given to assure that an accused person who is released from custody will appear at trial; verb: to deposit bail to get a person out of *jail*; also to remove water from the inside of a boat	canvass	verb: to solicit funds, votes, or the like
		censer	a container for in*cense*
		censor	a person who removes parts considered unauthorized or inappropriate from a work such as a letter or motion picture
bale	noun: a large bund*le*—for example, of paper, cotton, or hay		

Word	Meaning
cereal	noun: an edible grain, named for the Greek goddess *Ceres*
serial	adjective: occurring in a set of consecutive items (a *series*)
cite	verb: to refer to or note an action or statement, usually in writing ("She cited Shakespeare for the quotation"; "The sergeant was cited for bravery")
sight	noun: vision; ability to see; also a notable place seen
site	noun: location; the place where something, such as a camp or building *sits*
coarse	adjective: rough, the opposite of fine—for example, coarse fabric, hair, or words
course	a series of points along a *route*—for example, a race course, golf course, or course of study
complement	noun: a person or thing that *completes* or balances another ("The tomato sauce is a delicious complement for the chicken"); in grammar, the words that complete the sentence after a being verb ("He is *happy*"); verb: to complete or balance ("Harry's outgoing nature complements Marie's shyness")
compliment	noun: a flattering remark, a *nice* comment; verb: to say something nice, to give a compliment
council	noun: a governing board, especially of a *city* or the like
counsel	noun: advice; an advisor—for example, legal counsel; verb: to advise ("Noah counsels patients in a drug-abuse program")
descent	noun: a movement downward
dissent	verb: to *disagree*; to say no; to rebel
desert	noun, accented on the first syllable: a dry area with little vegetation; verb, accented on the second syllable: to leave, usually a place or person, to disappear, to leave empty

Word	Meaning
dessert	noun, accented on the second syllable: a sweet food served at the end of a meal—a French word related to *desert*, it is brought to the table after the table has been cleared or "deserted"
detract	to lessen value ("The trash detracted from the appearance of the yard")
distract	to take attention away ("Distract that hungry child until dinner is ready")
device	noun, pronounced with a soft *c*: an item created
devise	verb, with an *s* pronounced *z*: to create
disburse	to give out funds or material in a business situation
disperse	to scatter ("The police dispersed the crowd")
disinterested	objective, impartial, having no financial or emotional interest in the result ("The defendant wanted a disinterested jury")
uninterested	not paying attention, not interested
disapprove	to not approve ("My mother disapproves of cheating on one's income tax")
disprove	to prove false ("The witness disproved the defendant's alibi")
dual	adjective: double—for example, dual carburetors
duel	noun: a fight between two people, now illegal, formerly fought to the death; verb: to fight a duel
elicit	verb: to draw forth ("The teacher elicited answers")
illicit	adjective: unlawful; literally "shady, not lighted" ("He was charged with possession of illicit drugs")
eligible	qualified ("At eighteen, they are eligible to vote")
illegible	not legible, not readable

Word	Meaning
emigrate	to go out of a country, to *exit*
immigrate	to come *into* a country
expand	to grow larger, have a "wider *span*"
expend	to *spend*—for example, money or energy
extant	adjective: exist*ant*, the opposite of extinct;
extent	noun: the deg*ree*, range, or scope of something
fiscal	related to funds, money, a tax year
physical	related to material goods ("They sold the physical assets of the business when the fiscal assets were gone")
grate	noun: a pattern, usually in metal, of crossed pieces—for example, in a fireplace or across a window; verb: to scrape food or other matter into pieces using a utensil with such a pattern; also to annoy, disturb, or irritate emotionally
great	adjective: very large; very good
hear	verb: to discern with the *ear*
here	adverb: in this place, the opposite of "*there*"
heard	past tense of verb *hear*
herd	a group of animals, such as cattle
holy	revered in a religion
wholly	completely
human	noun: a person; adjective: having the qualities of a person
humane	adjective: kind, considerate, compassionate
ingenious	full of *genius*, clever
ingenuous	very naive, innocent, have the qualities of an *ingenue*, the innocent heroine in a melodrama
instance	a happening, an example
instants	plural of instant, meaning "moments"

Word	Meaning
lead	noun, pronounced to rhyme with *said*: a heavy metal; verb, pronounced to rhyme with *seed*: to guide by going in advance, the opposite of to follow
led	past tense and past participle of the verb *lead* ("She led them to water," "They were easily led")
lean	adjective: the opposite of fat; verb: to incline ("Lean the boards against the building")
lien	noun: a legal claim on property, frequently because of an unpaid bill
leased	past tense of verb *lease,* meaning "rent for a specified period of time, usually with a contract"
least	superlative of adjective *little* ("He was the least likely to succeed")
lesser	comparative of the adjective *little* between two items: ("Pat chose the lesser of the two pieces of cake")
lessor	a person who leases property to another for rent, a landlord
loan	noun: an item given temporarily to another; also now accepted as a verb: to lend
lone	adjective: only, alone, single
medal	noun: an object, usually made of *metal,* given to award an action or to recognize excellence
meddle	verb: to interfere in a situation unasked and unwanted
moral	adjective: ethical, good, right
morale	noun: the good mood or feeling of worth of a person or group ("His morale was high")
miner	a person working in a mine
minor	noun: a person under voting age; adjective: of little importance
overdo	verb: to *do* too much
overdue	adjective: past *due*—for example, a bill

Word	Meaning	Word	Meaning
pain	noun: extreme discomfort; verb: to inflict discomfort	reality	noun: the quality of being real
pane	noun: a flat surface, for example, of glass or bedding	realty	noun: real estate, property consisting of land or buildings
patience	ability to wait without agitation	recent	adjective, accented on the first syllable: not long ago
patients	plural of *patient*, a person under a doctor's care	resent	verb, accented on the second syllable: when the *s* is pronounced *z*, to feel angry about an event or a situation; when the *s* is pronounced *s*, sent again
picture	a de*pict*ion of something, for example, a painting or photograph		
pitcher	a container for a liquid; also a baseball player	right	adjective: correct; the opposite of left—these two meanings illustrate a prejudice in the Middle Ages against the left-handed, who were thought to be "sinister"
presence	abstract noun: being here, attendance, the opposite of *absence*		
presents	noun, accented on the first syllable: gifts; verb, accented on the second syllable: gives	rite	noun: a *rit*ual or planned series of events
		wright	noun: a worker in wood or a similar substance
principal	noun: the main person, the main money ("Mike's savings book listed his principal and interest); adjective: main or primary	write	verb: to inscribe letters on a surface
		shined	past tense of transitive verb *shine*, which takes an object ("I shined the shoes")
principle	noun: ru*le* ("They studied the principles of grammar," "He adhered to high principles")	shone	past tense of intransitive verb *shine*, which does not take an object ("The sun shone brightly on the pavement")
prophecy	noun, pronounced to rhyme with *see*: prediction		
prophesy	verb, pronounced to rhyme with *sigh*: to predict	shown	past participle of verb *show* ("He has shown me the paper")
quiet	adjective: the opposite of *noisy*	sleight	noun: deceitful craftiness; also adroitness and dexterity ("Sleight of hand is an almost unnoticeable hand movement used by magicians")
quit	verb, pronounced to rhyme with *fit*: to stop		
quite	adverb: very		
raise	verb, transitive: to lift something or cause something to go up	slight	noun: a humiliating discourtesy; verb: to neglect, to treat poorly; adjective: barely discernible in size or amount
raze	verb: to tear down—related to *razor*		
rap	noun: a knock; also an informal talk, a type of informal "talking song"; verb: to knock; also to talk informally, to sing a rap song	sole	noun: the bottom of a foot or shoe; also an edible fish shaped a little like the bottom of a shoe; adjective: only
wrap	noun: material used to enclose or surround, for example, a gift or a woman's shoulders; verb: to enclose or envelop ("He wrapped the puppy in his arms")	soul	noun: the spirit; adjective: related to the spirit or spiritual things; also related to African-American culture, for example, music or food

Word	Meaning	Word	Meaning
some	pronoun or adjective: a few, a small amount	vain	adjective: thinking very highly of oneself; also futile or useless ("She made a vain attempt to become fabulously wealthy")
sum	noun: the total quantity; verb: to add together	vane	a turning blade, especially one moved by wind ("The weather vane was spinning in the storm")
stake	a sharpened piece of wood or metal, usually used to mark boundaries of property; also used figuratively to represent property or an interest ("The Peabodys had a stake in the issue")	vein	a circulatory vessel that takes deoxygenated blood back to the lungs for oxygen
steak	a slice of meat, usually tender, from an animal or fish	wait	noun: a period of expectancy or watchfulness; verb: to expect, to defer until later
stationary	adjective: standing in position, not moving	weight	noun: the amount of mass of an object or person in pounds, kilograms, or the like
stationery	noun: paper and envelopes for writing letters		
statue	a sculpture, usually representing a person	waive	verb: to give up a legal right ("The defendant waived his right to a jury trial")
statute	a law	wave	noun: a recurrent curved motion of matter—for example, an ocean wave, a wave of the hand, or a radio wave; verb: to move back and forth in a curved motion
straight	adjective: uncurving, without bends or angles ("Two straight parallel lines are the same distance apart at any point along them")		
strait	noun: a narrow neck of water connecting two large bodies of water	weather	noun: the climate, especially changes in rainfall and temperature
suit	noun: an outfit of clothing; verb: to fit or be appropriate	whether	conjunction: if, expressing a question about two or more alternatives ("He asked whether she would marry him")
suite	noun: a group of interconnecting rooms, often in a hotel		

When you're not sure which word is the right one, look it up. The computer doesn't know which word you want.

Appendix D

Prefixes and Suffixes; Word Division

Prefixes are syllables added at the beginnings of root, or base, words. Suffixes are syllables added to the ends of root words. When you know the meanings of the most common prefixes and suffixes, you'll have excellent clues to meanings of the longer words. **"Pre"** means **"before;"** **"suff"** is related to **"sufficient."**

Memory Peg

Prefixes

Sometimes the spelling of a prefix changes to make the word easier to spell or pronounce. For example, the prefix *ad,* which means "to" or "for," can be spelled *a, ac, af, ag, al, an, ap, ar, as,* or *at.*

Prefix	Meaning of Prefix	Examples
ab (a, abs)	from, away, off	abject, absent
ad (a, ac, af, ag, al, an, ap, ar, as, at)	to, toward, for	adhere, admire
ante	before, prior to	antedate, antecedent
anti (ant, anth)	against, opposite	antifreeze, antitrust
bi	two, twice	bimonthly, binary
circum	around, about	circumscribe
com (co, col, con)	with, together	companion, collate, connect
contra (contro)	against, contrary	contradict, contraband
de	do the opposite, down	degrade, deprive
dia (di)	through, across	diagram, diameter
dis (di, dif)	separate, away	discontinue, digress, diffuse
ex (e, ef, es)	out of, former	expire, escape, ex-mayor
extra (extro)	outside, beyond	extraordinary, extrovert
in (ig, il, im, ir, en)	in, on, into, not	inland, ignore, illegal
inter	between, among	intervene, interview
intra	within	intrastate, intravenous
intro	inward, toward	introduce, introvert
mis	wrongly, badly	miscount, misjudge
non	not	nonentity, nondurable
ob (oc, of, op)	against, over	obstacle, oppress
per	through, throughout	persistence, pertain
post	after, behind	postdate, postwar
pre	before, prior, advance	previous, premature

Prefix	Meaning of Prefix	Examples
pro	take place, favor	prolong, promote
re	back, again	rebuild, repay, repeat
retro	backward	retroactive, retrospect
semi	half, partly	semiannual, semitrailer
sub (suc, suf, sug, sus)	under, below	subcontractor, suspect
super	over, above, more	supersensitive, superior
trans	across, over, beyond	transaction, transmit
ultra	beyond in space	ultraformal, ultraviolet
un	not, removal	unafraid, unhappy
uni	one, single	uniform, unified

Suffixes

Suffixes frequently can be classified by the part of speech that they usually represent—noun, adjective, verb, adverb, and versatile suffixes that represent more than one part.

Verb suffixes denote "to make."

Suffix	Example	Meaning of Example
fy	satisfy	to make sated (full)
ize (ise)	idolize	to make worship of idols

Noun suffixes denote "one who," "state of," "act of," "place of," "characteristic of," "art of," and "that which."

Suffix	Example	Meaning of Example
age	breakage	that which is broken
ance (ancy)	performance	act of performing
ard (art)	dullard	one who is dull
cy	accuracy	state of being accurate
dom	freedom	state of being free
ee	grantee	one who receives a grant
eer	auctioneer	one who auctions goods
ence (ency)	reference	act of referring
ery	cookery	art of cooking
ess	princess	one who is a female prince
hood	childhood	state of being a child
ia	hysteria	state of being hysterical (having excessive fear)
ician	beautician	one who styles hair
ion (sion, tion)	regulation	act of regulating
ism	criticism	act of criticizing

Suffix	Example	Meaning of Example
ist	florist	one who works with flowers
ity	possibility	that which is possible
ium	auditorium	hall for audience
ment	entertainment	that which entertains
ness	kindness	that which is kind
or	demeanor	outward behavior
ry	citizenry	those who are citizens
ship	friendship	state of being friends
ule	ductule	small duct

Adjective suffixes denote "full of," "capable of," "tending to," "resembling," "pertaining to," and "without."

Suffix	Example	Meaning of Example
able (ible)	breakable	capable of breaking
an	American	pertaining to America
ar	spectacular	resembling a spectacle
ial	custodial	pertaining to custody (guardianship)
ical	economical	capable of economy (thrift)
ious	tedious	tending to tedium (boredom)
ish	devilish	resembling a devil
ive	regressive	tending to regress
less	restless	without rest (unsettled)
ous	rigorous	full of rigor (strictness)
ulent	turbulent	full of turbulence (agitation, tumult)

Adverb suffixes denote "like," "way," or "manner."

Suffix	Example	Meaning of Example
ly	slowly	in a slow manner
ward (wards)	backward	in the back (previous) or opposite way
wise	clockwise	in the manner of the hands of a clock

Versatile suffixes may be used with more than one part of speech.

Suffix	Example	Meaning of Example
al	refusal	noun: the act of refusing
	fictional	adjective: pertaining to fiction
ant (ent)	claimant	noun: one who makes a claim
	pertinent	adjective: tending to pertain (be relevant)
ary	notary	noun: one who notarizes
	budgetary	adjective: pertaining to a budget
ate	advocate	noun: one who voices (pleads for) a cause
	immediate	adjective: pertaining to the present (not the middle)
	activate	verb: to make active

Suffix	Example	Meaning of Example
en	woolen	adjective: full of wool
	sharpen	verb: to make sharp
er	abstainer	noun: one who abstains
	drier	adjective: pertaining to dryness
	hotter	adjective or adverb: pertaining to hotness
ese	Chinese	noun: one who comes from China
	Japanese	adjective: pertaining to Japan
ful	roomful	noun: as many as a room can hold
	eventful	adjective: full of events
ile	percentile	noun: percent of distribution
	infantile	adjective: characteristic of a child
ine	chlorine	noun: chemical element
	equine	adjective: pertaining to horses (*equus* in Latin)
ite	Israelite	noun: one who comes from the tribes of Israel
	favorite	adjective: full of favor
ory	observatory	noun: place for observing
	exploratory	adjective: tending to explore
y (ie)	inquiry	noun: an act of inquiring
	angry	adjective: full of anger

Summary of Word Division Rules

As you learn suffixes and prefixes, your understanding of word division rules should increase, since words are usually divided into syllables according to the meaning of the various parts.

1. Divide words between pronounced syllables only; you can't divide *searched,* no matter how tempting.

2. Don't split off just one or two letters—that saves very little space (once you add the hyphen) and tends to confuse the reader.

3. Always divide so that the first part of the word is pronounced the way it will be in the final word. Don't divide *product* "pro-duct," because the "pro" would give the wrong pronunciation cue.

4. When a vowel is a separate syllable, divide after it, as in "vaga-bond."

5. Split double consonants, as in "writ-ten," unless the root word has the double letter, as in "spell-ing."

6. Usually divide between two consonants (see rule 5), unless the root word ends with the two consonants, as in "bond-ing."

7. Do not divide proper names, titles with proper names, abbreviations, contractions, or numbers.

Because word processing materials are so frequently moved around on the page, the modern trend in keyboarding is to divide very seldom if at all, and then only on the final copy. Some readers also contend that undivided words are easier to read and understand. Be sure to follow the instructions outlined by your teacher, employer, or reference manual (see page 330).

Appendix E

Recommended References;
Proofreading Symbols

Reference Sources

Many kinds of reference books are available for home, school, office, and library use. The following are recommended:

1. Every writer needs a good *pocket dictionary* to carry almost everywhere. Good inexpensive paperbacks are available; many contain useful capitalized biographical and geographical words. Be sure the publication date is recent, because the language changes rapidly. Pocket dictionaries usually do not contain such extras as spelling rules or helpful hints. Read the preface carefully to note what the dictionary does include. Find the pronunciation key, and learn how to use it; note the abbreviations your dictionary uses for terms such as the parts of speech.

2. At home, a writer should have a *desk or college dictionary.* These are usually hardcover; watch for sales. Desk dictionaries often have separate detailed sections for biographical and geographical names, spelling hints, grammar rules, symbols, and abbreviations.

3. You may also need some *specialized vocabulary references.* For example, if you are a computer major, you need a dictionary of computer terms; if you are a pre-law major, a legal dictionary is a necessity.

4. *Unabridged dictionaries,* found primarily in libraries, contain nearly all the words ever used in a language, including many archaic (obsolete) usages.

5. Anyone writing papers or working in an office needs a general *reference manual,* which gives basic information on typing, computer keyboarding, grammar, punctuation, spelling, and sometimes on reports, manuscripts, filing, job applications, and other subjects.

6. A *thesaurus* is an excellent "extra." This reference work offers vocabulary words and synonyms organized by subject, so that if you want to write about "love," you'll find the words about love, affection, friendship, sex, hate, family, and similar topics grouped in one area—it saves a lot of page-turning.

7. *Spellers* and *word division manuals* often cover both uses; they show how to spell and divide words, but do not show meanings.

8. *Desk encyclopedias* are sometimes published in one large volume or two small volumes. They include desk reference information, such as descriptions and history of people, places, and events, plus such extras as longer biographical and geographical sections, a grammar section, symbols, and abbreviations.

9. *Computer spell checkers* are computer programs to check the spelling of a long list of words—say 15,000—to which you can add your own (for example, brands and other names and business jargon). However, spell checkers do not distinguish between homonyms or recognize incorrect usage, so you must know which word you want. Some new computer grammar programs can catch certain basic mistakes, but they are quite limited.

10. Excellent reference materials of all kinds are available in your local libraries. The reference librarian is there to help you. Most libraries, in addition to tours and individual help from the librarian, also offer written handouts entitled something like "How to Use This Library," and "Writing Library Research Reports." These handouts are especially valuable because they explain how to take advantage of a particular library setup, as well as more general matters. Ask for the handouts and then read them.

Proofreading Methods and Symbols

Who needs to proofread? Why is it important? You may feel that proofreading is just a last detail that someone else can handle. Actually, everyone needs to proofread her or his written work—to look for simple typographical or spelling errors, more complex grammatical mistakes, and problems of clarity or tone. People who depend upon computer spell checker programs to correct their errors may be disappointed to find that many mistakes are not caught—a perfectly good word in the wrong place, such as "principle and interest," for example.

Here are some helpful tips for proofreading:

1. Proofread as you write—but don't count on that process to find all the mistakes.

2. Proofread each page before you print it or remove it from the machine. This will break up your work tasks, and you'll catch most errors.

3. Compare your copy with the original—especially complex material such as technical or scientific work. When possible, ask a coworker to read the new material aloud as you check the original.

4. When you are proofreading alone, do it line by line—sometimes even backwards. Then read the sentences in order (aloud if possible) to check for logic.

5. Use the customary proofreading symbols to help communicate clearly what your revisions are. A list of the most common symbols follows on the next page.

Common Proofreading Symbols

Command	Mark in Text	Result
Align	yesterday today tomorrow	yesterday today tomorrow
Capitalize	new york	New York
Close up space	Cali fornia	California
Delete	Texxas in the the spring	Texas in the spring
Insert	in _the_ spring	in the spring
Insert punctuation above	you won't	you won't
Insert punctuation below	Mobile Alabama	Mobile, Alabama
Let it stand	Each is _stet_	Each is
Lowercase	next Fall	next fall
Move down	down	down
Move right	move right	move right
Paragraph indent	The following	The following
Spell out	Calif.	California
Transpose	either I'll go	I'll either go

Index

Page numbers in boldface type indicate Memory Pegs.

Words used as words are in italic type.

Resources for the Instructor

Directions: In the blanks write S for complete sentence, F for fragment (incomplete sentence), or R for run-on (incorrect double sentence).

_____ 1. First he spoke quietly, then he started to yell.

_____ 2. Hoping that you would change your mind soon.

_____ 3. Angie is hard to please, she tends to be nervous.

_____ 4. I got a typing speed of 40, which is good for a beginner.

_____ 5. A school that has a very good reputation.

_____ 6. When I saw her, I laughed until I cried.

_____ 7. The path is stony, it hurts his feet.

_____ 8. One sister went to school, the other started working.

_____ 9. Exploring all the rooms, we walked around the school.

_____ 10. While she attended college, Sue worked as a receptionist.

_____ 11. She always plans her time, at least a few days at once.

_____ 12. Which made me change my mind about the job.

Directions: Add all necessary capital letters and punctuation marks, including apostrophes.

13. The childrens room is near ours

14. Its our stores policy to sell english imports on the first floor

15. The letter will be mailed I hope on thursday

16. The Joneses our neighbors have five siamese kittens

17. Well be at the stuart hotel 680 santa clara street until monday

    february 4.

18. Lick high and oak grove high are in the same area and the rivalry

    between them is great

19. This bill by the way is important to every pupil teacher and employer

    in this state

20. Expecting out-of-town guests we arranged for more bedding food and

    towels

21. The teacher replied we can't expect perfect scores

22. Why not asked jose

23. I hope karen that youll write a better letter after labor day

24. Sam for example is a better typist than elizabeth but his spelling still needs work

25. will mrs miller come to our class and demonstrate body language

26. When im busy i eat only juice toast and coffee for breakfast

27. Are all the names on the secretarys list

28. We celebrate thanksgiving day in november

29. I bought some groceries then i bought some new shoes

30. Please order the following items soap tea napkins milk

31. Give her many chances for example help her with her spanish lesson

Directions: Label N (noun), Pro (pronoun), V (verb), adj (adjective), adv (adverb), prep (preposition), and con (conjunction) in this sentence.

32. Look carefully at complete records of applicants before you hire them.

Directions: Put each prepositional phrase in parentheses.

33. The children spent the day hunting for shells.

34. We grew beans in a space near our driveway.

35. There was a garden between the two trees.

36. We learn much from the letters of friends.

37. The band played an old waltz by Chopin.

38. Mrs. Carbajal looked at my notes and shook her head.

39. All the students except Jean finished the word processing.

Directions: Circle the correct word in the parentheses.

40. There (was/were) no marks on my paper.

41. The class (don't/doesn't) start until 10 a.m.

42. My interest in flowers (go/goes) back to my childhood.

43. The results of this study (was/were) serious.

44. A razor blade or a stylus sometimes (is/are) used for correction.

45. One of the typewriters (need/needs) fixing.

46. Each one of these students (has/have) an interesting story.

47. The diamonds in this bracelet (is/are) genuine.

48. Several books were (threw/thrown) on the floor.

49. Someone must have (broke/broken) this window.

50. The textbook (came/come) with a key.

51. I (lay/laid) back in the chair and relaxed.

52. Mom had (laid/lain) down on the sofa.

53. Kim (lay/laid) her books on the chair.

54. John forgot where he had (laid/lain) his keys.

55. Sue had (set/sat) the cake on the floor.

56. Cheryl typed two more letters than (she/her).

57. Dad is taller than (I/me).

58. (We/Us) students want to fix up the parking lot.

59. I wonder where (its/it's) owner is?

60. The Browns don't eat as early as (us/we).

61. Between you and (I/me), English is hard.

62. This motor runs (well/good) on regular gas.

63. I stumbled very (awkward/awkwardly) on the rug.

64. Our roses look (beautifully/beautiful) in the spring.

65. I can't type (good/well) on this old typewriter.

66. She felt very (bad/badly) about the mistake.

67. Your wedding plans sound (delightful/delightfully).

68. There aren't (any/no) more days left.

69. Who is (faster/fastest), Jack or Tom?

70. The Powells have the (attractivest/most attractive) car in the lot.

71. We didn't like (neither/either) of the tests.

72. They should have used (more easy/easier/more easier) examples.

Directions: In the blanks write S for complete sentence, F for fragment (incomplete sentence), or R for run-on (incorrect double sentence).

_____ 1. Wondering if you can meet on Tuesday.

_____ 2. First turn on the power, then turn on the screen.

_____ 3. This equipment is sometimes slow, it needs to warm up.

_____ 4. Keyboarding is a valuable skill, one that everybody should learn.

_____ 5. A company known as a good employer.

_____ 6. When she called, I relaxed and drank a cup of coffee.

_____ 7. This machine is new, it confuses me occasionally.

_____ 8. One friend went to school fulltime, the other enrolled at night.

_____ 9. Walking around the work stations, we explored the office.

_____ 10. While she attended college, Lee worked as an assembler.

_____ 11. He always plans his time, at least a week ahead.

_____ 12. Which made me want to apply for the job.

Directions: Add any necessary capital letters and punctuation marks, including apostrophes.

13. The bosses office is near ours

14. Its our companys policy to send french shipments weekly

15. The fax will be sent I hope tomorrow

16. The Smiths our neighbors have two japanese cars

17. Well be at the maxim hotel 110 san jose avenue until friday june 10

18. Andrew hill high and independence high are in the same area and the rivalry between them is great

19. This bill by the way is important to every pupil teacher and employer in this state

20. Expecting out-of-town visitors we arranged for hotel car and restaurant reservations

21. The teacher explained we can't expect perfect scores

22. Why not asked lisa

23. I hope maria that youll write a better memo after new years day

24. Roberto for example is a better typist than gina but his spelling still needs work

25. Give her many chances for example help her with her computer lesson

26. Please order the following items paper correction fluid staples

27. I bought some groceries then i bought a paper

28. We celebrate memorial day in may

29. Are all the names on the leaders list

30. When im busy i eat only juice cereal and coffee for breakfast

31. Will mrs vasquez come to our class and demonstrate audiovisuals

Directions: Label N (noun), Pro (pronoun), V (verb), adj (adjective), adv (adverb), prep (preposition), and con (conjunction) in this sentence.

32. Read slowly all instructions before you begin any new procedure at work.

Directions: Put each prepositional phrase in parentheses.

33. The students spent the day looking at videos.

34. We grow plants in a space near our office window.

35. There is a garden between the two trees.

36. We learn much from the examples on the job.

37. The radio played an old waltz by Chopin.

38. Mrs. Bennett looked at my notes and shook her head.

39. All the students except Beverly finished the word processing.

Directions: Circle the correct word in the parentheses.

40. Several papers were (threw/thrown) on the floor.

41. The diamonds in this ring (is/are) genuine.

42. Each one of these workers (has/have) an interesting story.

43. One of the telephones (need/needs) fixing.

44. A razor blade or a stylus sometimes (is/are) used for repair.

45. The results of this meeting (was/were) serious.

46. My interest in computers (go/goes) back to my childhood.

47. My job (don't/doesn't) start until 10 a.m.

48. There (was/were) two changes on my outline.

49. They should have used (more easy/easier/more easier) questions.

50. We didn't like (neither/either) of the texts.

51. The Sanchezes have the (attractivest/most attractive) car in the lot.

52. Who is (faster/fastest), Jack or Tom?

53. There aren't (any/no) more cookies left.

54. Your vacation plans sound (delightful/delightfully).

55. She felt very (bad/badly) about the mistake.

56. I can't type (good/well) on this old typewriter.

57. Our roses look (beautifully/beautiful) in the spring.

58. I stumbled very (awkward/awkwardly) on the wire.

59. This motor runs (well/good) on unleaded gas.

60. Between you and (I/me), English is hard.

61. The Joneses don't leave as early as (us/we).

62. I wonder where (its/it's) owner is.

63. (We/Us) employees want to fix up the lounge.

64. Dad is taller than (I/me).

65. Cheryl typed two more letters than (he/him).

66. Sue had (set/sat) the typewriter on the floor.

67. Someone must have (broke/broken) this viewer.

68. Lee forgot where he had (laid/lain) his keys.

69. Sarita (lay/laid) her books on the car seat.

70. Mom had (laid/lain) down on the beach chair.

71. I (lay/laid) back on the sand and relaxed.

72. The textbook (came/come) with a workbook.

Directions: In the blanks write S for complete sentence, F for fragment (incomplete sentence), or R for run-on (incorrect double sentence).

_____ 1. Beginning to write a research report.

_____ 2. First decide on a general topic, later you can narrow it a little.

_____ 3. You may need to write for a specific audience, the subject may have been assigned to you.

_____ 4. In business, research is very important, a skill you should have.

_____ 5. A topic that is too general or too long.

_____ 6. When they ask you to write, relax and enjoy the process.

_____ 7. Starting is the hardest part, many people wait until the last minute.

_____ 8. Just start writing, see what appears on the page.

_____ 9. You can fix the problems later, polishing and organizing.

_____ 10. When you are first writing, try making lists or clusters.

_____ 11. Be sure you learn your way around the library, with the help of the research librarian.

_____ 12. Which may require taking careful notes about authors and page numbers.

Directions: Add any necessary capital letters and punctuation marks, including apostrophes.

13. My teachers desk is piled high with english books and papers

14. Its crowded but more organized than yours

15. Sally brown will leave for the convention in miami on tuesday

16. The airplane tickets will be here i think by november 22

17. Youre going to need a map to find the address on south tenth street in st. petersburg before december 1 1997

18. Its near south high school and across from a city fire department

19. this map by the way has every city county and highway in this state

20. Expecting weather problems we packed flashlights bottled water and a first-aid kit

21. The officer warned they cant drive near the beach today

22. Why not asked ken

23. I hope marika that youll have a good trip before christmas day

24. Lui for example is a better driver than lee but she needs to practice reading maps

25. Give him many opportunities for example help him with his computer program

26. Please order the following items disks paper and ink cartridges

27. I read the report then i summarized it

28. We celebrate thanksgiving day in november

29. Are all the names on the bosses list

30. When im busy i have just crackers soup and coffee for lunch

31. Will mrs lee come to our class and demonstrate the new video program

Directions: Label N (noun), Pro (pronoun), V (verb), adj (adjective), adv (adverb), prep (preposition), and con (conjunction) in this sentence.

32. List carefully each part of the job before you start a new project.

Directions: Put each prepositional phrase in parentheses.

33. My sister and I are planning a trip to Costa Rica.

34. We have maps in a folder on the coffee table.

35. There is a special fund marked "for the trip."

36. We save money for gifts and souvenirs.

37. Costa Rica has been a democracy for 100 years.

38. The tiny country has more species of plants and animals than there are in the United States.

39. A jungle train runs over the mountains as monkeys play on the beach.

Directions: Circle the correct word in parentheses.

40. The relationship between living things and environment (is/are) called "ecology."

41. Trash is often (threw/thrown) on beaches and trails.

42. Every piece of trash (has/have) an effect on the earth.

43. Plastic rings from one type of six-pack (kill/kills) birds and animals.

44. Many types of plastic (is/are) now labeled for recycling.

45. Our cities (need/needs) more recycling plants.

46. Each government (is/are) planning ways to solve pollution problems.

47. They (haven't/hasn't) learned to cooperate well yet.

48. There (was/were) some new laws recently about air pollution.

49. They have used (more hard/harder/more harder) air standards.

50. People will not use (neither/either) trains or buses if not convenient.

51. This new car has the (effectivest/most effective) fuel economy.

52. Which is (best/better) in cutting air pollution, this model or that?

53. There aren't (any/no) easy answers.

54. Your new job sounds (delightful/delightfully).

55. He felt quite (bad/badly) about the loss.

56. I can't study (good/well) in this light.

57. Your trees look (beautifully/beautiful) in the fall.

58. She stumbled (awkward/awkwardly) on the step.

59. This program runs (well/good) on this computer.

60. Between you and (I/me), writing English is not easy.

61. The teachers don't leave as early as (we/us).

62. I discovered where (its/it's) owner lived.

63. (We/Us) students want to take the test early.

64. Maria is taller than (I/me).

65. (Who/Whom) did you see at the meeting?

66. Tomas had (set/sat) the printer on the floor.

67. Someone must have (took/taken) the disk home.

68. Jana forgot where she had (laid/lain) the papers.

69. Lela (lay/laid) her briefcase on the car seat.

70. Dad had (laid/lain) down after dinner.

71. I (lay/laid) back on the sofa and relaxed.

72. The program (ran/run) very quickly.

Part One Examination: Version A _____
Covering Chapters 1–10; Structure

Directions: Label each group of words either declarative (dec), interrogatory (int), exclamatory (exc), imperative (imp), or fragment (fra). Use abbreviations if you wish.

_____ 1. Some weather announcers do a great job.

_____ 2. Working with the public early in the morning.

_____ 3. What a strange-looking cloud that is!

_____ 4. Check the symbols on the weather maps.

_____ 5. A small group of students with their teacher.

_____ 6. Do you watch weather reports on television?

_____ 7. A tornado is the smallest of destructive storms.

_____ 8. The opportunity for better planning of trips.

Directions: Label S above the simple subjects and V above the verb.

9. The satellite reports often are quite accurate.

10. Your neighborhood weather forecaster frequently predicts local weather as well as national weather.

11. Along with many others, he or she sometimes rises early and comes to work before breakfast.

12. Complete reports, as well as the weather map, come over your early morning airwaves.

13. Do you understand the symbols on the weather map?

14. Early in their careers, weather reporters take lessons in terminology.

15. They sometimes observe the sky through the telescopes at the observatory.

Directions: Put each prepositional phrase in parentheses.

16. The announcer spoke of many possibilities.

17. During the broadcast, he mentioned the earthquake prediction.

18. That weather forecaster is also a comedian at some points.

19. Although he is very funny, he also knows about weather.

20. The announcer who works with him sometimes laughs at his jokes.

Directions: Underline each dependent clause and put each prepositional phrase in parentheses.

21.   The professor started her lecture before the class was seated.

22.   Many students in the class were startled.

23.   One student who came in late ran to his seat.

24.   Here are the results of the tests that they took.

Directions: In the blanks write S for complete sentence, F for fragment (incomplete sentence), or R for run-on (two incorrectly joined sentences).

_____ 25.   L. Frank Baum, who wrote *The Wizard of Oz.*

_____ 26.   Judy Garland became famous in the movie as Dorothy, carried off by a tornado.

_____ 27.   Was Dorothy born in Kansas?

_____ 28.   Ray Bolger played the Scarecrow, Bert Lahr played the Cowardly Lion.

_____ 29.   Children have loved the book since about 1900.

_____ 30.   The Wonderful Wizard a humbug who faked magic.

_____ 31.   The Tin Woodsman needed a heart, the Scarecrow wanted a brain.

Directions: Label the part of speech of each word, using S, AV or BV, N, N (poss), Pro, rel pro, adj, adv, prep, con, interj, inf, and part, and put prepositional phrases in parentheses.

32.   Sitting in front of the television and studying her English, Priya was

soon asleep.

33.   Oscar, who knows the material well, will pass the test easily.

34.   If you study, you will learn.

35.   The time is available for studying.

Directions: Label each group of words either declarative (dec), interrogatory (int), exclamatory (exc), imperative (imp), run-on (R), or fragment (frag).

_____ 1. There is little we can do to help, he is too stubborn.

_____ 2. Mr. Hanson is out of town, however, he'll be back soon.

_____ 3. Speak to Mr. Ng about that.

_____ 4. Are you sure that is the right answer?

_____ 5. Since the plant operated on a 24-hour basis, we finished.

_____ 6. Because the sun had shone all day, melting the ice.

_____ 7. Our apple trees have grown amazingly you should see them.

_____ 8. What a beautiful day this is!

Directions: Label S above the simple subjects and V above the verb.

9. The imported goods often cost more.

10. Our friendly neighbor efficiently and quietly manages the store.

11. Majestic ships, with imported cargo, slip silently into port.

12. Along with many others, they bring the goods for the store.

13. This import house, called Green Jade, is one of my favorites.

14. The oriental furniture is expensive but durable.

15. In the shop we look at beautiful things for hours.

Directions: Put each prepositional phrase in parentheses.

16. We talked of many places.

17. During our visit, the wind chimes played.

18. The saleswoman with the happy smile is popular.

19. My uncle who lived in Burma knows about tropical woods.

20. Although he is older now, his memory for facts is very good.

Directions: Underline each dependent clause and put each prepositional phrase in parentheses.

21. The shop owner started to explain before we asked questions.

22. Many countries with tropical climates have economic problems.

23. Pauline Lee, who has been my friend for many years, knows this shop

    owner.

24. Here is the Christmas card which she sent.

25. After we buy a gift, I will call her.

Directions: In the blanks write S for complete sentence, F for fragment (incomplete sentence), or R for run-on (two incorrectly joined sentences).

_____ 26. First he asked questions, then he laughed.

_____ 27. Hoping that I would change my mind soon.

_____ 28. Beverly is easy to please, she likes my style.

_____ 29. We paid $60 for the chest, a very good bargain.

_____ 30. A store that has a very good reputation.

_____ 31. When I saw my old friend, we laughed until we cried.

Directions: Label the part of speech of each word, using S, AV or BV, N, N (poss), Pro, rel pro, adj, adv, prep, con, interj, inf, and part, and put prepositional phrases in parentheses.

32. Store owners place special importance on repeat customers.

33. Experienced managers usually do their work in order of importance.

34. I shopped at that store because I enjoy the atmosphere.

35. When I leave the store, I think about birthday gifts.

Directions: Add any necessary punctuation and delete any that is unnecessary. Use the standard proofreading symbols in your text.

1. He paid $2,000. for the used car

2. We'll drive it to Los Angeles on Tuesday; on Wednesday to San Diego

3. The valley may be very very hot for driving

4. We may drive part way at night; our car however should handle the heat well

5. Our next trip will be at Christmas but we're not sure exactly which day.

6. Jessica, Daniel and Ben are coming with us this time.

7. Anyone else who wants to come, should see me before Monday

8. Before we start we need to check luggage space.

9. Next Thursday—or is it on Wednesday—we should be in Death Valley

10. To see the desert blooming, is a great thrill

11. The owner of the restaurant (Wolfgang Puck,) says he'll give us a discount.

12. He is known in the area as a "creative careful chef

13. "As you see" said Kevin, "I dont carry much luggage".

14. "Yes Kevin but your skis and fishing poles are odd shapes"! says his mother

15. We'll stop at Monterey, California, Bakersfield, California, Tucson, Arizona, and Death Valley, California on that trip.

16. Dont forget to bring regular camera, camcorder, color film tapes etc.

17. "Are you looking forward to the trip" asked Jessica?

18. Daniel answered, that he certainly was

19. "Then come," his mother said and help get ready

20. Eventually early in the morning we all piled into the car

Directions: Mark letters that need to be capitalized or lowercased; in the space above the sentence, correct or spell out abbreviations as necessary.

21. We took with us the A.A.A. guide book Discovering The West

22. Our first stop was at 1212 46 street in Monterey, a famous pacific coast city.

23. Kevin's Mother works there in the Fisher building near the Red salmon restaurant.

24. Some of the salmon are four ft. long, the largest in CA.

25. 3 of us ordered salmon, along with about a 100 other people in the restaurant.

Directions: Add any necessary punctuation, and delete any that is unnecessary. Use the standard proofreading symbols in your text.

1. "Ive been thinking about my budget," said Rosa.

2. "Me too"! said Henry. "Should we start planning now

3. "I think wed better" she answered we want a vacation.

4. We could always fly now and pay much much later, he said grinning

5. Rosa said she didn't think that was a good idea.

6. "In one month we would pay an extra $150.00 for just $1000. of vacation money, she said.

7. They decided to save their money then they would go to Alaska on a cruise along the Inland Passage.

8. This beautiful summer cruise between the islands and the mainland of Canada and Alaska is very popular.

9. Because the ships are close to shore the tourists who watch from the decks can see reindeer grizzly bear and moose.

10. Sea life—such as whales, seals, otters, and thousands of birds,—also follow the passage.

11. When passengers go, on shore however they can walk on glaciers.

12. People who take cameras, and many rolls of film can photograph wildlife sea mountains and icebergs

13. For a ticket in a cabin for four people the cost is $595 which is quite inexpensive.

14. My sister wants to go to Alaska next vacation; my brother Tahiti.

15. Tahiti is better for a winter vacation; Alaska for summer.

16. When we go in July well stop in Anchorage Ketchikan and Homer where I have relatives who own a fishing boat.

17. Anyone else who wants to join us, should call soon.

18. To see the wildlife from the ship, is unforgettable.

19. To get a good price we need to have three or four people.

20. My travel agent Juanita Lopez calls these "bargain cruises

Directions: Mark letters that need to be capitalized or lowercased; circle any incorrect number or abbreviation forms and rewrite them correctly in the blanks.

21. Juanita's telephone number is 555,6745.   _____

22. Her address is at No. 16, 755 6th St.   _____

23. That is the Old mission bldg. in san Jose.   _____

24. Meet me at ken's pancake house to plan.   _____

25. They have ¼ inch pancakes 6 in across.   _____

Part Three Examination: Section 1, Version A _____
Covering Chapters 21–23; Plurals, Possessives

Directions: Write the correct possessives of the nouns by adding apostrophes in the right places.

1. This employees group is planning a surprise.

2. Its their boss birthday.

3. Two workers discovered that their boss likes Chinese food.

4. At tomorrows break, many mysterious dishes will appear.

5. Tonys job is to bring drinks.

6. Thuy makes great egg rolls with crispy crusts.

7. Several telephone calls have happened among employees houses.

8. A giant card will hold signatures and funny sayings from workers.

9. The members of the group hope for the boss permission to take a

   longer break.

10. Do you think shell let them do that?

Directions: Write the plural form of the noun in the blank following:

11. measles   _____

12. salmon   _____

13. knife   _____

14. handful   _____

15. woman   _____

16. soprano   _____

17. hero   _____

18. stereo   _____

19. mother-in-law _____

20. berry   _____

Directions: Write the possessive form of each phrase in the blank.

21. home of the Smiths   _____

22. rooms of the boys   _____

23. advice of the attorney-at-law _____

24. mothers of Jack and Maria   _____

25. clothing of the women   _____

R-21

Part Three Examination: Section 1, Version B _____
Covering Chapters 21–23; Plurals, Possessives

Directions: Circle the correct plural or possessive form in the parentheses.

1. Fantasy, myth, fairy tale—whether (children's/childrens') or (adults'/adult's) versions—occupy much of our leisure time.

2. Nursery school children dress up in (Supermans'/Superman's) cape, (Batmans'/Batman's) hood, and the Ninja (Turtles'/Turtle's) masks.

3. (Superheroes/Superheroes') make children feel their own power.

4. Young (boy's/boys') aggressive instincts are encouraged to "fight for the good," against the "bad guys."

5. In the better (stories/stories'), they are shown how to seek peaceful (solutions'/solutions).

6. Because our culture is changing, the more recent (girls'/girl's) (story's/stories) show young (girls'/girls) bravery and strength.

7. (Girls'/Girls) and (woman/women) are no longer limited to keeping house and having (babies/babys).

8. Even some adult fantasy—for example (mens/mens'/men's) and (womens/women's/womens') scenes in ads—is showing the new message.

9. (Girls/Girls') dreams for themselves can now include jobs as police (officers/officers') or (lawyers'/lawyers).

10. (Mens/Men's) strengths are now shown to include the difficult (arts/arts') of peace and understanding (ones/one's) family and caring for (ones/one's) children.

11. Look carefully to see the (culture's/cultures) messages.

Directions: Circle the correct pronoun in the parentheses.

1. Jean and (I/me) corrected the tests.

2. Dan met Ken and (him/he) at the library.

3. (We/Us) men are planning a bicycle race.

4. She was as much to blame as (I/me).

5. Stan took a picture of Sally and (her/she).

6. Lois and (them/they) got the high scores on the test.

7. The class chose Juan and (her/she) to represent them.

8. The other people caught more fish than (we/us).

9. (His/Him) studying the subject was important.

10. My high grades surprised my family more than (I/me).

11. The candlesticks are a gift from (her/she) and Tom.

12. Our teacher read an article about computers to Tony and (us/we).

13. Edgar Allen Poe, (who/whom) wrote the first detective stories, was a

    fascinating writer.

14. Writers (who/whom) are less gifted have tried to imitate him.

15. (Who/Whom) do I see for a new library card?

16. Another great writer (who/whom) I appreciate was Washington Irving.

17. Please tell me (who/whom) can write as well as Mark Twain.

18. William Faulkner is another author (who/whom) wrote great stories.

19. To (who/whom) did he dedicate that novel?

20. Give the prize to (whoever/whomever) deserves it.

Directions: Write in the blank at the right the correct *past* form of the verb in the parentheses.

21. What have you (do) to your car?   _____

22. You have already (drive) it too long.   _____

23. We (find) it on the freeway. _____

24. Have you (run) out of gas? _____

25. We (think) you had an accident. _____

26. Be sure that the gas gauge is not (break). _____

27. Last year I (lose) my owner's manual. _____

28. I (forget) to change the oil in the engine. _____

29. Then the car (begin) to overheat. _____

30. The mechanic said the seal had (begin) to leak. _____

31. He (say) that some problems are expensive. _____

32. I (feel) like giving the car away. _____

33. I wish that I had (saw) the problem sooner. _____

34. I probably (throw) the manual away. _____

35. I (write) to the car company for a new book. _____

36. The morning mail has (come) today. _____

37. Now I have (read) about proper car care. _____

38. (Do) you buy a used car last year? _____

39. I (buy) my car from a car rental agency. _____

40. Rental agencies have (sell) almost new cars. _____

41. My car (is) only a year old. _____

42. It (has) only 10,000 miles on it. _____

43. It was not very (wear) at all. _____

44. When I (bring) it home, my family cheered. _____

45. My other car had (be) 10 years old. _____

Directions: Circle the correct pronouns in the parentheses.

1. For my family and (I/me), foreign films are especially tempting.

2. My husband and (I/me) both like French and Spanish movies.

3. To (we/us) the subtitles are an interesting challenge.

4. You see, (he and I/him and me) like to try to understand the words by listening, but the subtitles are there if (we/us) need them.

5. Some family members are distracted by the subtitles, so (they/them) choose films that dub in English words instead.

6. Would you rather see a movie in a theater or rent one to see (it/them) at home?

7. Some of (we/us) in the family like fast-moving drama; others, like my sister and (I/me), choose romantic comedies for relaxation.

8. (We/Us) can rent or tape two films and take turns watching and playing table games or working.

9. My grandchildren tell me when (he and she/him and her) think the movie is too violent to suit my sister and (I/me).

10. "You can fast-forward through the scary part on this one," say (them/they).

11. My sister and (I/me) are concerned about violence in the media.

12. For my husband and (I/me), worries about film and television ratings always bring discussion about censorship.

13. He is more concerned than (I/me) about a possible computer "V" chip to use to block out violent or pornographic films.

14. (Who/Whom) should choose what is watched by your family?

15. Should the parents choose (who/whom) they think should watch?

16. Should television shows be rated like movies to recommend (who/whom) should be allowed to see (it/them)?

17. For (who/whom) do you think media ratings should be designed?

18. Should films be rented by (whomever/whoever) wants them?

19. Among my family and (I/me), these are frequent discussion questions.

20. Does your family argue as much as (us/we) about this topic?

21. Perhaps you are as concerned as (I/me).

Directions: Circle the correct past tense in the parentheses.

22. Why do you think human beings have always (fight/fighted/fought)?

23. When we study early humans, we discover that violence has always (be/been/being) with us.

24. We know that sometimes brothers have (kill/killed) brothers.

25. Some of the worst violence we have (see/seen) has been among those who are close.

26. Wars, feuds, and other disputes often have (begin/began/begun) among relatives or members of the same religion.

27. The First World War (begin/began/begun) in 1914 in an area of Europe not far from Bosnia, where recent fighting has again (arose/arisen).

28. The American Civil War (grow/grew/grown) out of arguments about individual, regional, and national rights that have (break/broke/broken) many families.

29. Any violent acts have (raised/rose/risen) questions about solutions.

30. Many historians say that World War II (had/has/have) its roots in an unjust settlement of World War I.

31. Arguments about territory, trade, and fairness have (show/showed/shown) up both in families and in nations.

32. Do you think that your childhood family was (ran/run) like a democracy or a dictatorship?

33. As a child, when you (choose/chose) a path, what was the result?

34. (Did/Do) your parents support your decision?

35. (Was/Were) your brothers or sisters and other family members helpful or jealous or both?

36. (Laying/Lying) deep in our minds have always (be/been) the memories of childhood and our related feelings about ourselves.

37. These feelings have (laid/lain) within us since early childhood.

38. We may remember being (set/sat) in a corner to regret our misdeeds.

39. Some may think about being (strike/struck/striked) with a strap or paddle.

40. When a belt is (laid/lain) across a back, does violence disappear?

41. Have you (spoke/spoken) to anyone about crime and punishment?

42. These are topics about which you may have (think/thinked/thought) or (write/wrote/written).

Part Three Examination: Section 3, Version A _____

Covering Chapters 27–29; Agreement, Modifiers

Directions: Circle the correct verb in the parentheses.

1. The players on the team (stands/stand) silently before the game.

2. The students in this school (use/uses) two colors to decorate.

3. There (is/are) several hundred cars in the lot.

4. Ricardo or Enrique (is/are) throwing the first ball.

5. Musicians or marchers (have/has) always performed at halftime.

6. The coaches on the bench (seem/seems) nervous.

7. Neither the players nor the fans (is/are) happy about the weather.

8. The mood in the stands (seem/seems) doubtful.

9. The dark clouds overhead (is/are) scheduled to disappear.

10. From behind one cloud, here (come/comes) the sun.

11. Nobody in the stadium (want/wants) the rain to come.

12. Sometimes it (rain/rains) while the sun shines.

13. Then everybody (see/sees) a rainbow.

14. Which kind of ballgame (do/does) your family enjoy?

15. Some people (play/plays) a game every day.

16. Others (watch/watches) games on television.

17. Today we all (is/are) seeing the game at the school.

18. Few of us (play/plays) ball as well as these players.

19. Some of them (have/has) practiced since age 3.

20. My daughter and son (love/loves) to play softball.

21. They especially (like/likes) to bat home runs.

22. That (seem/seems) to be more fun than catching balls.

23. Both batting and catching (is/are) important, I tell them.

24. Now the score (is/are) tied at 6–6.

25. In the ninth inning, the next run (win/wins) the game.

26. A new girls' team is playing (good/well) in Little League.

27. These young girls have practiced (diligent/diligently) for a year or more.

28. During their first year, they have proved that they can pitch and hit (real/really) well.

29. They need a little more practice in catching balls (safe/safely).

30. Their abilities are (different/differently) from those of boys.

31. In some ways, the girls are more (accurate/accurately) than the boys.

32. Girls tend to play more (careful/carefully).

33. In our culture, money is still given less (free/freely) for women's sports than for men's.

34. Everyone agrees that women can play (brave/bravely).

35. Many organizations are encouraging girls and women to practice sports (regular/regularly).

36. Exercise (sure/surely) improves health, for both men and women.

37. Does this trend mean that men and women will look (similar/similarly)?

38. There will (sure/surely) be some changes.

39. However, Superman's muscles will always work (good/well).

40. Superwoman will always move (swift/swiftly).

41. The average man will always seem more (strong/strongly) than the average woman is.

42. One major new problem in sports competition has developed (rapid/rapidly).

43. Steroid drugs have been given (illegal/illegally) to both men and women athletes at some international contests.

44. Such drugs (temporary/temporarily) strengthen and enlarge muscles.

45. They also cause (severe/severely) liver damage and major hormonal changes.

46. Athletes who are found to use (illegal/illegally) drugs are banned from competition.

47. Because these drugs cause both physical and emotional damage, some of the athletes (eventual/eventually) ruin their relationships or even die.

48. Sports competitions are (extreme/extremely) important to many of us.

49. Each of us needs to decide (thoughtful/thoughtfully) where sports activities belong in our lives.

50. Do we play games to exercise (good/well) or to beat other people?

Directions: Circle the correct verb in the parentheses.

1. Fantasy and myth (is/are) part of all our lives.

2. Some people (say/says) that fantasy (is/are) lies.

3. Others say that fantasy and myth (is/are) like our dreams.

4. Our dreams (tell/tells) us true things about ourselves.

5. Events in a dream (explain/explains) feelings in real life.

6. The stories we tell children (is/are) like the dreams of our culture.

7. Heroes in the story (inspire/inspires) us to try harder.

8. A villain who makes mistakes (warn/warns) us about results.

9. When you (set/sit) a story before a child, you help him or her.

10. As he or she (lies/lays) reading at bedtime, each child (learn/learns)

    more about life.

11. In the *Wizard of Oz*, each character (think/thinks) (he or she/they)

    must get help from the Wonderful Wizard.

12. At the end of the story, the Wizard (admits/admit) he cannot help.

13. He (doesn't/don't) have that kind of power.

14. Every character in the story (has/have) power to help

    (himself or herself/themselves).

15. The Good Witch (show/shows) Dorothy that the Ruby Slippers (is/are)

    a sign of her own power.

16. When Dorothy has (flew/flown) home from her dream, she

    (awakens/awakened) saying, "There's no place like home."

17. The Land of Oz, like Alice's Wonderland, (is/are) a beautiful, colorful

    place.

18. The world of our dreams (is/are) (given/gave) to us by our own minds.

Directions: Circle the correct modifier in the parentheses.

19. That wall color looks (different/differently) in daylight.

20. Clean the surface (good/well) before painting it.

21. This paint brush doesn't look (clean/cleanly).

22. Which dries (faster/fastest)—the acrylic or the oil?

23. This is the (difficultest/most difficult) job I've done.

24. We couldn't find the trim (anywhere/nowhere).

25. I stumbled (awkward/awkwardly) while climbing the ladder.

26. Your decorating plans sound (delightful/delightfully).

27. We should have used (brighter/more brighter) paint.

28. They didn't like (either/neither) of the colors we had.

29. The man wouldn't take (any/no) money for his advice.

30. Josh spent his money rather (foolish/foolishly).

31. This brush works (bad/badly) on the corners.

32. They talked very (cheerful/cheerfully).

33. We now have the (attractivest/most attractive) room in the building.

34. We saw (an/a) easy way to do it.

35. A (larger/more larger) brush would help.

36. He is the (more/most) helpful worker we've had.

37. I feel (bad/badly) about the cost.

38. The room looks (good/well) now after all our hard work.

Directions: Use proofreading symbols to correct any errors.

Part A: Spelling and Commonly Confused Words

1. Absents makes the heart grow fonder.

2. When he cheated on the test, his conscious bothered him.

3. They were accidently omitted from the graduation list.

4. It is convenent to know how to spell.

5. Can you discribe your goals after graduation?

6. They decided that they wanted to work for the two attornies.

7. Are you definitly sure about that?

8. We had to much cake at the party.

9. Tell us immediatly when you plan to graduate.

10. It will be nesessary to fill out the paperwork.

11. Your permenent record will always be here.

12. Has it occured to you that you need a job soon?

13. The principle speech will be given by Ms. Turnoy.

14. Then we will procede with the diplomas.

15. Have you had suffcent time to study for the final?

Part B: Punctuation

16. Do you realize Maria that we have only one more month?

17. We plan to attend the ceremony on Saturday, however, we'll have two more weeks of class.

18. The following staff will be at graduation the administration, the teachers, the counselors, and the office employees.

19. This ceremony—is it the only one this spring—is important to me.

20. Mr. Rosas asked, "Do you have the diplomas ready"?

21. When the teachers get here please call me.

22. Send the bill to Ms. Watkins (has she gone on leave yet).

23. On June 15, 1997 there will be a graduation.

24. We have been working hard for this, we deserve it.

25. The student who has been selected to give the speech is ready.

26. The party will be fun, won't it.

27. The new Dean of Admissions is Mr. Elfstrom who has just started.

28. This test is comprehensive, it covers all the English so far.

29. When you finish this test there will be no more grammar exams.

30. You can relax, therefore, and take a deep breath.

Part C: Capitals, Abbreviations, Numbers

31. Yes, the sale offers twenty % off.

32. The President of our school sometimes speaks at graduation.

33. Let's ask Mister Kapinski whether he wants to do that.

34. The Gold tower building is for sale.

35. Our school is in the North part of San Jose.

Part D: English Usage

36. Both the counselor and the teacher is now with the student.

37. The red jacket is hers; the blue one is our's.

38. Do you know whether the Johnson's are still here?

39. Between you and I, English is not an easy language.

40. Naturally, we feel badly when we make mistakes.

41. Don't Ms. Powell have that test ready?

42. Yes, I seen it on her desk.

43. Each teacher in these classes work many hours at home.

44. Ernest, not one of the other assistants, were ordering books.

45. I have risen my grade to a B this module.

Directions: In the blanks, rewrite the sentences.

46. Has Bonita cooked the dinner or Fred?

_____

_____

47. Sara got an invitation for her friend, which she decided to mail.

_____

_____

48. There is one hard problem on the test I took yesterday in my desk drawer.

_____

_____

Directions: Use proofreading symbols to correct errors.

Part A: Spelling and Commonly Confused Words

1. Job oppertunities are increased with more training.

2. Our calander shows the holidays planned.

3. It is disirable to review spelling.

4. Have you been writting down your goals?

5. Most people are surprized about how quickly they learn.

6. Have you been refered to the job placement office?

7. The pronounciation of the word helps the spelling.

8. They have studied the material very throughly.

9. The goverment is explaining its actions.

10. Have you made similiar statements?

11. Are you disatisfied with your performance this week?

12. This is the nineth week of the English classes.

13. Have you had continous time available to study?

14. There is not much more grammer to review.

15. Have the school accomodations been satisfactory?

Part B: Punctuation

16. Come and see us Antony after you get your job.

17. The graduation party will be on Saturday night, although the ceremony is in the morning.

18. I have invited the following people to graduation my mother, my sister, my husband, and my two kids.

19. This week—despite the engrossing national news! we still need to finish our classes.

20. The teacher asked, "Are you ready for your new job

21. If my mother calls let me know.

22. Order the party food from the bakery (do you have the phone number

23. On July 4, 1997 we will be on vacation.

24. My graduation present will be a computer, however, I haven't chosen the brand yet.

25. I have applied for jobs at several companies that seemed interesting.

26. Getting a job will be a relief I think.

27. One speaker at graduation will be Ms. Turnoy the school director.

28. This is the last main grammar test, we're almost done with English.

29. After this test is over well be writing letters.

30. You should practice typing therefore and review typing rules.

Part C: Capitals, Abbreviations, Numbers

31. 200 people are expected at graduation.

32. The Director of our school will make that announcement.

33. The ceremony will be in Clover hall.

34. That bldg. is on Bascom Ave.

35. Drive South on de la Cruz.

Part D: English Usage

36. She will attend the ceremony with Jane and I.

37. Each counselor and teacher are proud of the students.

38. I feel real good about that.

39. The new car is her's; that one is John's.

40. Leyla and Barbara don't need help with that course.

41. Obviously, well help if needed.

42. All the test materials is on the desk.

43. Every student in these classes have studied hard.

44. April, along with other assistants, were planning graduation.

45. Don't leave your tests laying around the classroom.

Part E: Rewriting Sentences

Directions: In the blanks, rewrite the sentences.

46. Climbing quickly, our eyes beheld the scenic view.

_____

_____

47. She bought a parrot for her brother, which was green and yellow.

_____

_____

48. We enjoy bike riding and to hike in the hills.

_____

_____

Evaluation and Placement Examination: Version A _____

Directions: In the blanks write S for complete sentence, F for fragment (incomplete sentence), or R for run-on (incorrect double sentence). *One point each sentence.*

__R__ 1. First he spoke quietly, then he started to yell.

__F__ 2. Hoping that you would change your mind soon.

__R__ 3. Angie is hard to please, she tends to be nervous.

__S__ 4. I got a typing speed of 40, which is good for a beginner.

__F__ 5. A school that has a very good reputation.

__S__ 6. When I saw her, I laughed until I cried.

__R__ 7. The path is stony, it hurts his feet.

__R__ 8. One sister went to school, the other started working.

__S__ 9. Exploring all the rooms, we walked around the school.

__S__ 10. While she attended college, Sue worked as a receptionist.

__S__ 11. She always plans her time, at least a few days at once.

__F__ 12. Which made me change my mind about the job.

Directions: Add any necessary capital letters and punctuation marks, including apostrophes. *Two points each sentence.*

13. The children's room is near ours.

14. It's our store's policy to sell english imports on the first floor.

15. The letter will be mailed, I hope, on thursday.

16. The Joneses, our neighbors, have five siamese kittens.

17. We'll be at the stuart hotel, 680 santa clara street, until monday, february 4.

18. Lick high and oak grove high are in the same area, and the rivalry between them is great.

19. This bill, by the way, is important to every pupil, teacher, and employer in this state.

20. Expecting out-of-town guests, we arranged for more bedding, food, and towels.

21. The teacher replied, "we can't expect perfect scores."

22. "Why not?" asked jose.

23. I hope, karen, that you'll write a better letter after labor day.

24. Sam, for example, is a better typist than elizabeth, but his spelling still

    needs work.

25. will mrs. miller come to our class and demonstrate body language?

26. When i'm busy, i eat only juice, toast, and coffee for breakfast.

27. Are all the names on the secretary's list?

28. We celebrate thanksgiving day in november.

29. I bought some groceries; then i bought some new shoes.

30. Please order the following items: soap, tea, napkins, milk.

31. Give her many chances; for example, help her with her spanish lesson.

Directions: Label N for noun, Pro for pronoun, V for verb, adj for adjective, adv for adverb, prep for preposition, and con for conjunction above each word in this sentence. *One point each word.*

      V   adv   prep adj   N   prep   N   con Pro V Pro

32. Look carefully at complete records of applicants before you hire them.

Directions: Put each prepositional phrase in parentheses. *One point each sentence.*

33. The children spent the day hunting (for shells.)

34. We grew beans (in a space) (near our driveway.)

35. There was a garden (between the two trees.)

36. We learn much (from the letters) (of friends.)

37. The band played an old waltz (by Chopin.)

38. Mrs. Carbajal looked (at my notes) and shook her head.

39. All the students (except Jean) finished the word processing.

Directions: Circle the correct word in the parentheses. *One point each.*

40. There (was/were) no marks on my paper.

41. The class (don't/doesn't) start until 10 a.m.

42. My interest in flowers (go/**goes**) back to my childhood.

43. The results of this study (was/**were**) serious.

44. A razor blade or a stylus sometimes (**is**/are) used for correction.

45. One of the typewriters (need/**needs**) fixing.

46. Each one of these students (**has**/have) an interesting story.

47. The diamonds in this bracelet (is/**are**) genuine.

48. Several books were (threw/**thrown**) on the floor.

49. Someone must have (broke/**broken**) this window.

50. The textbook (**came**/come) with a key.

51. I (**lay**/laid) back in the chair and relaxed.

52. Mom had (laid/**lain**) down on the sofa.

53. Kim (lay/**laid**) her books on the chair.

54. John forgot where he had (**laid**/lain) his keys.

55. Sue had (**set**/sat) the cake on the floor.

56. Cheryl typed two more letters than (**she**/her).

57. Dad is taller than (**I**/me).

58. (**We**/Us) students want to fix up the parking lot.

59. I wonder where (**its**/it's) owner is?

60. The Browns don't eat as early as (us/**we**).

61. Between you and (I/**me**), English is hard.

62. This motor runs (**well**/good) on regular gas.

63. I stumbled very (awkward/**awkwardly**) on the rug.

64. Our roses look (beautifully/**beautiful**) in the spring.

65. I can't type (good/**well**) on this old typewriter.

66. She felt very (**bad**/badly) about the mistake.

67. Your wedding plans sound (**delightful**/delightfully).

68. There aren't (~~any~~/no) more days left.

69. Who is (~~faster~~/fastest), Jack or Tom?

70. The Powells have the (attractivest/~~most attractive~~) car in the lot.

71. We didn't like (neither/~~either~~) of the tests.

72. They should have used (more easy/~~easier~~/more easier) examples.

Evaluation and Placement Examination: Version B _____

Directions: In the blanks write S for complete sentence, F for fragment (incomplete sentence), or R for run-on (incorrect double sentence). *One point each sentence.*

_F_ 1. Wondering if you can meet on Tuesday.

_R_ 2. First turn on the power, then turn on the screen.

_R_ 3. This equipment is sometimes slow, it needs to warm up.

_S_ 4. Keyboarding is a valuable skill, one that everybody should learn.

_F_ 5. A company known as a good employer.

_S_ 6. When she called, I relaxed and drank a cup of coffee.

_R_ 7. This machine is new, it confuses me occasionally.

_R_ 8. One friend went to school fulltime, the other enrolled at night.

_S_ 9. Walking around the work stations, we explored the office.

_S_ 10. While she attended college, Lee worked as an assembler.

_S_ 11. He always plans his time, at least a week ahead.

_F_ 12. Which made me want to apply for the job.

Directions: Add any necessary capital letters and punctuation marks, including apostrophes. *Two points each sentence.*

13. The bosses' office is near ours.

14. It's our company's policy to send french shipments weekly.

15. The fax will be sent, I hope, tomorrow.

16. The Smiths, our neighbors, have two japanese cars.

17. We'll be at the maxim hotel, 110 san jose avenue, until friday, june 10.

18. Andrew hill high and independence high are in the same area, and the rivalry between them is great.

19. This bill, by the way, is important to every pupil, teacher, and employer in this state.

20. Expecting out-of-town visitors, we arranged for hotel, car, and restaurant reservations.

21. The teacher explained, "we can't expect perfect scores."

22. "Why not?" asked lisa.

23. I hope, maria, that you'll write a better memo after new year's day.

24. Roberto, for example, is a better typist than gina, but his spelling still needs work.

(or colon)

25. Give her many chances; for example, help her with her computer lesson.

26. Please order the following items: paper, correction fluid, staples.

27. I bought some groceries; then i bought a paper.

28. We celebrate memorial day in may.

29. Are all the names on the leader's list?

30. When i'm busy, i eat only juice, cereal, and coffee for breakfast.

31. Will mrs. vasquez come to our class and demonstrate audiovisuals?

Directions: Label N for noun, Pro for pronoun, V for verb, adj for adjective, adv for adverb, prep for preposition, and con for conjunction above each word in this sentence. *One point each word.*

    V   adv   adj   N   con   Pro V adj adj   N   prep

32. Read slowly all instructions before you begin any new procedure at

   N

work.

Directions: Put each prepositional phrase in parentheses. *One point each sentence.*

33. The students spent the day looking (at videos.)

34. We grow plants (in a space) (near our office window.)

35. There is a garden (between the two trees.)

R-43

36. We learn much (from the examples) (on the job.)

37. The radio played an old waltz (by Chopin.)

38. Mrs. Bennett looked (at my notes) and shook her head.

39. All the students (except Beverly) finished the word processing.

Directions: Circle the correct word in the parentheses. *One point each.*

40. Several papers were (threw/thrown) on the floor.

41. The diamonds in this ring (is/are) genuine.

42. Each one of these workers (has/have) an interesting story.

43. One of the telephones (need/needs) fixing.

44. A razor blade or a stylus sometimes (is/are) used for repair.

45. The results of this meeting (was/were) serious.

46. My interest in computers (go/goes) back to my childhood.

47. My job (don't/doesn't) start until 10 a.m.

48. There (was/were) two changes on my outline.

49. They should have used (more easy/easier/more easier) questions.

50. We didn't like (neither/either) of the texts.

51. The Sanchezes have the (attractivest/most attractive) car in the lot.

52. Who is (faster/fastest), Jack or Tom?

53. There aren't (any/no) more cookies left.

54. Your vacation plans sound (delightful/delightfully).

55. She felt very (bad/badly) about the mistake.

56. I can't type (good/well) on this old typewriter.

57. Our roses look (beautifully/beautiful) in the spring.

58. I stumbled very (awkward/awkwardly) on the wire.

59. This motor runs (well/good) on unleaded gas.

60. Between you and (I/me), English is hard.

61. The Joneses don't leave as early as (us/**we**).

62. I wonder where (**its**/it's) owner is.

63. (**We**/Us) employees want to fix up the lounge.

64. Dad is taller than (**I**/me).

65. Cheryl typed two more letters than (**he**/him).

66. Sue had (**set**/sat) the typewriter on the floor.

67. Someone must have (broke/**broken**) this viewer.

68. Lee forgot where he had (**laid**/lain) his keys.

69. Sarita (lay/**laid**) her books on the car seat.

70. Mom had (laid/**lain**) down on the beach chair.

71. I (**lay**/laid) back on the sand and relaxed.

72. The textbook (**came**/come) with a workbook.

Evaluation and Placement Examination: Version C ___

Directions: In the blanks write S for complete sentence, F for fragment (incomplete sentence), or R for run-on (incorrect double sentence). *One point each sentence.*

<u>F</u>   1. Beginning to write a research report.

<u>R</u>   2. First decide on a general topic, later you can narrow it a little.

<u>R</u>   3. You may need to write for a specific audience, the subject may have been assigned to you.

<u>S</u>   4. In business, research is very important, a skill you should have.

<u>F</u>   5. A topic that is too general or too long.

<u>S</u>   6. When they ask you to write, relax and enjoy the process.

<u>R</u>   7. Starting is the hardest part, many people wait until the last minute.

<u>R</u>   8. Just start writing, see what appears on the page.

<u>S</u>   9. You can fix the problems later, polishing and organizing.

<u>S</u> 10. When you are first writing, try making lists or clusters.

<u>S</u> 11. Be sure you learn your way around the library, with the help of the research librarian.

___F___ 12. Which may require taking careful notes about authors and page numbers.

Directions: Add any necessary capital letters and punctuation marks, including apostrophes. *Two points each sentence.*

13. My teacher's desk is piled high with english books and papers.

14. It's crowded but more organized than yours.

15. Sally brown will leave for the convention in miami on tuesday.

16. The airplane tickets will be here, i think, by november 22.

17. You're going to need a map to find the address on south tenth street in st. petersburg before december 1, 1997.

18. It's near south high school and across from a city fire department.

19. this map, by the way, has every city, county, and highway in this state.

20. Expecting weather problems, we packed flashlights, bottled water, and a first-aid kit.

21. The officer warned, "they can't drive near the beach today."

22. "Why not?" asked ken.

23. I hope, marika, that you'll have a good trip before christmas day.

24. Lui, for example, is a better driver than lee, but she needs to practice reading maps.

25. Give him many opportunities; for example, help him with his computer program.

26. Please order the following items: disks, paper, and ink cartridges.

27. I read the report; then i summarized it.

28. We celebrate thanksgiving day in november.

29. Are all the names on the bosses' list?

30. When i'm busy, i have just crackers, soup, and coffee for lunch.

31. Will mrs. lee come to our class and demonstrate the new video program?

Directions: Label N for noun, Pro for pronoun, V for verb, adj for adjective, adv for adverb, prep for preposition, and con for conjunction above each word in this sentence. *One point each word.*

   V adv adj N prep adj N con Pro V adj adj N

32. List carefully each part of the job before you start a new project.

Directions: Put each prepositional phrase in parentheses. *One point each sentence.*

33. My sister and I are planning a trip (to Costa Rica.)

34. We have maps (in a folder) (on the coffee table.)

35. There is a special fund marked ("for the trip.")

36. We save money (for gifts and souvenirs.)

37. Costa Rica has been a democracy (for 100 years.)

38. The tiny country has more species (of plants and animals) than there are

  (in the United States.)

39. A jungle train runs (over the mountains) as monkeys play (on the beach.)

Directions: Circle the correct word in the parentheses. *One point each.*

40. The relationship between living things and environment (is/are) called

  "ecology."

41. Trash is often (threw/thrown) on beaches and trails.

42. Every piece of trash (has/have) an effect on the earth.

43. Plastic rings from one type of six-pack (kill/kills) birds and animals.

44. Many types of plastic (is/are) now labeled for recycling.

45. Our cities (need/needs) more recycling plants.

46. Each government (is/are) planning ways to solve pollution problems.

47. They (haven't/hasn't) learned to cooperate well yet.

48. There (was/were) some new laws recently about air pollution.

49. They have used (more hard/harder/more harder) air standards.

50. People will not use (neither/either) trains or buses if not convenient.

51. This new car has the (effectivest/most effective) fuel economy.

52. Which is (best/**better**) in cutting air pollution, this model or that?

53. There aren't (**any**/no) easy answers.

54. Your new job sounds (**delightful**/delightfully).

55. He felt quite (**bad**/badly) about the loss.

56. I can't study (good/**well**) in this light.

57. Your trees look (beautifully/**beautiful**) in the fall.

58. She stumbled (awkward/**awkwardly**) on the step.

59. This program runs (**well**/good) on this computer.

60. Between you and (I/**me**), writing English is not easy.

61. The teachers don't leave as early as (**we**/us).

62. I discovered where (**its**/it's) owner lived.

63. (**We**/Us) students want to take the test early.

64. Maria is taller than (**I**/me).

65. (Who/**Whom**) did you see at the meeting?

66. Tomas had (**set**/sat) the printer on the floor.

67. Someone must have (took/**taken**) the disk home.

68. Jana forgot where she had (**laid**/lain) the papers.

69. Lela (lay/**laid**) her briefcase on the car seat.

70. Dad had (laid/**lain**) down after dinner.

71. I (**lay**/laid) back on the sofa and relaxed.

72. The program (**ran**/run) very quickly.

Part One Examination: Version A
Covering Chapters 1–10

Directions: Label each group of words either declarative (dec), interrogatory (int), exclamatory (exc), imperative (imp), or fragment (fra). Use abbreviations if you wish. *Two points per numbered item.*

<u>dec</u>   1. Some weather announcers do a great job.

<u>fra</u>   2. Working with the public early in the morning.

<u>exc</u>   3. What a strange-looking cloud that is!

<u>imp</u>   4. Check the symbols on the weather maps.

<u>fra</u>   5. A small group of students with their teacher.

<u>int</u>   6. Do you watch weather reports on television?

<u>dec</u>   7. A tornado is the smallest of destructive storms.

<u>fra</u>   8. The opportunity for better planning of trips.

Directions: Label S above the simple subjects and V above the verb. *Two points per numbered item.*

9. The satellite **reports** often **are** quite accurate.
                S   V

10. Your neighborhood weather **forecaster** frequently **predicts** local weather as well as national weather.
                             S   V

11. Along with many others, **he** or **she** sometimes **rises** early and **comes** to work before breakfast.
                        S   S   V   V

12. Complete **reports**, as well as the weather map, **come** over your early morning airwaves.
               S   V

13. **Do you understand** the symbols on the weather map?
    V   S   V

14. Early in their careers, weather **reporters take** lessons in terminology.
                              S   V

15. **They** sometimes **observe** the sky through the telescopes at the observatory.
    S   V

Directions: Put each prepositional phrase in parentheses. *Two points per numbered item.*

16. The announcer spoke (of many possibilities.)

17. (During the broadcast,) he mentioned the earthquake prediction.

18. That weather forecaster is also a comedian (at some points.)

19. Although he is very funny, he also knows (about weather.)

20. The announcer who works (with him) sometimes laughs (at his jokes.)

Directions: Underline each dependent clause and put each prepositional phrase in parentheses.

21. The professor started her lecture <u>before the class was seated.</u>

22. Many students (in the class) were startled.

23. One student <u>who came (in late)</u> ran (to his seat.)

24. Here are the results (of the tests) <u>that they took.</u>

Directions: In the blanks write S for complete sentence, F for fragment (incomplete sentence), or R for run-on (two incorrectly joined sentences).

__F__ 25. L. Frank Baum, who wrote *The Wizard of Oz.*

__S__ 26. Judy Garland became famous in the movie as Dorothy, carried off by a tornado.

__S__ 27. Was Dorothy born in Kansas?

__R__ 28. Ray Bolger played the Scarecrow, Bert Lahr played the Cowardly Lion.

__S__ 29. Children have loved the book since about 1900.

__F__ 30. The Wonderful Wizard a humbug who faked magic.

__R__ 31. The Tin Woodsman needed a heart, the Scarecrow wanted a brain.

Directions: Label the part of speech of each word, using S, AV or BV, N, N (poss), Pro, rel pro, adj, adv, prep, con, interj, inf, and part, and put prepositional phrases in parentheses.

32.
    part prep N prep adj   N   con part (adj) Pro   N   S-N BV
Sitting (in front) (of the television) and studying her English, Priya was
    adv   adj
soon asleep.

33.
    S-N rel pro AV adj   N   adv   AV   adj N   adv
Oscar, who knows the material well, will pass the test easily.

34.
    con S-Pro AV S-Pro   AV
If you study, you will learn.

35.
    adj S-N BV   adj   prep   N
The time is available (for studying.)

Part One Examination: Version B
Covering Chapters 1–10

Directions: Label each group of words either declarative (dec), interrogatory (int), exclamatory (exc), imperative (imp), run-on (R), or fragment (fra). *Two points per sentence.*

_____R_____ 1. There is little we can do to help, he is too stubborn.

_____R_____ 2. Mr. Hanson is out of town, however, he'll be back soon.

imp 3. Speak to Mr. Ng about that.

int 4. Are you sure that is the right answer?

dec 5. Since the plant operated on a 24-hour basis, we finished.

fra 6. Because the sun had shone all day, melting the ice.

_R_ 7. Our apple trees have grown amazingly you should see them.

exc 8. What a beautiful day this is!

Directions: Label S above the simple subjects and V above the verb.

9. The imported goods often cost more.
        S   V

10. Our friendly neighbor efficiently and quietly manages the store.

11. Majestic ships, with imported cargo, slip silently into port.

12. Along with many others, they bring the goods for the store.

13. This import house, called Green Jade, is one of my favorites.

14. The oriental furniture is expensive but durable.

15. In the shop we look at beautiful things for hours.

Directions: Put each prepositional phrase in parentheses.

16. We talked (of many places.)

17. (During our visit,) the wind chimes played.

18. The saleswoman (with the happy smile) is popular.

19. My uncle who lived (in Burma) knows (about tropical woods.)

20. Although he is older now, his memory (for facts) is very good.

Directions: Underline each dependent clause and put each prepositional phrase in parentheses.

21. The shop owner started to explain <u>before we asked questions</u>.

22. Many countries (with tropical climates) have economic problems.

23. Pauline Lee, <u>who has been my friend (for many years,)</u> knows this shop owner.

24. Here is the Christmas card <u>which she sent</u>.

25. <u>After we buy a gift</u>, I will call her.

Directions: In the blanks write S for complete sentence, F for fragment (incomplete sentence), or R for run-on (two incorrectly joined sentences).

R 26. First he asked questions, then he laughed.

F 27. Hoping that I would change my mind soon.

R 28. Beverly is easy to please, she likes my style.

S 29. We paid $60 for the chest, a very good bargain.

F 30. A store that has a very good reputation.

S 31. When I saw my old friend, we laughed until we cried.

Directions: Label the part of speech of each word, using S, AV or BV, N, N (poss), Pro, rel pro, adj, adv, prep, con, interj, inf, and part, and put prepositional phrases in parentheses.

     adj   S-N   AV   adj   N   prep adj   N
32. Store owners place special importance (on repeat customers.)

     adj   S-N   adv   AV adj or Pro N prep N   prep   N
33. Experienced managers usually do their work (in order) (of importance.)

  S-Pro AV   prep adj   N   con S-Pro AV   adj   N
34. I shopped (at that store) because I enjoy the atmosphere.

   con S-Pro AV adj   N S-Pro AV   prep   adj   N
35. When I leave the store, I think (about birthday gifts.)

Part Two Examination: Version A
Covering Chapters 11–20

Directions: Add any necessary punctuation and delete any that is unnecessary. Use the standard proofreading symbols in your text. *Four points per sentence; partial credit possible.*

1. He paid $2,000 for the used car.

2. We'll drive it to Los Angeles on Tuesday; on Wednesday, to San Diego.

3. The valley may be very, very hot for driving.

4. We may drive part way at night; our car, however, should handle the heat well.

5. Our next trip will be at Christmas, but we're not sure exactly which day.

6. Jessica, Daniel, and Ben are coming with us this time.

7. Anyone else who wants to come should see me before Monday.

8. Before we start, we need to check luggage space.

9. Next Thursday—or is it on Wednesday?—we should be in Death Valley.

10. To see the desert blooming, is a great thrill.

11. The owner of the restaurant (Wolfgang Puck,) says he'll give us a

    discount. [or replace parentheses with commas]

12. He is known in the area as a "creative, careful chef."

13. "As you see," said Kevin, "I don't carry much luggage."

14. "Yes, Kevin, but your skis and fishing poles are odd shapes," says his

    mother.

15. We'll stop at Monterey, California; Bakersfield, California; Tucson,

    Arizona; and Death Valley, California, on that trip.

16. Don't forget to bring regular camera, camcorder, color film, tapes, etc.

17. "Are you looking forward to the trip?" asked Jessica.

18. Daniel answered, that he certainly was.

19. "Then come," his mother said, "and help get ready."

20. Eventually, early in the morning, we all piled into the car.

Directions: Mark letters that need to be capitalized or lowercased; in the space above the sentence, correct or spell out abbreviations as necessary. *Four points per sentence; partial credit possible.*

21. We took with us the A/A/A guide book, <u>Discovering The West</u>. [or the title can go in quotation marks]

22. Our first stop was at 1212 46th street in Monterey, a famous pacific coast city.

23. Kevin's Mother works there in the Fisher building near the Red salmon restaurant.

24. Some of the salmon are (four ft.) long, the largest in (CA). [4 feet / California]

25. (3) of us ordered salmon, along with about a (100) other people in the restaurant. [Three / hundred]

Directions: Add any necessary punctuation, and delete any that is unnecessary. Use the standard proofreading symbols in your text. *Four points per sentence; partial credit possible.*

1. "I've been thinking about my budget," said Rosa.

2. "Me too," said Henry. "Should we start planning now?"

3. "I think we'd better," she answered. "We want a vacation."

4. "We could always fly now and pay much, much later," he said grinning.

5. Rosa said she didn't think that was a good idea. OK

6. "In one month we would pay an extra $150.00 for just $1000 of

   vacation money," she said.

7. They decided to save their money; then they would go to Alaska on a

   cruise along the Inland Passage.

8. This beautiful summer cruise between the islands and the mainland of

   Canada and Alaska is very popular. OK

9. Because the ships are close to shore, the tourists who watch from the

   decks can see reindeer, grizzly bear, and moose.

10. Sea life—such as whales, seals, otters, and thousands of birds—also

    follow the passage.

11. When passengers go on shore, however, they can walk on glaciers.

12. People who take cameras and many rolls of film can photograph

    wildlife, sea, mountains, and icebergs.

13. For a ticket in a cabin for four people, the cost is $595, which is quite

    inexpensive.

14. My sister wants to go to Alaska next vacation; my brother, Tahiti.

15. Tahiti is better for a winter vacation; Alaska, for summer.

16. When we go in July, we'll stop in Anchorage, Ketchikan, and Homer, where I have relatives who own a fishing boat.

17. Anyone else who wants to join us, should call soon.

18. To see the wildlife from the ship, is unforgettable.

19. To get a good price, we need to have three or four people.

20. My travel agent, Juanita Lopez, calls these "bargain cruises."

Directions: Mark letters that need to be capitalized or lowercased; Circle any incorrect number or abbreviation forms and rewrite them correctly in the blanks. *Four points per sentence; partial credit possible.*

21. Juanita's telephone number is 555,6745.   555-6745
22. Her address is at No. 16, 755 6th St.   16755 Sixth Street
23. That is the Old mission bldg. in san Jose.   Building
24. Meet me at ken's pancake house to plan.   Ken's Pancake House
25. They have ¼ inch pancakes 6 in. across.   inches

Part Three Examination: Section 1, Version A
Covering Chapters 21–23

Directions: Write the correct possessives of the nouns by adding apostrophes in the right places. *Four points per sentence.*

1. This employees' group is planning a surprise.

2. It's their boss's birthday. [or boss']

3. Two workers discovered that their boss likes Chinese food. OK

4. At tomorrow's break, many mysterious dishes will appear.

5. Tony's job is to bring drinks.

6. Thuy makes great egg rolls with crispy crusts. OK

7. Several telephone calls have happened among employees' houses.

8. A giant card will hold signatures and funny sayings from workers. OK

9. The members of the group hope for the boss's permission to take a longer break.

10. Do you think she'll let them do that?
   ^

Directions: Write the plural form of the noun in the blank.

11. measles   *measles*
12. salmon   *salmon*
13. knife   *knives*
14. handful   *handfuls*
15. woman   *women*
16. soprano   *sopranos*
17. hero   *heroes*
18. stereo   *stereos*
19. mother-in-law   *mothers-in-law*
20. berry   *berries*

Directions: Write the possessive form of each phrase in the blank.

21. home of the Smiths   *the Smiths' home*
22. rooms of the boys   *the boys' rooms*
23. advice of the attorney-at-law   *the attorney-at-law's advice*
24. mothers of Jack and Maria   *Jack's and Maria's mothers*
25. clothing of the women   *the women's clothing*

Part Three Examination: Section 1, Version B
Covering Chapters 21–23

Directions: Circle the correct plural or possessive form in the parentheses.

1. Fantasy, myth, fairy tale—whether (**children's**/childrens') or
   (**adults'**/adult's) versions—occupy much of our leisure time.

2. Nursery school children dress up in (Supermans'/**Superman's**) cape,
   (Batmans'/**Batman's**) hood, and the Ninja (**Turtles'**/Turtle's) masks.

3. (**Superheroes**/Superheroes') make children feel their own power.

4. Young (boy's/**boys'**) aggressive instincts are encouraged to "fight for the
   good," against the "bad guys."

5. In the better ((stories)/stories'), they are shown how to seek peaceful (solutions'/(solutions)).

6. Because our culture is changing, the more recent ((girls')/girl's) (story's/(stories)) show young ((girls')/girls) bravery and strength.

7. ((Girls')/Girls) and (woman/(women)) are no longer limited to keeping house and having ((babies)/babys).

8. Even some adult fantasy—for example (mens/mens'/(men's)) and (womens/(women's)/womens') scenes in ads—is showing the new message.

9. (Girls/(Girls')) dreams for themselves can now include jobs as police ((officers)/officers') or (lawyers'/(lawyers)).

10. (Mens/(Men's)) strengths are now shown to include the difficult ((arts)/arts') of peace and understanding (ones/(one's)) family and caring for (ones/(one's)) children.

11. Look carefully to see the ((culture's)/cultures) messages.

Part Three Examination: Section 2, Version A
Covering Chapters 24–26

Directions: Circle the correct pronoun in the parentheses. *Two points each.*

1. Jean and ((I)/me) corrected the tests.

2. Dan met Ken and ((him)/he) at the library.

3. ((We)/Us) men are planning a bicycle race.

4. She was as much to blame as ((I)/me).

5. Stan took a picture of Sally and ((her)/she).

6. Lois and (them/(they)) got the high scores on the test.

7. The class chose Juan and ((her)/she) to represent them.

8. The other people caught more fish than (we/us).

9. (His/Him) studying the subject was important.

10. My high grades surprised my family more than (I/me).

11. The candlesticks are a gift from (her/she) and Tom.

12. Our teacher read an article about computers to Tony and (us/we).

13. Edgar Allen Poe, (who/whom) wrote the first detective stories, was a fascinating writer.

14. Writers (who/whom) are less gifted have tried to imitate him.

15. (Who/Whom) do I see for a new library card?

16. Another great writer (who/whom) I appreciate was Washington Irving.

17. Please tell me (who/whom) can write as well as Mark Twain.

18. William Faulkner is another author (who/whom) wrote great stories.

19. To (who/whom) did he dedicate that novel?

20. Give the prize to (whoever/whomever) deserves it.

Directions: Write in the blank at the right the correct *past* form of the verb in the parentheses. *Two points each.*

21. What have you (do) to your car?   _done_

22. You have already (drive) it too long.   _driven_

23. We (find) it on the freeway.   _found_

24. Have you (run) out of gas?   _run_

25. We (think) you had an accident.   _thought_

26. Be sure that the gas gauge is not (break).   _broken_

27. Last year I (lose) my owner's manual.   _lost_

28. I (forget) to change the oil in the engine.   _forgot_

29. Then the car (begin) to overheat.   _began_

30. The mechanic said the seal had (begin) to leak.   _begun_

31. He (say) that some problems are expensive.   _said_

32. I (feel) like giving the car away.   _felt_

33. I wish that I had (saw) the problem sooner.   _seen_

34. I probably (throw) the manual away.   _threw_

35. I (write) to the car company for a new book. _____wrote_____

36. The morning mail has (come) today. _____come_____

37. Now I have (read) about proper car care. _____read_____

38. (Do) you buy a used car last year? _____Did_____

39. I (buy) my car from a car rental agency. _____bought_____

40. Rental agencies have (sell) almost new cars. _____sold_____

41. My car (is) only a year old. _____was_____

42. It (has) only 10,000 miles on it. _____had_____

43. It was not very (wear) at all. _____worn_____

44. When I (bring) it home, my family cheered. _____brought_____

45. My other car had (be) 10 years old. _____been_____

Part Three Examination: Section 2, Version B
Covering Chapters 24–26

Directions: Circle the correct pronouns in the parentheses. *Two points each.*

1. For my family and (I/**me**), foreign films are especially tempting.

2. My husband and (**I**/me) both like French and Spanish movies.

3. To (we/**us**) the subtitles are an interesting challenge.

4. You see, (**he and I**/him and me) like to try to understand the words by listening, but the subtitles are there if (**we**/us) need them.

5. Some family members are distracted by the subtitles, so (**they**/them) choose films that dub in English words instead.

6. Would you rather see a movie in a theater or rent one to see (**it**/them) at home?

7. Some of (we/**us**) in the family like fast-moving drama; others, like my sister and (I/**me**), choose romantic comedies for relaxation.

8. (**We**/Us) can rent or tape two films and take turns watching and playing table games or working.

9. My grandchildren tell me when (he and she/him and her) think the movie is too violent to suit my sister and (I/me).

10. "You can fast-forward through the scary part on this one," say (them/they).

11. My sister and (I/me) are concerned about violence in the media.

12. For my husband and (I/me), worries about film and television ratings always bring discussion about censorship.

13. He is more concerned than (I/me) about a possible computer "V" chip to use to block out violent or pornographic films.

14. (Who/Whom) should choose what is watched by your family?

15. Should the parents choose (who/whom) they think should watch?

16. Should television shows be rated like movies to recommend (who/whom) should be allowed to see (it/them)?

17. For (who/whom) do you think media ratings should be designed?

18. Should films be rented by (whomever/whoever) wants them?

19. Among my family and (I/me), these are frequent discussion questions.

20. Does your family argue as much as (us/we) about this topic?

21. Perhaps you are as concerned as (I/me).

Directions: Circle the correct past tense in the parentheses. *Two points each.*

22. Why do you think human beings have always (fight/fighted/fought)?

23. When we study early humans, we discover that violence has always (be/been/being) with us.

24. We know that sometimes brothers have (kill/killed) brothers.

25. Some of the worst violence we have (see/seen) has been among those who are close.

26. Wars, feuds, and other disputes often have (begin/began/begun) among relatives or members of the same religion.

27. The First World War (begin/began/begun) in 1914 in an area of Europe not far from Bosnia, where recent fighting has again (arose/arisen).

28. The American Civil War (grow/grew/grown) out of arguments about individual, regional, and national rights that have (break/broke/broken) many families.

29. Any violent acts have (raised/rose/risen) questions about solutions.

30. Many historians say that World War II (had/has/have) its roots in an unjust settlement of World War I.

31. Arguments about territory, trade, and fairness have (show/showed/shown) up both in families and in nations.

32. Do you think that your childhood family was (ran/run) like a democracy or a dictatorship?

33. As a child, when you (choose/chose) a path, what was the result?

34. (Did/Do) your parents support your decision?

35. (Was/Were) your brothers or sisters and other family members helpful or jealous or both?

36. (Laying/Lying) deep in our minds have always (be/been) the memories of childhood and our related feelings about ourselves.

37. These feelings have (laid/lain) within us since early childhood.

38. We may remember being (set/sat) in a corner to regret our misdeeds.

39. Some may think about being (strike/struck/striked) with a strap or paddle.

40. When a belt is (laid/lain) across a back, does violence disappear?

41. Have you (spoke/spoken) to anyone about crime and punishment?

42. These are topics about which you may have (think/thinked/**thought**) or (write/wrote/**written**).

Part Three Examination: Section 3, Version A ____
Covering Chapters 27–29

Directions: Circle the correct verb in the parentheses. *Two points each.*

1. The players on the team (stands/**stand**) silently before the game.

2. The students in this school (**use**/uses) two colors to decorate.

3. There (is/**are**) several hundred cars in the lot.

4. Ricardo or Enrique (**is**/are) throwing the first ball.

5. Musicians or marchers (**have**/has) always performed at halftime.

6. The coaches on the bench (**seem**/seems) nervous.

7. Neither the players nor the fans (is/**are**) happy about the weather.

8. The mood in the stands (seem/**seems**) doubtful.

9. The dark clouds overhead (is/**are**) scheduled to disappear.

10. From behind one cloud, here (come/**comes**) the sun.

11. Nobody in the stadium (want/**wants**) the rain to come.

12. Sometimes it (rain/**rains**) while the sun shines.

13. Then everybody (see/**sees**) a rainbow.

14. Which kind of ballgame (do/**does**) your family enjoy?

15. Some people (**play**/plays) a game every day.

16. Others (**watch**/watches) games on television.

17. Today we all (is/**are**) seeing the game at the school.

18. Few of us (**play**/plays) ball as well as these players.

19. Some of them (**have**/has) practiced since age 3.

20. My daughter and son (**love**/loves) to play softball.

21. They especially (**like**/likes) to bat home runs.

22. That (seem/**seems**) to be more fun than catching balls.

23. Both batting and catching (is/**are**) important, I tell them.

24. Now the score (**is**/are) tied at 6–6.

25. In the ninth inning, the next run (win/**wins**) the game.

26. A new girls' team is playing (good/**well**) in Little League.

27. These young girls have practiced (diligent/**diligently**) for a year or more.

28. During their first year, they have proved that they can pitch and hit (real/**really**) well.

29. They need a little more practice in catching balls (safe/**safely**).

30. Their abilities are (**different**/differently) from those of boys.

31. In some ways, the girls are more (**accurate**/accurately) than the boys.

32. Girls tend to play more (careful/**carefully**).

33. In our culture, money is still given less (free/**freely**) for women's sports than for men's.

34. Everyone agrees that women can play (brave/**bravely**).

35. Many organizations are encouraging girls and women to practice sports (regular/**regularly**).

36. Exercise (sure/**surely**) improves health, for both men and women.

37. Does this trend mean that men and women will look (**similar**/similarly)?

38. There will (sure/**surely**) be some changes.

39. However, Superman's muscles will always work (good/**well**).

40. Superwoman will always move (swift/**swiftly**).

41. The average man will always seem more (**strong**/strongly) than the average woman is.

42. One major new problem in sports competition has developed (rapid/**rapidly**).

43. Steroid drugs have been given (illegal/**illegally**) to both men and women athletes at some international contests.

44. Such drugs (temporary/**temporarily**) strengthen and enlarge muscles.

45. They also cause (**severe**/severely) liver damage and major hormonal changes.

46. Athletes who are found to use (**illegal**/illegally) drugs are banned from competition.

47. Because these drugs cause both physical and emotional damage, some of the athletes (eventual/**eventually**) ruin their relationships or even die.

48. Sports competitions are (extreme/**extremely**) important to many of us.

49. Each of us needs to decide (thoughtful/**thoughtfully**) where sports activities belong in our lives.

50. Do we play games to exercise (good/**well**) or to beat other people?

Part Three Examination: Section 3, Version B
Covering Chapters 27–29

Directions: Circle the correct verb in the parentheses. *Two points each.*

1. Fantasy and myth (is/**are**) part of all our lives.

2. Some people (**say**/says) that fantasy (**is**/are) lies.

3. Others say that fantasy and myth (is/**are**) like our dreams.

4. Our dreams (**tell**/tells) us true things about ourselves.

5. Events in a dream (**explain**/explains) feelings in real life.

6. The stories we tell children (is/**are**) like the dreams of our culture.

7. Heroes in the story (**inspire**/inspires) us to try harder.

8. A villain who makes mistakes (warn/**warns**) us about results.

9. When you (**set**/sit) a story before a child, you help him or her.

10. As he or she (**lies**/lays) reading at bedtime, each child (learn/**learns**) more about life.

11. In the *Wizard of Oz,* each character (think/**thinks**) (**he or she**/they) must get help from the Wonderful Wizard.

12. At the end of the story, the Wizard (**admits**/admit) he cannot help.

13. He (**doesn't**/don't) have that kind of power.

14. Every character in the story (**has**/have) power to help (**himself or herself**/themselves).

15. The Good Witch (show/**shows**) Dorothy that the Ruby Slippers (is/**are**) a sign of her own power.

16. When Dorothy has (flew/**flown**) home from her dream, she (**awakens**/awakened) saying, "There's no place like home."

17. The Land of Oz, like Alice's Wonderland, (**is**/are) a beautiful, colorful place.

18. The world of our dreams (**is**/are) (**given**/gave) to us by our own minds.

Directions: Circle the correct modifier in the parentheses. *Five points each.*

19. That wall color looks (**different**/differently) in daylight.

20. Clean the surface (good/**well**) before painting it.

21. This paint brush doesn't look (**clean**/cleanly).

22. Which dries (**faster**/fastest)—the acrylic or the oil?

23. This is the (difficultest/**most difficult**) job I've done.

24. We couldn't find the trim (**anywhere**/nowhere).

25. I stumbled (awkward/awkwardly) while climbing the ladder.

26. Your decorating plans sound (delightful/delightfully).

27. We should have used (brighter/more brighter) paint.

28. They didn't like (either/neither) of the colors we had.

29. The man wouldn't take (any/no) money for his advice.

30. Josh spent his money rather (foolish/foolishly).

31. This brush works (bad/badly) on the corners.

32. They talked very (cheerful/cheerfully).

33. We now have the (attractivest/most attractive) room in the building.

34. We saw (an/a) easy way to do it.

35. A (larger/more larger) brush would help.

36. He is the (more/most) helpful worker we've had.

37. I feel (bad/badly) about the cost.

38. The room looks (good/well) now after all our hard work.

Advanced Comprehensive Examination: Version A
Covering All 30 Chapters

Directions: Use proofreading symbols to correct any errors. *Two points each; partial credit possible.*

Part A: Spelling and Commonly Confused Words

1. Absents makes the heart grow fonder.

2. When he cheated on the test, his conscious bothered him.

3. They were accidently omitted from the graduation list.

4. It is convenent to know how to spell.

5. Can you discribe your goals after graduation?

6. They decided that they wanted to work for the two attornies.

7. Are you definitly sure about that? [e]

8. We had to much cake at the party. [o]

9. Tell us immediatly when you plan to graduate. [e]

10. It will be nesessary to fill out the paperwork. [c]

11. Your permenent record will always be here. [a]

12. Has it occured to you that you need a job soon? [r]

13. The principle speech will be given by Ms. Turnoy. [al]

14. Then we will procede with the diplomas. [i]

15. Have you had sufficent time to study for the final? [i]

Part B: Punctuation

16. Do you realize, Maria, that we have only one more month?

17. We plan to attend the ceremony on Saturday; however, we'll have two more weeks of class.

18. The following staff will be at graduation: the administration, the teachers, the counselors, and the office employees.

19. This ceremony—is it the only one this spring?—is important to me.

20. Mr. Rosas asked, "Do you have the diplomas ready?"

21. When the teachers get here, please call me.

22. Send the bill to Ms. Watkins (has she gone on leave yet?).

23. On June 15, 1997, there will be a graduation.

24. We have been working hard for this; we deserve it.

25. The student who has been selected to give the speech is ready. OK

26. The party will be fun, won't it?

27. The new Dean of Admissions is Mr. Elfstrom, who has just started.

28. This test is comprehensive; it covers all the English so far.

29. When you finish this test, there will be no more grammar exams.

30. You can relax, therefore, and take a deep breath. OK

Part C: Capitals, Abbreviations, Numbers

31. Yes, the sale offers ~~twenty~~ 20 percent ~~%~~ off.

32. The ~~P~~president of our school sometimes speaks at graduation.

33. Let's ask ~~Mister~~ Mr. Kapinski whether he wants to do that.

34. The Gold <u>t</u>ower <u>b</u>uilding is for sale.

35. Our school is in the ~~N~~north part of San Jose.

Part D: English Usage

36. Both the counselor and the teacher ~~is~~ are now with the student.

37. The red jacket is hers; the blue one is our~~'~~s.

38. Do you know whether the Johnson~~'~~s are still here?

39. Between you and ~~I~~ me, English is not an easy language.

40. Naturally, we feel bad~~ly~~ when we make mistakes.

41. ~~Don't~~ Doesn't Ms. Powell have that test ready?

42. Yes, I ~~seen~~ saw it on her desk. [or "have seen"]

43. Each teacher in these classes ~~work~~ works many hours at home.

44. Ernest, not one of the other assistants, ~~were~~ was ordering books.

45. I have ~~risen~~ raised my grade to a B this module.

Part E: Rewriting Sentences

Directions: In the blanks rewrite the sentences. *Two points each.*

46. Has Bonita cooked the dinner or Fred?

    Has Bonita or Fred cooked the dinner?
    _____

47. Sara got an invitation for her friend, which she decided to mail.

    Sara decided to mail the invitation for her friend.
    _____

48. There is one hard problem on the test I took yesterday in my desk
    drawer.

The test in my desk drawer has one hard problem. OR, In my desk drawer is the test I took yesterday.

It has one hard problem.

Advanced Comprehensive Examination: Version B
Covering All 30 chapters

Directions: Use proofreading symbols to correct errors. *Two points each; partial credit possible.*

Part A: Spelling and Commonly Confused Words

1. Job opportunities are increased with more training.

2. Our calander shows the holidays planned.

3. It is disirable to review spelling.

4. Have you been writting down your goals?

5. Most people are surprized about how quickly they learn.

6. Have you been refered to the job placement office?

7. The pronounciation of the word helps the spelling.

8. They have studied the material very throughly.

9. The goverment is explaining its actions.

10. Have you made similiar statements?

11. Are you disatisfied with your performance this week?

12. This is the nineth week of the English classes.

13. Have you had continous time available to study?

14. There is not much more grammer to review.

15. Have the school accomodations been satisfactory?

Part B: Punctuation

16. Come and see us, Antony, after you get your job.

17. The graduation party will be on Saturday night, although the ceremony

    is in the morning. OK

18. I have invited the following people to graduation: my mother, my sister, my husband, and my two kids.

19. This week—despite the engrossing national news!--we still need to finish our classes.

20. The teacher asked, "Are you ready for your new job?"

21. If my mother calls, let me know.

22. Order the party food from the bakery (do you have the phone number?).

23. On July 4, 1992, we will be on vacation.

24. My graduation present will be a computer; however, I haven't chosen the brand yet.

25. I have applied for jobs at several companies that seemed interesting. OK

26. Getting a job will be a relief, I think.

27. One speaker at graduation will be Ms. Turnoy, the school director.

28. This is the last main grammar test; we're almost done with English.

29. After this test is over, we'll be writing letters.

30. You should practice typing, therefore, and review typing rules.

Part C: Capitals, Abbreviations, Numbers

31. *Two hundred* ~~200~~ people are expected at graduation.

32. The Director of our school will make that announcement.

33. The ceremony will be in Clover hall.

34. That *building* ~~bldg.~~ is on Bascom *Avenue* ~~Ave.~~

35. Drive South on de la Cruz.

Part D: English Usage

36. She will attend the ceremony with Jane and *me* ~~I~~.

37. Each counselor and teacher *is* ~~are~~ proud of the students.

38. I feel *really* ~~real~~ good about that.

39. The new car is her's; that one is John's. *[her's corrected to hers]*

40. Leyla and Barbara don't need help with that course. OK

41. Obviously, we'll help if needed. *[^]*

42. All the test materials is on the desk. *[is corrected to are]*

43. Every student in these classes have studied hard. *[have corrected to has]*

44. April, along with other assistants, were planning graduation. *[were corrected to was]*

45. Don't leave your tests laying around the classroom. *[laying corrected to lying]*

Part E: Rewriting Sentences

Directions: In the blanks rewrite the sentences. *Two points each.*

46. Climbing quickly, our eyes beheld the scenic view.

   Climbing quickly, we beheld the scenic view.
   _____

47. She bought a parrot for her brother, which was green and yellow.

   She bought a green and yellow parrot for her brother.
   _____

48. We enjoy bike riding and to hike in the hills.

   We enjoy bike riding and hiking in the hills.
   _____

Directions: Add any necessary punctuation and delete any that is unnecessary. Capitalize as necessary.

1. Tim is happy about the book he has found however that it is too long for his needs

2. How you did that is amazing to me?

3. The order arrived Friday, therefore, the package was shipped on Monday

4. Did you hear about her new job it's better than anybody expected

5. Run that elevator is about to leave

6. Please send the following materials (1.) books, (2.) computer paper, (3.) disks

7. Can you estimate the cost of the heat? Light? Maintenance service?

8. Will you be going to that conference Of course I will

9. The computer printout showed the following words to be omitted assignment and optional

10. Would you please correct the errors and rerun it today

11. Capitalize the first word of:
    a. Every sentence
    b. Direct quotations
    c. Line items in an outline

12. Please order the following supplies:
    1. Flow pens.
    2. Typewriter paper.
    3. Photocopy paper.

13. We can count on getting those in time, can't we.

14. There are two reasons I want to work overtime first, I'm going back to school next year. Second, this is a busy time on the job.

15. On Mondays people tend to come in late on Fridays they would like to leave early

16. Wanda asked whether we had the records ready?

17. Why were you absent Monday.

18. We signed the card and took her: books, flowers, fruit, and her assignments.

19. Two skills are required: keyboarding speed and keyboarding accuracy.

20. This new computer is fast and accurate; perfect for word processing.

21. My next project I can't wait to show it to you is in the computer.

22. Will you meet me at: the desk, the elevator, or the restaurant?

23. There is one main reason for coming in early it's very quiet.

24. Call Martin Schmidt he's with the publishing company and get his opinion.

25. We keyboarded all morning then we proofread all afternoon.

26. The following assignments were given: be sure to check them.

27. Did you enclose the check for $62.00?

28. Will you be able to proofread the manuscript by Friday.

29. That English 3. course is very thorough.

30. They had no plans for the holiday, consequently, we had Thanksgiving together.

31. You got it congratulations on your new job.

32. The meeting was called for 8 a.m. it started at 9:00.

33. We're ready to relax now, therefore, this assignment is over.

Directions: Add any necessary commas and delete any that are unnecessary. Use standard proofreading symbols where possible.

1. One of the first things a person looks for in a new town, is a good inexpensive grocery store.

2. Unfortunately many smaller neighborhood stores, must charge higher prices to stay in business.

3. In the very small local stores, however, sometimes fresh fruit vegetables and meat are good buys.

4. The small stores must sell these things very quickly and they cannot afford to throw them away as the big stores might.

5. Let's take a tour of a large American supermarket to see the best ways to shop there.

6. First because frozen goods should be bought last we begin at the opposite side of the store; if necessary we go back to a center aisle just before leaving the store.

7. Since fresh vegetables and fruit are sometimes bargains in season we look for these early in our trip, and plan menus around them.

8. We try to adjust our grocery list to the best prices, and quality we see.

9. Today the mushrooms look good but expensive; the green peppers an excellent bargain; the apples rather stale.

10. Since we decided to have stuffed peppers for dinner, we'll need some type of bread, or meat for stuffing.

11. We think about cholesterol, calories, and expense; then we plan to make a bread stuffing with egg whites, and herbs.

12. At 7 p.m. the next Saturday, February 12 we're having a dinner party and inviting Maria, Jose, Tom and Janet, and Victor and Sally.

13. Now we're looking for ingredients for a party dessert that we can make ahead of time perhaps even to freeze.

14. Oh good! Here are the first strawberries of the season and they freeze beautifully.

15. We can make a simple sponge cake, (much cheaper than buying one), and have strawberry shortcake with a low-calorie nonfat topping.

16. Because many people make a list and then hunt for just what's on the list they miss some good bargains spending too much money.

17. People often pay twice as much for a ready-made dish, that is really simple to make.

18. Shoppers often don't read the ingredients or notice which ready-made items list nutrition information.

19. We also tend to get into a destructive pattern of eating high-fat or high-calorie foods without thinking of alternatives.

20. Unfortunately some of the least nutritious food tends to be most heavily advertised on television, and in magazines.

21. A large hamburger for example usually contains much of the worst kind of fat although some companies are changing this recipe.

22. Vegetarian pizza on the other hand is relatively nutritious especially if the cheese is low-fat.

23. Most cultures use one excellent complex carbohydrate which gives much of the necessary nutrition; for example, potatoes, beans, rice, noodles and other pasta.

24. When cooked at home such dishes are quite inexpensive.

25. Americans learned to eat large amounts of meat in frontier days when the weather and their travels kept them from gardens and they needed long-lasting calories for warmth and energy.

26. Now we live in heated homes and no longer cut wood or plow the land; therefore we need far fewer calories and much less meat.

27. As the culture changes we must change with it.

28. Does this mean, that we should all be extremely thin?

29. Most of us are born with a certain body pattern that feels healthy for us; for some, the muscles and bones are larger; for others smaller.

30. You may say "That's all very fine if you have time but I don't."

31. I will answer, "It's not really time but interest. If you want to you'll do it."

32. Back at the local supermarket we discover that we have bought almost everything on the list without buying canned goods or prepared frozen dishes.

33. "Congratulations!", we say to ourselves. "Now for a treat—how about some frozen juice bars? The budget and the nutrition charts can accept that much."

Covering Chapter 17

Directions: Use proofreading marks to insert quotation marks or parentheses where necessary, before or after other punctuation. Delete punctuation as necessary.

1. At the Personnel Office, the receptionist said, Follow me

2. Because I wanted the job, I said enthusiastically, "Of course

3. Ms. Jackson will be ready in just a moment, explained the assistant.

    Just sit here. Would you like coffee?

4. I wondered whether that would be a good idea.

5. Not just now, thank you I answered.

6. The receptionist smiled. Just let me know if I can get you anything.

7. Do you have a general brochure about the company I asked.

8. Oh, yes here's the latest information! she answered.

9. I was glad I asked. "Thanks a lot"!

10. I sat down and started reading. (I should have gotten this before).

11. Next time I apply for a job, I'll get all the information ahead of time, I

    said to myself.

12. (This is known as "second-guessing).

13. My teacher tells me, "Apply for lots of jobs." "This gives good

    practice."

14. "Practice makes perfect", I think to myself.

15. "Ms. Jackson will see you now", says the receptionist.

Directions: Mark any letters that should be capitalized or lowercased.

1. when you get a new job and plan to move to a new town, what are some of the places you watch for?

2. If there are children in the family, most people look for a good Elementary School and a good High School.

3. In some School Districts, bus service is provided to children outside a certain area.

4. In a Unified School District, such as Minneapolis Unified, children may be registered in a wide choice of schools.

5. Hennepin county has many different school districts.

6. when i moved, i interviewed the Superintendent or Principal to learn about the school programs in various districts.

7. Administrators like Superintendent Beck, who used to be my neighbor, can be very helpful.

8. Another item to investigate in a new area is the public transportation system, served by rapid transit (like twin cities transit).

9. Do you live near Hennepin county transit bus lines?

10. As oil becomes scarcer, we need to think of Samtrans, caltrain, and other similar methods of transport.

11. When you plan to move, you'll also think about Police, Sanitation, Emergency medical, and other services.

12. The polk county sheriff's department has a good reputation.

13. For shopping, you need to note big stores (dayton's, sears, wards, or penney's) and transport nearby.

14. Many people choose a home because it is near recreation; they think of florida beaches, rockies skiing, or the chicago symphony, opera, theaters, and museums.

15. Good recreational possibilities for children might include parks like disney world and marine world, or educational museums such as Discovery museum.

16. Inexpensive family facilities such as the Ymca swimming, crafts, exercise, and camping programs also help.

17. Organizations like the greenwood park recreational department or the youth science institute may offer Science classes, Tennis lessons, or Diving in an olympic-size pool.

18. Most states in the United States offer educational programs for adults; for example, the Metropolitan Adult education program in Duchess county or the cuny System in New York city.

19. For a small fee anyone can continue education at any level, from beginning english lessons to graduate programs at universities such as columbia.

20. First, however, comes the job; you can begin the job search by reading a paper like the *st. louis post dispatch*.

Directions: Circle any incorrect number or abbreviation forms and write the correct forms in the space at the right.

1. Are you applying at that empl. agency? _____

2. Enclosed is the appl. card from the mgr. _____

3. Write down the Soc. S. Number for me. _____

4. The agency is on 8th Ave. _____

5. It opens at nine o'clock a.m. _____

6. I need 2 twenty-five cent stamps. _____

7. My appt. is on March ninth. _____

8. The cost of the call is $.75 cents. _____

9. The ad was in a mag. owned by Time

    Incorporated. _____

10. The manager's name is Jose Rivas Junior. _____

Adjectives/Adverbs

Directions: Circle the correct words in the parentheses.

1. Lorena was (real/really) happy about her grade.

2. When John arrives, give him all (those/them) papers.

3. These materials will be (more useful/usefuler) after you study.

4. Sam (hasn't/has) scarcely come to school at all this week.

5. Doesn't the new computer look (good/well) in that room?

6. It was the (less/least) expensive of the two models.

7. When she called, she sounded very (critical/critically).

8. This typewriter does not work as (good/well) as the old one.

9. This application is for (no fault/no-fault) insurance.

10. I saw on television (where/that) a thousand people were laid off.

11. This school has better teachers than (any/any other) in this area.

12. Sara enjoyed her (500 mile/500-mile) trip to Mexico.

13. Jack's speech was (more/more nearly) unique than Carl's.

14. Have you looked very (careful/carefully) for your test paper?

15. This book is (better/more better) than that one.

16. Maria has a higher grade than (anyone/anyone else) in her class.

Conjunctions/Prepositions

Directions: Insert or delete any words or word groups as necessary.

17. The reason for two versions of the test is because we need practice.

18. Does anyone know where the new teacher is at?

19. The long holiday weekend is near, and we do have some homework.

20. This test is a little different than the other one.

21. Will the material to study be retroactive from English 1?

22. Driving a car is easy, but to get a license is not so simple.

23. When she enrolled in school, she was accompanied with her sister.

24. He gives paper away like it cost nothing.

25. Do you know where Sarita went to?

26. I don't remember whether this test is identical to that one.

27. See the Dean in regards to your schedule.

28. Being that this is the last grammar unit, we'll review next week.

29. Don't leave early except you have the Dean's permission.

30. Divide the sandwich between your three friends.

31. Are you angry at that child?

32. Give this note to the teacher which comes in early.

33. Anyways, I'm glad this is the end of the test.

Directions: In the blanks, rewrite sentences to make their meaning clear.

1. They teach primarily business students, and so we should try community college for history classes.

_____

_____

2. After eating the spicy food, my eyes were watering.

_____

_____

3. Punctuation is important, but to spell well is important also.

_____

_____

4. A rise in prices is sure. This should be kept in mind when you make your budget.

_____

_____

5. I'm really happy about the way I studied now.

_____

_____

6. We sent the graduation card to Sonya addressed to her mother.

_____

_____

7. It says in the catalog that we have lifetime placement.

_____

_____

8. Please empty these wastebaskets when thoroughly full.

_____

_____

9. She sat at the desk on a new chair.

_____

_____

10. Help wanted: receptionist to type letters and two secretaries.

_____

_____

Quiz 1: Punctuation
Covering Chapters 11–12

Directions: Add any necessary punctuation and delete any that is unnecessary. Capitalize as necessary. *Three points per sentence; partial credit given.*

1. Tim is happy about the book; he has found, however, that it is too long for his needs.

2. How you did that is amazing to me?!

3. The order arrived Friday; therefore, the package was shipped on Monday.

4. Did you hear about her new job? It's better than anybody expected! [or .]

5. Run! That elevator is about to leave!

6. Please send the following materials: (1) books, (2) computer paper, (3) disks.

7. Can you estimate the cost of the heat? Light? Maintenance service?

8. Will you be going to that conference? Of course I will!

9. The computer printout showed the following words to be omitted: assignment and optional.

10. Would you please correct the errors and rerun it today.

11. Capitalize the first word of:
    a. Every sentence.
    b. Direct quotations.
    c. Line items in an outline.

12. Please order the following supplies:
    1. Flow pens
    2. Typewriter paper
    3. Photocopy paper

13. We can count on getting those in time, can't we?

14. There are two reasons I want to work overtime: first, I'm going back to school next year. Second, this is a busy time on the job.

15. On Mondays people tend to come in late; on Fridays they would like to leave early. [Optional commas after *Mondays* and *Fridays*.]

16. Wanda asked whether we had the records ready.

17. Why were you absent Monday?

18. We signed the card and took her books, flowers, fruit, and her assignments.

19. Two skills are required: keyboarding speed and keyboarding accuracy. OK

20. This new computer is fast and accurate, perfect for word processing. [Or, dash instead of comma]

21. My next project--I can't wait to show it to you--is in the computer. [Could add an exclamation point after *you*]

22. Will you meet me at the desk, the elevator, or the restaurant?

23. There is one main reason for coming in early: it's very quiet.

24. Call Martin Schmidt--he's with the publishing company-- and get his opinion.

25. We keyboarded all morning; then we proofread all afternoon. [Or, a period after *morning* and a capital T in *Then*]

26. The following assignments were given; be sure to check them.

27. Did you enclose the check for $62.00?

28. Will you be able to proofread the manuscript by Friday?

29. That English 3 course is very thorough.

30. They had no plans for the holiday; consequently, we had Thanksgiving together.

31. You got it! Congratulations on your new job!

32. The meeting was called for 8 a.m.; it started at 9:00.

33. We're ready to relax now; therefore, this assignment is over.

Quiz 2: Commas
Covering Chapters 13–16

Directions: Add any necessary commas and delete any that are unnecessary. Use standard proofreading symbols where possible. *One point per comma.*

1. One of the first things a person looks for in a new town, is a good inexpensive grocery store.

2. Unfortunately, many smaller neighborhood stores, must charge higher prices to stay in business.

3. In the very small local stores, however, sometimes fresh fruit, vegetables, and meat are good buys.

4. The small stores must sell these things very quickly, and they cannot afford to throw them away, [or no comma] as the big stores might.

5. Let's take a tour of a large American supermarket to see the best ways to shop there. OK

6. First, because frozen goods should be bought last, we begin at the opposite side of the store; if necessary, we go back to a center aisle, just [or no comma] before leaving the store.

7. Since fresh vegetables and fruit are sometimes bargains in season, we look for these early in our trip, and plan menus around them.

8. We try to adjust our grocery list to the best prices, and quality we see.

9. Today, the mushrooms look good but expensive; the green peppers, an excellent bargain; the apples, rather stale. [or no comma]

10. Since we decided to have stuffed peppers for dinner, we'll need some type of bread, or meat for stuffing.

11. We think about cholesterol, calories, and expense; then, we plan to make a bread stuffing with egg whites, and herbs. [or no comma]

12. At 7 p.m. the next Saturday, February 12, we're having a dinner party and inviting Maria, Jose, Tom and Janet, and Victor and Sally.

13. Now we're looking for ingredients for a party dessert that we can make ahead of time, perhaps even to freeze.

14. Oh, good! Here are the first strawberries of the season, and they freeze beautifully.

15. We can make a simple sponge cake, (much cheaper than buying one), and have strawberry shortcake with a low-calorie nonfat topping.

16. Because many people make a list and then hunt for just what's on the list, they miss some good bargains, spending too much money.

17. People often pay twice as much for a ready-made dish, that is really simple to make.

18. Shoppers often don't read the ingredients or notice which ready-made items list nutrition information. OK

19. We also tend to get into a destructive pattern of eating high-fat or high-calorie foods, without thinking of alternatives.

20. Unfortunately, some of the least nutritious food tends to be most heavily advertised on television, and in magazines.

21. A large hamburger, for example, usually contains much of the worst kind of fat, although some companies are changing this recipe.

22. Vegetarian pizza, on the other hand, is relatively nutritious, especially if the cheese is low-fat.

23. Most cultures use one excellent complex carbohydrate, which gives much of the necessary nutrition; for example, potatoes, beans, rice, noodles, and other pasta.

24. When cooked at home, such dishes are quite inexpensive.

25. Americans learned to eat large amounts of meat in frontier days, when

the weather and their travels kept them from gardens, and they needed

long-lasting calories for warmth and energy.

26. Now we live in heated homes and no longer cut wood or plow the

land; therefore, we need far fewer calories and much less meat.

27. As the culture changes, we must change with it.

28. Does this mean, that we should all be extremely thin?

29. Most of us are born with a certain body pattern that feels healthy for

us; for some, the muscles and bones are larger; for others, smaller.

30. You may say, "That's all very fine if you have time, but I don't."

31. I will answer, "It's not really time, but interest. If you want to, you'll

do it."

32. Back at the local supermarket, we discover that we have bought almost

everything on the list without buying canned goods or prepared frozen

dishes.

33. "Congratulations!" we say to ourselves. "Now for a treat—how about

some frozen juice bars? The budget and the nutrition charts can accept

that much."

Quiz 3: Quotation Marks and Parentheses
Covering Chapter 17

Directions: Use proofreading marks to insert quotation marks or parentheses where necessary, before or after other punctuation. Delete punctuation as necessary. *Six points per sentence; partial credit possible.*

1. At the Personnel Office, the receptionist said, "Follow me."

2. Because I wanted the job, I said enthusiastically, "Of course!"

3. "Ms. Jackson will be ready in just a moment," explained the assistant.

"Just sit here. Would you like coffee?"

4. I wondered whether that would be a good idea. OK

5. "Not just now, thank you," I answered.

6. The receptionist smiled. "Just let me know if I can get you anything."

7. "Do you have a general brochure about the company?" I asked.
   [or comma]

8. "Oh, yes--here's the latest information!" she answered.

9. I was glad I asked. "Thanks a lot."

10. I sat down and started reading. (I should have gotten this before.)

11. "Next time I apply for a job, I'll get all the information ahead of time," I said to myself.

12. (This is known as "second-guessing.")

13. My teacher tells me, "Apply for lots of jobs." "This gives good practice."

14. "Practice makes perfect," I think to myself.

15. "Ms. Jackson will see you now," says the receptionist.

Quiz 4: Capitalization
Covering Chapter 18

Directions: Mark any letters that should be capitalized or lowercased. *Five points per sentence. One point per error.*

1. when you get a new job and plan to move to a new town, what are some of the places you watch for?

2. If there are children in the family, most people look for a good Elementary School and a good High School.

3. In some School Districts, bus service is provided to children outside a certain area.

4. In a Unified School District, such as Minneapolis Unified, children may

   be registered in a wide choice of schools.

5. Hennepin county has many different school districts.

6. when i moved, i interviewed the Superintendent or Principal to learn

   about the school programs in various districts.

7. Administrators like Superintendent Beck, who used to be my neighbor,

   can be very helpful. OK

8. Another item to investigate in a new area is the public transportation

   system, served by rapid transit (like twin cities transit).

9. Do you live near Hennepin county transit bus lines?

10. As oil becomes scarcer, we need to think of Samtrans, caltrain, and

    other similar methods of transport.

11. When you plan to move, you'll also think about Police, Sanitation,

    Emergency medical, and other services.

12. The polk county sheriff's department has a good reputation.

13. For shopping, you need to note big stores (dayton's, sears, wards, or

    penney's) and transport nearby.

14. Many people choose a home because it is near recreation; they think of

    florida beaches, rockies skiing, or the chicago symphony, opera,

    theaters, and museums.

15. Good recreational possibilities for children might include parks like

    disney world and marine world, or educational museums such as

    Discovery museum.

16. Inexpensive family facilities such as the Ymca swimming, crafts,

    exercise, and camping programs also help.

17. Organizations like the greenwood park recreational department or the

youth science institute may offer Science classes, Tennis lessons, or

Diving in an olympic-size pool.

18. Most states in the United States offer educational programs for adults;

for example, the Metropolitan Adult education program in Duchess

county or the cuny System in New York city.

19. For a small fee anyone can continue education at any level, from

beginning english lessons to graduate programs at universities such as

columbia.

20. First, however, comes the job; you can begin the job search by reading

a paper like the *st. louis post dispatch.*

Quiz 5: Numbers and Abbreviations
Covering Chapter 19

Directions: Circle any incorrect number or abbreviation forms and write the correct forms in the space at the right. *Ten points per sentence.*

1. Are you applying at that empl. agency?   *employment*

2. Enclosed is the appl. card from the mgr.   *application, manager*

3. Write down the Soc. S. Number for me.   *Social Security number*

4. The agency is on 8th Ave.   *Eighth Avenue*

5. It opens at nine o'clock a.m.   *9 a.m.*

6. I need 2 twenty-five cent stamps.   *two 25-cent*

7. My appt. is on March ninth.   *appointment, 9*

8. The cost of the call is $.75 cents.   *75 cents*

9. The ad was in a mag. owned by Time

   Incorporated.   *magazine, Inc.*

10. The manager's name is Jose Rivas Junior.   *Jr.*

Quiz 6: Usage of Modifiers and Connectors _____
Covering Chapter 29

Adjectives/Adverbs

Directions: Circle the correct words in the parentheses. *Three points each sentence.*

1. Lorena was (real/**really**) happy about her grade.

2. When John arrives, give him all (**those**/them) papers.

3. These materials will be (**more useful**/usefuler) after you study.

4. Sam (hasn't/**has**) scarcely come to school at all this week.

5. Doesn't the new computer look (**good**/well) in that room?

6. It was the (**less**/least) expensive of the two models.

7. When she called, she sounded very (**critical**/critically).

8. This typewriter does not work as (good/**well**) as the old one.

9. This application is for (no fault/**no-fault**) insurance.

10. I saw on television (where/**that**) a thousand people were laid off.

11. This school has better teachers than (any/**any other**) in this area.

12. Sara enjoyed her (500 mile/**500-mile**) trip to Mexico.

13. Jack's speech was (more/**more nearly**) unique than Carl's.

14. Have you looked very (careful/**carefully**) for your test paper?

15. This book is (**better**/more better) than that one.

16. Maria has a higher grade than (anyone/**anyone else**) in her class.

Conjunctions/Prepositions

Directions: Insert or delete any words or word groups as necessary. *Three points per sentence.*

17. The reason for two versions of the test is ~~because~~ that we need practice.

18. Does anyone know where the new teacher is ~~at~~?

19. The long holiday weekend is near, ~~and~~ but we do have some homework.

20. This test is a little different ~~than~~ from the other one.

21. Will the material to study be retroactive ~~from~~ ^to^ English 1?

22. Driving a car is easy, but ~~to get~~ ^getting^ a license is not so simple.

23. When she enrolled in school, she was accompanied ~~with~~ ^by^ her sister.

24. He gives paper away ~~like~~ ^as if^ it cost nothing.

25. Do you know where Sarita went ~~to~~?

26. I don't remember whether this test is identical ~~to~~ ^with^ that one.

27. See the Dean in ~~regards~~ to your schedule.

28. ~~Being that~~ ^Since^ this is the last grammar unit, we'll review next week.

29. Don't leave early ~~except~~ ^unless^ you have the Dean's permission.

30. Divide the sandwich ~~between~~ ^among^ your three friends.

31. Are you angry ~~at~~ ^with^ that child?

32. Give this note to the teacher ~~which~~ ^who^ comes in early.

33. ~~Anyways~~, I'm glad this is the end of the test.

Quiz 7: Modifiers, Reference, and Balance (Advanced) _
Covering Chapter 30

Directions: In the blanks, rewrite sentences to make their meaning clear.

1. They teach primarily business students, and so we should try

   community college for history classes.

   Because that school teaches primarily business students, we should try community college for

   history classes.

2. After eating the spicy food, my eyes were watering.

   My eyes watered after I ate the spicy food.

3. Punctuation is important, but to spell well is important also.

   Punctuation is important, but spelling well is important also.

4. A rise in prices is sure. This should be kept in mind when you make

your budget.

A rise in prices is sure. This problem should be kept in mind when you make your budget.
_____

5. I'm really happy about the way I studied now.

I'm really happy now about the way I studied.
_____

6. We sent the graduation card to Sonya addressed to her mother.

We sent Sonya's graduation card addressed to her mother.
_____

7. It says in the catalog that we have lifetime placement.

The catalog says that we have lifetime placement.
_____

8. Please empty these wastebaskets when thoroughly full.

Please empty these full wastebaskets.
_____

9. She sat at the desk on a new chair.

She sat on a new chair at the desk.
_____

10. Help wanted: receptionist to type letters and two secretaries.

Help wanted: receptionist and two secretaries to type letters.
_____